DEUTERONOMY–KINGS AS
EMERGING AUTHORITATIVE BOOKS

Society of Biblical Literature

Ancient Near East Monographs

General Editors
Ehud Ben Zvi
Roxana Flammini

Editorial Board
Reinhard Achenbach
Esther J. Hamori
Steven W. Holloway
René Krüger
Alan Lenzi
Steven L. McKenzie
Martti Nissinen
Graciela Gestoso Singer
Juan Manuel Tebes

DEUTERONOMY–KINGS AS EMERGING AUTHORITATIVE BOOKS

A CONVERSATION

Edited by
Diana V. Edelman

Society of Biblical Literature
Atlanta

Copyright © 2014 by the Society of Biblical Literature

All rights reserved. No part of this work may be reproduced or transmitted in any form or by any means, electronic or mechanical, including photocopying and recording, or by means of any information storage or retrieval system, except as may be expressly permitted by the 1976 Copyright Act or in writing from the publisher. Requests for permission should be addressed in writing to the Rights and Permissions Office, Society of Biblical Literature, 825 Houston Mill Road, Atlanta, GA 30329 USA.

Library of Congress Control Number: 2014931428

The Ancient Near East Monographs/Monografias Sobre El Antiguo Cercano Oriente series is published jointly by the Society of Biblical Literature and the Universidad Católica Argentina Facultad de Ciencias Sociales, Políticas y de la Comunicación, Centro de Estudios de Historia del Antiguo Oriente.

For further information, see:
    http://www.sbl-site.org/publications/Books_ANEmonographs.aspx
    http://www.uca.edu.ar/cehao

Printed on acid-free, recycled paper conforming to
ANSI/NISO Z39.48-1992 (R1997) and ISO 9706:1994
standards for paper permanence.

To the memory of my father, Arthur T. Vikander, who was so proud of my scholarly pursuits and accomplishments.

The final editing of this volume was completed during our last weeks together.

CONTENTS

Abbreviations ix

Introduction
    Diana V. Edelman 1

The Authority of Deuteronomy
    Philip R. Davies 27

Rereading Deuteronomy in the Persian and Hellenistic Periods:
The Ethics of Brotherhood and the Care of the Poor
    Christoph Levin 49

Why "Joshua"?
    E. Axel Knauf 73

The Case of Joshua
    Serge Frolov 85

Who Was Interested in the Book of Judges in the Persian-
Hellenistic Periods?
    Yairah Amit 103

Memories Laid to Rest: The Book of Judges in the Persian Period
    Susanne Gillmayr-Bucher 115

1–2 Samuel and Jewish *Paideia* in the Persian and Hellenistic
Periods
    Thomas M. Bolin 133

What Made the Books of Samuel Authoritative in the Discourses
of the Persian Period? Reflections on the Legal Discourse in
2 Samuel 14
Klaus-Peter Adam 159

The Case of the Book of Kings
Thomas Römer 187

On the Authority of Dead Kings
James R. Linville 203

Contributors..223

Bibliography..225

Primary Sources Index 257

Modern Authors Index..273

Subject Index...279

Abbreviations

AB	Anchor Bible
ABD	*Anchor Bible Dictionary*. Edited by David Noel Freedman. 6 vols. Garden City, N.Y.: Doubleday, 1992.
ABRL	Anchor Bible Reference Library
AnBib	Analecta biblica
AOAT	Alter Orient und Altes Testament
BA	*Biblical Archaeologist*
BASOR	*Bulletin of the American Schools of Oriental Research*
BEATAJ	Beiträge zur Erforschung des Alten Testaments und des antiken Judentums
BETL	Bibliotheca ephemeridum theologicarum lovaniensium
Bib	*Biblica*
BibInt	*Biblical Interpretation*
BWANT	Beiträge zur Wissenschaft vom Alten (und Neuen) Testament
BZAW	Beihefte zur Zeitschrift für die alttestamentliche Wissenschaft
CahRB	Cahiers de la Revue biblique
CBET	Contributions to Biblical Exegesis
CBQ	*Catholic Biblical Quarterly*
GAT	Grundrisse zum Alten Testament
GKC	*Gesenius' Hebrew Grammar*. Edited by Emil Kautzsch. Translated by A. E. Cowley. 2nd. ed. Oxford: Oxford University Press, 1910.
ESHM	European Seminar in Historical Methodology
FAT	Forschungen zum Alten Testaments
FOTL	Forms of Old Testament Literature
FRLANT	Forschungen zur Religion und Literatur des Alten und Neuen Testament

HKAT	Herders theologischer Kommentar zum Alten Testament.
HSM	Harvard Semitic Monographs
ICC	International Critical Commentary
IEJ	*Israel Exploration Journal*
JBL	*Journal of Biblical Literature*
JHS	*Journal of Hebrew Scriptures*
JJS	*Journal of Jewish Studies*
JNSL	*Journal of Northwest Semitic Languages*
JRAS	*Journal of the Royal Asiatic Society*
JSOT	*Journal for the Study of the Old Testament*
JSOTSup	Journal for the Study of the Old Testament Supplement Series
JSPSup	Journal for the Study of the Pseudepigrapha Supplement Series
KHC	Kurzer Hand-Commentar zum Alten Testament
LHBOTS	Library of Hebrew Bible/Old Testament Studies
LSTS	Library of Second Temple Studies
NCBS	New Century Bible Series
NICOT	New International Commentary on the Old Testament
OBO	Orbis biblicus et orientalis
OTL	Old Testament Library
OTP	*Old Testament Pseudepigrapha*. Edited by James H. Charlesworth. 2 vols. New York: Doubleday, 1983–1985.
OtSt	Oudtestamentische Studiën
PEQ	Palestine Exploration Quarterly
QD	Quaestiones disputatae
SAA	State Archives of Assyria
SBAB	Stuttgarter biblische Aufsatzbände, Altes Testament
SBL	Society of Biblical Literature
SBLAIL	Society of Biblical Literature Ancient Israel and Its Literature
SBLSymS	Society of Biblical Literature Symposium Series
SBT	Studies in Biblical Theology
SCSS	Septuagint and Cognate Studies Series
SJOT	*Scandinavian Journal of the Old Testament*
SOTSMS	Society for Old Testament Studies Monograph Series
STAR	Studies in Theology and Religion

STW	Suhrkamp Taschenbuch Wissenschaft
STTSB	Suomalainen Tiedakatemie Toimituksia, Sarja B.
TB	Theologische Bücherei
ThWAT	*Theologisches Wörterbuch zum Alten Testament.* Edited by G. J. Botterweck and H. Ringgren. Stuttgart: Kohlhammer, 1970–2006.
TransSup	Supplément à Transeuphratène
VT	*Vetus Testamentum*
VTSup	Vetus Testamentum Supplements
WBC	Word Biblical Commentary
WMANT	Wissenschaftliche Monographien zum Alten und Neuen Testament
ZAR	*Zeitschrift für Altorientalische und Biblische Rechtsgeschichte*
ZAW	*Zeitschrift für die alttestamentliche Wissenschaft*
ZBKAT	Zürcher Bibelkommentare Altes Testament

INTRODUCTION

Diana V. Edelman

The existence of a "Deuteronomistic History," consisting of the books of Deuteronomy, Joshua, Judges, Samuel, and Kings, is under review.[1] Is this scholarly construct an accurate understanding of what ancient writers of the Hebrew Bible conceived to be a coherent sequence of books that should be read together? Did the books ever form an independent collection, without Exodus, Leviticus and Numbers prefixed, or without Genesis-Numbers prefixed? If we are not as certain as past generations that they ever formed a recognized literary unit,[2] why ask what was deemed

---

1. For convenient summaries of the history of the theory of the existence of Deuteronomistic historiography, see Douglas A. Knight, "Deuteronomy and the Deuteronomists," in *Old Testament Interpretation Past, Present, and Future: Essays in Honour of Gene M. Tucker* (ed. James L. Mays, David L. Petersen and Kent H. Richards; Edinburgh: T&T Clark, 1995), 61–79; Thomas Römer and Albert de Pury, "Deuteronomistic Historiography (DH): History of Research and Debated Issues," in *Israel Constructs its History: Deuteronomistic History in Recent Research* (ed. Albert de Pury, Thomas Römer, and Jean-Daniel Macchi; JSOTSup 306; Sheffield: Sheffield Academic Press, 2000), 24–141.

2. For essays and studies dealing with various aspects of this debate, see conveniently, A. Graeme Auld, *Joshua, Moses and the Land: Tetrateuch-Pentateuch-Hexateuch in a Generation since 1938* (Edinburgh: T&T Clark, 1980); Claus Westermann, *Die Geschichtsbücher des Alten Testaments: gab es ein deuteronomistisches Geschichtswerk?* (TB 87; Gütersloh: Kaiser, 1994); James R. Linville, *Israel in the Book of Kings: The Past as a Project of Social Identity* (JSOTSup 272; Sheffield: Sheffield Academic Press, 1998), 46–73; Reinhard G. Kratz, *The Composition of the Narrative Books of the Bible* (trans. J. Bowden; New York: T&T Clark, International, 2000), 1–5, 153–221; Albert de Pury, Thomas Römer, and Jean-Daniel Macchi, eds., *Israel Constructs its History: Deuteronomistic History in Recent Research* (JSOTSup 306; Sheffield: Sheffield Academic Press, 2000); Christian Frevel, "Deuteronomistisches Geschichtswerk oder Gechichtswerke? Die These Martin Noths zwischen Tetrateuch, Hexateuch und

authoritative about these five books in the late Persian and early Hellenistic periods, by which time it is generally agreed they existed close to their current final forms?

The purpose of the present volume is not to focus on the important debate about the status of the so-called Deuteronomistic History, though the results might contribute toward framing arguments on one side or the other. Instead, it is to try to understand the element of authority in relation to each book, which can be construed in two different ways. On the one hand, it can lead us to ask why we have each of the five individual books and what concerns led to their creation using which older materials to address those issues, because these earlier traditions carried some weight of authority for the community of scribes who penned the narratives as well as for their implied target audience(s). Currently, the dates of composition for the various books are generally assigned to the late monarchic period, the Neo-Babylonian period, or the early Persian period. In all three cases, a second question naturally arises then that needs a reasoned response: once created, why would the concerns addressed have had ongoing relevance and resonance for audiences in the late Persian and early Hellenistic periods?

On the other hand, the concept of authority can lead us to ask why the five individual books gained authoritative status, regardless of the age or of the materials in them; why was it desirable to give authority to written narratives about YHWH's relation to the people of Israel? Many of the essays in the volume emphasize the close connection between authority and group identity, where the texts can help define a group by serving as a written, authoritative depository of valued social memories that are

---

Enneateuch," in *Martin Noth: Aus der Sicht heutiger Forschung* (ed. Udo Rüterswörden; biblisch-theologische Studien 58; Neukirchen-Vluyn: Neukirchener Verlag, 2004), 60–94; Philippe Guillaume, *Waiting for Josiah: The Judges* (JSOTSup 385; London: T&T Clark, 2004), 227–36; Eckhard Otto and Reinhard Achenbach, eds., *Das Deuteronomium zwischen Pentateuch und deuteronomistischem Geschichtswerk* (FRLANT 206; Göttingen: Vandenhoeck & Ruprecht, 2004); Markus Witte et al., *Die deuteronomistischen Geschichtswerk: redaktions- und religionsgesichtliche Perspektiven zur "Deuteronomismus"- Diskussion in Tora und Vorderen Propheten* (BZAW 365; Berlin: de Gruyter, 2006); Thomas B. Dozeman, Thomas Römer, and Konrad Schmid, eds., *Pentateuch, Hexateuch, or Enneateuch? Identifying Literary Works in Genesis through Kings* (SBLAIL 8; Atlanta: Society of Biblical Literature, 2011); Konrad Schmid and Raymond F. Person Jr., eds., *Deuteronomy in the Pentateuch, Hexateuch, and the Deuteronomistic History* (FAT 2/56; Tübingen: Mohr Siebeck, 2012).

to be learned and passed on by those considering themselves to belong to the group. In this case, the book of Deuteronomy had audiences in both Samaria and Yehud/Judea who considered themselves to belong to Israel, while Joshua, Judges, Samuel and Kings eventually were considered authoritative only for Judean-rooted Israel. Thus, the volume is primarily concerned with the issues of authority, identity, and social memory, though only that of authority is addressed directly in each contribution. The other two will surface in varying degrees as each scholar seeks to answer "why" their book gained authority.

The five essays by C. Levin, Y. Amit, E. A. Knauf, K.-P. Adam, and T. Römer were initially presented at the European Association of Biblical Studies Meeting in Tartu, Estonia, July 25–29, 2010, in a session of the research program "Israel and the Production and Reception of Authoritative Books in the Persian and Hellenistic Periods," co-chaired by Ehud Ben Zvi and myself. The announced theme was "What made these books authoritative within the discourse of Persian Yehud/early Hellenistic Judah?" It was worthwhile to commission a second set of essays on each book from scholars who would not likely agree with the first group, as a way of teasing out issues and beginning a conversation about why the books of Deuteronomy–2 Kings became authoritative as individual compositions and, it was hoped, secondarily, as part of a larger grouping, whether that be conceived as a Deuteronomistic collection or the traditional "Deuteronomistic History." Ehud had many other commitments at the time, and thus I took full and sole control of this project. The current volume is the result of my efforts. The authors of the first five papers were encouraged to make any necessary revisions to ensure they engaged directly with the thematic question while the second group was being assembled. The most successful conversations have been initiated when both essays on a given book have focused the majority of their discussion on the central theme.

The contributors were asked to focus on a single book as an individual unit, though they were encouraged to explore links between their book and the other four. Two essays are devoted to each book. What was deemed authoritative in or about Deuteronomy? Joshua? Judges? Samuel? Kings? Individual scholars have been encouraged to state whether they believe the author of their book also wrote one or more of the other books, or whether one or more editors joined together independently created compositions to create a larger, intentional literary unit. Like the debate about the existence of a "Deuteronomistic History," the compositional and redactional history of these books is not the primary focus.

A case has been made for seeing a set of theologically coherent ideas and certain idiomatic words or phrases in these five books, suggesting they formed a literary unit or subunit.³ Yet, ultimately, Judaism identified the first five books, Genesis-Deuteronomy, as a literary unit and joined Joshua-Kings with the ensuing collection of prophetic books to create a unit dubbed "The Prophets." Taking a closer thematic look at the initial nine books in the Hebrew Bible, it can be argued that Exodus-Deuteronomy comprise a "biography of Moses," a "Quatrateuch," to which a narrative about the forefathers was prefaced—Genesis—creating the authorized "Pentateuch." But it has also long been debated whether originally, a Pentateuch was envisioned by the ancient authors or a Hexateuch that included Joshua, since the promise of the land is a prominent theme in Genesis that only finds it final fulfilment in the occupation of Canaan in Joshua.⁴ Still others propose that Genesis–Kings comprises a single, coherent narrative that should not be subdivided, because Judges, Samuel, and Kings cannot stand independently from what precedes. They, too, exemplify the theme of the Promised Land, justifying its eventual loss for the repeated failure of the people of Israel and its leaders to keep the terms of the covenant made by YHWH with the ancestors. It has even been suggested that an original Pentateuch included Genesis, Exodus, Leviticus, Numbers and Joshua, with Deuteronomy being placed in its current position later on, when the Enneateuch was created, to extend the original narrative later in time, to the exile.⁵

In these many debates, Deuteronomy plays a pivotal role, creating a bridge between the ancestors and a series of divine covenants made outside the land and the failure to observe the terms of many of the covenants once inside the land. It becomes somewhat moot whether the book ends

---

3. See the classical formulation of the hypothesis of the existence of a Deuteronomistic History developed by Martin Noth in *The Deuteronomistic History* (2d ed.; JSOTSup 15; Sheffield: Sheffield Academic Press, 1991; German original *Überlieferungs-geschichtliche Studien* I [Halle: M. Niemeyer, 1943]). For a list of allegedly Deuteronomic phraseology, see Moshe Weinfeld, *Deuteronomy and the Deuteronomic School* (Winona Lake, IN: Eisenbrauns, 1992), 320–65; idem, *Deuteronomy 1–11: A New Translation with Introduction and Commentary* (AB 5; New York: Doubleday, 1991), 35–37. For unifying techniques amongst the books, see e.g. Richard D. Nelson, *The Historical Books* (Interpreting Biblical Texts; Nashville: Abingdon, 1998), 70–77.

4. For an evaluation of the Hexateuch hypothesis, see, for example, Frevel, "Deuteronomistisches Geschichtswerk oder Gechichtswerke," 80–86.

5. E. Axel Knauf, *Josua* (ZBKAT 6; Zürich: TVZ, 2008), 18.

a plot-line that began in Genesis or begins a new plot-line that ends in Kings, with exile.[6] Endings are beginnings; the introduction of idiomatic language that will recur throughout the story developed in Joshua, Judges, Samuel, and Kings can come at the beginning of a new direction in which the plot moves or can be anticipated already in the ongoing plot before dramatic new events unfold. After all, there is arguably a single story being narrated from Genesis-Kings, whether a preconceived one meant to be developed over a multivolume project or an *ad hoc* one that evolved over time as individual compositions that worked with similar themes, motifs, and concerns were placed side by side, resulting in the emergence of a series of successive, discrete periods.[7] Bearing this in mind, it is possible to examine the five books of Deuteronomy–2 Kings as a subunit of a larger whole, whether or not one chooses to designate them officially by the scholarly moniker, "The Deuteronomistic History," with all the presuppositions that label and construct entails.

Authority

The ten contributors have understood authority in different ways. These include: a socially constructed interpretative framework into which a readership places texts they consider to embody truths or insights considered to be necessary or valuable resources for public discourse on socially sig-

---

6. One should take note with E. A. Knauf of how the end of Kings is a very weak conclusion to the proposed Enneateuch but serves well as an opening to a continuing history instead, consituting an excellent introduction to the prophetic books ("Does 'Deuteronomistic Historiography' Exist?" in *Israel Constructs Its History: Deuteronomistic History in Recent Research* [ed. Albert de Pury, Thomas Römer, and Jean-Daniel Macchi; JSOTSup 306; Sheffield: Sheffield Academic Press, 2000], 388–98 [397]). As such, it could be seen to occupy a pivotal role, similar to Deuteronomy.

7. An interesting question is whether the literary technique of interweaving has been used to join together two formerly independent cycles; a "Pentateuch" that included Gen-Num + Josh, and a "Quatrateuch" that included Deut + Judg-Kgs. To combine the two, the first book of the second unit has been placed immediately before the last book of the first cycle, creating anticipation. It is noteworthy that the internal justification given to explain the two law-giving accounts in Exod and Deut is that two sets of laws were revealed to Moses by God: the first was to apply while the people remained outside the Promised Land, and the second was to come into force once the people were settled in the Promised Land. Thus, Exod applies to the narrative through the occupation in Josh, while Deut applies through to the exile.

nificant topics such as matters of religious practice, belief, the symbolic boundaries of society, and social order; the final form of the text; the definitive version of certain past events; the torah-based ethic expressed in many texts in the Hebrew Bible; a text that has become established by virture of having being read and reread; an established text that is updated to maintain its authority; an established text that prompts the composition of a new text that leaves it intact but creates an updated version as an independent compostion, as in the cases of Deuteronomy and Chronicles; and the ability to understand the enigmas and the disjunctions in a collection of texts containing a matrix of stories and myths that allowed different views of what makes an ideal society and its norms to be considered and debated. This fluidity opens a vital conversation about who created these books initially, for whom, why, and when, and additionally, who were subsequent audiences who read them, and why? Were the books authoritative from their inception and creation or did they only become so over time, and if so, why? Who had authority to "update" the texts for subsequent audiences?

The essay by T. Bolin situates their authoritative use as educational texts for the children of priests, Levites, and the influential families of Yehud, on analogy with the Greek and Hellenistic educational system in particular, as opposed to former scribal training in Mesopotamia and Egypt. Certainly, Ben Sira indicates that the texts were being used to educate Jewish youth whose fathers could afford to send their children to a private tutor by ca. 190 B.C.E. But it is unclear if this were a relatively new development during the Hellenistic period, which emulated the Greek system but used "native" texts instead of Homer to enculturate Jewish youth, emphasizing Jewish ideals, morals, and ethics, or if it had begun already during the Persian Empire or earlier. The depiction of Ezra's memorization and interiorization of YHWH's teaching in Ezra 7:10 so that he was "skilled" in it (Ezra 8:6) and of his study of it with priests, Levites, and the heads of the ancestral clans of all the people with in Neh 8:13 seems to presume a Hellenistic educational system.

Like most biblical books, the dating of Ezra and Nehemiah is disputed. While many presume a Persian-era date close to the events depicted, a minority favor a Hellenistic date.[8] The former group would likely see the books to provide evidence for the use of such an educational system in

---

8. For the varying dates of composition and the rationales underlying them, see, for example, Jacob M. Myers, *Ezra Nehemiah: Introduction, Translation, and Notes* (AB 14; Garden City, N.Y.: 1965), lxviii-lxx; Leonard H. Brockington, *Ezra, Nehemiah and*

the mid-fifth century, under Persian imperialism, while the latter group would see them to confirm the picture presented in Ben Sira. They would argue it is logical to associate this educational system with social memories about the group's "new beginning," when Jerusalem was reinhabited, the temple was rebuilt, and Torah was to play a new, central role in defining the people.

Were the books of Deuteronomy, Joshua, Judges, Samuel and Kings created as educational texts, or did they eventually come to serve that as one purpose among others, as they gained authoritative status? Here we return to the conundrum about their original purposes and audiences. The early work by A. Lemaire on scribal schools argued there was a widespread educational system in monarchic Judah that featured royal scribal schools in various cities as well as local schools in outlying sites like Arad, Kadesh-Barnea and Kuntillet 'Ajrud and separate schools for the training of priests and prophets. He argued the biblical canon developed from the curricula used in these various schools.[9] His theories have not gained wide support. E. Ben Zvi has proposed a model for their composition and early use that sees them to be created for the small circle of "literati" as a means of exploring vital issues and pressing concerns in the present and future by drawing on lessons from the past, without pushing for a consensus view.[10] He emphasizes the didactic and socializing roles of reading and rereading these works within that group. D. M. Carr similarly thinks that the original intended audience was a small group. He defines its members as scribes, priests, administrators, and kings. He also argues that the purpose was educational. According to him, students memorized and recited long passages from an authoritative curriculum, which simultaneously served as templates for the composition of new texts. The written corpus served at the same time as a means of enculturation and preservation of national tradition. For Carr literacy was training in and mastery of the tradition

---

Esther (NCBS; London: Thomas Nelson, 1969), 24–25; Hugh G. M. Williamson, *Ezra, Nehemiah* (WBC 16; Waco, Tex.: Word Books, 1985), xxv–xxxvi.

9. André Lemaire, *Les Écoles et la formation de la Bible dans l'ancien Israël* (OBO 39; Fribourg: University Press, 1981).

10. See, for example, Ehud Ben Zvi, "The Concept of Prophetic Books and Its Historical Setting," in *The Production of Prophecy: Constructing Prophets and Prophecy in Yehud* (ed. Diana V. Edelman and Ehud Ben Zvi; BibleWorld; London: Equinox, 2009), 73–95; idem, "Reconstructing the Intellectual Discourse of Ancient Yehud," *Studies in Religion/Sciences Religieuses* 39 (2010): 7–23.

and not necessarily alphabetic competency.[11] He concludes that much of what is currently contained in the literature of the Hebrew Bible had served as key parts of an indigenous curriculum for early Israelite scribes and other literate members of the upper class.[12]

K. van der Toorn considers the biblical texts to have been created for the scribal community by Levitical scribes attached to the temple, though the contents of the scrolls became more widely disseminated and known due to oral recitation. He identifies six ways scribes produced written texts: transcription of oral lore, invention of a new text, compilation of existing lore, either oral or written, expansion of an inherited text, adaptation of an existing text for a new audience, and integration of individual documents into a more comprehensive composition and then asserts no text in the Hebrew Bible is the explicit invention of a scribe.[13] However, he has not attempted to understand scribal compositional techniques, *per se*, and has not addressed the purpose of the creation of this written literature.

J. A. Sanders, on the other hand, has identified seven modes of intertextuality that were involved in the creation of the biblical literature. The literature is presumed to be be made up of previous literature, which is reflected through citation, allusion and paraphrases of the preceding literature so that the existing texts serve as the "generating force" underlying the elaboration of narrative or other textual expansion.[14] These include: citation with or without formula, weaving of scriptural phrases into newer composition, paraphrasing scriptural passages, reflection of the structure of scriptural passage, allusions to scriptural persons, episodes, or events, and echoes of Scripture passages in a later composition.[15] Unlike van der

---

11. David M. Carr, *Writing on the Tablet of the Heart: Origins of Scripture and Literature* (Oxford: Oxford University Press, 2005), 116–73.

12. Carr, *Writing on the Tablet*, 156. Although the approaches of Carr and Ben Zvi share significant similarites, key differences emerge from their different dating of the texts and from Carr's willingness to address forerunners or earlier versions of texts and Ben Zvi's reticence to do so.

13. Karel van der Toorn, *Scribal Culture and the Making of the Hebrew Bible* (Cambridge: Harvard University Press, 2007), 92, 110, 115.

14. James A. Sanders, "Canon as Dialogue," in *The Bible at Qumran: Text, Shape, and Interpretation* (ed. Peter W. Flint; Studies in the Dead Sea Scrolls and Related Literature; Grand Rapids, Mich.: Eerdmans, 2001), 7–26 (17).

15. James A. Sanders, "Intertextuality and Canon," in *On the Way to Nineveh: Studies in Honor of George M. Landes* (ed. Stephen L. Cook and Sarah C. Winter; Atlanta: Scholars Press, 1999), 316–33; idem, "Canon as Dialogue," 19.

Toorn, whose list seems to address what scribes typically did when working with texts, Sanders has addressed how they created literature.

P. Davies notes that some texts, like Esther, Ruth and Jonah, appear to have been written for enjoyment by a wider public and not just scribes, but he also notes this might have arisen in the Hellenistic setting, where the spread of literacy led to the adaptation of scribal education and its "canon" to a wider nonprofessional education, which led to changes to the "canon." He cautions against assuming the Masoretic-rabbinic canon represented solely a school curriculum and notes that the canonizing process seems to have involved debate over the movement of history, internationalizing, and universalizing, with a deliberate move to include texts that prevented a consensus view.[16] This brief survey demonstrates our lack of information about formal or informal education in Judah during the monarchy or in Yehud in the Persian period as well as the ultimate purpose behind creating a collection of written works of literature to be read and reread.

AUTHORITY, IDENTITY, AND SOCIAL MEMORY

A shared common past is a typical trait along with perceived kinship, a common language, a common religion, shared culture and customs, and sometimes regionalism, which help a group establish its identity and define who is an ethnic "insider" and who is an "outsider."[17] Those in

---

16. Philip R. Davies, *Scribes and Schools: The Canonization of the Hebrew Scriptures* (Library of Ancient Israel; Louisville: Westminster John Knox, 1998), 85, 124.

17. So, for example, Clifford Geertz, *The Interpretation of Cultures: Selected Essays by Clifford Geertz* (New York: Basic Books, 1973); especially germane are "The Integrative Revolution," The Interpretation of Cultures," 255–310 (261–63) and "Politics Past, Politics Present: Some Notes on the Uses of Anthropology in Understanding the New States," 327–41 (331–35); Harry C. Triandis, "Theoretical and Methodological Approaches to the Study of Collectivism and Individualism," in *Individualism and Collectivism: Theory, Method, and Applications* (ed. Uichol Kim et al.; Cross-Cultural Research and Methodology Series 18; London: Sage, 1994), 41–51; Anthony D. Smith, "Culture, community, and territory: the politics of ethnicity and nationalism," *International Affairs* 72/3 (1996): 445–58; Steve Fenton, *Ethnicity* (2nd rev. and updated ed.; Key Concepts in the Social Sciences; Cambridge, UK: Polity, 2013), 63–64. For a discussion of characteristics of collectivism in social groups in contemporary Indian culture, see Jai B. P. Sinha, "Collectivism, Social Energy, and Development in India," in *From a Different Perspective: Studies of Behavior Across Cultures* (ed. Isabel Reyes Lagunes and Ype H. Poortinga; Lisse: Swets & Zeitlinger, 1985), 109–19. For the relationship between individual and gender identity and ethnic identity, see Peter Wein-

power or with authority tend to control what is remembered and how, as well as what is forgotten in the collective memory of the larger group. They also are involved in the means used to make those memories familiar to, and inculcated in, members across society, which usually involves institutionalizing them to provide a material as well as intellectual existence in society.[18]

While subgroups exist that can have different understandings of communal memory that challenge hegemonic ones, they still are reacting to the established authoritative accounts that are accepted by either a majority of the wider group or those in power, who control what is considered to be "orthodox." Subgroups also often create and perpetuate a set of their own additional memories that they recall in particular gatherings and contexts, which are meaningful primarily for them. These, in turn, influence their understandings of the "orthodox" texts. An individual in a given society will assign meaning to the common social past, however it is expressed, on the basis of his or her cumulative experience and memories, individual and shared.[19] But even though the human brain operates in this way, socialization and enculturation from the time of birth predispose individuals to assign similar values and meanings to "concepts" consisting of semantic and sensory patterns that derive from interaction with one's environment.[20]

---

reich, "The Operationalization of Ethnic Identity," in *Ethnic Psychology: Research and Practice with Immigrants, Refugees, Native Peoples, Ethnic Groups and Sojourners* (ed. John W. Berry and Robert C. Annis; Amsterdam: Swets & Zeitlinger, 1988), 149–68.

18. For the content of knowledge and mode of thought in traditional social settings, see Robin Horton, "African Traditional Thought and Western Science: Part 1: From Tradition to Science," *Africa* 37 (1967): 50–71; idem, "African Traditional Thought and Western Science: Part 2: The Closed and Open Predicaments," *Africa* 37 (1967): 155–87.

19. For essays from multidisciplinary perspectives on how an individual's self-concept and constructed identity affect his or her behavior, see, e.g., Anita Jacobson-Widding (ed.), *Identity: Personal and Socio-Cultural* (Acta Universitatis Upsaliensis Uppsala Studies in Cultural Anthropology 5; Stockholm: Almqvist & Wicksell International, 1983).

20. For a study of how mother-child communication helps impart the prevailing socio-cultural system, see Soo Hang Choi, "Communicative Socialization Processes: Korea and Canada," in *Innovations in Cross-Cultural Psychology: Selected Papers from the Tenth International Conference of the International Association for Cross-Cultural Psychology* (ed. Saburo Iwawaki, Yoshihisa Kashima and Kwok Leung; Amsterdam: Swets & Zeitlinger, 1992), 103–22; more generally, see James Fentress and Chris Wick-

One of the most common ways to remember is narrative emplotment, oral or written. It is generally recognized amongst those engaged in memory studies in various disciplines that facts and details relating to selected events and experiences are lost in the early stages of the formulation of social memory as stories are created so the group can easily recall the incidents. There is a filtering process at work in the transformation of experienced events into images and "concepts" that will be easy to grasp, which will evoke a shared value-system and meaning amongst the group, and which will be capable of transmission.[21] By definition then, social memory is a deliberately simplified version of the past that has eliminated specific, nontypical details for the sake of easy recall, using standard elements and plot-lines that will evoke shared meanings that have been inculcated through socialization and informal or formal education.

The move to create a canon of authoritative texts within a society involves the selection and organization of certain texts from a larger group and putting in place a means to ensure their transmission.[22] Canons serve multiple functions in a society. They create collective identities, legitimate political power, and uphold or undermine value systems.[23] As the collective self-identity or value systems of the group change over time, the corpus of texts can be modified or adapted to reflect the new situation. The Hebrew Bible represents such a canon for emergent Jewish communities that self-identified as "children of Israel" and eventually, for Jewish-Christian and Christian communities as well, with modifications via truncation and expansion over time.

---

ham, *Social Memory* (New Perspectives on the Past; Oxford: Blackwell, 1992), 47; Pascal Boyer, *Religion Explained: The Human Instincts that Fashion Gods, Spirits, and Ancestors* (London: Vintage Books, 2002), 21, 47–51; Astrid Erll, *Memory in Culture* (trans. S. B. Young; Palgrave Macmillan Memory Studies; New York: Palgrave Macmillan, 2011), 82–89.

21. See, for example, Paul Connerton, *How Societies Remember* (Themes in the Social Sciences; Cambridge: Cambridge University Press, 1989), 76; Fentress and Wickham, *Social Memory*, 47–48, 71–74. It has also been noted that the inclusion of an element that does not fit with an expected plot-line or which is counter-intuitive makes it more memorable.

22. For the role of literature more generally in individual and social memory, see Erll, *Memory in Culture*, 75–82, 89–91, 160–71.

23. For these functions, see, for example, Jan Assmann, *Religion and Culture Memory: Ten Studies* (trans. R. Livingstone; Cultural Memory in the Present; Stanford, Calif.: Stanford University Press, 2006).

12   DEUTERONOMY–KINGS AS EMERGING AUTHORITATIVE BOOKS

Chapter Summaries and Conversation Openers

Deuteronomy

P. Davies begins his investigation of Deuteronomy by examining questions of authorship before moving on to questions about its growing authority. He notes its author blends the two genres of vassal treaty and law code and has the suzerain, unusually in this case, the deity YHWH, use an intermediary patron, secondarily identified as Moses, to address the vassal Israel directly, rather than its king, as would have been standard. In contrast to the call for the centralization of the temple cult in the book, the administration of Torah is not centralized or located in that temple cult; it is separate. He posits the need to give careful consideration to the book's creation in Samaria rather than in Yehud in the early Persian period.

He then argues that Deuteronomy did not have intrinsic authority when it was composed but gained it subsequently, through giving it secondary endorsement via the two institutions that are central to the book of Kings: kingship (King Josiah) and prophecy (Huldah). Deuteronomy envisages a society in which the token king rules by the law book (Deut 17:14–20) and in which prophets can only give messages that are consistent with the commandments in the law book (Deut 13). It also envisages Levites working in towns and villages throughout Samaria and Yehud to implement the law book, in accordance with requirements of the Persian Empire. Yet, Davies also argues the book of Deuteronomy was never *taught* outside the scribal schools in Jerusalem and Samaria or Gerizim; the text remained for the most part the domain of the clerics and educated laity. He thinks we can infer from the move to give it added authority by introducing it into the book of Kings that its contents did not carry sufficient authority or that they were challenged by another group, such as those responsible for Chronicles.

Deuteronomy is seen to be a utopian book in its vision of an Israel bound by a religious treaty to create a specific, "ideal" society. It represents a program for the new religion of YHWH and its new "Israel" to become not just a cult but a *culture*, in which Torah replaces monarchy and prophecy and indeed almost everything else, and its ministers are Levites—priests, but mostly without a sanctuary. It advocates a new pattern of religion in which the people become responsible for their own behavior and fate by choosing or not choosing to observe the community and domestic laws commanded by YHWH, which serve as the conditional basis of his election of Israel. Its authority resides in its ethic, the set of principles it contains, by which its reenvisioned, new "Israel" was to define itself.

The pilgrimage festivals, especially Passover, become the most important element of the envisioned ongoing, centralized temple cult; its daily priestly rituals are of little or no import. Deuteronomy has Moses deliver the "book of the law" as part of a larger speech that recalls the exodus. It thus identifies the exodus story as the founding event and the law book as the founding constitution of the new nation and in the process, assigns itself the status of a foundational *text*.

In the second article on Deuteronomy, C. Levin accepts that the earliest nucleus of Deuteronomy is a reworking of the Covenant Code to emphasize centralization of the national cult; it contains social-ethical intentions in its paraenetic sections, like the Covenant Code. This nucleus dates from the time of Josiah at the end of the seventh century B.C.E. and, by implication, was to give divine weight to the desired centralization program by associating its promotion by YHWH himself as a part of the stipulations to be obeyed by Israel when the covenant was made at Mt Sinai. It is presented as something that is to apply once the people enter the Promised Land, revealed to the people by Moses only on the eve of the conquest, when the need for cult centralization would become directly relevant. Subsequently, at the beginning of the sixth century when the country was under impending Neo-Babylonian conquest, the code was set into its historical framework. He then argues that, at the end of the sixth century B.C.E, after Yehud had become a Persian province and hope for the rebirth of the Davidic monarchy had died, the cultic community of Jerusalem considered itself to be YHWH's direct vassal in place of the former Davidic line and the law code of Deuteronomy was revised to take on the form of a treaty between YHWH Elohim and Israel directly, and thus, to serve as a code of behavior toward YHWH Elohim himself.

The main thrust of the paper focuses on further adaptations to the book undertaken in the Persian and Hellenistic periods that center on two themes: the ethics of brotherhood and the care of the poor. Careful, analytical readings of Deut 15:1-6, 7-11, 12-18; 19:16-21; 22:1-4; 23:20-2; 24:7, 10-13, 14-15; 25:1-3 in various versions are undertaken to tease out editorial layers. Levin argues that passages that develop the theme of the ethics of brotherhood assume the presence of the covenant theology revisions and so reflect a chronologically subsequent development. They were not part of the original law code, as commonly assumed. Rather, they reflect the morality of the Jewish temple community, which constituted an ethno-religious minority within the larger population of Yehud in the Persian period. The theme of the care of the poor reflects links with the "devout poor" in the Psalms and similar supplements also made to the prophetic books that identify "the poor" as a religiously devout group with a special closeness to God who will survive the eschatological judgment. It reflects concerns that developed in the Hellenistic period.

There is little direct conversation between the two papers, yet together, they raise a number of important issues for futher reflection. One posits the monarchic era as the time of composition and the other the Persian period; each provides a rationale for the proposed socio-historical context. How does a decision about origin impact on the book's authority? How does purpose relate to authority? While one sees authority from the beginning, inherent in the book's composition, the other posits authority being a secondary development, which accounts for the story of the finding of the law scroll during temple renovations in the reign of King Josiah. What clues can be used to deduce or understand a text's primary or secondary authority? When can we identify the existence of something we would call a book of Deuteronomy; would it only be once the law code was set in its narrative framework? How did authority work in emerging Jewish communities such that it was possible to alter the text of an authoritiave book over centuries, on the one hand, and yet create a different book from Exodus, rather than simply updating that book? Why did this book form a core for both the Samarian and Judean communities?

Joshua

E. A. Knauf tackles the twofold question of authority relating to the book of Joshua: why the Joshua character grew in authority, and why his story was formulated as a book, which became authoritative. He answers the first by noting that the narrative beginning either in Genesis or Exodus needs an ending other than what is in Deut 34, where the Israelites are still in the desert, outside time and space. The account of how they came into their land and possessed it under Moses' appointed prophetic successor, Joshua (Deut 31–34 if not Exod 15–Deut 34), is required. Its specific format as a book derives from the growth of the corpora of texts that eventually became the two collections that comprise Torah and Prophets. As the first book of the latter corpus, it exemplifies the role of the prophets who will succeed Moses but never be his equal: God talks to them and they may perform miracles but primarily, they are to learn, teach, and apply Torah and write down their divine encounters. The core of the book is the distribution of the land for Israelite tenure. This theology was particularly germane to two developments in the Persian period: 1) the imperial bureaucracy was interested in confiscating communal land to create military fiefs; and 2) once money was introduced, land could be used to secure agricultural credit. The book offers its intended Persian audience a utopian political vision of every person under his or her vine and fig tree, forever. Jerusalem is conspicuously absent but is implied: a new Jerusalem, regulated by Torah and associated with the Second Temple.

In the second article on Joshua, S. Frolov argues that, like the book of Judges, Joshua is not likely to have been read independently. It cannot be known if it were created as a separate unit prior to the formation of the canonical Enneateuch, but the internal use of the opening formula, "And it happened after the death of PN" in Josh 1:1; Judg 1:1; 2 Sam 1:1 and 2 Kgs 1:1suggests it was part of an integral composition. It also fits the roughly symmetrical distribution of the most prominent genres (narratives, genealogies, commandments and admonitions) in the Enneateuch. As a result, he thinks we can only ask how Joshua affected the reception of the larger corpus of Genesis–2 Kings, of which it was an integral part. He notes it functions in the larger whole by highlighting the rewards that come from observing Torah, especially keeping the First Commandment, in contrast to the transgression of Torah and the associated punishment and decline in Judges–Kings. As such, it serves to represent blessing, as opposed to curse, matching blessing in Lev 26:3–39 and curse in Deut 28:1–68 and helping to shape the Enneateuch as a suzerain treaty, with the preamble in Gen 1–Exod 19; the stipulations in Exod 20–Deut 34, and the blessings and curses in Joshua–Kings.

For Frolov, the reassurance that YHWH will reward those who observe Torah with uncontested control over land of their own and "rest round about" was particularly important for a group whose collective memory included forced relocation. Yet, he also notes how the political situation in the Persian period did not correspond to what is depicted in either Joshua or in Kings, which could generate doubts about the portrayed causal link between land and Torah observance as well as doubts that the entrenched imperial system could ever change. At the same time, by the later Persian period, Joshua's depiction of a nondynastic, non-Davidic leader working in tandem with the high priest could provide a working model for Israel beyond monarchy, even if it originally were meant to be an inadequate, temporary solution. In the Hellenistic period, however, the "transformative" plot-line of the book, where the Canaanite landscape becomes reapportioned to Torah-observant Israelites, but not under Davidic leadership, was closer to experienced reality. As a result, an original Enneateuch, which had been truncated in the Persian period to create a Pentateuch without a problematic link between land and Torah observance, could be restored, but now as two collections instead of one: the Torah and the Former Prophets.

Both of these essays grapple with the role of the book of Joshua within a story-line that extends from Genesis through 2 Kings. Both authors agree that a main focus in the book is ownership of the Promised Land, which fulfils the Abrahamic promise. Both also tend to argue that Joshua would not have existed as an independent composition set side by side with other existing compositions so that over time, a periodized "time-line" would have developed via juxtaposition; rather, it would have been composed as part of a multivolume project. Yet, as the first book of the eventual prophetic collection in Jewish tradition, it seems odd that Joshua is never called a prophet. His leadership role in Israel after Moses is dependent upon accounts in earlier Pentateuchal books that depict or describe him directly as Moses' "assistant" (*mešeret*) (Exod 17, 24, 33; Num 11, 13, 14; Deut 1:38; 3:21, 28; 31:3, 7; 34:9) and which depict YHWH selecting him to be the new leader (Num 14; 27:18–22) and directly commissioning him (Deut 31:14, 23). The audience is left to infer that Joshua is the "prophet like Moses."

How can we sort out the dual depiction of Joshua as military leader and yet as an obedient Torah-follower and Torah-interpreter, who also follows direct commands from YHWH? Were both an integral part of the original plot and if so, why? Is the opening line of the book original or part of the redactional process that has created the Hexateuch or Enneateuch? Is the unstated prophetic function actually intended at the compositional or redactional level? As noted by Knauf, Jerusalem is not mentioned directly either but certainly is implied.

While both scholars seem to favor a date of composition in the Persian period, neither addresses directly the relationship between purpose and authority. Both, however, seem to assume that the meta-story line was meant to carry social authority as a definitive version of a shared past, lending the book of Joshua authority because of the role it plays in developing a definitive version of the past. Does it also serve to endorse a form of political leadership that is relevant for its originating community as well as for subsequent communites? Does it both uphold a Torah-based value system and undermine another competing system at the time of writing?

Judges

Y. Amit argues that a book of Judges was the earliest composition that is now part of the collected books that can be classified as ancient "history-writing." It was composed in Judah near the end of the eighth century B.C.E. to understand and justify the conquest of Israel by the Assyrians in 722 B.C.E. and its conversion to a province. It was meant to explore how Judah could avoid a similar fate in the future. It also explored whether foreign imperial kings derived their power from YHWH or not, and whether history has meaning or is arbitrary. This preliminary composition, which was authoritative by virtue of having gained a certain status from being read and reread, was subsequently taken up by Deuteronomistic editors and made into a description of the period from the death of Joshua to the birth of Samuel, with chapters 19–21 being a subsequent addition to address concerns of a later audience.

Evidence of the book's ongoing authority in the Persian and Hellenistic periods is then provided; not only did it enjoy status as part of the so-called Deuteronomistic History, but it dealt with a number of issues the Judean intellectuals of the time deemed central: divine mercy, the status of "the north" vis à vis Yehud; the paradigmatic character of history; divine kingship; Saulide-Davidic rivalry, and the legitimacy of foreign women. It allowed the past to serve as a source of inspiration and brain-storming about central issues of concern in later generations.

In the second article on Judges, S. Gillmayr-Bucher, on the other hand, argues two central themes in Judges ensured its ongoing relevance in the Persian period, leading to its growing authoritative status: the search for Israel's identity and the question of leadership. While the specific tribes vary within the book, there is, nevertheless, an emphasis throughout on Israel as a distinct ethnic unit to be distinguished from other groups living in the area and defined particularly by its religion. The borders are established, so the issue is not primarily conquest, which is mentioned in chapters 1 and 18–19, but rather, maintaining supremacy over the land in the face of threats from outside nations. Israel's self-identity is reflected in two key elements: a shared origin story—the exodus from Egypt—and solidarity, which is vital to its survival. The same ideas appear in the book of Joshua.

Leadership is also a central focus in the book. By depicting the achievement of individual leaders over a span of time, the book shows they accomplish nothing; the behavior of the people remains wayward and unacceptable to YHWH. Judges 2:11–19 reduces the heroic judges to instruments of God, who fail, ultimately, to guide Israel, raising the question, can anyone do so? It is unclear if the references to the lack of a king in chapters 17–21 are an appeal to an ideal king as a solution to leadership or not, but there is a strong implication that the temporal leader must teach the people Torah so they have a guideline for how to live their lives as a united community of tribes on its land, even if not necessarily as an independent political entity.

Judges offered readers and rereaders in the Persian era a critique of the forms of heroic and royal leadership depicted in the books of Joshua and Kings; neither worked, ultimately. It also offered an alternate vision to that set forth in Ezra-Nehemiah that focuses on Judah/Yehud only; in Judges, Judah is not a leader and is not on its own; it is one of the constituent tribes that comprise Israel. The debate over the relationship and common identity of those living in the adjoining provinces of Samaria and Yehud finds support for wider unity, in spite of its problematic nature, not for isolationism.

Both contributors understand Judges to have as a central focus the issue of leadership; however, is that only leadership by foreign imperial kings, native leaders, or both? How does the other focus on Israelite identity play out and interact with the emphasis on leadership? Does the book ultimately advocate a form of theocracy based on Torah-teaching and group solidarity expressed through torah-observance, without a temporal leader? Or, does it accept that there inevitably will be a temporal leader, native or foreign, who most likely will exhibit many failings and rule inadequately, but that his policies and shortcomings are ultimately irrelevant since the people of Israel have Torah and can survive and even thrive if they, as a group, follow it? Who does this book understand should be the teacher(s) of Torah? Is it civil or religious authorities? Can Israel rely on divine mercy and leniency if the people disobey Torah or is exile from the homeland a possible catastrophe that can be repeated?

How can we firmly identify earlier versions of a current biblical book and locate their period and place of composition? Is the "all-Israel" perspective part of the original shaping of the book or the product of later editing, when Judges found its location amongst other books that resulted in its current place in the periodization of the past that envisioned a twelve-tribe premonarchic Israel? Does the failure of judges who have tribal affiliations other than with Judah and Benjamin intentionally denigrate Samaria in favor of Yehud? When the past serves as a source of inspiration and brainstorming, should we assume that the past as depicted is historically accurate or might it equally be idealized or fashioned to examine painful or potentially dangerous present situations safely by setting them in a different time period and exploring likely consequences of certain courses of present action? What concerns are addressed by chapters 19–21?

SAMUEL

T. Bolin focuses his essay on those who read 1–2 Samuel in the Persian and Hellenistic periods and what they saw as authoritative in this narrative. He concentrates on the educational system in Jerusalem in Yehud in order better to understand the context in which collecting, copying, and the incorporation of texts, including Samuel, took place. Arguing for the likely clearing away of Persian-era remains in Jerusalem for building projects undertaken in the Hellenistic and Roman periods, he suggests that the population in the city and its environs in the Persian period would have been sufficiently large to have supported an educational system. Noting the presence of Greek imports and, therefore, Greek influence in the southern Levant already in the Persian period, he suggests the Judean educational system was likely to have been modeled already under the Persians on the goals current in Greece and western Asia Minor rather than on those of the older ancient Near Eastern and Egyptian systems, but definitely was set up in this way by the Hellenistic period. While both involved the mastery of a canon of set texts, the latter aimed at acquiring knowledge that was to be used in the ongoing service of kings and gods, while the former aimed at instilling the inherited cultural norms in the next generation of elite priestly and nonpriestly boys.

The only clues we have about how 1–2 Samuel were understood in these two periods are in the partially paralleled sections in 1–2 Chronicles, in the fourteen psalms with superscriptions related to the life of David, twelve of which allude to stories in Samuel, and apparent allusions to events in Samuel found in Qohelet, whose speaker has assumed the persona of Solomon. It is suggested that the fourteen psalms with superscriptions associated with the life of David represent recorded exemplars of the best oral recitations of advanced students who were set the task of generating a response to a morally or theologically problematic episode in the learned canon as the culmination of their years of training.

In the second article on the books of Samuel, K.-P. Adam suggests the way to determine how the books were authoritative in the Persian period is to focus on the themes, Deuteronomistic language, and traditions that grew or were revised in this era. Different versions of the text help establish these later developments. Typical modes of reception also determine their authority. He then examines the contribution the books make to legal debates in the Persian period in a number of narratives that comment in detail on decision-making and legal authority, procedure, and content. These include rights of the king (2 Sam 8:10–22; 2 Sam 7*) and violence between individuals, including homicide and revenge (1 Sam 18–27*; 2 Sam 1–4; 11–14). He examines two legal parables in more depth, 2 Sam 12 and 2 Sam 14:2–22, the latter of which he suggests was created in Yehud in the Persian period. 2 Sam 12:1–4 is considered a secondary unit, invented to reveal the legal liability David bears for Uriah's death, while 2 Sam 12:15–24b is seen to be a later insertion rebutting claims that Solomon had dishonorable origins. It is based on the principle of individual retributive justice typical of the Chronicler but not the Dtr.

A number of other likely Persian-era expansions are identified in the footnotes. These include 1 Sam 8*, 12*; 1 Sam 14:23–46; 1 Sam 17:1–18:5 MT; the feud-like quarrel between the protagonists Saul and David in 1 Sam 18–27*; the theme of the fundamental solidarity of the living with the dead (1 Sam 17:44, 46; 2 Sam 21:1–14); the fascination with heroic scenes of single combat (1 Sam 17; 2 Sam 23:9–12, 20–23); the Greek tradition of lists of heroes (2 Sam 23:24–39), the superiority of prophet over king (e.g.1 Sam 19:18–24) and the tragic character of Saul (1 Sam 10:8; 13:7–13a; 10:17–27; 14:24–46; 26*; 28* and 1 Sam 31*). The reasons for their appeal to a Persian-era audience are not explored, however, since the focus of the chapter is on legal narratives in the book, especially 2 Sam 14.

The incident involving the wise woman of Tekoa in 2 Sam 14:2–22 is identified as an inserted, stylized case narrative or "judicial parable" on various grounds: 1) the change in David's attitude between 13:39 and 14:1, which likely prompted the episode's insertion; 2) the use of generic designations for the protagonists that typify inserted case narrative; 3) the failure of the wise woman episode otherwise to be referenced; 4) the story's consideration of legal aspects of Absalom's return, whose short plot is an excursus on a closely related theme of relevance for key characters in the books of Samuel; and 5) the use of nuanced categories of guilt. The narrative modifies the existing laws on homicide, asylum, and revenge in the Pentateuch while juxtaposing two contrasting images of David in connection with royal judicial authority in the macro-text. 2 Samuel 14 depicts him as a mellow king, but 1 Kgs 1–2 portrays him as a law-abiding hardliner who defers the execution of justice in the case of Joab to his successor. The possibility is raised that the judicial parable in 1 Sam 14, which uses the device of entrapment like Greek drama and is framed primarily as direct speech, had an origin in oral performance. Be that as it may, the current written form is directed at a particular audience whose sociohistorical, religious and social contexts are acknowledged to need further investigation.

There is no real intersection between these two essays, each of which focuses on aspects of authority or the compositional history of the books of Samuel more than on the issue of the way(s) in which the books of Samuel would have been deemed authoritative by audiences in the later Persian and early Hellenistic periods. Nevertheless, each essay generates a few questions. The date of the use of the texts for scribal education or a more widely based philosophical and moral education has already been raised in an earlier section of the Introduction. What is the relationship between the books of Samuel and the books of Kings, both of which focus on kings during the time of the monarchies of Israel and Judah but which are developed in different ways? Why was the social memory of David shifted over time from being founding hero and warrior to being a paragon of personal piety? Was this a deliberate expansion of David as a memory node, or an attempt to reshape and privilege a new image over an older one? Which social subgroup might have been responsible, and what might be revealed about the issue of the eternal Davidic covenant? How does a focus on the themes, Deuteronomistic language, and traditions that grew or were revised in the later Persian or early Hellenistic period help us determine how the books were authoritative in these two periods?

Were the proposed additions necessary in order for the book to be seen to be relevant and gain some sort of authority, or was the earlier form already authoritative to some degree so that such expansions, which it is assumed reflect live issues in the reading community at the time of their additions, enhance it existing status? Was the administration of law a new key issue in one or both of these time periods, or does 1 Sam 14 help qualify the portrait of David as a fallible human, which might be intended to counter the growing trend in other circles to idealize him, which found expression in the books of Chronicles? Was there a perceived need to undermine royal authority in the administration of justice in favor of priestly or Levitical administration of local law? Why would the biblical redactors be so open to using Greek literary techniques and trends to shape the shared account of their own group's past, which is meant to define them as an ethnos with a distinctive value system? Would any of these literary techniques or trends have been utilized in a way to oppose Hellenistic culture, or would their use have been an embracing of some of it elements?

Kings

T. Römer begins by noting that the Septuagint translators considered 1–2 Kings to belong together with 1–2 Samuel; they called this history of the monarchies of Israel and Judah 1–4 Reigns, so it is uncertain that Kings was ever intended to be read without Samuel preceding it. In the Persian period, Kings was not authoritative in the sense of its having reached a final, agreed form, as indicated by the divergent form from the MT that underlies the Greek translation. It was also not yet authoritative in Yehud or Babylonia for its implied, intended Judean audiences in the sense of being "the" accepted view of the era of the monarchies or else Chronicles would not have been composed in the later Persian or early Hellenistic period and included in the Hebrew and Christian canons. However, by implication, the story of the monarchies was deemed an important tradition to be preserved and transmitted to future generations. The ambiguous ending allows for different meanings and functions; if Kings is read in isolation or as the end to an Enneateuch, then 2 Kgs 25:27–30 is an acceptance of the exile; but read as part of the Prophets, as it is in Jewish tradition, it is a transition to prophetic oracles concerning an ideal king in Isaiah or a new David in Ezekiel.

The condemnation of Solomon's mingling with foreign women reflects one ideological option in the discussion taking place in the Persian period about how nascent Jewish identity should be built: via segregation. The book relates how kingship finally failed, due to the actions of people and kings, and suggests another authority is needed. Read in the second half of the Persian period, this message would have resonated with the acceptance of the loss of political autonomy by the economic and intellectual leaders of nascent Judaism.

Kings contains a discourse about good kings and bad kings and the limitation of royal authority. Good kings follow two prescriptions from the book of Deuteronomy: the exclusive veneration of YHWH and the acceptance of the temple in Jerusalem as the only legitimate place to worship him. In the Persian period, most of the prophetic narratives in Kings were added to foster its prophetic character and authority. By the end of the book, prophets move from being messengers of doom to kings to preachers of *tōrâ*. In the Persian period, then, the book of Kings ranks prophetic authority above royal authority for its readers, but both types become relative and subordinate to the final authority of Moses and the Torah, which would have been understood to be the Pentateuch or a forerunner to it. In 2 Kgs 22–23, Torah replaces the traditional markers of religious identity: temple, prophet, and king. For those who accepted integration into the Persian Empire, prophetic proclamations of the restoration of the Davidic kingship would have been seen to be problematic and were to be curbed by making Torah the authoritative word of God.

In the second article on the books of Kings, J. Linville argues that the authority of Kings lay not in its endorsement of certain ideological points but rather, in its being part of a flexible, open-ended social discourse that allowed readers to use ritual episodes and prototypical events to reflect on the differences between their lives and the social constructions found in Kings and other texts. It was part of a larger matrix of stories and myths that allowed different views of what makes an ideal society and its norms to be considered and debated, while also establishing status and authority for those who could understand the enigmas addressed in, and the disjunctions between, different texts. The key to understanding Kings is to compare and contrast it with other myths of Israel's history and identity. The book endorses acceptance of a unified Israel willingly bound to YHWH by a covenant, an ideal that would have been open to debate and reinterpretation in the late Persian and early Hellenistic periods. The ending, which leaves Judah in exile, also would have raised questions about the status of Second Temple Jerusalem.

"Exilicist" thought is not the purview of a single ideology but rather, an ancient Judean way of conceptualizing the past and present that found expression in various forms in the books that now constitute the Hebrew Bible. It was not the only lens used to understand the termination of the monarchic past in the Persian and Hellenistic periods; Chronicles views the exile as the end to Sabbath rest (2 Chr 36:20–21). Kings gained authority from recognizing the authority of Moses but at the same time, produced a new myth at odds with aspects of the old myth in order to provoke new ways of imagining society.

The book, as well as the entire collection of books comprising the Former Prophets, can be seen to constitute a myth about the myth of how Torah was revealed and how its covenant curses became reality. It turns the myth of exile into the myth of exodus but omits the myth of a new, successful conquest, thereby providing a useful, alternate reality in which readers in the late Persian and early Hellenistic periods could question, affirm, or perhaps subvert both the *status quo* and projected social or political agendas. In its myths concerning the rituals of Sukkot (1 Kgs 8–9) and Passover (2 Kgs 22–23), as well as in stories dealing with regular temple rituals, the book authorizes the ongoing significance of all three types of rituals in the social situations of its readers while also contributing to important discourses on the boundaries, characteristic features, and defining social actions of the group identifying itself as Israel in the target periods, and later.

An interesting dialogue emerges from reading these two articles in succession. There is agreement over an emphasis on Torah and on exile, but a different view of how readers would have interacted with the stories they encountered in Kings and the message they would have taken away. For Römer, the addition of prophetic authority to the texts in the Persian period has resulted in a relegation of royal authority to third-place, with Moses and Torah becoming the central authority taught by the prophets that ultimately replaces king, prophet, and temple, the traditional markers of religious identity. Originally, the book had been a discourse over good kings and bad kings, and so, more generally, about the limitations of royal authority. For Linville, the stories that highlight temple rituals and pilgrimage festivals send a clear signal that the temple and its calendar continued to play a central role in the social fabric of Judeans in the Persian and Hellenistic periods. He agrees that Torah is operative in the book in that the plot-line tells how the covenant curses from Sinai/Horeb were made reality but does not see it to be a central aspect, although he thinks the authority of the book was enhanced by its acceptance of the authority of Moses. Yet Linville also sees scope for readers not only to affirm the implied *status quo* of the temple of their day but also to question or subvert it, offering two additional options that reflect what Römer considered to be the only option. Linville sees the book to allow hearers to reflect over their own situation in contrast to what is found in the texts, as part of a larger flexible discourse over what makes an ideal society, with no endorsement of certain ideologies and rejection of others. Römer, on the other hand, seems to think the book is modeling certain ideologies that it wants hearers to endorse, though perhaps he would agree that some ideas are floated without necessarily expecting full agreement, as ways to prompt reflection and debate.

Since both Kings and Chronicles, which cover much of the same ground but also differ in terms of overall scope, were accepted as authoritative, can we assume Chronicles could only have been written at a point in time before Samuel had gained authority? Does authoritative status mean no further changes to a given book can be introduced? If so, does this necessitate the writing of a new work if one wants to object to ideas in the authoritative one? How can we infer authorial intent from finished, edited products? Don't authors usually have points of view they want their readers to accept and endorse, over against competing views? If so, does any single composition encourage open reflection and debate, or is this only the net result of a collection of compositions that advocate different views, forcing the reader to reflect and take a personal stand amongst the options on offer? If we were to read Samuel and Kings as a single literary composition, as the LXX translators did, would it modify any of the views expressed by the two contributors or reinforce their points implicitly or explicitly?

It is time for you, the reader, to engage directly with the full text of the ten essays in this volume and discover what questions and further thoughts they trigger in your mind, whether as monologues or as dialogues. There are many interesting ideas on offer here, relating to authority as well as to other aspects of individual books.

The Authority of Deuteronomy

Philip R. Davies

Introduction

The reception of a text does not necessarily depend upon the nature of its conception. However, the imputed origins of Deuteronomy given in the book itself (1:1) and its "rediscovery" in 2 Kgs 22 are themselves part of the book's own reception, and we must therefore try to determine what we regard as its historical origin, not for its own sake, but to evaluate the stories told of its origin and history.

How Deuteronomy came about and what kind of a composition it is are mutually entailed questions that still need to be addressed separately and in the right sequence. Unfortunately, the question of dating (for reasons connected with the classical documentary theory of Pentateuchal formation) has too often taken priority over the question of purpose, and, having been widely regarded as settled, has rather predetermined the more basic questions of nature and purpose. How this scroll became "authorized" in the first place can only be determined with some probability if we begin not with an accepted date and setting but by asking what it was seeking to achieve. What do its implied objectives—or its vision of Israelite society—tell us about the circumstances of its conception? To answer this question is not, of course, the primary purpose of this essay, which is about its reception as an authoritative book: but at the very least the purpose should disclose its *intended* reception, and so very probably its *initial* reception.

Deuteronomy's "Israel"

Deuteronomy defines a novel conception of the manner of the relationship between "Israel" and its "tribes" (1:13,15; 5:23; 12:5,14; 16:18; 18:5 etc.) on the one hand and its deity on the other. This relationship is articulated in terms of a "covenant" (ברית *běrît* occurs twenty-seven times in the book) between the deity and the people, and encompasses nearly all aspects of social and domestic life. "Israel" is also strongly distinguished from its neighbors in the land given to it by its god, with whom it is not to intermarry nor share any cultural traits; such an imposition of strict boundaries suggest an ethnicizing agenda. Such an agenda is further indicated by regular allusions to the land as promised to Israel's ancestors (forty-seven references to "fathers/ancestors") and to an original event of ethnogenesis, the deliverance from Egypt (forty-six references to "Egypt").[1] Deuteronomy seeks to define Israel in terms of its *religion* and not by its genealogical descent or its cult or its political status. Its religion, moreover, embraces most aspects of its cultural life. In addition, Deuteronomy is not as such concerned with monotheism as we now understand that: the question of the existence of other gods remains obscure. What is crucial is that Israel's exclusive identity is mirrored by the exclusive identity of its own god.[2]

But what *is* Deuteronomy's "Israel"? It is not the kingdom of that name, nor its political successor, the province of Samerina. Its "tribes" are enumerated as twelve in the blessing-and-curse ritual of ch. 27 and include six on Mt. Ebal and six on Mt. Gerizim; both kingdoms or provinces are thus included in what is a religious and cultural entity, a tribal people. But when and how did such an entity—or such a concept—come into existence? In a detailed examination of this question, I have proposed that the only possible *terminus a quo* for such a concept is after 586 B.C.E., with the ending of the royal dynasty in Jerusalem and the emergence of Benjaminite hegemony in Yehud.[3] One important consequence of this shift of political power was a reversal of previous hostile relations between the two

---

1. Festive meals have also recently been suggested by as a further identity-forming practice; see Peter Altmann, *Festive Meals in Ancient Israel: Deuteronomy's Identity Politics in Their Ancient Near Eastern Context* (BZAW 424; Berlin: de Gruyter, 2011).

2. The nature of Deuteronomy's "monotheism" might provide an important clue to its historical context. But the major study by Nathan MacDonald confines itself to theological definitions and does not engage with the diachronic aspect of the emergence of "high god" beliefs within the imperialized world of the Levant (*Deuteronomy and the Meaning of "Monotheism"* [FAT 2/1; Tübingen: Mohr Siebeck, 2003]). Elsewhere I have termed such beliefs "imperial theism"; see Philip R. Davies, "M*n*th**sm" (paper presented at the SBL International Meeting, London, July 6, 2011).

3. Philip R. Davies, *The Origins of Biblical Israel* (LHBOTS 485; London: T&T Clark, 2007).

former kingdoms, and, more importantly, the adoption of the cult of the "god of Israel" within Judah, a cult centered on the temple of Bethel, which lay at this time within the borders of Judah but had previously functioned as a royal temple in the kingdom of Israel. Its association with Jacob probably dates from the monarchic period, in which the patriarch was also given the name "Israel." One result of this cultic integration of Samaria and Judah was, therefore, the adoption of the patriarch Judah as a son of Jacob, the eponymous "Israel," and thus the adoption of a *religious* Israelite identity within Judah. Hereafter "Israel" remains a religious and never a political designation.[4] This is the "Israel" of Deuteronomy—and of the Pentateuch as a whole—and hence both populations shared these documents. We can thus conclude that Deuteronomy is at least in part about providing a new or recently developed "Israel" with a number of crucial ethnic characteristics: cult, ancestry, founding legend, legal customs.

The Genre of Deuteronomy

The literary form that this definition takes, at least in its canonized shape, seems to have been inspired by two standard diplomatic-scribal genres: the vassal treaty and the law code. Both genres are of considerable antiquity and no doubt comprised part of the scribal repertory of the kingdoms of Israel and Judah and also later of the provinces of Samaria and Yehud. There remains some disagreement[5] over whether the Hittite vassal treaty

---

4. That the inhabitants of Samaria continued to be addressed as "Israel," however, can be deduced from a number of oracles in the book of Jeremiah that are clearly addressed to Samaria and not to Judah. See Davies, *Origins of Biblical Israel*, 119–20.

5. The similarities between Deuteronomy and the Hittite vassal treaty were first pointed out by George E. Mendenhall, "Covenant Forms in Israelite Tradition," *BA* 17 (1954): 49–76. Later studies extended the comparison to Assyrian treaties or "loyalty oaths"; see, for example, Dennis J. McCarthy, *Treaty and Covenant: A Study in Form in Ancient Oriental Documents and in the Old Testament* (AnBib 21; Rome: Pontifical Biblical Institute, 1963). Moshe Weinfeld provides an excellent review (*Deuteronomy and the Deuteronomic School* [Oxford: Clarendon, 1972], 59–157), as do George E. Mendenhall and Gary Herion ("Covenant," *ABD* 1:1179–1202). Thomas Römer argues against any possibility of dependence on Hittite treaties and favors the loyalty oaths of Esarhaddon (*The So-Called Deuteronomistic History: A Sociological, Historical and Literary Introduction* [London: T&T Clark, 2007], 74–78). Compare the views of Bernard M. Levinson, *Deuteronomy and the Hermeneutics of Legal Innovation* (New York: Oxford University Press, 1998); Simo Parpola and Kazuko Watanabe, eds., *Neo-Assyr-*

or the Neo-Assyrian loyalty oath furnishes the more precise model. The historical prologue (chs. 1–11) is characteristic of Hittite treaties and is followed by stipulations, provision for the deposit of the treaty or public reading, witnesses, and finally, blessing and curses. Apart from the invocation of witnesses, all these are present in Deuteronomy. The vassal treaties of Esarhaddon are characterized by demands to "love" the king; the identical language is present in Deuteronomy. Both also contain curses. These options are not exclusive: if the authors knew both genres, they could well have been combined. Nor should either model be taken to imply either a *terminus a quo* date[6] or an anti-imperial device. The laws in Deuteronomy's central section (chs. 12–26), after all, bear comparison with a very ancient Akkadian tradition. These law codes, like Deuteronomy's, govern most aspects of social life (unlike vassal treaties). But unlike the law codes, Deuteronomy expresses the laws in a hortatory style that utilizes both singular and plural second person forms (explanations for this alternation are numerous and mostly unconvincing.[7]) What this rhetorical style implies

---

ian *Treaties and Loyalty Oaths* (SAA 2; Helsinki: Helsinki University Press, 1988); and John Van Seters, *A Law Book for the Diaspora: Revision in the Study of the Covenant Code* (Oxford: Oxford University Press, 2003), 99–101. On the forms of the ancient Mesopotamian law code, see Martha T. Roth, *Law Collections from Mesopotamia and Asia Minor* (Writings from the Ancient World 6; Atlanta: Society of Biblical Literature, 1995). For a recent convenient summary, see Diana Edelman et al., *The Books of Moses: Opening the Books* (BibleWorld; Sheffield: Equinox, 2012), 147–54.

6. So pointed out by E. Axel Knauf, "Observations on Judah's Social and Economic History and The Dating of The Laws In Deuteronomy," *JHS* 9:18 (2009), available online at http://www.jhsonline.org/Articles/article_120.pdf and in *Perspectives in Hebrew Scriptures VI: Comprising the Contents of Journal of Hebrew Scriptures, vol. 9* (ed. Ehud Ben Zvi; Piscataway, N.J.: Gorgias, 2010), 387–93.

7. Explanations include the presence of different redactional layers, that the singular is addressed to the king, and that it is a rhetorical device to address each Israelite individually. The book itself nowhere suggests that any particular individual is being addressed, and the notion of a king, for example, as the addressee is an inference from the book's conjectured original context in the reign of Josiah and the injunction that the king is to be presented with a copy (17:18–19). But the possibility that a later writer would expand an existing singular text, or attach it to another, in a plural address, while leaving the singular mode of address, is problematic. For discussion and critique of the major alternatives, see Timothy A. Lenchak, *Choose Life! A Rhetorical-Critical Investigation of Deuteronomy 28, 69–30,20* (AnBib 129; Rome: Pontifical Biblical Institute, 1993), 10–16. The view taken here, that they are stylistic, follows, among others, Norbert Lohfink, *Das Hauptgebot: eine Untersuchung literarischer Einleitungsfragen zu Dtn 5–11* (AnBib 20; Rome: Pontifical Biblical Institute, 1963); Walter Beyerlin, "Die

by way of speech is given a concrete setting (1:1) in the mouth of Moses on the steppes of Moab prior to initial entry into Canaan, and with Deuteronomy's "Israel" as the audience.

The radical character of Deuteronomy's restructuring of the national religion has been eloquently described by B. M. Levinson, though he treats the operation essentially as an exegetical revision of the Covenant Code, the *mišpāṭîm* (Exod 20:22–23:33).[8] He notes the elements of "cultic centralization … sacrificial procedure, the festival calendar, judicial procedure, and public administration, including the monarchy" as the chief innovations.[9] As for the questions of by whom, and why, such a radical and ambitious work was initially authorized or commissioned, Levinson, like many other scholars, regards it as a turning of the Assyrian loyalty oath against its inventors in the time of Josiah, but he does not defend this view, taking it rather for granted, as if such a radical reorganization of every aspect of life were not rather improbable under a monarchic system of government. The observations that follow here on the intended effects of the contents of Deuteronomy are broadly in line with Levinson's, though with a rather different evaluation; in particular, I reserve judgment on Levinson's claim that Deuteronomy is essentially an exegesis, especially given the contention of J. Van Seters that the "Book of the Covenant" is actually later than Deuteronomy.[10] This position has much in common with K. Berge's argument that Deuteronomy's didactic tone does not reflect any

---

Paranäse im Bundesbuch und ihre Herkunft," in *Gottes Wort und Gottes Land: Hans-Wilhelm Hertzberg zum 70. Geburtstag am 16 Januar 1965 dargebracht* (ed. Henning G. Reventlow; Göttingen: Vandenhoeck and Ruprecht, 1965), 9–29; Georg Braulik, "Das Deuteronomium und die Geburt des Monotheismus," *Gott, der einzige: Zur Entstehung des Monotheismus in Israel* (ed. Georg Braulik et al.; Quaestiones disputatae 104; Freiburg: Herder, 1985), 115–59; Casper J. Labuschagne, "The Literary and Theological Function of Divine Speech in the Pentateuch," in *Congress Volume Salamanca* (ed. John A. Emerton; VTSup 36; Leiden: Brill, 1985), 154–73; and J. Gordon McConville, "Singular Address in the Deuteronomic Law and the Politics of Legal Administration," *Journal for the Study of the Old Testament* 26 (2002): 19–36.

8. Bernard M. Levinson, *Deuteronomy and the Hermeneutics of Legal Innovation* (New York: Oxford University Press, 1998).

9. Levinson, *Deuteronomy and Legal Innovation*, 144.

10. Van Seters, *Law Book*. The point here is not that Van Seters is correct but that the textual relationship between the two corpora is not so clear as to preclude the possibility of reversing the chronology and literary influence. His arguments have as yet not been widely accepted.

teaching function but rather, that it constitutes a utopian project aimed at the small circle of literate readers.[11] But the crucial question is not whether the vision of Deuteronomy is utopian, but to what extent the book also betrays signs of its implementation. And here we come to one of the basic questions of Deuteronomy's reception.

The Original Reception of Deuteronomy

The reception of the scroll itself is of course to be confined to literate circles. But were the contents disseminated more widely in an attempt to create its "Israel"? Berge is surely right to doubt the widely held view that the text of Deuteronomy was disseminated by public reading: Deut 31:11 prescribes this only every seven years, hardly adequate for the purpose, even if the law was "explained" in the manner that Neh 7:7–8 narrates.[12] But it is possible that Deuteronomy is not the *beginning* (of a utopian project) but the *culmination* of a process, a codification and not a proposal: not the beginning, but the end—or some intermediate point—of a venture. Before Deuteronomy is classified as a *purely* literary and utopian project, we need to consider in what ways it might be related to the actual legal and customary practices of the period in which it originated. For example, was its "utopian" proposal for the major festivals not put into practice, as was its "utopian" proposal of a single sanctuary? In this respect, then, Deuteronomy was not, or did not remain, "utopian." With the disappearance of the local monarchy and its replacement by an empire that did not impose an imperial law, how were the judicial functions carried out in the two provinces that succeeded the kingdoms of Israel and Judah? What relationship, if any, existed between legal customs and ethnic identity? The possibility that behind the book of Deuteronomy lies some kind of effort at creating or standardizing a set of cultural behaviors that defined the "descendants of Jacob," that is, the populations of Samerina and Yehud, or "Israel" should not be discounted.

---

11. Kåre Berge, "Literacy, Utopia and Memory: Is There a Public Teaching in Deuteronomy?" *Journal of Hebrew Studies* 12:3 (2012).

12. There must be doubts about the historical reliability of this narrative. Whether a scroll of Deuteronomy, let alone a proto-Pentateuch existed in the mid-fifth century B.C.E. is questionable. Like the anti-Samari(t)an tenor of the book, this seems to be an anachronism, reflecting conditions of a later period.

For the majority of contemporary scholars, as for Levinson, Deuteronomy, or some form of it, is to be identified with the law book found in the reign of Josiah (2 Kgs 22), though on this theory the exact circles responsible are not certain: they are clearly not among those whose authority depended upon the king and on traditional royal patronage, since the composition undermines royal patronage, withdrawing the king's authority in the management of justice, the making of war and mediation between the people and the deity (Deut 17: 14–20). Nor is it clear how the text of a law book proposed to have been discovered and implemented under a *Judahite* king at a time when the kingdom of Israel had been replaced by a province of Samerina could have been adopted in Samaria—as it clearly was. The scholarly tendency to assume a *Judahite* or *Judean* origin for Deuteronomy, or at least for its implementation, stems from this "Josianic" setting. And yet there exists a longstanding scholarly opinion that the contents of Deuteronomy originated within the kingdom of Israel.[13] But there is no indication with the book itself of a Judahite or Judean origin, and the question should be left open. The suggestion that the book, written under Josiah, was preserved through the reigns of Josiah's successors and subsequently among Judean exiles in Babylonia and reintroduced into Judah in the late sixth or fifth century is perhaps a necessary speculation, but somewhat fanciful nevertheless—and still leaves the question of its adoption in Samerina problematic.

There is, however, no sound reason to read the legend of 2 Kgs 22 as a reliable historical account and compel oneself to propose possible reasons for its composition in such a context. The view that Deuteronomy was created in a postmonarchic context is attracting a growing number of scholars[14] because such a context seems more appropriate for the kind

---

13. Among the proponents of a "northern" origin or of "northern traditions" are Adam C. Welch, *The Code of Deuteronomy: A New Theory of Its Origin* (London: Clarke, 1924); Albrecht Alt, "Die Heimat des Deuteronomiums," in *Kleine Schriften zur Geschichte des Volkes Israel* (3 vols.; Munich: Beck, 1953–1959), 2:250–75; Georg Fohrer, *Introduction to the Old Testament* (trans. D. Green; Nashville: Abingdon, 1968), 174; G. Ernest Wright, "Deuteronomy," in *The Interpreter's Bible* (ed. Leander Keck et al.; 12 vols.; Nashville: Abingdon, 1953), 2:311–30; Gerhard von Rad, *Studies in Deuteronomy* (trans. D. M. G. Stalker; SBT 9; London: SCM, 195, 1953), 68; and Ernest W. Nicholson, *Deuteronomy and Tradition* (Oxford: Blackwell, 1967).

14. For a recent presentation of this alternative view, see Philip R. Davies, "Josiah and the Law Book," in *Good Kings and Bad Kings: The Kingdom of Judah in the Seventh Century* (ed. Lester L. Grabbe; ESHM 5/LHBOTS 393; London: T&T Clark, 2005),

of radical agenda just discussed, for its implicitly postmonarchic constitution (see Deut 17:14–20), and most of all, for its agenda of building an *ethnos* based on common religious and judicial practices. Given its patent, anti-Samarian bias (see, e.g., 17: 24–41), assigning Deuteronomy a purely Judean origin might itself stem from the consciousness that it was largely Samarian in origin.

But the geographical origin is perhaps less important than the social origin. From which circle does the agenda of Deuteronomy emanate? In an influential short monograph, G. von Rad argued that Deuteronomy began its life in Levitical sermons, a view prompted especially by the book's rhetorical character.[15] This conclusion still seems worth consideration as an alternative to the view that this rhetorical character stems from an initial conception as a Mosaic pseudepigraphon. At any rate, Deuteronomy's "Levitical priests" are given ultimate authority in the writing, interpretation and implementation of its stipulations, and so it is here that we should most naturally expect to find the authorship:

> where you shall consult with the Levitical priests and the judge who is in office in those days; they shall announce to you the decision in the case. (17:9; cf. 19:17; 21:5)

> Then Moses wrote down this law, and gave it to the priests, the sons of Levi, who carried the ark of the covenant of YHWH, and to all the elders of Israel. (31:9)

> When he [the king] has taken the throne of his kingdom, he shall have a copy of this law written for him in the presence of the Levitical priests. (17:18)

Deuteronomy insists that Levites have priestly status ("priest" being nearly always qualified by the word "Levite," e.g., 17:9,18; 18:1; 24:8; 27:9). But they do not function primarily in the cult of the central sanctuary. Any Levite is permitted to come to the chosen sanctuary and "serve" there (ch.

65–77 and responses by Rainer Albertz, "Why a Reform Like Josiah's Must Have Happened," in *Good Kings and Bad Kings: The Kingdom of Judah in the Seventh Century* (ed. Lester L. Grabbe; ESHM 5/LHBOTS 393; London: T&T Clark, 2005), 27–46; and Knauf, "Observations on Judah's Social and Economic History."

15. Gerhard von Rad, *Studies in Deuteronomy* (trans. David Stalker; SBT 9; London: SCM, 1953).

18), but here and elsewhere it is assumed that they reside for the most part throughout the land (12:12,18; 14:27; 16:11; 26:11)— where Deuteronomy does not permit sacrificial offerings—and sustained by the benefit of the tithe offering (26:12). Moreover, the function of the Levites in the central sanctuary is not necessarily cultic at all, for one of its functions is to act (in place of the previous royal court) as the "supreme court" to which judicial decisions can be referred, in which Levites play a major role:

> If a judicial decision is too difficult for you to make between one kind of bloodshed and another, one kind of legal right and another, or one kind of assault and another—any such matters of dispute in your towns— then you shall immediately go up to the place that YHWH your god will choose, where you shall consult with the Levitical priests and the judge who is in office in those days; they shall announce to you the decision in the case. Carry out exactly the decision that they announce to you from the place that YHWH will choose, diligently observing everything they instruct you. (Deut 17:8–10)

The Levitical function in the central sanctuary, therefore, is probably not cultic, but juridical. Indeed, for Deuteronomy, the requirement of a single sanctuary apparently has much more to do with cultic (more precisely, sacrificial) matters than with the consolidation of an ethnic consciousness through a central legal institution that could replace the monarchic function in an imperial regime.

The connection between Levites and *tōrâ* is certainly indissoluble: in 31: 9, 25 the Levites bear the ark that contains the tablets of the law and in this they are the successors of Moses, who was himself a Levite and the primary mediator of the *tōrâ*. In the Pentateuch it is Aaron who is regularly designated as "the priest" and receives the instructions concerning sacrifice, while his sons serve as priests (cf. Exod 31:10; 40:13; Lev and Num *passim*). Deuteronomy, however, says nothing of Aaron's privileges and mentions him only three times, once somewhat disparagingly (9:20). This again indicates the rather peripheral role in Deuteronomy of the sacrificial cult, compared with the centrality of *tōrâ*. Nehemiah 8:7, which recounts an actualization of the reading of the Deuteronomic law as stipulated in the book itself, provides for Levitical interpretation of the *tōrâ* in a story that should be taken less as historical than paradigmatic. But should this function of disseminating and regulating *tōrâ* be regarded as postdating the creation of the book of Deuteronomy or as a practice from which the book itself arose? This question is important for understanding whether the reception of Deuteronomy as authoritative consists in its recognition as a written codification of an already recognized *tôrâ* or essential as a self-authenticating writing, a purported Mosaic or Josianic bequest.

Deuteronomy thus sees the role of its "priestly Levites" not within the cult but within the national and local judicial processes.[16] M. Leuchter provides a generally excellent and well-documented discussion of "the Levites within your gates" as "official regional jurists," though, following M. A. Sweeney, he interprets this function as a Josianic arrangement.[17] Was this role a utopian proposal or did it reflect historical activity? We cannot neglect the rather different presentation of the role of Levites in the books of Chronicles. Here they are singers, treasurers (2 Chr 24:11); guards (2 Chr 34:9)—in general "scribes, and officials, and gatekeepers" (2 Chr 34:13). To some extent the portraits are not contradictory, and it must be borne in mind that Chronicles' portrait of the temple is set in the fictional monarchic context of the reign of David and not the postmonarchic society of the authors. Nevertheless, there is undoubtedly a tension between Deuteronomy and Chronicles—or between Deuteronomy and the Priestly writings as a whole—concerning the relative importance of cult and *tôrâ* in the religious life of "Israel."[18]

---

16. See also Nadav Na'aman, "Sojourners and Levites in the Kingdom of Judah in the Seventh Century BCE," *ZAR* 14 (2008): 237–79. For a response, dating the Deuteronomic laws to the sixth century B.C.E., see Knauf, "Observations on Judah's Social and Economic History."

17. Mark Leuchter, "The Levite in Your Gates: The Deuteronomic Redefinition of Levitical Authority," *JBL* 126 (2007): 417–36; Marvin A. Sweeney, *King Josiah, the Lost Messiah of Israel* (New York: Oxford University Press, 2001), 151–53.

18. Ideological competition on this issue can be seen in the manner in which Leviticus, and especially chs. 17–26, seeks to extend priestly notions of holiness to embrace those areas of life covered by Deuteronomy: to spread the temple courts across the whole land and implicate each domestic act in the sanctity of the temple. Whether or not this reflects a conscious response to the Levitical sphere of influence (or desired sphere of influence), the reader is left with two fairly comprehensive systems within the books of Moses that articulate the manner in which Israel and its deity are essentially related: *tôrâ* and cult. "There is also a considerable degree of agreement on an understanding of the Torah as a 'compromise document', in which different narratives and legal collections were gathered together in an attempt to accommodate the different ideological points of view of the Priestly school on one hand and a lay group, which one may call the Deuteronomists, on the other hand" (Thomas Römer, "Moses Outside the Torah and the Construction of a Diaspora Identity," *JHS* 8:15 [2008] available online at http://www.jhsonline.org/Articles/article_92.pdf and in *Perspectives in*

If the portrait of Levites in Chronicles may be suspected of some anachronism or of ideological manipulation, whether Deuteronomy offers a historically accurate portrait of Levites as a whole or is equally unrealistic is hard to say.[19] But a central question of much recent scholarship has been the emergence of *tôrâ* and its place within the society of Persian period Yehud (and implicitly Samerina)—frequently focusing on how far imperial authorization was involved in the creation of a "law" for this part of the empire. The book of Ezra testifies to the belief that the *tôrâ*, the "words of the commandments of YHWH" (elsewhere "law of the god of heaven"), are already in Ezra's possession ("in your hand," 7:14), though their enforcement *within the satrapy of Beyond the River* is a matter of imperial command (7:25–26). Ezra is commanded also to "appoint magistrates and judges who may judge all the people" (7:25: cf. Deut 16:18). This episode should not, as it too often has, be understood as factual history[20] but instead, at least as a claim that the *tôrâ* has the authority of both heaven and earth, as also an official institution of enforcement.

Deuteronomy seems to reflect exactly the outcome of this part of the Ezra narrative (and, as observed, also the ceremony of Neh 8), and we should consider whether Ezra and Nehemiah are not providing a somewhat idealized and dramatized account of how a historical state of affairs— an "Israelite" *tôrâ*, though not necessarily in a strict literary form even after its literary codification in Deuteronomy came about.[21] If Deuteronomy is utopian, it describes a utopia that, as already remarked, seems to have come into existence. But there is of course one important utopian feature of Deuteronomy: the possession of the land, the divine part of the covenant agreement. For the writers of the book of Nehemiah's prayer (Neh 9:36–37):

Hebrew Scriptures V: Comprising the Contents of Journal of Hebrew Scriptures, vol. 8 (ed. Ehud Ben Zvi; Piscataway, N.J.: Gorgias, 2009), 269–81.

19. On the necessity of distinguishing various types of Levite, see Joachim Schaper, *Priester und Leviten in achämenidischen Juda: Studien zur Kult- und Sozialgeschichte Israels in persischer Zeit* (FAT 31; Tübingen: Mohr Siebeck, 2000), esp. 294–95.

20. On the historicity of Ezra and his achievements, see Lester L. Grabbe, *Ezra–Nehemiah* (Old Testament Readings; London: Routledge, 1998).

21. On this one (of many) identities of Ezra, see Mark Leuchter, who very accurately calls this identity a "Deuteronomistic Levite" ("Coming to Terms with Ezra's Many Identities in Ezra–Nehemiah," in *Historiography and Identity [Re]formulation in Second Temple Historiographical Literature* [ed. Louis Jonker; LHBOT 534; London: T&T Clark, 2010], 41–63 [49–57]).

> Here we are, slaves to this day—slaves in the land that you gave to our ancestors to enjoy its fruit and its good gifts. Its rich yield goes to the kings whom you have set over us because of our sins; they have power also over our bodies and over our livestock at their pleasure, and we are in great distress.

So must Deuteronomy be read, of course: as a law to be observed in return for a land *in the future—as also in the setting of the book*. However far the Deuteronomic law was authorized—or claimed to be authorized—by the emperor, its adoption was believed to be a condition of future release from the empire. This understanding is also an important element of the reception of Deuteronomy and a source of its authority.

It is by now surely clear that a monarchic context makes no sense whatever of the contents of Deuteronomy, where national identity can no longer be expressed in terms of feudalism or patronage but only through religion, lineage and custom. It is by these features that *ethne* recognize themselves and are organized within large empires in which divisions into monarchic states and their corresponding feudal allegiances have disappeared. Gone too are national deities, who increasing become ministers of the high god or "angels" or the heavenly equivalent of "governors" (e.g., *sārîm*)—or in typical colonial manner they become the "true" manifestations of the imperial high god, in a belief system often misdiagnosed as "monotheism."

The creation of a pan-"Israelite" ethnic identity requires both local and "national" dimension. The indoctrination and implementation of Israelite "law" requires, as law always required, local enforcement: justice cannot be dispensed at a geographical distance, nor will such justice be adopted as indigenous. But ethic solidarity requires communal participation also. Deuteronomy creates this through its use of centralized cultic occasions. However irrelevant the daily sacrificial cult, nevertheless three times a year (Deut 16:16) the sanctuary becomes the scene of a pan-Israelite celebration of the story of its birth. At both Passover and Weeks there is a call to remember the servitude in Egypt, although the agricultural associations of these festivals is maintained. The later specific associations of Weeks with lawgiving and Booths with wilderness are not found in Deuteronomy but may be seen as a development in the direction already set. But while the bringing of offerings is mentioned, nothing is said directly of any sacrificial obligations. The relationship between "Israel" and its god appears to lie almost entirely outside the realm of the cult in this narrow sense.

Developments in the Reception of Deuteronomy

We have now already begun to adumbrate the way in which Deuteronomy was received as authoritative—if the intentions of the work itself were more or less fulfilled. The book becomes a codification of mechanisms of self-definition. But there are several additional and more specific mechanisms by which this book was accorded authoritative status. We are better able to understand these mechanisms than we are with any other scriptural book, and it is sometimes possible to suggest their sequence (which will be followed below). What is worth pointing to at the outset, however, is that the range and number of these "authorizing" mechanisms suggests that Deuteronomy was probably not originally endowed with the intrinsic authority of a person or an institute. Rather, it was seen to require such associations in order to achieve its ultimate canonized status as the core of Mosaic Torah in both Yehud and Samerina.

Royal (Davidic) and Prophetic Vindication

Despite the shared authority of Deuteronomy within both provinces, *royal* authorization was manufactured only in Yehud (unless Samerina has a corresponding, but now lost, equivalent). Certainly, it is unlikely that the authority of Josiah would carry any weight in the north. Deuteronomy's agenda of shifting authority over religion and justice (and some other matters of government as well as warfare) away from monarchy towards the Levitical priests may have required no explanation in a postmonarchic province, but nevertheless, it was apparently felt important, within Yehud at any rate, to have this transfer explicitly endorsed *by the monarchy itself*, in the form of a legend.[22] The story of the finding of a "scroll of the law" in the Jerusalem temple is told in 2 Kgs 22–3 and in 2 Chr 34–5, but it is only the Kings account that points directly to Deuteronomy as the scroll in question, by describing the nature of the reform subsequently introduced by the king (the destruction of images to gods other than YHWH and of altars outside Jerusalem) and describing the celebration of the Passover

---

22. I have already suggested above that an additional motivation may have been to embed the "discovery" of Deut with Yehud and to ignore its Samarian dimension, though 2 Kgs 17:27–28 gives the faintest of acknowledgements that Samarians also worshiped YHWH and followed his *tōrâ*.

according to the Deuteronomic prescription.²³ Other hints as to its identity are the oracle of Huldah, which refers to the worship of other gods (22:17), and the phrase "scroll of the law," occurring twice in 2 Kgs 22 and three times in Deuteronomy (29:21; 30:10; 31:26).

A number of scholars have questioned whether the accounts of the discovery of the book and of the cultic reform constitute a literary unity, that is, a single narrative.²⁴ If not, then either the story of the scroll-finding is an elaboration and justification of the reform,²⁵ or the account of the reform is an elaboration of the scroll-finding. In either case, the addition of the second story to the first achieves the same purpose: to show that Deuteronomy was known *in the monarchic era* and was made the basis of a religious reform by a righteous king, whose death prevented it from being permanently enshrined in the Judahite kingdom.

The book receives, however, a prophetic as well as a royal vindication—not by the most famous prophet of the age (Jeremiah, a book whose Deuteronomistic editing nevertheless indirectly serves to add a prophetic endorsement to its ideology) but by the otherwise obscure Huldah.²⁶ Here again, there is scholarly disagreement about whether her introduction represents an addition to the story; if so, then prophetic endorsement should be counted as another, separate, authorizing device.

---

23. Whether the account in Chronicles is directly a reworking of the Kings account can be left aside. What seems clear is that the Chronicler does not base the reform on the law book itself and so denies the legitimating function in the Kgs account, because for Chronicles the "law of Moses" is cultic; see P. R. Davies, "Moses in the Books of Kings," in *La Construction de la Figure de Moïse—The Construction of the Figure of Moses* (ed. Thomas Römer; TransSup 13; Paris: Gabalda, 2007), 77–87. The Chronicler's lack of reference to the exodus and its portrayal of Levites as cultic functionaries seems to constitute a rejection of the Deuteronomic program.

24. For a discussion of the issues, see Norbert Lohfink, "Zur neueren Diskussion über 2 Kön 22–23," in *Das Deuteronomium: Entstehung, Gestalt und Botschaft* (ed. N. Lohfink; BETL 68; Leuven: Leuven University Press, 1985), 24–48; Nadav Na'aman, "The 'Discovered Book' and the Legitimation of Josiah's Reform," *JBL* 130 (2011): 47–62.

25. So, e.g., Na'aman, "Discovered Book."

26. On Huldah and Jeremiah as part of a mechanism for replacing temple with prophet and prophet with scribe, see Thomas Römer, "From Prophet to Scribe: Jeremiah, Huldah and the Invention of the Book," in *Writing the Bible: Scribes and Scribalism in Ancient Judah* (ed. Philip R. Davies and Thomas Römer; BibleWorld. Durham: Equinox, 2013), 89–96.

For the entire reign of Josiah we have nothing but the biblical account: no inscription, no archaeology.[27] There is no firm basis on which to make a judgment about its historicity, other than the unlikelihood of such a text as Deuteronomy being written and established in this context. The scholarly elaborations of this reign are therefore as shallow as they are implausible.[28] Stories of book-finding are also a well-attested device, sometimes historical[29] but sometimes fictitious.[30] For our purposes, the historicity of any of the events recorded about Josiah is unimportant; what matters is the authorizing of Deuteronomy by the two institutions that are central to the books of Kings: monarchy and prophecy. Let us not overlook, either, that while monarchy and prophecy endorse the book, each is in fact being emphatically *supplanted* by it within Deuteronomy, whose society is not ruled by an effective king (merely one who is given the law book to rule by) nor an effective prophet, namely, one who can utter messages that in any way transgress the commandments of the law book (Deut 13).

Mosaic Endorsement

For Deuteronomy, there is one great prophet—and leader—Moses (34:10), and he fulfills the Deuteronomic requirement of a prophet—to preach the Torah. The Mosaic authorship of Deuteronomy is certainly clear from the beginning of the book, which is presented as his speech before Israel on the plains of Moab. The laws themselves are also clearly identified as coming through him in the opening chapters (4:44–45; 5:1) and again in 29:1 and

---

27. As Na'aman remarks: "This conclusion rests on the assumption that Josiah's reform was a historical event and that the account in 2 Kings 22–23 describes it in a fairly reliable outline" ("Discovered Book," 49 n. 7). For a different opinion, see Ernst Würthwein, "Die josianische Reform und das Deuteronomium," *ZTK* 73 (1976): 395–423; Christoph Levin, "Joschija im deuteronmistischen Geschichtswerk," *ZAW* 96 (1984): 351–71; Lowell K. Handy, "The Role of Huldah in Josiah's Cult Reform," *ZAW* 106 (1994): 46–52.

28. See, e.g. Marvin A. Sweeney, *King Josiah, the Lost Messiah of Israel* (New York: Oxford University Press, 2001).

29. So Na'aman, "Discovered Book."

30. So David Henige, "In Good Company: Problematic Sources and Biblical Historicity," *JSOT* 30 (2005): 29–47; Kathryn Stott, "Finding the Lost Book of the Law: Re-reading the Story of 'the Book of the Law' (Deuteronomy–2 Kings) in Light of Classical Literature," *JSOT* 30 (2005): 153–69.

31:9–24—where he writes them down. But is the connection with Moses original to Deuteronomy, or has it been subsequently added—along with the setting on the steppes of Moab? The question arises chiefly from the story of Josiah's law book and reform in Chronicles, where two major differences need to be taken into account.[31] First, in 2 Chr 34 Josiah's reform *precedes* the discovery of the law book and is, therefore, not its cause. Hence, the identity of the law book cannot be inferred from the nature of the reform.[32] The fact that in Chronicles a celebration of Passover follows the discovery might hint that Deuteronomy was indeed the scroll in question. But the Passover is not said to be occasioned by the discovery, since Hezekiah, the Chronicler's great hero, had previously celebrated it too. The account of this celebration, moreover, pays great attention to the cultic role of the Aaronide priests, who are totally neglected in Deuteronomy generally, let alone in its prescriptions for Passover. Perhaps the Chronicler, aware of the connection made in other scribal circles between Josiah, Deuteronomy, and the reform, allowed that Josiah's reform was *consistent* with Deuteronomy (removal of other temples and alien cult objects) and that his Passover celebration followed the reform and the finding of the scroll. But if so, he has done as much as possible to deny the notion of a "Deuteronomic reform." He does, nevertheless, name "the scroll of the law that YHWH had given through Moses" (34:14).

Yet elsewhere in Chronicles "the law of Moses" is concerned with cultic and not with Deuteronomic issues.[33] Thus, in 2 Chr 8:13 we read how Solomon's sacrificial cult followed the rules laid down by Moses; in 2 Chr 23:18 Jehoiada commissions the *Levitical priests* (their only occur-

---

31. Niels-Peter Lemche points out other important shifts in the evaluation of Josiah: he is killed on the battlefield, implicitly because he disobeyed the divine will imparted to him by the pharaoh Necho (35:21-22) ("Did a Reform Like Josiah's Happen?" in *The Historian and the Bible: Essays in Honour of Lester L. Grabbe* [ed. Philip R. Davies and Diana V. Edelman; LHBOT 530; London: T&T Clark, 2010], 11–19).

32. The question of the relationship between Kings and Chronicles is another matter that cannot be discussed in detail here: the work of A. Graeme Auld has challenged the conventional understanding, as much through textual criticism as through literary criticism (*Kings Without Privilege: David and Moses in the Story of the Bible's Kings* [Edinburgh: T&T Clark, 1994]). What seems clear, however, is that there exists between the two works a basic ideological disagreement between a cult-centered polity and a *tôrâ*-centered one.

33. Davies, "Moses in Kings," 77–87.

rence in Chronicles) to perform the burnt offerings (with singing) "as written in the law of Moses." In 2 Chr 24:6, 9 we are told of the tax for the upkeep of the tent of meeting, "which Moses the servant of God laid upon Israel in the wilderness" (v. 9). Finally, in 2 Chr 30:16, in celebrating the Passover under Hezekiah, the priests take their positions "according to the law of Moses." Perhaps the Chronicler means in every case the Pentateuch, including Deuteronomy—if it can be referred to as a single "scroll," as it is in chapter 34. But perhaps he had other documents than Deuteronomy in mind.

This discussion, otherwise inconsequential, derives some relevance in that 2 Kgs 22 does not connect the law book with Moses at all: it is called only "the scroll of the law." This seems a strange omission. There is a statement in 23:25 that Josiah "turned to YHWH with all his heart, with all his soul, and with all his might, according to all the law of Moses," but this curiously fails to make any connection with his law book. Indeed, it belongs with a number of standard phrases with which bad or good kings are characterized: the same is said of Hezekiah (18:4, 6, 12), while in 14:6 Amaziah "did not put to death the children of the murderers, according to what is written in the book of the law of Moses, where YHWH commanded, 'The parents shall not be put to death for the children, or the children be put to death for the parents; but all shall be put to death for their own sin'" (cf. Deut 24:16).

Thus, according to the books of Kings, Hezekiah obeyed the "law of Moses," presumably knowledgeable of its contents, while the last reference shows that the "book of the law of Moses" is indeed understood to be Deuteronomy. In light of this, the finding of a scroll fairly clearly identified as Deuteronomy would have to be understood as a *rediscovery* of something known (and implemented) earlier. If the statement that Josiah's Passover had not been performed since the "days of the judges" (23:22) implies that Deuteronomy was not known during the monarchic period, it clearly lies in contradiction with other texts from the same book. According to 2 Kgs 21:8 (concluding the reign of Manasseh):

> I will not cause the feet of Israel to wander any more out of the land that I gave to their ancestors, if only they will be careful to do according to all that I have commanded them, and according to all the law that my servant Moses commanded them.

There is no space here to explore this contradiction between a law *known and unheeded* and a law *unknown*.[34] We can merely note that in the whole of the books of Kings, Moses is mentioned only ten times, and five of these are in chs. 18–23. It is as if the narrative were building to the climax in which failure to observe the Mosaic law led to disaster. If so, this narrative implies that the law *was* known and willfully disregarded, almost (if not completely) to the time of Josiah. The appearance of a righteous king, complete with reform, obeying the law of Moses, would be an appropriate climax to this plot. But the sudden finding of a hitherto forgotten *Mosaic* law book would create a huge problem. And the account in 2 Kgs 22 does not identify a *Mosaic* law book.

Various explanations are possible. One is that Josiah was originally described as a pious king who lived according to the "law of Moses," as in ch. 23, and who carried out a religious reform accordingly. In this case, the story of the finding of a law book is a later insertion that ignores the wider implications for the role of Deuteronomy's law in 2 Kings. However, the absence of any reference to the Mosaic character of the law book actually avoids a direct contradiction, even though the accounts of the reform and the Passover point to Deuteronomy. Another possibility is that Deuteronomy was for a period of time *not* ascribed to Moses and that the few references to the "law of Moses" elsewhere in 2 Kings (including that in 2 Kgs 23) are secondary. The former view has been argued by many, including C. Levin,[35] the second by A. G. Auld.[36]

If 2 Kgs 22–23 is composed of two or more originally separate sources, then Davidic, prophetic, *and Mosaic* authorization/validation of Deuteronomy may have been separate processes (the sequence being indeterminable). The possibility that for the Chronicler also Deuteronomy was *not* "the law of Moses" should also be taken into account. When Ben Sira 24:23 alludes to "the scroll of the covenant of El 'Elyon, the law that Moses commanded us," is he following Kings or Chronicles? Is it Deuteronomy or a scroll of ritual prescriptions? The word "covenant" suggests the former but is by no means exclusive to Deuteronomy.

But if, as is the scholarly consensus, the laws themselves are earlier than the framing material and constitute the earliest form of the scroll,

---

34. On the whole issue of Moses in Kings, see Auld, *Kings without Privilege*.

35. Christoph Levin, "Joschija im deuteronomistischen Geschichtswerk," *ZAW* 96 (1984): 351–71.

36. Auld, *Kings without Privilege*; see also Davies, "Moses in Kings."

then on that conclusion that scroll may have been originally anonymous; one may also speculate (or reason) endlessly about the various layers of Mosaic attribution (the earliest and briefest being perhaps 5:1–5) and how the announcement of the laws by Moses became part of a longer *speech* (including historical summary) by Moses and, ultimately, a *book* written by Moses. As remarked earlier, the study of reception, while it may entail the recognition of literary history, does not need to probe such a history for its own sake. But the literary history of Deuteronomy itself, insofar as we can unravel it, suggests an increasing association with the *name* of Moses and, correspondingly, a development of the "Deuteronomic" profile of Moses as prophetic lawgiver.

Deuteronomy as Torah and as History

Since the thesis of M. Noth on the "Deuteronomistic History," the status of Deuteronomy as belonging both with the Pentateuch and with the books of Joshua to Kings has been central to the history of its early reception.[37] Is it, as originally conceived or first employed, a historiographical prologue or a (second) lawgiving? Whether, or to what extent, one accepts the detailed arguments for, on the one hand, an original Tetrateuch or, on the other, a single "Deuteronomistic" composition, it cannot be denied that Deuteronomy was finally received within the canonical grouping called "Torah"—all of which was later associated with the name of Moses—nor that its ideology and language provided a foundation for much of the narrative in Joshua–Kings. That Deuteronomy replaced Numbers as the final book of the Mosaic canon can certainly be argued, but whether it belonged with a "Deuteronomistic History" as a prologue (with chs. 1–3 or possibly chs. 1–4 as an introduction to the entire composition) depends on the perception of a single "Deuteronomistic" work, and after a half-century of almost complete consensus, this thesis is being eroded, though not yet widely abandoned.[38] But beyond Joshua–Kings, Deuteronomy has directly influenced the formation of the book of Jeremiah and perhaps less directly the collection of the Book of the Twelve. It thus fuelled a consider-

---

37. Martin Noth, *Überlieferungsgeschichtliche Studien* (Halle: Niemeyer, 1943; ET = *The Deuteronomistic History* (JSOTSup 15; Sheffield: JSOT Press, 1981).

38. For an excellent discussion, see Thomas Römer, *The So-Called Deuteronomistic History: A Sociological, Historical and Literary* Introduction (London: T&T Clark, 2007). He still—just—accepts the core of Noth's thesis.

able editorial and canonizing process that dominated both historiography and prophecy, to the extent that "Deuteronomic" has tended to become so all-pervasive as to lose much of its definition. But can it be doubted that Deuteronomy became the most authoritative book in the entire canon? If so, how was this ideological influence achieved?

The "Publication" of Deuteronomy

It is asserted with increasing frequency in the last few decades that the books of the Jewish scriptural canon were composed, read, and reread within the circles of the Jerusalem *literati*.[39] It is hard to disagree with this conclusion as applied to all the canonized literature. But there are indications that the contents of Deuteronomy were intended to be disseminated—and were disseminated—more widely. As noted, the book itself mandates a public reading every seven years, though such an infrequent event during a pilgrimage festival would hardly secure wide knowledge, let alone achieve any kind of enculturation of its values within the societies of Yehud and Samaria. The "law of Moses" (that is, the book of Deut) was not introduced with explicit Persian support by a single individual in Jerusalem but by an entire cohort of Levites working perhaps in accordance with the requirements of the Persian Empire, in towns and villages throughout the two provinces. No doubt scribal communities existed in Jerusalem and Samaria or Gerizim, but to these we ascribe only the evolving *text* of the book. Of course, the book was never *taught* outside this elite circle as a text. But the Levitical priests are portrayed in Deuteronomy as playing a role in the local administration of justice, along with the elders, and whether or not this is an accurate reflection of the manner in which the idea of an "Israelite" law came into existence, it remains true that such a law *was* created and its observance was, however theoretically, entailed in being part of "Israel."

---

39. See especially the work of Ehud Ben Zvi; two useful articles by him are "Reconstructing the Intellectual Discourse of Ancient Yehud," *Studies in Religion/Sciences Religieuses* 39 (2010): 7–23 and "Towards an Integrative Study of the Production of Authoritative Books in Ancient Israel," in *The Production of Prophecy: Constructing Prophecy and Prophets in Yehud* (ed. Diana V. Edelman and Ehud Ben Zvi; BibleWorld; London: Equinox, 2009), 15–28.

Through control of the administration of justice at the local level and by liturgical gatherings at the pilgrim festivals, the "Levitical priests" were supposed by the contents of Deuteronomy to ensure that their ideology became authoritative for those outside the scribal circles as well as within. As with the Latin Bible of mediaeval Christendom, its contents were disseminated not through text but through image, through instruction, through ritual celebration, and through social memory. Was the agenda laid out in Deuteronomy actually carried out? There seems to be general scholarly agreement that it was, in some manner. Does Deuteronomy, then, carry the key to the puzzle of why and how the *idea* as well as the content of *tōrâ* came into existence, and indeed how it became part of the self-identification of "Israel?

Rereading Deuteronomy in the Persian and Hellenistic Periods: The Ethics of Brotherhood and the Care of the Poor

Christoph Levin

Introduction

One of the fundamental problems in the exegesis of Deuteronomy is the book's utopian character. It is "u-topian" in the sense that its location in history is not unequivocally clear. The biblical setting is fictitious, and this not by chance. It is supposed to be Moses' discourse on the last day of his life, immediately before the conquest of West Jordan. But the church fathers already connected Deuteronomy with the politico-cultic measures ascribed to King Josiah in 2 Kgs 22–23, identifying it with "the book of the law" (סֵפֶר הַתּוֹרָה) mentioned there, and W. M. L. de Wette concluded the book was never, in fact, rediscovered at that time but was actually written then.[1]

I find de Wette's hypothesis about the origins of Deuteronomy still to be the most probable. Even if the record of the rediscovery of the book in 2 Kgs 22 may be legendary, there are good reasons to see the law book as a product of Judahite royal politics during the last third of the seventh century B.C.E., even though the king was not originally mentioned in the book. In this case, the orginal form of Deuteronomy, whose core was Deut 12–26, would have been an official document from the outset. Being part of the royal archives that survived the Babylonian conquest, it would have

---

1. Wilhelm Martin Leberecht de Wette, "Dissertatio critica-exegetica qua Deuteronomium a prioribus Pentateuchi libris diversum alius cuiusdam recentioris auctoris opus esse monstratur" (diss. phil., University of Jena, 1805); repr. in *Opuscula theologica* (Berlin: Reimer, 1830), 149–68, esp. 164–65 n. 5.

been seen as authoritative thereafter. Then, during the Second Temple period, the book would have served as a matrix used by the scribes to express their modified view of the community's relation to its God and human social relations. The intention was to establish the people as the vassal of the deity in place of the king in order to adapt and recycle former monarchic ideology after the monarchy had been terminated by the Neo-Babylonians in 586 B.C.E.

It seems that the Deuteronomic law existed as an independent scroll for a long time. This holds also for the so-called Covenant Code in Exod 20:22–23:19, which served as the *Vorlage* of Deuteronomy in the seventh century and later was incorporated into the Sinai pericope in the book of Exodus. The Covenant Code served as a literary matrix to meet the needs of the Jewish Diaspora, whereas Deuteronomy, with its focus on the central sanctuary, was read by the Jewish community in Judah. The third law book of this kind, the so-called Holiness Code in Lev 17–26, is the latest of the three and was used in Judah, like the Deuteronomic law. Beginning as an exposition of the Decalogue (Lev 19), it presupposes both the Covenant Code and Deuteronomy. Regardless of the differences among these law books, all eventually were incorporated into the Torah because all were seen as authoritative, each reflecting in its own way the recorded will of God. Having gained authoritative status, their texts could not be changed except to add new prescriptions that addressed the changed conditions in the life of the community. Outdated or superceded regulations were not omitted but maintained as part of the inherited, authoritative scroll, resulting in the present forms of the texts.

Today, the centralization of the cult is merely one subject among others in Deuteronomy. What strikes the eye is, above all, its social legislation. In its present form at least, Deuteronomy reads as being the order for a socially well-balanced, religious community. This religious community has much more in common with Second Temple Judaism than with the people of Judah at the time of the monarchy. For that reason above all, G. Hölscher assigned Deuteronomy to the postexilic period.[2] He ascribed "unwordly idealism" to the lawgiver, calling the law about release from debt in Deut 15:1–3, 7–11 "impracticable," for example. "He (i.e., the writer) does not consider the actual application of this law in economic

---

2. Gustav Hölscher, "Komposition und Ursprung des Deuteronomiums," *ZAW* 40 (1923): 161–255.

life; for him it is merely a humanitarian institution." Similarly, the law about the freeing of slaves in Deut 15:12–18, compared with the earlier law in Exod 21:2–6, proceeds from presuppositions that show "the theoretical rigidity of this legislation, which completely loses sight of any practical application."[3]

The problem of determining the social situation to which the reforming intention was directed and to which degree the demands could be translated into down-to-earth reality is certainly not solved but is perhaps alleviated if we take the literary growth of the book of Deuteronomy into account. Fortunately, we know what the *Vorlage* of the original lawbook was, because it is easy to see that Deuteronomy's earliest nucleus goes back to the Covenant Code.[4] Its legislative material was reworked from the standpoint of the centralization of the official Judahite cult. It was only in a clearly later step that this law was then seen, and accordingly revised, as a code of behavior for the relationship to the god YHWH himself.[5] This took place at the end of the sixth century B.C.E. when, with the incorporation of Judah into the Persian provincial system, hope for a rebirth of the Davidic monarchy died, and the cultic community of Jerusalem adopted the role of YHWH's direct vassal.

This by no means completes the history of the revisions. The following paper has as its subject the sections of the law book that have as their most immediate subject the ethic of brotherhood and/or the care of the poor. How can the additions that focus on the ethic of brotherhood be fitted into the literary history? Do they belong to the Deuteronomic editor,[6] or were they added by a later hand? In order to decide, the relevant sections must be viewed in the framework of the whole literary development of the lawbook. There are instances where the Deuteronomic redaction and the

---

3. Hölscher, "Komposition und Ursprung," 195–97.

4. See, among many others, Bernard M. Levinson, *Deuteronomy and the Hermeneutics of Legal Innovation* (New York: Oxford University Press, 1997).

5. See esp. Timo Veijola, "Bundestheologische Redaktion im Deuteronomium," in *Moses Erben: Studien zum Dekalog, zum Deuteronomismus und zum Schriftgelehrtentum* (BWANT 149; Stuttgart: Kohlhammer, 2000), 153–75; also idem, *Das 5. Buch Mose: Deuteronomium Kapitel 1,1-16,17* (ATD 8,1; Göttingen: Vandenhoeck & Ruprecht, 2004).

6. Thus, e.g., the thorough study of Lothar Perlitt, "'Ein einzig Volk von Brüdern': Zur deuteronomischen Herkunft der biblischen Bezeichnung 'Bruder,'" in *Deuteronomium-Studien* (FAT 8; Tübingen: Mohr Siebeck, 1994), 50–73.

brotherhood ethic can be distinguished, so that their relationship in time becomes clear.

It will emerge that Deuteronomy's brotherhood ethic did not belong to the original features of the law, as has often been thought, but that it, too, is a later insertion.[7] It had its immediate setting in the community of the Second Temple in the Persian period. The specific theology of the poor, which also has traces in Deuteronomy even if they are less distinct, is even later. The distribution of the instances is striking. "The two expressions אביון and עני appear in Deuteronomy only in the laws which have to do with the problem-complex 'procedure in the case of debt.' That is an astonishing phenomenon."[8] Comparable texts show that this revision should be assigned to the Hellenistic period.[9]

On Release, on Loan, and on Slaves (Deut 15:1–6, 7–11, 12–18)

The first examples in the sequence of the book are the social directives in Deut 15.[10] Their gradual literary development can best be followed if we look at the section as a whole.[11]

(1)At the end of every seven years you shall grant a release.

---

7. Christoph Levin, "Das Deuteronomium und der Jahwist," in *Fortschreibungen: Gesammelte Studien zum Alten Testament* (BZAW 316; Berlin: de Gruyter, 2003), 96–110.

8. Norbert Lohfink, "Das deuteronomische Gesetz in der Endgestalt – Entwurf einer Gesellschaft ohne marginale Gruppen," in *Studien zum Deuteronomium und zur deuteronomistischen Literatur* (3 vols.; SBAB 8, 12, 20; Stuttgart: Katholisches Bibelwerk, 1990–1995), 3:205–18, esp. 212.

9. Christoph Levin, "The Poor in the Old Testament: Some Observations," in *Fortschreibungen*, 322–38.

10. Heinz-Josef Fabry presents a thorough analysis of the section ("Deuteronomium 15: Gedanken zur Geschwister-Ethik im Alten Testament," ZAR 3 [1997]: 92–111). Veijola offers the most recent interpretation, together with important insights into the literary history (*Das 5. Buch Mose*, 310–23).

11. In the following translations the old prescriptions, i.e., the **Vorlage** of the Deuteronomic editor, are printed in bold type, and the text of the *Deuteronomic editor* in italics. The history edition as well as the covenant edition and finally the edition that stresses Israel's election over against the other nations are printed in normal types and marked by indentation. The brotherhood edition is underlined; the edition regarding the poor is given in plain font.

(2)*And this is the manner of the release: every creditor shall release what he has lent to his neighbor; he shall not exact it of his neighbor*[12]
  and[13] *of his brother* (אָחִיו),
because YHWH's release has been proclaimed.
   (3)*Of a foreigner* (הַנָּכְרִי) *you may exact it; but whatever of yours is with your brother* (אָחִיךָ) *your hand shall release,*
    (4)because there will be no poor (אֶבְיוֹן) among you. For YHWH <your God>[14] will bless you in the land which YHWH your God gives you for an inheritance to possess,
    (5)if only you will obey the voice of YHWH your God, being careful to do all this commandment which I command you today.
    (6)For YHWH your God has blessed you, as he promised you, and you shall lend to many nations, but you shall not borrow; and you shall rule over many nations, but they shall not rule over you.

(7)*If there is among you (sg.) a poor man* (אֶבְיוֹן),
  one of your brethren (מֵאַחַד אַחֶיךָ),
within any of your gates (= settlements)
  within your[15] *land that YHWH your God gives you,*
you shall not harden your heart
  or shut your hand against your poor brother (מֵאָחִיךָ הָאֶבְיוֹן),
(8)*but you shall open your hand to him.*
  < >[16] Lend him sufficient for his need, whatever it may be.
    (9)Take heed lest there be a base thought in your heart, and you say, The seventh year, the year of release is near, and your eye be hostile to your poor brother (בְּאָחִיךָ הָאֶבְיוֹן), and you give him nothing, and he cry to YHWH against you, and it be sin in you.
    (10)You shall give to him freely, and your heart shall not be grudging when you give to him; because for this YHWH your God will bless you in all your work and in all that you undertake.
    (11)For the poor (אֶבְיוֹן) will never cease out of the land.

---

  12. In the Greek text אֶת־רֵעֵהוּ "his neighbor and" is missing: καὶ τὸν ἀδελφόν σου οὐκ ἀπαιτήσεις.
  13. The Samaritan Pentateuch reads without copula.
  14. Insert אֱלֹהֶיךָ with the Samaritan Pentateuch, the Septuagint, the Peshitta, and the Vulgate.
  15. The Samaritan Pentateuch, the Septuagint, the Peshitta, and the Vulgate read without the suffix.
  16. The Samaritan Pentateuch and the Septuagint read without copula.

Therefore I command you, You shall open wide your hand to your brother (לְאָחִיךָ),
to your needy and to your poor (לַעֲנִיֶּךָ וּלְאֶבְיֹנֶךָ) in your land.

⁽¹²⁾**If**
your brother (אָחִיךָ),
a Hebrew man, or a Hebrew woman, is sold to you, he shall serve you six years, and in the seventh year you shall let him go free from you.
⁽¹³⁾And when you let him go free from you, you shall not let him go empty-handed; ⁽¹⁴⁾you shall furnish him liberally out of your flock, out of your threshing floor, and out of your wine press; <just as>¹⁷ YHWH your God has blessed you, you shall give to him.

⁽¹⁵⁾You shall remember that you were a slave in the land of Egypt, and YHWH your God redeemed you; therefore I command you this today.

⁽¹⁶⁾**But if he says to you, I will not go out from you, because he loves you and your household,**
because he fares well with you,
⁽¹⁷⁾**then you shall take an awl, and thrust it through his ear into the door, and he shall be your bondman for ever. And to your bondwoman you shall do likewise.**

⁽¹⁸⁾It shall not seem hard to you, when you let him go free from you; for at half the cost of a hired servant he has served you six years. So YHWH your God will bless you in all that you do.

(1) The earliest basis for the series are the regulations about release in v. 1, which pick up the regulation from the Covenant Code in Exod 23:10–11 and the law about slaves in vv. 12–17, which constitutes the Deuteronomic parallel to the slave law in Exod 21:1–11.¹⁸

---

17. Read כַּאֲשֶׁר with the Samaritan Pentateuch and probably with the Septuagint (καθὰ or καθότι).

18. Norbert Lohfink has thoroughly compared both passages ("Fortschreibung? Zur Technik der Rechtsrevisionen im deuteronomischen Bereich, erörtert an Deuteronomium 12, Ex 21,2–11 und Dtn 15,12–18," in *Das Deuteronomium und seine Querbeziehungen* [ed. Timo Veijola; Schriften der Finnischen Exegetischen Gesellschaft 62; Helsinki: Finnische Exegetische Gesellschaft and Göttingen: Vandenhoeck & Ruprecht, 1996], 127–71, esp. 149–65). Eckart Otto presents a useful synopsis of the parallel texts (*Das Deuteronomium: Politische Theologie und Rechtsreform in Juda und Assyrien* [BZAW 284; Berlin: de Gruyter, 1999], 304–5).

(2) The *Deuteronomic reworking* of these directives begins with v. 2. The introduction shows that it is meant to be understood as the way the regulation in v. 1 is to be applied: "And this is the manner of the release...." "The שמטה is ... not put forward as something new, but is newly interpreted, as the 'legal application' in v. 2 immediately shows. Here v. 2aα ... should be viewed as an actual 'quotation formula,' or—better—as a transition to the interpretation."[19] What is applied to the practice of fallowing in the Covenant Code is transferred in Deuteronomy to the relationship between a lender and a debtor:[20] "...every creditor shall release what he has lent to his neighbor; he shall not exact it of his neighbor, because YHWH's release has been proclaimed." The same ethical turn of mind can be found at the core of vv. 7–8: "If there is among you a poor man in any of your gates, you shall not harden your heart, but you shall open your hand to him." A regulation of this kind is no longer a legal enactment; it is pure paraenesis, aimed at the ideal common life. Although the intention is not that the difference in wealth should disappear completely, it is to be alleviated through compassion. The possibility that the slave may lead a contented existence with his master, "because he fares well with you," which in v. 16bβ is expanded over and above the reason taken over from the Covenant Code, "because he loves you and your household" (v. 16bα), reflects the same ideal.

(3) The next redactional level relates the directives to the situation existing immediately before the conquest of the land west of the Jordan. This revision has gone hand in hand with the subsequent *insertion of Deuteronomy into the historical account*. The expansion can easily be detected because of the double place mention in v. 7, "within any of your gates (= settlements)/within your land which YHWH your God gives you." The same kind of localization can also be found in v. 4b: "For YHWH your God will bless you in the land which YHWH your God gives you for an inheritance to possess." The required forgiveness of debt becomes possible because of the blessing YHWH has promised the people once they have entered the country.

(4) In v. 5 this blessing is subsequently linked with obedience; for this Deut 28:1 is cited, word for word. The *Shemittah* thereby is declared to be a component in the obedience to which Israel is said to have committed

---

19. Perlitt, "Ein einzig Volk von Brüdern," 55.
20. See Fabry, "Deuteronomium 15," 104.

itself when YHWH concluded his covenant with it (cf. Deut 26:17–18). In this way the *covenant-theology revision* of Deuteronomy comes into play. The freeing of slaves is based on similar reasoning in v. 15. The wording is largely identical with that in the reason given for the Sabbath commandment in the Decalogue in Deut 5:15.[21] A comparison between v. 15b and v. 5bβ shows that vv. 5 and 15 are probably the work of the same hand: "Therefore I command you (אָנֹכִי מְצַוְּךָ) this today (הַיּוֹם)" // "which I command you this day (אָנֹכִי מְצַוְּךָ הַיּוֹם)." The conditional promises in v. 10 that are supposed to provide the reason for helping the poor, and in v. 18, which are supposed to justify the freeing of slaves, are governed by the same intention: they see blessing as being dependent on the fulfillment of the commandments.[22]

(5) The *brotherhood ethic* was only incorporated after the covenant-theology revision.[23] The restriction in v. 3, which exempts the foreigner from the release, is alien to the original enactment: "Of a foreigner (הַנָּכְרִי) you may exact it; but whatever of yours is with your brother (אָחִיךָ) your hand shall release." "The comment has been added at a later point, only following the reason given in v. 2bβ, which is based on the specially privileged relationship with YHWH, and in its second part (v. 3b) repeats the substance and the terminology of v. 2abα, thus showing itself to be a later addition."[24] The catchword וְאֶת־אָחִיו "and his brother" in v. 2 is connected with this obvious addition. "The words are a gloss on his neighbour."[25] It is quite clearly a literary augmentation. At the same time, "this doublet is quite inadequately, or even inappropriately, termed a 'gloss' or a 'corrective addition.'"[26] On the contrary, it is part of a systematic revision.

In the two following directives as well, the same catchword has been added at the beginning in a very similar way. That מֵאַחַד אַחֶיךָ "one of

---

21. See also Deut 16:12; 24:18, 22.

22. Where vv. 5 and 18 are concerned, my previous analysis must be corrected; see Levin, "Das Deuteronomium und der Jahwist," 106.

23. For the literary history of the section, see also Fabry, "Deuteronomium 15," 103–4.

24. Veijola, *Das 5. Buch Mose*, 314; see also Carl Steuernagel, *Das Deuteronomium* (2d ed.; HK series 1, 3/1; Göttingen: Vandenhoeck & Ruprecht, 1923), 109.

25. Andrew D. H. Mayes, *Deuteronomy* (NCBS; London: Marshall, Morgan & Scott, 1979), 248; also Hölscher, "Komposition und Ursprung," 194 n. 1 ("simply a doublet besides את־רעהו"); Perlitt, "Ein einzig Volk von Brüdern," 55; Veijola, *Das 5. Buch Mose*, 311.

26. Perlitt, "Ein einzig Volk von Brüdern," 55.

your brethren" in v. 7 is an addition is made plain by the "unhappy repetition אביון מאחד אחיך באחד שעריך."[27] "The first אחד 'one' in the Masoretic text is a dittography of the second, as the Septuagint and Deut 24:14 show."[28] The purpose is to integrate the catchword אָחִיךָ. In the slave law, "the preceding apposition אָחִיךָ"[29] in v. 12 is clearly a subsequently added interpretation.

The commandment concerning a loan for the poor in its original form speaks for itself: "You shall not harden your heart, but you shall open your hand to him" (vv. 7bα¹, 8a). Now it is given sharper form through the prohibition of the opposite behavior: "You must not shut your hand against your poor brother" (v. 7bα²b). The text is no longer focused on the poor man (אֶבְיוֹן) as such. He is the recipient of care because he is a member of the religious-ethnic community. The ethic is no longer based solely on the social duty to care for others, as it was in the original Deuteronomy, nor does it rest solely on the special position of God's people, as was the case in the covenant-theology revision; it now ministers to the cohesion of the religious community and, at the same time, sets it apart from its environment. What was formerly a general requirement: "You shall open your hand to him" is now precisely defined: "Lend him sufficient for his need, whatever it may be." With the same intention, the covenant-theology reason (v. 10) has been subsequently related to the brotherhood ethic: "Therefore I command you, 'You shall open wide your hand to your brother'" (v. 11bαβ¹). Here the requirement in v. 8a is repeated word for word but now no longer related to "him" (לוֹ),—i.e., to the poor man (אֶבְיוֹן)—but to the brother: לְאָחִיךָ.

In the law about slaves, too, we do not find the application to the brother only in the catchword אָחִיךָ in v. 12. The admonition to be generous in material matters in vv. 13–14 breathes the same spirit as the additions in vv. 7bα²b, 8b, 11bαβ¹, which are based on the brotherhood ethic: "And when you let him go free from you, you shall not let him go empty-handed; you shall furnish him liberally out of your flock, out of your threshing floor, and out of your wine press; [just as] YHWH your God has blessed you, you shall give to him." The word-for-word repetition of וְכִי־תְשַׁלְּחֶנּוּ חָפְשִׁי מֵעִמָּךְ, which links to v. 12bβ, identifies the two verses as an addition.

---

27. Perlitt, "Ein einzig Volk von Brüdern," 56 n. 23.

28. Veijola, *Das 5. Buch Mose*, 310 n. 1092, with Perlitt, "Ein einzig Volk von Brüdern," 59 n. 33.

29. Perlitt, "Ein einzig Volk von Brüdern," 56.

(6) The literary development of Deut 15 was not yet finished with the brotherhood ethic. In vv. 4a and 6 we hear a voice which, by way of a word-for-word pointer to the blessing promised in v. 4b, maintains that among God's people no loans will be necessary, "because there will be no poor among you." The assertion frankly contradicts v. 7 and makes the instruction in vv. 7–11 pointless. Consequently, vv. 4–6 are widely held to be a later interpolation.[30] This becomes evident also from the literary hiatus between vv. 3 and 4.

However, as was shown above, vv. 4b and 5 must already have belonged to the earlier text. The interpolation in vv. 4a and 6 solves the problem presented by the earlier directive that interest-free loans have no point, economically speaking, referring to the promise of blessing. The difference between the "brother" (אָח) and the "foreigner" (נָכְרִי) that was established in v. 3 is generalized: "For YHWH your God has blessed you, as he promised you, and you shall lend to many nations, but you shall not borrow."[31] Its foundation is *Israel's election* (cf. Deut 7:6, 14–16; 14:2).

(7) The assertion that "there will be no poor among you" did not remain undisputed. In v. 11a the exact opposite is maintained: "The poor will never cease out of the land."[32] At first sight, it would seem that the choice lies between seeing v. 11a as corrected by v. 4a, or vice versa. In

---

30. Alfred Bertholet, *Deuteronomium* (KHC 5; Freiburg im Breisgau: Mohr Siebeck, 1899), 48; Johannes Hempel, *Die Schichten des Deuteronomiums: Ein Beitrag zur israelitischen Literatur- und Rechtsgeschichte* (Leipzig: Voigtländer, 1914), 226; Hölscher, "Komposition und Ursprung," 194 n. 1; Karl Marti, *Das fünfte Buch Mose oder Deuteronomium* (Die Heilige Schrift des Alten Testaments 1; 4th ed.; Tübingen: Mohr Siebeck, 1922), 287; Steuernagel, *Deuteronomium*, 108–9; Mayes, *Deuteronomy*, 247–48; Rosario P. Merendino, *Das deuteronomische Gesetz: Eine literarkritische, gattungs- und überlieferungsgeschichtliche Untersuchung zu Dt 12–26* (Bonner biblische Beiträge 31; Bonn: Hanstein, 1969), 110–11; Gottfried Seitz, *Redaktionsgeschichtliche Studien zum Deuteronomium* (BWANT 93; Stuttgart: Kohlhammer, 1971), 169; Fabry, "Deuteronomium 15," 104; Eckart Otto, *Gottes Recht als Menschenrecht: Rechts- und literaturhistorische Studien zum Deuteronomium* (Beihefte zur Zeitschrift für altorientalische und biblische Rechtsgeschichte 2; Wiesbaden: Harrassowitz, 2002), 219 n. 523.; Veijola, *Das 5. Buch Mose*, 315.

31. Verse 6bβγ may again be a later addition: "and you shall rule over many nations, but they shall not rule over you."

32. For Lohfink, the contradiction between Deut 15:4 and 15:11 is only apparent: "There may be poverty in 'the land,' but not in 'Israel,' if it is truly 'Israel'" ("Das Deuteronomische Gesetz in der Endgestalt," 216). This interpretation is in danger of replacing the divine promise with the demand for a certain kind of behavior.

the first case, the reality of poor and rich would be contrasted with the goal of a society without marginal groups;[33] in the second case, the social utopia would be subjected subsequently to the test of reality.[34] But in actual fact, it is a question neither of the one nor the other. It is rather that the author of v. 11a is resisting the notion that the commandment threatens the existence of the poor. For him, poverty is not a condition that ought to be overcome; it is the mark of a religious group characterized by its special closeness to God. To say "the poor will never cease out of the land" is as much as to say "the poor (עֲנָוִים) will inherit the land" (Ps 37:11; cf. Matt 5:5).

Consequently, in v. 11bβ² this writer defines the brother who is to be the recipient of solicitous care as one who is "humble and poor" (עָנִי וְאֶבְיוֹן). These paired terms introduce into Deuteronomy a particular connotation that otherwise can be found above all in the Psalms: the *devout poor* (see Ps 35:10; 37:14; 40:18 par. 70:6; 74:21; 86:1; 109:16, 22). In this case, poverty is not in the first instance a social category; it is a religious one. It is evidence of nearness to God. The poor are the people who seek YHWH and who will be justified in the eschatological judgment. In contrast to the wicked, they will survive doomsday (see Zeph 2:2–3; 3:8, 12).

This is the presupposition for an understanding of the warning that is added in v. 9. It is a precaution lest the institution of the Year of Release, in which the debtor was freed of his debts (vv. 1–2), should diminish the readiness to help the humble and poor. It is clearly secondary, over against the earlier provision. Again, the poor man's special relationship to YHWH is presupposed: that is the reason why not to have helped him will count as sin (חֵטְא) in the divine judgment. The same threat is to be found later in Deut 24:15.[35] This confirms that in this case, too, we are not looking at a gloss but at a more thoroughgoing revision.

---

33. Fabry: "The goal of the brotherhood/sisterhood ethic of Deut 15 is the utopian precept: 'Really there should be no poor people among you' (v. 4), over against the objective fact of experience: 'The poor will never entirely disappear from your land' (v. 11)" ("Deuteronomium 15," 107).

34. Otto states about 15:11a: "Verse 15:11 again corrects v. 4 and brings it into line with postexilic circumstances. The utopian program of the exilic period has not been fulfilled" (*Gottes Recht als Menschenrecht*, 220 n. 523).

35. See below in the subsection, "On Pledges, and on the Wages of the Day Laborer (Deut 24:10–13, 14–15)."

On False Witness (Deut 19:16–21)

The procedure to be adopted against a malicious witness is determined as follows:

> **(16)If a malicious witness rises against someone**
>   to accuse him of apostasy
> **(17)then both parties to the dispute shall appear before YHWH**
>   before the priests and the judges who are in office in those days.
>   (18)And the judges shall inquire diligently, and if the witness[36] proves to be a false witness,
>   <u>having testified falsely against his brother</u> (בְּאָחִיו), (19)<u>then you (pl.) shall do to him as he had meant to do to his brother</u> (לְאָחִיו).
>   then you (sg.) shall purge the evil from the midst of you.
>   (20)And the rest shall hear, and fear, and shall never again commit any such evil in the midst of you.
>   (21)< >[37] Your eye shall not pity.
> [It shall be] **life for life, eye for eye, tooth for tooth, hand for hand, foot for foot.**

(1) This directive again goes back basically speaking to the Covenant Code. It rests on the appeal in Exod 23:1 not to come forward as a malicious witness (עֵד־חָמָס).[38] In Deuteronomy this is modified so that if the truthfullness of a witness is in doubt, a divine judgment should be sought (vv. 16a, 17a). The punishment to be imposed on a malicious witness is accordingly determined by the *ius talionis* (v. 21b), which is taken over from Exod 21:23–24.

(2) In the context of *Deuteronomy's historization*, v. 17b has been added later. This can be detected from the temporal clause בַּיָּמִים הָהֵם "in those days." This is also made the occasion for laying down the constitution of the cultic court. "La répétition *lifnê* … *lifnê* montre que le second membre de phrase est une explication postérieure."[39] "Verse 17b interprets

---

36. The Septuagint reads הָעֵד as a verbal form ἐμαρτύρησεν (הֵעִיד), similar the Peshitta. As a consequence, the second שֶׁקֶר was seen as the object of הֵעִיד "he testified," not of עָנָה "he answered." This reading certainly misses the original meaning.
37. The Samaritan Pentateuch, 4QDeut^f, the Septuagint, the Peshitta, and the Vulgate read without copula.
38. The term עֵד־חָמָס can be found otherwise only in Ps 35:11.
39. Jean L'Hour, "Une législation criminelle dans le Deutéronome," *Bib* 44 (1963):

the לפני יהוה in v. 17a:"⁴⁰ The divine judgment is to be put into force by the appointed priests and judges (cf. Deut 17:9; 26:3). That this is an addition can also be seen from the expression used: "'פ לפני עמד is employed when someone appears before the king, but not when he comes before the priests or judges."⁴¹ The Samaritan Pentateuch, the Septuagint, and the Peshitta read the second לִפְנֵי as וְלִפְנֵי. The copula is not original, however, but shows the inconsistency has been noted and an attempt has been made to smooth it out. Modern exegesis has found it necessary to intervene in a number of different ways.⁴² The simplest and most probable solution is that v. 17b has been added in a single act.⁴³

(3) A second, extensive expansion of the instruction took place in the framework of the revision made in the interests of *covenant theology*. The additions can be detected from their agreement with the relevant passages in 13:2–19 and 17:2–5: compare v. 16b with 13:6,⁴⁴ v. 18abα with 13:15 and 17:4,⁴⁵ the בִּעַרְתָּ-formula in v. 19b with 13:6; 17:7, 12; 19:13, 19; 21:9, 21; 22:21, 22; 24:7,⁴⁶ and v. 21a with 7:16; 13:9; 19:13; 25:13. The matter is now considered to affect the relationship to God. Consequently, the false accusation counts as סָרָה "apostasy."⁴⁷ For hearing the evidence, the judges are

---

1–28, esp. 18 n.1. See earlier, Bertholet, *Deuteronomium*, 62; Marti, *Das fünfte Buch Mose*, 295.

40. Merendino, *Das deuteronomische Gesetz*, 215.

41. Hölscher, "Komposition und Ursprung," 206 n. 3.

42. See Steuernagel, *Deuteronomium*, 125; Bertholet, *Deuteronomium*, 62; Marti, *Das fünfte Buch Mose*, 295; Hölscher, "Komposition und Ursprung," 206 n. 3; Seitz, *Redaktionsgeschichtliche Studien*, 114.

43. Thus Hempel, *Die Schichten des Deuteronomiums*, 221; L'Hour, "Une Législation criminelle," 18; Merendino, *Das deuteronomische Gesetz*, 215; Mayes, *Deuteronomy*, 290.

44. Steuernagel, *Deuteronomium*, 125, perceived that v. 16b was an addition.

45. Jan Christian Gertz presents a synopsis of 13:15 and 17:4 (*Die Gerichtsorganisation Israels im deuteronomischen Gesetz* [FRLANT 165; Göttingen: Vandenhoeck & Ruprecht, 1994], 111). When he assigns v. 18 to the original text, however, he misses the significance of the concurrence.

46. See the relevant study of L'Hour, "Une Législation criminelle."

47. See Marti, *Das fünfte Buch Mose*, 295; Steuernagel, *Deuteronomium*, 125. According to Samuel R. Driver, סָרָה "appears from the context to be used more generally" (*A Critical and Exegetical Commentary on Deuteronomy* [3d ed.; ICC; Edinburgh: T&T Clark, 1902], 235); Bertholet agrees (*Deuteronomium*, 62). However, it is Deut 13 that provides the original context. According to Mayes, "except for the doubtful case of Isa. 59:13, there is no example of *sārāh* having the general sense of 'wrongdoing,'

"to initiate a careful investigation" (דרש), a different procedure from the earlier one לִפְנֵי יהוה, according to which "the divine decision was declared not by way of a precise investigation but by means of an oracle."[48] A striking fact is that the key term is now no longer עֵד־חָמָס, but עֵד־שָׁקֶר. This points to the Decalogue (Exod 20:16)[49] as the foundational law for covenant theology. In a further step, the regulation in v. 20 has been developed into a warning. Its aim is to ensure as far as possible that the harsh judgment need not be applied in the future to members of God's people. We find similar additions—probably the work of the same hand—in 13:12; 17:13; and 21:21b.[50]

(4) Finally, the edict is particularized as false witness against the *brethren*. The addition begins in v. 18bβ as asyndetic explication: שֶׁקֶר עָנָה בְּאָחִיו. "Verse 18bβ repeats what is said in v.18bα, and is also secondary."[51] The words are not "merely repetitions of the idea"[52] but pick up the existing text in order to introduce the regulation in v. 19a, which also shows itself to be an addition through the shift into the plural form of address. The choice of the verb ענה "to answer" shows that on this level, too, the Decalogue is in the writer's mind. The premise of the command for sincerity towards the court is now the special relationship to YHWH defined in the First Commandment, which thereby is given particular importance. In the light of Exod 20:16, it is understood as being a norm that determines the behavior of members of God's people towards one another. God's people count as a community of brethren.

On Loss of Lifestock (Deut 22:1–4)

An especially significant example of the brotherhood ethic is the commandment to render help in case of a strayed beast or one that has fallen

---

whereas it is used of apostasy in Dt. 13:6; Isa. 1:5; 31:6; Jer. 28:16; 29:32" (*Deuteronomy*, 290).

48. Hempel, *Die Schichten des Deuteronomiums*, 221; also Gertz: "The cultic method of proof required in v. 17a … and the thorough judicial investigation which is to be carried out according to v. 18a are mutually exclusive procedural methods" (*Die Gerichtsorganisation Israels*, 108).

49. L'Hour, "Une Législation criminelle," 19; Merendino, *Das deuteronomische Gesetz*, 215.

50. See L'Hour, "Une Législation criminelle," 10 n. 3.

51. Merendino, *Das deuteronomische Gesetz*, 215.

52. Seitz, *Redaktionsgeschichtliche Studien*, 114 n. 73.

down. In this case, the regulation does not rest on a traditional legal edict but is in very respect an ethical maxim.

> (1)You shall not see your brother's (אָחִיךָ) ox or his sheep go astray, and withhold your help from them; you shall take them back to your brother (לְאָחִיךָ).
> (2)And if your brother (אָחִיךָ) is not near you, or if you do not know him, you shall bring it home to your house, and it shall be with you until your brother (אָחִיךָ) seeks it; then you shall restore it to him.
> (3)<So>[53] you shall do with his ass; so you shall do with his garment; so you shall do with any lost thing of your brother's (אָחִיךָ), which he loses and you find; you may not withhold your help.
> (4)You shall not see your brother's (אָחִיךָ) ass or his ox fallen down by the way, and withhold your help from them; you shall help him to lift them up again.

The reference to "your brother" is essential for the appeal. It cannot be removed by literary intervention. Consequently, the instruction "in this brotherhood stratum ... must have been constituted by its author himself."[54] The context shows that the commandment as a whole is an addition, made at a later literary level: it interrupts the sequence of tabu regulations in 21:22–23 and 22:5–12, which has itself been interpolated into the family law in 21:10–21; 22:13–23:1. In this way this commandment, too, is evidence that the *brotherhood ethic* was not originally a feature of Deuteronomy.

Its late origin did not hinder the commandment from being expanded twice more. Verses 2 and 3 are later interpolations.[55] They envisage a case in which the beast's owner cannot be contacted immediately (v. 2), and they include the whole of the brother's property in the obligation, over and above the beast itself (v. 3). The earlier version of the commandment, which consisted only of vv. 1 and 4, is closely paralleled in Exod 23:4–5, but there, too, it is not original,[56] because the commandment interrupts

---

53. Read כֵּן with the Samaritan Pentateuch, the Septuagint, the Peshitta, and the Vulgate.
54. Perlitt, "Ein einzig Volk von Brüdern," 61.
55. August Klostermann, *Der Pentateuch: Beiträge zu seinem Verständnis und seiner Entstehungsgeschichte* (2d ed.; Leipzig: Deichert, 1907), 325–26.
56. Steuernagel, for example, labels it "a later addition to the Covenant Code" (*Deuteronomium*, 131).

the order for the legal proceeding given in Exod 23:1–3, 6–8. Compared with Deut 22, the ethical requirement has been heightened, since it applies to the *enemy's* ox and ass. Therefore, it is possible in this particular case that the line of the tradition-history has run from Deuteronomy to the Covenant Code.

On Interest (Deut 23:20–21)

Another example of brotherhood ethic is the prohibition of charging interest. Again, it is easy to see the sequence of the revisions:

⁽²⁰⁾**You shall**
    <u>to your brother (לְאָחִיךָ)</u>
not lend upon interest, interest on money, interest on victuals,
   interest on anything that is lent for interest.
     ⁽²¹⁾<u>To a foreigner (לַנָּכְרִי) you may lend upon interest, but to your brother (וּלְאָחִיךָ) you shall not lend upon interest</u>;
   so that YHWH your God may bless you in all that you undertake
    in the land which you are entering to take possession of it.

(1) The basis of the decree is confined to v. 20a: interest on money (silver) as well as on foodstuffs is prohibited. The age of this decree, the social context in which it must be viewed, and the question as to whether it is practicable at all in economic life are matters with which we need not concern ourselves here. What can be clearly seen is that the edict has been expanded and given a general reference through the apposition in v. 20b. It would seem plausible to see in this expansion the ethic of the *original Deuteronomy* and to link it with the promise of blessing in v. 21bα: "interest on anything that is lent for interest, so that YHWH your God may bless you in all that you undertake" (see esp. 14:29; 24:19). The *historicization* "in the land which you are entering to take possession of it" in v. 21bβ (that otherwise can be found in this form only outside Deut 12–26)[57] can easily be detached and, like all these comments, has been added later.

(2) In v. 21a a sharp line is drawn between brother and foreigner. This sentence, and with it the *brotherhood ethic*, is obviously an alien element in the framework of the regulation. "23:21 is a subsequent interpretation

---

57. See Deut 7:1; 11:10, 29; 28:21, 63; 30:16.

of 23:20."⁵⁸ On the one hand, a loophole is opened for the requirements of economic life. It is permissable to lend to a foreigner in return for the commercially customary interest; but, on the other hand, the regulation is given a specific reason. Within one's own ethnic-religious group special rules apply, rules differing from those generally in force. The addition touches on internal relationships in the community of the Second Temple, which wished to differentiate itself from its environment in its social ethic. In order that this reinterpretation should apply to the regulation as a whole, the catchword לְאָחִיךָ "to your brother" was added to v. 20 as well. It is certainly wrong to see here "the own voice of the author of Deuteronomy."⁵⁹

On Kidnapping (Deut 24:7)

The three directives for social behavior in Deut 24:7, 10–13, 14–15 form a direct sequence, interrupted only by the regulation to be observed in the case of leprosy, which was added subsequently in vv. 8–9.⁶⁰ The self-contained sequence makes it possible to determine the order of the revisions with comparative certainty.

> **⁽⁷⁾If a man is found stealing someone**
>   of his brethren (מֵאֶחָיו)
>   of the Israelites
>   and if he violently oppresses him
> **and sells him, then that thief shall die.**
>   So you shall purge the evil from the midst of you. [...]

The foundation of the directive is the sentence in Exod 21:16. It appears in a new version in Deut 24:7: "If a man is found stealing someone and sells him, then that thief shall die."⁶¹ The *covenant theology revision* comes to the fore once again, as it does in 19:19, with the בִּעַרְתָּ-formula.⁶² The restricting reference to God's people מִבְּנֵי יִשְׂרָאֵל, the Israelites, may be

---

58. Perlitt, "Ein einzig Volk von Brüdern," 57; compare Steuernagel, *Deuteronomium*, 137.
59. Against Seitz, *Redaktionsgeschichtliche Studien*, 175.
60. See further Steuernagel, *Deuteronomium*, 33, 140; Hölscher, "Komposition und Ursprung," 214; Seitz, *Redaktionsgeschichtliche Studien*, 166.
61. See Otto, *Deuteronomium*, 298–99.
62. See above, and again L'Hour, "Une Législation criminelle."

connected with this expansion. The asyndetic מֵאֶחָיו "of his brethren" before מִבְּנֵי יִשְׂרָאֵל "of the Israelites" has been added during the *brotherhood-ethic revision*. The fact that this is an addition has often been noted. "The two expressions מאחיו and מבני ישראל are not connected, so that they give the impression of being variants."[63] The doublets וְהִתְעַמֶּר־בּוֹ "and if he violently oppresses him" and וּמְכָרוֹ "if he sells him" can also be connected with the brotherhood revision.[64]

On Pledges, and on the Wages of the Day Laborer (Deut 24:10–13, 14–15)

The heart of the commandment about pledges and that of the regulation about the wages of the day laborer probably goes back to the author of the Deuteronomic law.

> (10) *When you make your neighbor a loan of any sort, you shall not go into his house to fetch his pledge.* (11) *You shall stand outside, and the man to whom you make the loan <he himself>*[65] *shall bring the pledge out to you.*
> > (12) *And if he is a poor man* (אִישׁ עָנִי), *you shall not sleep in his pledge;* (13) *when the sun goes down, you shall restore to him the pledge that he may sleep in his cloak and bless you; and it shall be righteousness to you before YHWH your God.*
>
> (14) *You shall not oppress a hired servant*
> > who is poor and needy (עָנִי וְאֶבְיוֹן),
> > <u>of your brethren</u> (מֵאַחֶיךָ), or of your sojourner (מִגֵּרְךָ) who are in your land[66]
>
> within your towns; (15) *you shall give him his hire on the day he earns it, before the sun goes down.*

---

63. Seitz, *Redaktionsgeschichtliche Studien*, 123; see also Steuernagel, *Deuteronomium*, 140.

64. The same phrase can be found in Deut 21:14 and there, too, has apparently been added at a later point, possibly under the influence of 24:7: "Then, if you have no delight in her, you shall let her go where she will; but you shall not sell her (וּמָכֹר לֹא־תִמְכְּרֶנָּה) for money [you shall not violently oppress her (לֹא־תִתְעַמֵּר בָּהּ)], since you have cohabited with her."

65. Add הוא with the Samaritan Pentateuch.

66. The Septuagint and the Peshitta omit בְּאַרְצְךָ "in your land" to eliminate the doublet "within your land in your towns" that was produced by the addition of the brethren-edition.

For he is poor (עָנִי), and sets his heart upon it; lest he cry against you to YHWH, and it be sin in you.

(1) The reason for the provision relating pledges (vv. 10–11) is obvious. The debtor has to be given the liberty to decide about his property, which is very limited in any case, and is to be protected against extortion. Also, the purpose of the provision that regulates the remuneration to be paid to the day laborer (vv. 14–15) is to prevent inequitable extortion and exploitation, in line with Deuteronomy's humanitarian ideal. The *brotherhood revision* has left its traces in v. 14b: "one of your brethren, or of your sojourner who are in your land."[67] The double localization בְּאַרְצְךָ בִּשְׁעָרֶיךָ "in your land within your towns" shows that the interpretation of the hired servant as brother is a later addition. The humanitarian ideal now counts as an expression of the special relationship obtaining among members of God's people.

(2) To the provision on pledges in vv. 12–13, a subsidiary case is added: "And if he is a poor man (אִישׁ עָנִי)...." The preciseness of this provision has rightly caused surprise: "For even in the main case the person concerned must surely have been a poor man, otherwise he would not have been liable for the loan."[68] Moreover, this poor person is said to have a close relationship to YHWH; for when he blesses the author of the charitable act, YHWH counts this as righteousness (צְדָקָה). Thus, *commitment to the poor* becomes a "good work" that appears on the credit side in the divine Judgment. All of a sudden, the postscript no longer talks about some random pledge but about the cloak; yet "we learn this only from the continuation."[69] It is only explicable at all if what the writer had in mind was the corresponding provision in the Covenant Code (Exod 22:25–26). In the continuation we have to do with comparative inner-biblical exegesis, no longer with a legal precept.

In addition, the day laborer is undoubtedly one of the poor. Therefore, it is all the more surprising that the circumstance is now again especially stressed. The "hired servant" (שָׂכִיר) is defined in asyndetic apposition as being עָנִי וְאֶבְיוֹן "poor and needy." These paired terms correspond precisely to the devout man's definition of himself in those psalms that have been revised from the standpoint of the theology of the poor; see Ps 40:18//70:6;

---

67. Perlitt, "Ein einzig Volk von Brüdern," 59 n. 33.
68. Seitz, *Redaktionsgeschichtliche Studien*, 178.
69. Seitz, *Redaktionsgeschichtliche Studien*, 178.

86:1; 109:22. In a postscript, this definition is repeated: כִּי עָנִי הוּא "for he is poor," and the provision justified by his particular need: "he sets his heart upon it." Again, the poor man is seen in a close relationship to YHWH, so that one could even say that a person's relation to God is decided by his behavior toward the poor. This time the negative variant is chosen, just as in 15:9: the refusal of commitment counts as sin (חֵטְא) in the divine Judgment. The two provisions in Deut 24:10–13 and 14–15 stand side by side as conditional blessing and conditional curse.

On Corporal Punishment (Deut 25:1–3)

The final example is the rule about corporal punishment. Here, too, the sequence of literary revisions is repeated:

> ⁽¹⁾**If there is a case between men, and they come into court, and they** [i.e. the people in the court] **decide between them,**
>> they shall justify the righteous (הַצַּדִּיק) and condemn the wicked (הָרָשָׁע),
>
> ⁽²⁾**then if the guilty man (הָרָשָׁע) deserves to be beaten, the judge shall cause him to lie down and be beaten in his presence, according to what is sufficient for his offence (רִשְׁעָתוֹ) by number.**
>> ⁽³⁾*Forty (stripes) he may beat him, he shall not exceed;*
>>> <u>lest, if he exceeds to beat him with more stripes than these, your brother (אָחִיךָ) be dishonored in your sight.</u>

(1) The regulation rests on a traditional legal tenet that can be detected in vv. 1a and 2. Corporal punishment is to be subjected to a proper procedure. It requires a decision before a public court, and the punishment must be carried out under the judge's supervision. The number of lashes is determined in proportion to the gravity of the offence, "according to what is sufficient for his offence." To this extent, the regulation is complete in itself.

What is in dispute exegetically is the point at which the legal consequence (apodosis) begins. Verse 2 is generally understood as a sub-section. In that case, v. 1aβb would already define a first legal consequence:[70] "If there is a case between men, they shall come into court...." That is not very probable, for to say that a legal matter (רִיב) should be decided before

---

70. Thus emphatically, Gertz, *Die Gerichtsorganisation Israels*, 98–100.

a court would merely be to state the matter-of-course conditions for the administration of justice; as a legal consequence, it would be meaningless. The וְהָיָה אִם "then if" in v. 2 rather states the outcome of the court's investigation. The apodosis follows only with וְהִפִּילוֹ "he shall cause him to lie down."[71]

(2) In v. 3a the directive was expanded for the first time. The number of lashes is to be limited to forty. To define the utmost extent of the punishment cuts across the court's right of decision that was previously declared.[72] "The disputed case and a just decision ('according to what is sufficient,' v. 2) are now forgotten."[73] This limitation reflects the *Deuteronomic humanitarian ideal*, which differs from that of the earlier edict. The addition probably goes back to the editor of the first edition of the Deuteronomic law.

(3) In a third step, the limitation is justified. For this the style changes into the form of address: the disproportionate corporal punishment would affect "your brother's" honor. The repetition פֶּן־יֹסִיף / לֹא יֹסִיף "he shall not exceed / lest, if he exceeds" shows that the negative purpose clause v. 3b is a further addition. A continuous text would have read: אַרְבָּעִים יַכֶּנּוּ לֹא יֹסִיף פֶּן־יַקְלֶה אָחִיךָ לְעֵינֶיךָ "forty he may beat him, he shall not exceed lest your brother be dishonored in your sight."[74] Here, once again, we can detect the *brotherhood revision*.

(4) Finally, the revisions that have to do with the *poor* and with justice have also left their traces behind them. For the judicial procedure וּשְׁפָטוּם "and they decide between them" to be developed in the sense of "they shall justify the righteous and condemn the wicked" is in law no more than a matter of course and can, therefore, hardly belong to the original version. Its sense is to make a clear distinction *coram Deo* between "the righteous" (הַצַּדִּיק) and "the wicked" (הָרָשָׁע).

Conclusion

The sequence of revisions undergone by the Deuteronomic law can be clearly observed in all the pericopes we have treated, and that sequence

---

71. Thus explicitly, Bertholet, *Deuteronomium*, 77. See also the translation by Marti, *Das fünfte Buch Mose*, 305 and by Steuernagel, *Deuteronomium*, 141.
72. Seitz, *Redaktionsgeschichtliche Studien*, 126.
73. Perlitt, "Ein einzig Volk von Brüdern," 60.
74. Compare the observations by Merendino, *Das deuteronomische Gesetz*, 318; however, he maintains the unity of v. 3, seeing it as being added in its entirety.

remains the same throughout. The individual analyses thus support each other and lend the findings as a whole a high degree of certainty.

The foundation of the text's structure is the Covenant Code. A selection of its regulations has been taken over and newly interpreted for the changed conditions obtaining at the end of the seventh century. The centralization of the cult was probably an essential motivation for the revision, even though this is not in the foreground in the relevant sections (the changed procedure in 15:17 is an exception). Here what is already noticeable is a certain social-ethical intention, just as the Covenant Code itself, indeed, also already contains parenetic sections.

When the law was incorporated into the historical account, it was related to the impending conquest of the country. This new direction is a distinct individual step in the literary history of Deuteronomy, a step that in many places (here: Deut 15:4b, 7aβγ; 19:17b; 23:21bβ) can be detached both from the original version and from the later theological revision.

The decisive theological step that fundamentally changed the character of Deuteronomy and enduringly determined its present form is the covenant-theology revision. It makes the law book the documentary record of a treaty. For this, not only was the loyalty obligation put at the head of the book in Deut 6:4–5, but also, Deut 26:17–18 added a covenant agreement of which blessing and, especially, curse in Deut 28 form a part. Corresponding references can be found scattered throughout the book (here: Deut 15:5, 10, 15, 18; 19:16b, 18abα, 19b, [20], 21a; 24:7a [only מִבְּנֵי יִשְׂרָאֵל], bβ). The casting forward to Deut 28 as well as the casting back to the Decalogue in Deut 5 are characteristic.

Contrary to a widely held view, what has emerged here is that the brotherhood ethic was not a feature of the original Deuteronomy. In every instance it has been added to the earlier directives at a later point: 15:2 (only וְאֶת־אָחִיו), 3, 7aα (only מֵאַחַד אַחֶיךָ), b (from וְלֹא onward), 8b, 11b (until יָדֶךָ), 12 (only אָחִיךָ), 13–14; 19:18bβ–19a; 22:1–4; 23:20 (only לְאָחִיךָ), 21a; 24:7 (only מֵאֶחָיו and וְהִתְעַמֶּר־בּוֹ), 14b (without בִּשְׁעָרֶיךָ); 25:3b.[75] The regularity of the additions suggests that they go back to a planned revision. They represent the internal morality of a religious-ethnic group, which can best be understood as a minority. The brotherhood ethic in Deuteronomy reflects the self-understanding of the Jewish temple community in

---

75. Instances such as Deut 14:21 (only אוֹ מָכֹר לְנָכְרִי) and 17:15b not dealt with in this paper also belong to the same level in the literary history.

the ongoing Persian period, a community forced to share the country with a population that differs ethnically and religiously (even if its members do not actually live in the Diaspora) and with its ethical maxims begins to develop a morality of its own. Subsequently, the brotherhood ethic was added to the framework of the Holiness Code in Lev 25:25, 35–55.

Finally, Deuteronomy's concern with the interests of the devout poor belongs to the late period. The traces of this revision found in Deut 15:9, 11a, bβ (only לַעֲנִיֶּךָ וּלְאֶבְיֹנְךָ בְּאַרְצֶךָ); 24:12–13, 14a (only עָנִי וְאֶבְיוֹן), 15 (from כִּי onward); 25:1b belong to the same era—probably in the Hellenistic period—when the prophetic books and the psalms were also supplemented to meet the needs of this devout minority, with its devotion to the Torah. They lend even the Torah a characteristic thrust in the direction of the divine eschatological judgment. Traces of this revision can also be found in the book of Exodus in Exod 22:24 (only אֶת־הֶעָנִי); 23:1bα, 6 (only אֶבְיֹנְךָ בְּרִיבוֹ), 7b, and 11a (from וְאָכְלוּ onward).

WHY "JOSHUA"?

E. Axel Knauf

PRELIMINARY THOUGHTS

Why is there a book of Joshua in the Hebrew Scriptures? The question is twofold: why is there a book of *Joshua*, and why is there a *book* of Joshua? In the hypothetical beginnings of Joshua's literary existence, the core of the book just served as the last chapter of an Exodus-Eisodus narrative.[1] In the present biblical canon, Joshua (656 verses[2]) and Judges (618 verses) rank among the shortest biblical books:

Rank (bottom up)	Book	Number of verses
1	Daniel	357
2	Judges	618
3	Joshua	656
4	Ezra-Nehemiah	685

Even combined, the two books (1,274 verses) would not make the top of the list:

---

1. See Konrad Schmid, *Erzväter und Exodus: Untersuchungen zur doppelten Begründung der Ursprünge Israels innerhalb der Geschichtsbücher des Alten Testaments* (WMANT 81; Neukirchen-Vluyn: Neukirchener Verlag, 1999); Konrad Schmid, *Literaturgeschichte des Alten Testaments: Eine Einführung* (Darmstadt: Wissenschaftliche Buchgesellschaft, 2008); E. Axel Knauf, *Josua* (ZBKAT 6; Zürich: TVZ, 2008); E. Axel Knauf, "History in Joshua," in *Israel in Transition: From Late Bronze II to Iron IIa (c. 1250–850 B.C.E.)* (ed. Lester L. Grabbe; 2 vols; LBHOTS 521 = ESHM 8; New York: T&T Clark, 2010), 2:130–39.

2. The verse counts used here are from the final *masora* of the individual books in Codex L.

Rank (top down)	Book	Number of verses
1	Chronicles	1,765
2	Genesis, Kings	1,534
3	Psalms	1,527
4	Samuel	1,506
5	Jeremiah	1,364
6	Isaiah	1,291
7	Numbers	1,288
8	Joshua and Judges	1,274
9	Ezekiel	1,273

That they are nevertheless not combined in the canon is one of the more striking arguments against the hypothesis of some "DtrH," once comprising the whole series Joshua–Kings as one literary unit.[3]

Looking Back

To address the first of the two questions, let us briefly imagine there were no book of Joshua, or nothing of the "Former Prophets" at all. In this case, our biblical narrative would jump from the death of Moses to the building of the (Second) Temple and the first reading of Torah. We would know from Deut 31–34 (if not from Exod 15–Deut 34) that Joshua was supposed to succeed Moses and actually did so (Deut 34:9), and from Neh 8:17 that under Joshua, the Israelites had kept Succoth as they were doing again since the days of Ezra. Our perception of Israel's history would come very close to the narrative of an anonymous Jew from Alexandria as recorded by Hecataeus of Abdera:[4] Moses led the Israelites into an empty land where no kings had ever ruled and founded Jerusalem and the temple.

If we had Judges and Kings, but not Joshua, we could conclude that Joshua was an utter failure: he was supposed to distribute the land of Canaan as described in Num 34:1–12 to the Israelites (Num 34:13–29).

---

3. Judges has been secondarily inserted between Josh and Sam; see Walter Groß, *Richter* (HKAT; Freiburg: Herder, 2009), 85–86; Knauf, *Josua*, 21–22.

4. Menahem Stern, ed., *Greek and Latin Authors on Jews and Judaism* (3 vols.; Jerusalem: Israel Academy of Sciences and Humanities, 1974–1984), 1:26–35.

Instead, we find in Judg 1, after the death of Joshua, each tribe acting on its own and all of them far from able to occupy the "whole land." Based on 1 Kgs 16:34, we might conclude that Joshua suffered a devastating defeat at Jericho, cursed the city, and died. Then Judg 1 sets in.

The narrative that begins in Gen 1 or perhaps in Exod 1 simply needs another ending in addition to Deut 34. There, the Israelites are still in the "desert," outside of time and space. How they came into their land and came to possess it needs to be told. Joshua 24, the last chapter of the book, concludes the mega-narrative that started when Abraham left his hometown and his relations for a future yet veiled. That is why there is a book of *Joshua*.[5]

Looking Forward

That there is a *book* of Joshua is due to the ranked canon of "Torah and Prophets." Both canonical corpora have, to begin with, clearly marked beginnings and ends:

In the beginning, when God created heaven and earth—but earth had been for long a watery mess, darkness had covered the abyss, and the spirit-storm of God had stood in the air like an eagle opposite the waters—God said: "Be there Light!" There was light....	בראשית ברא אלהים את השמים ואת הארץ והארץ היתה תהו ובהו וחשך על פני תהום ורוח אלהים מרחפת על פני המים ויאמר אלהים יהי אור ויהי אור ...
... Never again there arose in Israel a prophet like Moses, whom YHWH had known from face to face, with respect of all the signs and wonders that YHWH had sent him to do in the land of Egypt, to	ולא קם נביא עוד בישראל כמשה אשר ידעו יהוה פנים אל פנים לכל האתות והמופתים אשר שלחו יהוה לעשות בארץ מצרים לפרעה ולכל עבדיו

---

5. For the same reason, there is a Joshua narrative among the Samaritans, even though they do not have authoritative "Prophets": according to them, he was the first king of Israel and built the temple on Mount Gerizim; see Moses Gaster, "On the Newly Discovered Samaritan Book of Joshua," *JRAS* (New Series) 40 (1908): 795–809; Moses Gaster, "The Samaritan Hebrew Sources of The Arabic Book of Joshua," *JRAS* (New Series) 62 (1930): 597–99; Robert T. Anderson and Terry Giles, *Tradition Kept: The Literature of the Samaritans* (Peabody, Mass.: Hendrickson, 2005).

Pharaoh, all his staff, and all of his land; and with respect of the wholly strong hand and all the great terror that Moses had enacted before the eyes of all Israel.	ולכל ארצו ולכל היד החזקה ולכל המורא הגדול אשר עשה משה לעיני כל ישראל

It has been observed for some time[6] that the colophon of the Torah corresponds to the colophon of the Prophets, Mal 3:22–24 (MT; 4:4–6 in the Latin and English Bibles). But the two canonical corpora have also *incipits*, which relate both to each other and to the colophons. In the case of the Torah, the fact is quite clear, there is no stronger *incipit* imaginable than "In the beginning." Beginning and end of the Torah, seen together, link the Torah of Moses to creation, and vice versa[7] (cf. Ps 19). By creation, all humankind might recognize God in general (אלהים); by the Torah of Moses, Israel knows him by his first name (יהוה). *Incipit* and colophon of the Prophets link the Prophets to the Torah. Because Josh 1:1–5 sets in where Deut 34:9 has left the audience, it is Josh 1:6–9 that relates to Deut 34:10–12 and to Mal 3:22–24, and forms the *incipit* of the Prophets:

Josh 1:6 Be strong and courageous; for you shall put this people in possession of the land that I swore to their ancestors to give them.	חזק ואמץ כי אתה תנחיל את העם הזה את הארץ אשר נשבעתי לאבותם לתת להם
7 Only be strong and very courageous, being careful to act in accordance with all the law that my servant Moses commanded you; do not turn from it to the right hand or to the left, so that you may be successful wherever you go.	רק חזק ואמץ מאד לשמר לעשות ככל התורה אשר צוך משה עבדי אל תסור ממנו ימין ושמאול למען תשכיל בכל אשר תלך
8 This book of the law shall not depart out of your mouth; you shall meditate on it day and night, so that you may be careful to act in accordance with all that is written	לא ימוש ספר התורה הזה מפיך והגית בו יומם ולילה למען תשמר לעשות ככל

---

6. See Hans-Peter Mathys, "Bücheranfänge und -schlüsse," in *Vom Anfang und vom Ende: Fünf alttestamentliche Studien* (ed. Hans Peter Mathys; BEATAJ 47; Frankfurt am Main: Lang, 2000), 1–29; also "Anmerkungen zu Mal 3,22-24," 30–40 in the same volume.

7. See Othmar Keel and Silvia Schroer, *Schöpfung: Biblische Theologien im Kontext altorientalischer Religionen* (Freiburg: University Press, 2002), 218–36.

in it. For then you shall make your way prosperous, and then you shall be successful. 9 I hereby command you: Be strong and courageous; do not be frightened or dismayed, for the LORD your God is with you wherever you go." (NRSV)	הכתוב בו כי אז תצליח את דרכך ואז תשכיל הלוא צויתיך חזק ואמץ אל תערץ ואל תחת כי עמך יהוה אלהיך בכל אשר תלך
Mal 4:4 Remember the teaching of my servant Moses, the statutes and ordinances that I commanded him at Horeb for all Israel. 5 Lo, I will send you the prophet Elijah before the great and terrible day of the LORD comes. 6 He will turn the hearts of parents to their children and the hearts of children to their parents, so that I will not come and strike the land with a curse. (NRSV)	(3:22) זכרו תורת משה עבדי אשר צויתי אותו בחרב על כל ישראל חקים ומשפטים (3:23) הנה אנכי שלח לכם את אליה הנביא לפני בוא יום יהוה הגדול והנורא (3:24) והשיב לב אבות על בנים ולב בנים על אבותם פן אבוא והכיתי את הארץ חרם

Referring to the Torah-colophon, Josh 1:6–9 relates Joshua (and all prophets following him) to Moses: he/they are prophets "like Moses" (Deut 18:15–18) but not equal to him (Deut 34:10–12) for, regardless of what God has in store to say to them, he/they are bound by the limits set by the Torah of Moses, which they are meant to learn by heart "and recite day and night."

Malachi 3:22–24 relates to Deut 34:10–12 by the principle of "Torah first," other prophet second: whatever the future might hold, Torah will never be invalidated. But the terror that Moses inflicted on Egypt now threatens Israel and the whole world (Mal 3:23–24). The colophon of the Prophets refers to their *incipit* by commanding all Israel to do what is decreed to Joshua in Josh 1:8; in other words, זכר does not mean "think of the Torah (when you have nothing else on your mind)," but "be in the presence of Torah," which cannot be done without recitation, according to the ancient standards of reading. Joshua, the first "prophet like Moses after Moses," Elijah reincarnated, is now declared to be the last. Turning "the hearts of parents to their children and the hearts of children to their parents" might be interpreted as an allusion to the third part of the Tanak, but the *ketuvim* have tended to be designated instead metonymically as "the book of David," "psalms," or "psalms and the other scriptures."[8] The climate of intellectual agreement between the generations[9] recalls the teacher-pupil relationship and thus also חכמה "wisdom," which has become, however, a synonym of Torah[10] by the time Mal 3:22–24 was penned. The three biblical admonitions "When your son(s) ask you …" are restricted to the Torah (Exod 13:14; Deut 6:20) and Joshua (4:6). Thus, Mal 3:24 probably thinks of the Torah plus Joshua, which constitutes a nice chiasm: v. 22: Torah (and Josh)—v. 23: Prophets—v. 24: Torah and Joshua, for the conclusion והכיתי את הארץ חרם contains another not-so-hidden reference to Joshua.[11]

At the beginning of Joshua, the book's hero is entrusted with the "Torah of Moses"; at the end, he adds his own story to the "Torah of God" (Josh 24:26). His supplement to the "Torah of Moses" necessarily became a book of its own, when the Torah was finalized and "published" (by reading to the people) without it. The first book of what was becoming the corpus of "Prophets" provides the role model for all its successors: a prophet[12] is a person who is spoken to by God (Josh 1:1, e.g.) and may work miracles (Josh 10:12–14) but who is obliged to learn Torah (1:6–9), teach it (8:30–35), apply it (Josh 7), and, in the course of its application, fill in some of the lacunae the sages who collected its text wisely left (e.g., Josh 5:1–7). Finally, a prophet is someone who writes down his personal story with God. This is why there is a *book* of Joshua.

---

8. The Psalter is added (as "Book of David") to Torah and Prophets in 4QMMT; see Jonathan G. Campbell, "4QMMT and the Tripartite Canon," *JJS* 51 (2000): 181–90; Eugene Ulrich, "The Non-attestation of a Tripartite Canon in 4QMMT," *CBQ* 65 (2003): 202–14; for "Moses/the Law, the Prophets and the Psalms," see further Luke 24:44.

9. על instead of אל is indicative of Late Biblical Hebrew; the syntagms השיב/שוב לב might be postclassical as well, the only other attestation being 1 Kgs 12:27. For the ideal of harmony among the generations, see Ps 78:5; Prov 17:6; for the opposite, see Jer 47:3; Ezek 5:10; 20:18.

10. Keel and Schroer, *Schöpfung*, 228–30.

11. Of the thirty co-occurrences of נכה and חרם, fourteen are in Josh (46.67%), and make up 0.88% of its text; the two references in Mal account for 1.53% of that twelfth of the Book of the Twelve, and there are no other references from that biblical book.

12. It should not be necessary to point out that the theological construct of the "canonical prophet" has nothing to do with the socio-historical reality of prophecy in the ancient Near East and in Israel and Judah—but it still might be necessary in order not to be misunderstood by less-enlightened readers.

Looking Left and Right

The Torah was received by the "Israelites" of the Persian provinces of Yehud, Samaria and Idumea. Joshua unites these three provinces through the "distribution of the land at Gilgal" (Josh 14:1–18:1) in the guise of Judah,[13] Ephraim and Manasseh, and Caleb. The status of the numerous Judeans[14] living in Idumea is reflected by Caleb receiving his land both outside (Josh 14:6–15) and inside (Josh 15:13–19) Judah. This is more than a harmonization of the provincial system in the fourth century B.C.E. with the town list inherited from the Judahite monarchy—rather, it is an invitation to all of Idumea to join the "biblical Israel" constituted by Yehud and Samaria (see also Deut 23:7 [MT: 23:8]).[15]

The inclusion of Samaria in the "basic Israel" of Josh 14–17 indicates that the book of Joshua originally was free from any anti-Samarian attitude. The final assembly at Shiloh (Josh 24:1 LXX) points in the same direction: Shiloh is "neutral ground," halfway between Jerusalem and Mount

---

13. Benjamin is here represented as the lacuna between the northern border of Judah and the southern border of Ephraim, i.e. included in Judah, and later treated together with the "lost tribes" of the Negev and Galilee (Josh 18:11–28). For conflicts between the returnees and Benjamin in the Persian period, see E. Axel Knauf, "Bethel: The Israelite Impact on Judean Language and Literature," in *Judah and the Judeans in the Persian Period* (ed. Oded Lipschits and Manfred Oeming; Winona Lake, Ind.: Eisenbrauns, 2006), 291–349; Joseph Blenkinsopp, "Benjamin Traditions Read in the Early Persian Period", in *Judah and the Judeans in the Persian Period* (ed. Oded Lipschits and Manfred Oeming; Winona Lake, Ind.: Eisenbrauns, 2006), 629–45; Yairah Amit, "Saul Polemic in the Persian Period," in *Judah and the Judeans in the Persian Period* (ed. Oded Lipschits and Manfred Oeming; Winona Lake, Ind.: Eisenbrauns, 2006), 647–61.

14. See Nikos Kokkinos, *The Herodian Dynasty: Origins, Role in Society and Eclipse* (JSPSup 30; Sheffield: Sheffield Academic Press, 1998), 51, 75–79; André Lemaire, "New Aramaic Ostraca from Idumea and Their Historical Interpretation," in *Judah and the Judeans in the Persian Period* (ed. Oded Lipschits and Manfred Oeming; Winona Lake, Ind.: Eisenbrauns, 2006), 413–56; Manfred Weippert, *Historisches Textbuch zum Alten Testament* (GAT 10; Göttingen: Vandenhoeck & Ruprecht, 2010), 501–14.

15. In 1 Chr 2 and 4, the genealogies of "Caleb" consist to a high degree of Edomite/Idumean names. Hasmonean contributions to Chronicles, even after Hyrcanus's annexation of Idumea, are possible. See Israel Finkelstein, "Rehoboam's Fortified Cities (II Chr 11,5–12): A Hasmonean Reality?" *ZAW* 123 (2011): 92–107.

Gerizim. The anti-Samarian/Samaritan[16] bias comes into Joshua late: in the Hasmonean period, "Shiloh" is changed into "Shechem" in Josh 24:1, turning Joshua's farewell speech into a revivalist address to the apostates to return to the Jewish flock. On the level of the book's redaction, it might already play a role in Mount Ebal being the place the first altar was built in Canaan and where Torah was first read (Josh 8:30–35), in accordance with Deut 27:1–8, but in slight disagreement with Deut 11:29; 27:11–13, where "the Gerizim" is the mountain of blessing, and "the Ebal" the mountain of curse. In Josh 8:33, both the blessing and the cursing party is assembled on the Ebal, the non-Gerizim.

The book of Joshua is, like most biblical books, complex and expresses the point of view of more than one party or one set of politics.

Looking Down

Joshua is the book that has its feet (if books had such) most firmly on the ground. Joshua has the highest frequency[17] of geographical names of all biblical books. In the introduction, Josh 1:1–9, the distribution of the Land to the Israelites figures much more prominently than its conquest, and this reflects faithfully the perception of Joshua in the Torah. Joshua and Caleb are the only members of the exodus generation who will actually see the Land (Num 14:30, 38; 26:65; 32:12). Joshua sees it in order to distribute it to the Israelites as their possession (not property, for YHWH remains the sole proprietor, Lev 25:23); the "conquest motif" is played down in the Torah as far as possible (Deut 1:38; 3:28; 31:7).[18]

---

16. I use "Judeans/Samarians" to refer to the inhabitants of the Persian provinces and "Jews/Samaritans" to the two sides of the schism, which did not operate before Hellenism.

17. 13.23% of the text consists of proper names; that frequency is higher only in Chr (around 15%), where, especially in 1 Chr 1–9, personal names outrank place names by far—as opposed to Joshua (unfortunately, my version of Accordance™ does not allow me to search for the different types of "proper names" separately and presents statistics according to the books of the Christian Bible—1 Chronicles is not a "book" in the Tanak).

18. Hinted at in Deut 3:21–22; 31:23. In Exod 17, Joshua enters the stage as a warrior, but at the end of the scene he is promoted to prophetic assistant (or apprentice) and given words of God to commemorate. For Num 27:15–23, see Norbert Lohfink, "Die Schichten des Pentateuch und der Krieg," in *Gewalt und Gewaltlosigkeit im Alten Testament* (ed. Ernst Haag et al; QD 96; Freiburg: Herder, 1983), 51–110 (78–80) =

Quite contrary to its Christian reception, the book of Joshua has its center in chs. 13–21; chs. 1–12 is only the introduction, chs. 22–24 the finale. In these chapters, the land of Canaan is distributed to the tribes and families of Israel. In the course of this distribution, it is defined,[19] circumscribed, role-called, enchanted, and celebrated. Lists become litanies, repetitive narrative (as in Josh 10:28–39; 18:10–19:48) becomes liturgy. We ought to try to imagine the rhetorical effect of Josh 13–21 being heard, recited, and perhaps chanted. Learn it by heart, and you have a mantra. H. Heine once called the Torah the Jews's *portatives Vaterland*.[20] With Joshua, the Torah is embellished with quite an amount of real estate, which again, as part of a literary composition, enjoys all the restrictions and liberties of literature: the freedom of imagination wherever you are, the restriction that a narrated land does not bear edible fruit.

The political interest discernable in the "theology of the Land" exposed by the Torah and Joshua points to the Persian period. The possession of its land by the individual Judean family is inalienable, because YHWH is the proprietor. This theology is motivated by the threat by the Persian government to confiscate communal land to establish military fiefs, as they evidently did in Idumea. In the town list of Simeon, we find Beth-marcaboth "house of the chariots" next to Hazar-susah "Hamlet of a Horse" (Josh 19:5)—the fiefs bestowed by the Babylonian and Persian military administration consisted of "houses of bow" for the infantry, "houses of horse" for the cavalry, and "houses of chariot" for the chariot corps.[21] The drama of Naboth's vineyard is a Persian-period text on a Persian-period problem.[22]

Norbert Lohfink, *Studien zum Pentateuch* (SBAB 4; Stuttgart: Katholisches Bibelwerk, 1988), 255–315 (282–84).

19. And not in a one-dimensional way: there are several concepts of the borders of the Promised Land in Joshua. In Josh 10:40–42 the terminus of the Exodus is the kingdom of Judah, whose borders reflect those at the end of the seventh century B.C.E. In Josh 14–17 (concluded by 18:1), Eretz Israel consists of Idumea (Caleb), Yehud, and Samaria. In Josh 18–19, Galilee is added, and in Josh 13, Transjordan. The system of tribal borders follows the notion of "Canaan" presented in Num 34:1–12.

20. Heinrich Heine, "Geständnisse," in *Vermischte Schriften* (14 vols.; Sämmtliche Werke; Hamburg: Hoffmann und Campe, 1854–76), 1:97–179 (138).

21. See Jeremy Black, Andrew George & Nicholas Postgate, *A Concise Dictionary of Akkadian* (2d corr. printing; Santag: Arbeiten und Untersuchungen zur Keilschriftkunde 5; Wiesbaden: Harrassowitz, 2000), 47 sub *bīt narkabti/qašti*, 325 sub *sisû*.

22. See E. Axel Knauf, "Inside the Walls of Nehemiah's Jerusalem: Naboth's Vineyard," in *The Fire Signals of Lachish: Studies in the Archaeology and History of Israel*

The second front at which the biblical theology of the land fought was the impact of monetarization, also setting in by that time. The system secures agricultural credit, safeguarding concomitantly against insolvency both on the parts of the debtor and the creditor.²³

The main topic of the book of Joshua is not the narration of things from the distant past, nor is there any interest in a future different from the Persian-period present, which it reflects. The political program is "Each man (and woman) under his (and her) vine and fig tree, and may things stay that way for ever." As for utopias, this is not one of the worst.

Looking Up

The narrative of Joshua begins in the section of the Jordan valley of Moab opposite Jericho (בערבות מואב מעבר לירדן ירחו) (Num 22:1; Josh 13:32). Whoever lifts up his or her eyes to the hills opposite knows that they culminate in the Mount of Olives, overlooking Jerusalem. Jerusalem is one of the most intriguing lacunæ in Joshua. In Josh 6–10, Jerusalem is not conquered, but everything around it to the east, north, and west is. The king of Jerusalem is defeated, but unlike in the cases of the other kings, his city remains unconquered. Joshua 15:20–62; 18:21–28 is based on a town list of the kingdom of Judah at the end of the seventh century B.C.E., neatly divided into twelve districts. The list documents, in its way, the four-tier settlement hierarchy of the full-blown ancient Near Eastern state: capital city [Jerusalem]—district capital [unmarked]—town (עיר)—satellites

---

in the Late Bronze Age, Iron Age, and Persian Period in Honor of David Ussishkin (ed. Israel Finkelstein and Nadav Na'aman; Winona Lake, Ind.: Eisenbrauns, 2011), 185–94. 1 Sam 8:14–15 also is a text from the Persian period.

23. See Philippe Guillaume, *Land and Calendar: The Priestly Document from Genesis 1 to Joshua 18* (LHBOTS 391; New York: T&T Clark, 2009), 138–39; Philippe Guillaume, *Land, Credit and Crisis: Agrarian Finance in the Hebrew Bible* (BibleWorld; London: Equinox, 2011). Biblical law on landed property was neither inherited from the Iron I period nor was primarily directed against capitalist land grabbing. It did, though, necessitate Jewish would-be *latifundistas* to invest in a non-Jewish neighborhood like Idumea or Nabataean Arabia, and it also forced third and fourth sons to go colonize Galilee from the fourth century B.C.E. onwards; see E. Axel Knauf, "Biblical References to Judean Settlement in Eretz Israel (and Beyond) in the Late Persian and Early Hellenistic Periods," in *The Historian and the Bible: Essays in Honour of Lester L. Grabbe* (ed. Philip R. Davies and Diana V. Edelman; LBHOTS 530; New York: T&T Clark, 2010), 175–93.

(חצריה). Jerusalem is the point from which Judah and Benjamin are seen in this list, around which everything is centered—but Jerusalem, maybe because it takes for granted it is such a center, is not named.[24] In Josh 22, the problem that the elite of the Second Temple had was with other "second temples"—the attested "legitimate" altar of Shiloh and its "illegitimate" counterpart "across the Jordan." The solution finally reached looks like the Jerusalemite version of Bagawayhi's final response to the petitioners of Elephantine: the temple may be rebuilt, but bloody sacrifices are henceforward not permitted—the altar across the Jordan is not a "real" altar but a "model altar" to symbolize the "legitimate altar" in regions "far from Shiloh-Jerusalem." Jerusalem is only summarily "conquered" in the town-list in Josh 12:10, a redactional bridge between the conquest narrative in chs. 1–11 and the distribution narrative in chs. 14–21. If Joshua had to distribute "all the Land" (Josh 21:43), then he had better have conquered it first, as is stated against the evidence of the narrative in Josh 11:23; the narrative only covers Jericho, Ai, Gibeon, the Shephelah, and Galilee. Joshua 12:9–24 desperately and quite unsuccessfully tries to fill in the gaps.

In the three main parts of Joshua (chs. 1–11, 14–21, and 22–24), Jerusalem is conspicuously absent and central at the same time. Jerusalem is there but as an enemy of Israel still to be conquered. This conquest of Jerusalem is narrated in Ezra 7–10, where Israel's primeval enemies from the Torah and Joshua appear for the last time: "The people of Israel, the priests, and the Levites have not separated themselves from the peoples of the lands with their abominations, from the *Canaanites*, the *Hittites*, the *Perizzites*, the *Jebusites*, the Ammonites, the Moabites, the Egyptians, and the *Amorites*..." (Ezra 9:1). The Jerusalem to be conquered is "Old Jerusalem" from the time of the monarchy, with its polytheistic cult, the Jerusalem of the past without Torah. The Jerusalem hidden in the text of Joshua is the "New Jerusalem" of the Second Temple (that was, in fact, the very first of its kind), the Jerusalem under Torah.

Reading our various Bibles in the form of (usually one-volume) books with different but always standardized sequences of the biblical books, we have forgotten how it was to read the Scriptures when they still existed in the form of single scrolls. After Joshua, we are accustomed to continue

---

24. It is referred to in glosses as "Jebus" (Josh 15:8; 18:28), and in a redactional harmonization of Joshua and Judges (15:63), the city is attributed to Judah, in opposition to 18:28.

with Judges, and this certainly is what the redaction of the book of Judges intended. But actually, we could skip Judges and continue with Samuel, where the ark is still at Shiloh, where it was taken in Josh 18:1. And we could equally skip all the other prophets and jump to Ezra-Nehemiah where, after that tragedy of errors that was the time of the monarchy and the exile, and the turmoil and pity of it all, the Israel materializes that is intended by the Torah and the book of Joshua. This Israel might well regard itself as the fulfillment of everything announced by the prophets, rendering their books no more than historical memories that may or may not be read.

Joshua is a self-contained book so that its readers have the freedom to read it in the context of various other books of their choice with one exception: it is impossible to read Joshua without the Torah.

THE CASE OF JOSHUA

Serge Frolov

Form-critical exegesis, of which the present writer is a proud if not always committed practitioner, regards the text as a product of two different but related settings or contexts. On the one hand, it is generated by a certain communicative situation, traditionally referred to as *Sitz im Leben*, which shapes the sender's objectives as well as his or her ideas of the target audience and of the way(s) in which these objectives could be efficiently met with it. On the other hand, any composition emerges and circulates among other texts, linked to some of them by authorial or redactional design and to others in the minds of intended or unintended recipients; in other words, it has its own *Sitz in der Literatur*.[1]

Although this approach has never been applied, at least not explicitly, to the receiving end of the communication that is the HB, there is no obvious reason why it could not or should not be. The perspective of listeners or readers upon the text is doubtlessly affected by the interests, concerns, presuppositions, and the like that stem from their socio-historical background, in other words, from their *Sitz im Leben*. But just as consequential in this respect is the way they perceive the composition's literary context—its *Sitz in der Literatur*. Do they view it as an entity in its own right or part of a larger whole? What kind of intertextual connections might they be likely to draw? Does their repertoire include a touchstone of some

---

1. The term *Sitz in der Literatur* was, to my knowledge, coined by Wolfgang Richter (*Exegese als Literaturwissenschaft: Entwurf einer alttestamentlichen Literaturtheorie und Methodologie* [Göttingen: Vandenhoeck & Ruprecht, 1971], 117). For an outline of form-critical methodology in its most recent incarnation, see Marvin A. Sweeney, "Form Criticism," in *To Each Its Own Meaning: An Introduction to Biblical Criticisms and Their Application* (ed. Steven L. McKenzie and Stephen R. Haynes; 2d ed.; Louisville: Westminster John Knox, 1999), 58–89.

sort against which to check the ideological legitimacy or artistic merits of the piece? These and related factors powerfully affect the text's reception, which makes them impossible to ignore in any discussion of the issue. In fact, when the audience's *Sitz im Leben* is not sufficiently known or understood, *Sitz in der Literatur* may wax paramount.

This is precisely the case with the reception of Deuteronomy-Kings, including the book of Joshua, in the late Persian and early Hellenistic times. Contemporary sources pertaining to the Jewish community from Ezra and Nehemiah (mid-fifth century B.C.E.) through at least the establishment of Ptolemaic rule (301 B.C.E.) are scant and discrete, and the period left little trace in the collective memory of the Jews. In particular, *Pirke Aboth* offers only one name (Simon the Just) to fill it, and Josephus has little to say beyond paraphrasing the book of Esther and telling a story of no historical value that traces the origins of the Samaritan cult to a renegade Jerusalemite priest and has Alexander acknowledge the power of the Jewish God.[2] As a result, scholarly assumptions about the *Sitz im Leben* of the period's audiences are mostly projections or retrojections from earlier or later times, adjusted for changes in the broader historical picture (the gradual decline of the Persian Empire, Egypt's secessions, Alexander's takeover, etc.). Furthermore, since the most basic facts of the matter are not in doubt (e.g., the homeland Jewish community enjoyed a degree of autonomy under Persian rule) and finer, if crucial details can only be speculated about (How did the socioeconomic system function? How was power distributed? What role did organized religion play?), there seems to be relatively little to discuss.

By contrast, there is a wealth of information of every degree of magnitude—and, accordingly, much scholarly disagreement, simultaneously vexing and vibrant—concerning the *Sitz in der Literatur* of the biblical texts. Specifically, a relatively small but steadily growing group of exegetes has argued in the last two decades that the constituent books of what we know as Deuteronomy-Kings, perhaps even of the Enneateuch (Gen–Kgs) as a whole, emerged and initially circulated as self-contained opera.[3] This

---

2. *Ant.* 11.6–12.1.

3. E.g., Claus Westermann, *Die Geschichtsbücher des Alten Testaments: gab es ein deuteronomistisches Geschichtswerk?* (TB 87; Gütersloh: Kaiser, 1994); Ernst Axel Knauf, "L'Historiographie Deutéronomiste' (DtrG) existe-t-elle?" in *Israël construit son histoire. L'historiographie deutéronomiste à la lumière des recherches récentes* (ed. Albert de Pury, Thomas Römer and Jean-Daniel Macchi; Le monde de la Bible 34;

would have major consequences as far as the reception of Joshua in the late Persian and early Hellenistic periods is concerned, especially if it were possible to argue that at the time, the canonical or proto-canonical process that eventually shaped the corpus had not yet begun or was still in its incipient stages. Yet, a closer look at Joshua reveals that it is not likely ever to have existed as a stand-alone piece and, accordingly, to have been privately or publicly read on its own—a conclusion that is further supported by the present writer's similar findings with regard to the adjacent book of Judges.[4] If so, the question is not how Joshua was received roughly between 450 and 300 B.C.E. but rather, how it affected the reception of the larger corpus (the Enneateuch or Deut-Kgs), of which it is an integral part.

1. Joshua: A Volume or a Book?

Division into "books" is an inescapable feature of the biblical canon: in any Bible that a reader might encounter today, there are unmistakable signs of this division, such as titles, *masora finalis*, or at the very least (in the case of the traditional Torah scrolls created for liturgical purposes), major breaks in the text. When it comes to commentaries, each book often has a separate volume (or sometimes several volumes) devoted to it. A similar situation apparently obtained already in ancient times: in Qumran, biblical texts were preserved, in essence, as a collection of scrolls; as to the codices, making it physically possible to copy the entire Bible as a single tome, the extant exemplars hardly ever fail to demarcate the constituent books by one means or the other.

At the same time, anyone who has ever taken the time to read the HB closely would vouch that its books are not born equal. Many of them clearly are literary entities in their own right, connected to what precedes them and what follows mostly or exclusively by the canonical arrangement, which, accordingly, may differ from one religious tradition, group, or even manuscript to another. Some, however, just as clearly belong with each other, forming, in terms of their content, an easily traceable continuum; this is especially true of the Enneateuch but also pertains to 1–2 Chronicles plus Ezra. Specifically, Joshua picks up the narrative thread precisely where Deuteronomy drops it—as indicated by the reference back

---

Genève: Labor et fides, 1996), 409–18; Philippe Guillaume, *Waiting for Josiah: The Judges* (JSOTSup 385; London: T&T Clark, 2004), 227–36.

4. Serge Frolov, "Rethinking Judges," *CBQ* 71 (2009): 24–41.

to Moses' death (reported right across the canonical divide, in Deut 34) in Josh 1:1 as well as to the Torah as commanded by Moses (i.e. to Moses' discourses that make up the entire Deut) in Josh 1:7. In exactly the same fashion, the death of Joshua recounted at the very end of the book bearing his name (Josh 24:29) is identified in the opening verse of the book that follows (Judg 1:1) as its point of departure. This continuity of content is reflected in the highly stable canonical order of books in the Enneateuch, the only variation being the presence of Ruth between Judges and Samuel in the LXX and the Christian Bibles that go back to it. This stability far exceeds anything that can be found elsewhere in the HB, admittedly including the Chronicles-Ezra-Nehemiah complex that in the Jewish tradition ends with Chronicles, the unique catch-line 2 Chr 36:22–23 = Ezra 1:1–3αβ^{1a} be damned.

In and of itself, the fact that a text fits well into its canonical slot does not prove that it was created for this slot, in other words, as a part of a larger whole. But by the same token, the fact that the paratextual canonical markers mentioned above identify this text as a "book" does not necessarily prove that it was created as such or could be treated as such for hermeneutical purposes at any time or place prior to the canon's formation. It is only in the text proper, in other words, in the Masoretic consonantal sequence of the appropriate biblical book (emended, if needed, on the basis of ancient translations), that compelling indications of its self-contained character can be found.

One type of these indications, common in the HB, is a superscription—an opening line that "stands … apart from the text it heads" and contains information uniquely pertaining to this text as a whole.[5] A superscription can go a long way in defining a composition as a literary entity unto itself: for example, Isa 1:1 implicitly identifies everything between it and the next fragment of a similar kind (that in all existing canons is Jer 1:1–2) as "Isaiah's vision," although no one by this name is mentioned in the book's last twenty-seven chapters.[6] In a similar, if perhaps more ambig-

---

5. Michael H. Floyd, *Minor Prophets, Part 2* (FOTL 22; Grand Rapids: Eerdmans, 2000), 649.

6. This obviously does not preclude the possibility of the chapters in question being a redactional interpolation (as widely accepted in critical scholarship since at least the late eighteenth century; see Christopher R. Seitz, "Isaiah, the Book of [First Isaiah]," *ABD* 3:472–88 [472–73]). However, even if this trajectory of the book's emergence is accepted (for one radically different view, see Edgar W. Conrad, *Reading*

uous fashion, by specifying that the events of Ruth took place "in the days when judges ruled," its first clause (1:1aα) isolates it not only from Samuel but, paradoxically, from Judges as well and thus indicates that it does not properly belong between these two books.[7] But there is nothing identifiable as a superscription in what we know as the book of Joshua—or, for that matter, in any of the nine books of Genesis–Kings according to the Jewish canon. Josh 1:1a draws a line between Joshua and Deuteronomy by describing the events that follow as taking place "after the death of Moses," but that applies to the entire Joshua–Kings and thus does not circumscribe Joshua as a self-contained composition. Further militating against seeing it as such is the presence of the formula PN ויהי אחרי מות "and it happened after the death of PN" also in the opening lines of Judges, 2 Samuel, and 2 Kings. It is much more economical to assume that divisions in a previously integral composition (made for technical, liturgical, or other reasons) were consistently and conveniently tied to the characteristic expression, unique to the Enneateuch, than that four texts (two of which are not viewed by the Jewish canon as "books") were independently created with identical or almost identical beginnings.

Another aspect of the biblical text that may, on occasion, define it as an entity unto itself is its literary format: to cite just one example, although Psalms does not have an overall superscription, its status as a collection of liturgical compositions sets it apart from adjoining books in all canons of the HB. That, however, is not the case with Joshua. It fully shares the groundwork generic pattern of the Enneateuch, with narratives (essentially strings of clauses governed by *waw*-consecutive imperfect verbs) forming the text's more or less continuous backbone and other literary formats for the most part subordinated to it.[8] This pattern is especially prominent in chs. 15–19, where lists of localities apportioned to the tribes or outlines of their allotments are subsumed under what is essentially a single, if extremely sparse, account of the lot-casting procedure (note the

---

Isaiah [Minneapolis: Fortress, 1991]), it does mean that the interpolator wanted the audience to read them as Isaiah's discourse (or perhaps as the continuation of Hezekiah's address to Isaiah in Isa 39:8b).

7. Cf. David Jobling, *1 Samuel* (Berit Olam; Collegeville: Liturgical Press, 1998), 34–35.

8. On *waw*-consecutive imperfect as the main narrative form of biblical Hebrew, see, e.g., GKC §111a–h; Alviero Niccacci, *The Syntax of the Verb in Classical Hebrew Prose* (JSOTSup 86; Sheffield: Sheffield Academic Press, 1990), 29–32, 47–72, 175–80.

introductory ויעל/ויצא/ויהי הגורל in 15:1; 16:1; 17:1; 18:11; 19:1, 10, 17, 24, 32, 40).

In terms of the text's distribution between genres, Joshua differs, of course, from Deuteronomy, with its glut of admonitions and commandments (presented as Moses' discourses and thus subordinated to the Enneateuch's narrative master sequence), but so do Judges, Samuel and Kings, not to mention Genesis and Exod 1-19. Indeed, from this point of view, Joshua—dominated by narratives in chs. 1-11, 22 and nonnarrative formats in chs. 12-21, 23-24—helps ensure a smooth transition from Deuteronomy (and, more remotely, Exod 20-Num 36), where the narrative thread of the Enneateuch is barely traceable, to Judges-Kings, where nonnarrative pieces are few and far between. Joshua also fully fits into a roughly symmetrical distribution scheme of the Enneateuch's most prominent genres:[9]

> A Narratives and genealogies; some commandments, no admonitions (Gen 1-Exod 19)
>   B Mostly commandments (Exod 20-Lev 27)
>   C Commandments and narratives (Num 1-36)
>   B' Commandments and admonitions (Deut 1-33)
> A' Narratives and admonitions; no genealogies (Deut 34-2 Kgs 25)

In more specific terms, the relatively long and complex narratives of Josh 1-9, 22 are also common in Judges (to say nothing of Sam, Kgs, Gen, and Exod 1-19). Even the relatively rare, fast-paced battle reports and stereotyped conquest accounts of Josh 10-11 have counterparts in this adjoining book (Judg 1:1-26; compare also 2 Sam 8:1-14; 10:1-19), as do otherwise unique lists of localities and ethnic groups in Josh 12-21 (Judg 1:27-36; 3:1-6).[10]

The biblical text within the canonical boundaries of Joshua displays no signs of a harmonious organization that might be expected of a self-contained composition. Some scholars regard the paraenetic discourses of

---

9. Serge Frolov, *Judges* (FOTL 6B; Grand Rapids: Eerdmans, 2013), 335-36.

10. Some also see similarities between the latter lists and the so-called priestly portions of the Pentateuch; see especially Enzo Cortese, *Josua 13-21: Ein priesterschriftlicher Abschnitt im deuteronomistischen Geschichtswerk* (OBO 94; Freiburg: Universitätsverlag; Göttingen: Vandenhoeck & Ruprecht, 1990).

the book's titular character in its concluding chapters as elements of such organization; in particular, T. Römer argues that ch. 23 originally functioned as a wrap-up of stand-alone Joshua, while ch. 24 was added upon its inclusion in the Hexateuch (Gen-Josh) to serve as a grand finale to the entire corpus.[11] Yet, the scribal circles that produced the HB apparently did not consider discourses of this type indispensable or, for that matter, even appropriate as endings of corpora or books. On the one hand, there is nothing of the kind close to the conclusion of the Enneateuch or its constituent "books," except, that is, for Joshua; in fact, sundry poetic pieces are considerably more common in the vicinity of the "book" divisions (Gen 49:3–27; Deut 32:1–43; 33:2–29; 2 Sam 22:2–51; 23:2–7). On the other hand, several pronouncements akin to those in Josh 23–24 are not associated with any canonical boundaries (1 Sam 12:6–17, 20–25; 1 Kgs 9:3–9; 2 Kgs 17:7–23).

While there is thus no indication of Joshua being compositionally well-rounded within its canonical boundaries, on at least two counts it plays an indispensable role in the well-proportioned and meaningful composition of the Enneateuch as a whole. First, by showcasing the rewards of Torah observance and especially of worshiping YHWH alone, it contrasts with the account of Israel's gradual decline caused by transgressions, especially foreign worship, in Judges-Kings. This symmetry of the blessing and the curse matches that found in Lev 26:3–39; Deut 28:1–68 (significantly, in all three cases curses heavily preponderate in terms of sheer volume). On a broader scale, it contributes to the harmonious arrangement of the entire corpus, approximating that of ancient Near Eastern suzerain-vassal treaties, with bipartite preamble (suzerain's introduction in Gen 1–11 and an account of his spontaneous benevolence toward the vassal in Gen 12–Exod 19) mirrored by bipartite blessings-and-curses in the conclusion:[12]

A   Preamble (two parts) (Gen 1–Exod 19)
    B   Stipulations (Exod 20–Deut 34)
A'   Blessings and curses (two parts) (Josh–Kgs)

---

11. Thomas Römer, "Doppelte Ende des Josuabuches," *ZAW* 118 (2006): 523–48.

12. On these treaties, see Dennis J. McCarthy, *Treaty and Covenant: A Study in Form in the Ancient Oriental Documents and in the Old Testament* (AnBib 21; Rome: Pontifical Biblical Institute, 1963); Klaus Baltzer, *The Covenant Formulary in Old Testament, Jewish, and Early Christian Writings* (trans. D. E. Green; Philadelphia: Fortress, 1971), 1–93.

Second, by having an Ephraimite (Num 13:8) and, therefore, a descendant of Joseph spearhead Israel's conquest and reorganization of the Promised Land, Joshua introduces an intriguing element of symmetry into the Enneateuchal pattern of leadership; in this respect, it is hardly accidental that the narrator mentions Joseph's reburial in Shechem right after reporting Joshua's death and burial (Josh 24:29–32):[13]

> A   The patriarchs (Israel represented by a single individual; personal covenant with YHWH) (Gen 12–36)
> B   Joseph (out of the land) (Gen 37–50)
> C   Moses (Exod-Deut)
> B' Joshua the Josephite (into the land) (Josh)
> A' The monarchy (Israel represented by a single individual; personal covenant with YHWH) (Judg–Kgs)

The above observation may appear to suggest that since canonical Joshua covers a well-defined period when Israel was led by its titular character, the book is self-contained in terms of its subject matter. It should be noted, however, that this subject matter not only ensures a smooth transition between those of the Pentateuch, on the one hand, and Judges-Kings, on the other, but also presupposes both in multiple respects. This can be seen with the greatest clarity in the deity's address to Joshua in Josh 1:2–9: it expects the audience to know that Joshua had been chosen as Moses' successor (Deut 31:14–23; 34:9; note the verbal echoes of Deut 31:23 in Josh 1:5–7), that Israel is encamped on the Jordan's left bank (Deut 1:1), and, above all, that the people had received the Torah through Moses. Likewise, Joshua's address to the Transjordanian tribes in Josh 1:12–15 would be rather enigmatic without Num 32 in the background, and someone who has never read or heard Num 13–14 would have a hard time grasping what

---

13. Of course, the Israelite monarchy is established only in 1 Sam 8–12, and the Davidic dynasty, complete with a personal covenant with the deity, emerges only in 2 Sam—not to mention that competing royal houses remain in the picture until as late as 2 Kgs 17. However, from a rhetorical standpoint, the preparation for a transition to kingship begins already in Judg (see especially Marvin Sweeney, "Davidic Polemics in the Book of Judges," *VT* 47 [1997]: 517–29; Serge Frolov, "Fire, Smoke, and Judah in Judges: A Response to Gregory Wong," *SJOT* 21 [2007]: 127–38), and the Enneateuch consistently singles out the Davidic line as the only legitimate one (Serge Frolov, "Evil-Merodach and the Deuteronomist: The Sociohistorical Setting of Dtr in the Light of 2 Kgs 25,27–30," *Bib* 88 [2007]: 174–90 [176–78]).

Caleb says in Josh 14:7–8. (How did his fellow spies make the people's hearts melt? What is meant by his "fully following YHWH"?)[14] On the other end of the narrative continuum, the references in Josh 15:63; 16:10; 17:12–13 to the tribes' inability or unwillingness to take over their allotments fully foreshadow a much more comprehensive picture of such failures in Judg 1 (where these reference are cited with some modifications).[15] And the comment concerning "Israel worshiping YHWH all the days of Joshua and all the days of the elders that outlived him" in Josh 24:31 anticipates the time when things will be different—which is why Judges does not have any difficulty repeating the remark (2:7) right before reporting the expected change (2:10–13).

To sum up: there is hardly any reason to believe that what we know as the book of Joshua emerged and circulated as a composition in its own right. It is, consequently, highly unlikely that the Jewish audiences of the late Persian and early Hellenistic periods encountered it as anything but an integral part of the Enneateuch. The question, therefore, is not what made Joshua more or less authoritative during this period but rather, whether Joshua contributed to the authority of the Enneateuch or detracted from it. The second part of the article will attempt to answer this question.

2. Joshua and the Authority of the Enneateuch

In a certain sense, any text claims authority by the very fact of its existence; it is by no means accidental that the word "author" comes from the

---

14. Caleb, however, cogently explains how Moses, at the deity's behest, promised him that the Hebron area, which he had toured with other spies (Num 13:22), would become his hereditary estate (Josh 14:6b, 9–12). That no such promise is mentioned in Numbers tells volumes about the author of Joshua having the Pentateuch in mind.

15. Undeniably, Judg 1:27–35, with its extensive enumeration of locations that the Israelites failed to take over, clashes with the summary statement of Josh 21:41 that "YHWH gave Israel the entire country that he had sworn to give to their ancestors, and they inherited it and dwelt in it"; but so do the above-mentioned verses in Joshua. On the integral, rhetorical design possibly underlying this tension, see Serge Frolov, "Joshua's Double Demise (Josh. xxiv 28–31; Judg. ii 6–9): Making Sense of a Repetition," *VT* 58 (2008): 315–23. Even the scholars who see a "caesura" between Joshua and Judges usually do not interpret it as evidence that the former emerged as a self-contained piece (e.g., Konrad Schmid, *Erzväter und Exodus: Untersuchungen zur doppelten Begründung der Ursprünge Israels innerhalb der Geschichtsbücher des Alten Testaments* [WMANT 81; Neukirchen-Vluyn: Neukirchener Verlag, 1999] 374; Guillaume, *Josiah*, 227–40).

same root. However, the authority claimed by the Enneateuch goes much further than that. It does not simply educate, edify, entertain, counsel, or explore; like the ancient Near Eastern vassal-suzerain treaties to which, as pointed out above, it bears an overall generic semblance, the Enneateuch presumes to tell the members of its target audience what they should and should not do.

That said, in one crucial respect the Enneateuch differs from its generic precursors. The authority of the latter was buttressed by the raw material power of the promulgators—the Hittite and Assyrian sovereigns in charge of vast territorial states. That does not mean they eschewed rhetorical means of persuading their vassals to do the right thing, that is, to abide by the treaty. Among other things, the treaty's overall structure, with the stipulations preceded by an account of the suzerain's grace (essentially saying that the vassal owes him one) and followed by blessings and curses, was certainly meant not only to inform the addressee of his obligations but also to convince him that fulfilling them would be an honorable and smart move. Yet, an unspoken but presumed reality behind such treaties is the suzerain's ability to inflict, if needs be, severe penalties upon a recalcitrant vassal, up to and including his total destruction (which is why the extant exemplars of the genre never say a word about the suzerain's responsibilities).

This, of course, is not the case with the Enneateuch. It portrays YHWH as a numinous counterpart of a Hittite or Assyrian king, but unlike the latter, the deity's ability or willingness to enforce the Enneateuchal commandments—not to mention the very fact of these commandments coming from the deity—was wide open to doubt. As to the secular powers-that-be in the postexilic period, especially in the late Persian and early Hellenistic periods, their stance is unclear at best. In the book of Ezra, the Persian king charges its titular character with implementing the "law of his God"—a possible reference to the normative sections of the Enneateuch—in "Judah and Jerusalem" (7:14, 25–26). However, the entire royal edict cited in Ezra 7:12–26 and having the monarch speak as a faithful devotee of YHWH hardly qualifies as a reliable source. Tellingly, Ezra subverts his own claim to the mantle of a royal emissary, when toward the end of the book he convinces fellow Jews to agree to the expulsion of foreign wives by invoking the wrath of YHWH rather than that of the Persian king and giving a daylong prophetic-style performance (9:3–10:1) rather than a curt order. It is possible that the Persian administration permitted or even encouraged local populations to operate their own normative systems, to the extent that they did not clash with its purposes, but the likelihood of it throwing its full weight behind such a system, especially in a small, obscure community, was negligible. Moreover, even if such a policy was in place in the early part of the Persian period, its extrapolation to the fourth century B.C.E. would be highly speculative, given the multiple political upheavals and policy shifts of the intervening decades, not to mention the mother of all discontinuities: Alexander's invasion in the 330s B.C.E.[16]

Chances are, therefore, that throughout the first postexilic centuries and almost certainly in the late Persian and early Hellenistic times, there was no external authority to prop up that of the Enneateuch; it had to fend for itself, or rather, its constituent parts had to fend for the whole. Even with corrections made for the well-known research bias that makes the object of study look larger than life, Joshua seems to have been a major chip in this game. Moreover, it was both an asset and a liability, if increasingly more of the former than of the latter.

As already mentioned, Joshua plays a central role in the Enneateuch's rhetorical strategy by serving as a primary demonstration that YHWH is serious about rewarding observance, above all by granting the people of Israel uncontested control of a land of their own as well as "rest round about" (21:42). In a population with a forced relocation in its collective memory, such a demonstration could not fail to strike a sensitive chord, especially in tandem with Judges and Kings, where oppression by foreigners and exile are explained by sustained violations of the norms promulgated by the corpus. Yet, collective memory is dynamic, and it is not of a

---

16. Richard C. Steiner maintains that codification and approbation of the Jewish law would be in line with the much broader strategy of the Persian government ("The *mbqr* at Qumran, the *episkopos* in the Athenian Empire, and the Meaning of *lbqr'* in Ezra 7:14: On the Relation of Ezra's Mission to the Persian Legal Project," *JBL* 120 [2001]: 623–46). He explicitly argues against the view of David Janzen that this would not have been part of Persian policy ("The 'Mission' of Ezra and the Persian-Period Temple Community," *JBL* 119 [2000]: 619–43). The evidence Steiner cites, however, consists mostly of a papyrus text, according to which in his fourth year (518 B.C.E.), Darius I convened a commission to codify the Egyptian laws (630–36). The contrast between Egypt and Judah could not be greater: the first was a densely populated, economically and strategically invaluable, and ever restive part of the empire (as demonstrated above all by the temporary secessions in 460–54 and ca. 400–343 B.C.E.), while the latter was a small, sparsely populated, and generally docile sub-province of minor consequence. Given this contrast, there is no way to be sure that what we know about Persian policies in Egypt is also applicable to Judah.

piece. Jewish children born in the fourth century B.C.E. would be at least seven and perhaps as many as fifteen generations removed from 538 B.C.E., when the first group of deportees returned to Judah. By this time, those living there would perceive it as their ancestral estate, and those voluntarily living in Mesopotamia for just as many generations would be no more likely to regard themselves as landless than are today's American Jews. Only with the literate elite, possibly having access to written records pertaining to the exile and perhaps learning about it as a part of their training, would the picture be somewhat different though not altogether dissimilar, given that abstract knowledge does not fully compensate for the lack of lived experience.

Even more problematically, the Enneateuchal rhetoric, in which Joshua plays a pivotal part, leaves no place for the actual conditions that obtained between the restoration and the Hasmonean revolt, in other words, over three and a half centuries. The corpus moves between two polar opposites: in Joshua, sovereign Israel is securely settled in Canaan as a reward of observance; towards the end of Kings, dependent Israel is forcibly relocated elsewhere by a foreign power as punishment for nonobservance. The postexilic realities did not fit in with any of these scenarios: Israel's descendants, the Jews, were continuously settled in Canaan without being either sovereign or secure; rather, their tenure of the land was a function of dependence on a foreign power.[17] This discrepancy was, in its turn, liable to generate doubts whether the causal link between observance and Israel's fortunes really works in the way the Enneateuch claims it does, and even whether such a link exists at all. If a lack of regard for the Enneateuchal commandments is to blame for the current situation bearing little semblance to the dreamscape of Joshua, why are the people still in what they consider their homeland rather than in exile? And if, conversely, the relatively benevolent attitude of the dominant power that permits the Jews to stay in their ancestral land and keeps them relatively safe is a sign of divine satisfaction with their ways, what prevented this satisfaction from

---

17. The situation that recurs six times in Judges and the opening chapters of Samuel—that of Israel living in its land but under foreign domination—bears a closer resemblance to that of the postexilic homeland community. Yet, even here it is the difference that matters most: in Judges and Samuel, foreign ascendancy is invariably a "servitude" (e.g., Judg 3:8, 14) or "oppression" (e.g., Judg 4:3; 10:8) that causes Israel to "cry to YHWH," whereas until Antiochus Epiphanes, Jews must have seen their overlords as mostly benign, if not outright supportive.

finding a much more gratifying expression on a par with the sweeping triumphs recounted in Joshua? In either case, how much warrant is there to believe that a shift in the people's stance vis-à-vis the commandments, be it positive or negative, would result in a concomitant adjustment of their condition? Conceivably, the longer the postexilic situation remained unchanged, the more urgent such questions would become, creating an increasing drag on the normative authority claimed by the Enneateuch.

Another area where the picture painted by Joshua—this time on its own—would sharply disagree with the Jewish experience of the first postexilic centuries is that of continuity versus change. If there is anything that Joshua as a whole is about it is about the latter. Modern commentators see two main parts in the book, conquest in chs. 1–12 and distribution of land among the tribes in chs. 13–21, with the account of a cultic misunderstanding in ch. 22 and Joshua's farewell discourses in chs. 23–24 functioning as a denouement of sorts.[18] Yet, the two main parts also have an important theme in common; this theme is the organization of geographical space.[19] When the narrator brings the Israelites led by Joshua across the Jordan, they encounter a land divided between Canaanite city-states, and they explore it little by little, starting with the reconnaissance in Jericho (ch. 2), until a full picture emerges in 12:7–24 (notably tucked onto an outline of the Transjordan, 12:1–5, already familiar to them and the audience). In what follows, the same area is remade into tribal allotments punctuated (or, perhaps, anchored in place?) by the Levitical cities and cities of refuge. In other words, apart from its two or three concluding chapters, Joshua is a dynamic map of Canaan morphing into ארץ ישראל, the Land of Israel.[20]

---

18. E.g., J. Alberto Soggin, *Joshua: A Commentary* (OTL; Philadelphia: Westminster, 1972), 2–3; Martin Holland, *Das Buch Josua erklärt* (Wuppertaler Studienbibel; Wuppertal: Brockhaus, 1997); Richard D. Nelson, *Joshua: A Commentary* (OTL; Louisville: Westminster John Knox, 1997), 12–14.

19. This proves how precarious thematic segmentation of the biblical text might be, although in the case of Joshua, the tendency of modern scholarship to see ch. 12 as a primary watershed is also justified by a major syntactic break (two enormous nominal clauses in 12:1–5, 7–24) and generic shift from mostly stories and conquest accounts in chs. 1–11 to mostly lists in chs. 12–21. The structure of the book's ending is less clear, with ch. 22 generically dissimilar from chs. 23–24 but implicitly lumped together with them by the summary in 21:43–45.

20. Nelson aptly calls Joshua "a book of mental maps" (*Joshua*, 2).

From Judah of the Persian period, such dynamism must have increasingly looked improbable, if not altogether impossible, for the simple reason that the area had not seen a major political reorganization, much less one effected by an invading force, since the period's very beginning, when resettlement by former Israelite exiles led to its constitution as a subprovince. For almost two hundred years, it remained under largely the same administration and was not involved in wars or power struggles.[21] Under such conditions, its residents must have felt more strongly with each passing generation that the established order could not be altered, much less overthrown. Again, the educated elite, having access to written evidence of past turmoil and change, and also being more likely to be informed about such manifestations of the instability reigning in the larger world such as the Greco-Persian wars and the Egyptian revolts of the fifth and early fourth centuries B.C.E., would be less prone to this perception but not entirely immune from it.

On one count, Joshua may have contributed indirectly to the authority of the Enneateuch by counterbalancing, at least to a certain degree, what must have been another major liability of the corpus in the postexilic times—its pro-monarchic, and more specifically, pro-Davidic agenda. Wary as it may be about kingship (as seen, above all, in the stringent controls placed on the monarch by Deut 17:14–20) and cognizant of its deficiencies (note the less-than-flattering portrait of David, especially in 2 Sam, to say nothing of other kings), the Enneateuch nevertheless singles out Davidic rule as the only postconquest regime holding at least some promise. In particular, while both judgeship and the northern, non-Davidic monarchy inexorably decline over time and ultimately collapse, leaving (parts of) Israel in the gutter, David's dynasty redeems itself towards the end with Hezekiah and especially Josiah, and the corpus ends with a Davidic scion not only still around but also exalted on his throne above other monarchs

---

21. Discussing material and textual evidence pro and contra a Jewish revolt in the first half of the fifth century B.C.E., Mary Joan Winn Leith concludes that "the picture of disturbances in Judah … can no longer be affirmed or denied" ("Israel among the Nations: The Persian Period," in *The Oxford History of the Biblical World* [ed. Michael D. Coogan; New York: Oxford University Press, 1998], 367–419 [404]). For arguments against the hypothesis that Jews participated in the Phoenician rebellion against Persia around 350 B.C.E., see Geo Widengren, "The Persian Period," in *Israelite and Judaean History* (ed. John H. Hayes and J. Maxwell Miller; Philadelphia: Westminster, 1977), 489–538 (500–502).

(2 Kgs 25:27–30).²² Put differently, for the Enneateuch the problems of the Davidic monarchy lie in unworthy individuals (such as Solomon in his late years and especially Manasseh), while other modes of government are inherently flawed. The overall trajectory of leadership in the corpus, outlined above, likewise contributes to the composition's pro-Davidic slant by rendering David and his dynasty counterparts of the patriarchs, that is, individual embodiments of Israel as a whole.

Influential as it could be in exile and even in the first decades thereafter, when hopes for political independence associated with Zerubbabel (see especially Hag 2:20–23)—and probably earlier with his grandfather Jehoiachin—were still alive, this stance was later increasingly out of sync with the community's experiences. Davidides may have been around throughout the fifth century B.C.E., if 1 Chr 3:19–24 is any indication, but there is no evidence of them waging any power or influence, and by the fourth century many if not most in Judah likely saw any discussion of the advantages, or otherwise, of the Davidic rule as hopelessly outdated. Joshua would somewhat temper this impression by showing that Israel can be united and successful under a nonroyal, nondynastic leader working in tandem with the high priest—a better, if still very rough, approximation of Judah's postexilic governors, probably non-Davidic after Zerubbabel but likely Jewish (as suggested by their Hebrew and mostly YHWHistic names in various inscriptions as well as by Nehemiah's appointment in the HB). The Enneateuch may have created this figure simply because having the conquest happen under a monarch would have deprived it of an opportunity to run a test of other modes of government (and find them lacking), but the rhetorical maneuver also likely had the unintended consequence of rendering the corpus more relevant in the Persian period.

Given Joshua's close association with sovereign control of the land and its profound reorganization, in the Persian period this boost could still be insufficient to salvage the authority of the Enneateuch as a whole. That may have been one of the impulses behind the constitution of its first five books—which did not suffer from the problems outlined above—as the

---

22. Admittedly, Samuel seems to vindicate judgeship in 1 Sam 7; appropriately, in 1 Sam 8 kingship is uncompromisingly denounced by YHWH as another kind of idolatry (vv. 7–8). However, 1 Sam 1–8, which also undermines the Enneateuch's stance on cultic centralization, is identifiable as an interpolation in the corpus; see Serge Frolov, *The Turn of the Cycle: 1 Samuel 1–8 in Synchronic and Diachronic Perspectives* (BZAW 342; Berlin: de Gruyter, 2004), 176–94, and "Conclusions" below.

Torah/Pentateuch, a normative corpus in its own right. In any case, if the latter emerged as an excerpt from a larger whole (as the analysis offered in the first part of the present article seems to suggest), it must have happened before Alexander's invasion in the 330s B.C.E. After it, there would have been little reason to draw the line before Joshua rather than after the book—or even to draw it at all.

The reason is that starting around 332 B.C.E. the homeland Jewish community—and eventually all Jews within the boundaries of the Persian Empire—witnessed a series of events that entirely transformed their world. They saw a relatively small band of outsiders enter the land, defeat its established government, overthrow it, and establish a new administration. They watched the emergent power crumble in its turn a mere decade later and a series of military campaigns (the Diadochi wars and related conflicts) roll through the area, with it changing hands every few years. Finally, when the dust settled they found themselves in the immediate vicinity of a border between two rival empires, those of the Ptolemies and the Seleucids, and in constant anticipation of further perturbations (even though in actuality they took more than a century to happen).

Under the new conditions, the transformative scenario of Joshua would no longer look implausible; indeed, it would raise few, if any, eyebrows. And with the book demonstrating that a Davidic king is not a *conditio sine qua non* of Israel's triumph, the resultant conclusion would be that all that is needed for the sovereign possession of the land to come true is YHWH's support. Joshua would thus become instrumental in making the Jews listen to and hear Torah's claim that YHWH's disposition is contingent upon observance of its norms, in other words, upon recognition of its authority. The integrity of the Enneateuch would thus be restored, but with Joshua and the books that follow now identified as a corpus of their own, the Former Prophets. And later, the book's scenario would be played out almost to a letter in the Hasmonean revolt, with the homeland Jewish community gaining independence under non-Davidic (if eventually dynastic) leaders and establishing control over the entire area, except for the northern and southwestern fringe (cf. Josh 13:2–6). That, of course, would further enhance the Enneateuch's authority.

Conclusions

Tentative as they of necessity might be, the results of the preceding discussion can be summarized in two pithy sentences. First, there is no evidence that Jewish audiences in the fourth century B.C.E. knew Joshua as anything but a section of the Enneateuch. Second, as such, Joshua largely constituted an impediment to the normative authority of the larger whole throughout the Persian period and a major boost to this authority thereafter.

At the same time, there is little doubt that already in Persian times the Enneateuch exercised some kind of traditional (or, perhaps, intellectual?) authority, at least in educated circles. Irrefutably proving as much is the simple fact of the scribes keeping the corpus alive over centuries, repeatedly copying it (which required substantial effort, time, and financial outlay) regardless of its more problematic aspects, both associated with Joshua and unrelated to it. Moreover, literate Jews may have tried to resolve these problems by creating new texts. For example, the impetus for such compositions as Isa 53, Jonah, Ecclesiastes, and Job, dealing with the issue of theodicy, may have had to do with the Enneateuch's inability to account for the condition of the postexilic Jewish community. Interpolations like 1 Sam 1–8 and 2 Sam 10–12 can be interpreted as attempts to correct the Enneateuch's stance on the issue of kingship; the same is true of the rewritten account of the Israelite monarchy in Chronicles that, among other things, fashions the temple, complete with its priestly orders and services, as the surviving Davidic heir.[23] More remotely, the portrayal of Cyrus as YHWH's משיח "anointed one" and his "shepherd" in Isa 44:24–45:7 and the entire messianic tradition, removing Davidic restoration to the eschatological realm, may also be responses to the Enneateuch's pro-monarchic and pro-Davidic agenda, obsolete in the postexilic period. It is possible, then, that the exposure of the corpus to the crucible of the Persian period became a major formative factor of the biblical canon—in much the same way that this canon's exposure to the crucible of the late Roman period became a major formative factor of the rabbinic library.

---

23. On 1 Sam 1–8 as an anti-monarchic interpolation, see the previous footnote; on 2 Sam 10–12, see Serge Frolov, "Succession Narrative: A 'Document' or a Phantom?" *JBL* 121 (2002): 81–104 (102–3).

Who Was Interested in the Book of Judges in the Persian-Hellenistic Periods?

Yairah Amit

Introduction

For almost thirty years I have been trying to convince all those who are ready to hear or to read my arguments that an early version of the book of Judges was written and edited on the basis of northern traditions in Judah at the end of the eighth century B.C.E. or the beginning of the seventh.[1] In other words, I am convinced that the book of Judges is the beginning of history-writing in Judah and is the product of those intellectuals who reacted to the Assyrian conquests of the eighth century and to the fall of the northern kingdom (722 B.C.E.).[2] Those writers tried to understand and explain the historical disaster they had faced and enable those who came after them to study and analyze the past, learn some lessons from it, and draw inferences for their present and for the future.

The early Judahite edition of the book of Judges was a single composition, different to some extent from the book we know today. The version in our hands includes the prominent and obvious changes that were done by the Deuteronomistic editors who took the early Judahite version and turned it into a document that describes the period when there was no

---

1. I have remained loyal to this dating from the beginning of the 1980s; see my doctoral thesis, "The Art of Composition in the Book of Judges" [Hebrew] (Ph.D. diss., Tel Aviv University, 1984), which led to my book *The Book of Judges: the Art of Editing* (Leiden: Brill, 1999 [Heb.: 1992]). I repeated this view recently in "The Book of Judges: Dating and Meaning," in *Homeland and Exile: Biblical and Ancient Near Eastern Studies in Honour of Bustenay Oded* (ed. Gershon Galil, Mark Geller, and Alan Millard; VTSup 130; Leiden: Brill, 2009), 297–322.
2. See Amit, *Book of Judges*, 358–83.

king in Israel, that is, from the death of Joshua to the birth of the prophet Samuel, who appointed the first two kings of Israel.[3] The pre-Deuteronomistic editors were less severe in applying Deuteronomic principles. For example, they did not criticize the building of altars in different places (see Judg 6:24, 26–32; 13:19–20 and more). On the other hand, they put much effort into the opening to the book in general and to its stories specifically,[4] because as writers, they would have known that the opening of a text and its ending influence the whole reading process.[5]

As an independent book, Judges was intended to answer questions typical of the agenda of the writers' time. Does history have any meaning, or follow laws of justice, or is it simply arbitrary? Is it possible to understand and justify the fate of northern Israel? How can Judah avoid a similar fate? Is the God of Judah and Israel the God of other nations too, or whence does a foreign king derive his power? These questions are not new; we find them in the writings of the prophets of the eighth century B.C.E.[6] It seems that the answers provided by the book of Judges met the needs of the Deuteronomistic editors; therefore, they adopted the book and included it as a link in the chain of their historical description. This teaches us that the book of Judges gained authority at an early stage, which is why the Deuteronomistic editors were interested in including it with minimal changes.

I point out these three issues—dating, editing and intention—as background to the main subject, which asks why the book of Judges was still authoritative in the Persian or Hellenistic period and who was interested in it. Is it because it was part of the DtrH? Or, does the book have its own qualities and reasons for meeting the needs of later periods?

---

3. On my view of the role of the Deuteronomistic editorial work, see Amit, *Book of Judges*, 297–309.

4. On the complex exposition to the book of Judges and on its pre-Deuteronomistic units, see Amit, *Book of Judges*, 120–26; 363–83.

5. On beginnings and endings in general, see Yairah Amit, *Reading Biblical Narratives: Literary Criticism and the Hebrew Bible* (rev. and annotated ed.; trans. Y. Lotan; Minneapolis: Fortress, 2001), 33–35; Yairah Amit, "Endings: Especially Reversal Endings," *Scriptura* 87 (2004): 213–26.

6. One example will suffice; see Isa 10:1–19.

What Makes Judges an Authoritative Book in the Late Persian Period?

Before answering this question, I would like to clarify that, when I use the term "authoritative," I do not mean canonical writings whose contents and even letters are frozen. Rather, I am thinking about literary materials that have gained a certain status and importance within a circle or group of people that set it apart from other books, continued to use it, read, and reread it for themselves and for others. This kind of authority does not preclude its ongoing editing; the opposite is true. Those who consider such literary materials important enough are interested in updating them for the needs of their audience or in preserving them by inclusion in a larger sequence of writings. Therefore, I would like to show that there were sufficient reasons for Judges to be an authoritative book in the Persian and Hellenistic periods, not only because it might have been part of the DtrH but because it dealt with central issues that interested Judean intellectuals of that time. Thus, the focus of this discussion will be on those subjects that interested both the early addressees and the later audience.

Supporting the Idea of the Merciful God

The Levites' confessional prayer in Neh 9:6–37, which reflects the late Persian period (= LPP) while recounting the history of the people of Israel, emphasizes the transgression of Israel in the land and God's continued mercy and repeated forgiveness. The reference in this prayer to the judges as "deliverers" who were sent by God on many occasions (vv. 27–28) is explicit, in spite of the option to interpret this term in a more comprehensive way that might include some of the kings, too.[7] But what is more important is that this prayer shows how later generations understood the

---

7. See 2 Kgs 13:5, but see e.g. 1 Kgs 12–15:8. Many interpreters of the Levites' prayer emphasize the period of the judges in this context, see e.g. Herbert E. Ryle, *The Books of Ezra and Nehemiah* (CBCS; Cambridge: Cambridge University Press, 1893), 262; Loring W. Batten, *The Books of Ezra and Nehemiah* (ICC 12; Edinburgh: T&T Clark, 1913), 369; Leonard H. Brockington, *Ezra, Nehemiah and Esther* (NCBS; London: Nelson, 1969), 175; F. Charles Fensham, *The Books of Ezra and Nehemiah* (Grand Rapids, Mich.: Eerdmans, 1982), 233; Joseph Blenkinsopp, *Ezra-Nehemiah: A Commentary* (OTL; Philadelphia: Westminster, 1988), 306; Ralph W. Klein, "The Books of Ezra and Nehemiah," in *The New Interpreter's Bible* (ed. Leander Keck et al.; 12 vols.; Nashville: Abingdon), 3:671–851 (811–12).

past and interpreted it, and how much the period of the judges could serve as an explanation for the present, as a source for hopes for the future, and as a proof of the existence of a merciful God, because after he punishes, he always pities his people, sends them deliverers, and gives them another opportunity.

A similar pattern we find in Ps 106, which is postexilic (v. 47).[8] Here, too, the period of the judges and the kings is described as one sequence (vv. 33–42) and ends with a message of mercy: "He saved them time and again, but they were deliberately rebellious. … When He saw that they were in distress, when He heard their cry, He was mindful of His covenant and in His great faithfulness relented" (vv. 43–45).[9]

THE NEGATIVE PRESENTATION OF THE NORTHERN KINGDOM

The relationship between the province of Samaria and the small province of Yehud in the Persian period was complicated, although they worshiped the same God. The books of Ezra and Nehemiah provide the reasons for the hostility between the two groups and the need and intention of Ezra and his followers to slander the people of the north, "the adversaries of Judah and Benjamin" (Ezra 4:1: צרי יהודה ובנימין), as much as possible. The book of Judges, which serves as "a Judahite indictment of the northern kingdom,"[10] supports this direction and atmosphere. It could, therefore, serve as an important document and proof for understanding that the people of the north were a negative element from the minute they settled in the land and more so after the Assyrian deportations and the settling of foreign inhabitants in their places (Ezra 4:2).[11]

---

8. Edward J. Kissane rightly thinks: "From verse 47 it is clear that Israel is now scattered among the nations, because they had been unfaithful like their fathers. The restoration is still in the future (v. 4). The Psalm was written before the end of the Exile" (*The Book of Psalms* [Dublin: Browne and Nolan, 1964], 485). Hans-Joachim Kraus even notes that "It has correctly been emphasized again and again that this middle section [vv. 7–48] surely also has a literary dependence on the completed Pentateuch narrative … which would place Psalm 106 in post-exilic times" (*Psalms 60–150: A Commentary* [trans. H. C. Oswald; Minneapolis: Augsburg, 1989], 317).

9. Here and throughout this paper biblical quotations are taken from the JPS translation.

10. See Amit, *Book of Judges*, 313–15.

11. According to Sara Japhet and her followers, the book of Chronicles espouses a different position regarding the inhabitants of the north, who later will be called

Northern Israel is the central focus of the book of Judges. Except for Othniel son of Kenaz, all the judges—the deliverers as well as the "consecutive" or "minor" judges[12]—are from the north, and most of the events take place in the territories of what was the northern kingdom. In order to condemn the north, the Judahite editors shaped the opening of the book as an indictment composed of three accusations:

(a) The northern tribes, and not the tribe of Judah, are responsible for not inheriting the land. Judah went to battle together with Simeon, his brother, and took possession of the Canaanite areas (Judg 1:1–20). However, the northern tribes preferred instead to subjugate the Canaanites, to use them as forced labor, and even to dwell among them (1:21–36).[13]

(b) The Judahite editor is interested in emphasizing that Benjamin, the southernmost tribe of the north, is responsible for not dispossessing the Jebusite inhabitants of Jerusalem (1:21), whereas in Josh 15:63 the same blame is imposed on Judah, but in Judg 1:8, in the description of the conquest of Jerusalem by the Judahites, there is no hint that any local inhabitants were left. In other words, Benjamin, a northern tribe, is the one blamed for the existence of Jebusites in Jerusalem. However, the preferred city of the north is notorious Bethel, mentioned here twice: first, by telling about its conquest by the House of Joseph (Judg 1:22–26); and second, by using hidden polemic and describing Bochim (2:1–5),[14] which is Bethel,[15] as the place of rebuke where the messenger of God[16] was sent to the northern tribes that sinned in not dispossessing the inhabitants and were punished there for violating the covenant with God.

"Samaritans"; see Yairah Amit, "The Samaritans: Biblical Positions in the Service of Modern Politics," in *Samaritans: Past and Present: Current Studies* (ed. Menachem Mor and Friedrich V. Reiterer; Studia Judaica 53; Studia Samaritana 5; Berlin: de Gruyter, 2010), 247–66, esp. 251–55.

12. On the term "consecutive judges" instead of "minor judges," see Amit, *Book of Judges*, 81–85.

13. Amit, *Book of Judges*, 145–52.

14. On hidden polemic, see Yairah Amit, *Hidden Polemics in Biblical Narrative* (trans. J. Chipman; Leiden: Brill, 2000). Judges 2:1–5 is discussed on 119–20 specifically, but see the entire chapter dedicated to the case of Bethel (99–129).

15. See Judg 20:26; 21:2; see also 20:17–23. LXX Judg 2:1 uses the name Bethel in a kind of double reading: "to Bochim and to Bethel and to the House of Israel."

16. It does not matter if this messenger was an angel or a prophet; see the different commentaries.

(c) The third accusation is expressed indirectly, by including the segment about Othniel (3:7–11), a collection of formulaic phrases that report his deliverance with no story of salvation. This segment precedes the sequence of the northern judges and distinguishes the Judahite Othniel from the other judges, because he battled a "dark" (כוש) "doubly wicked" (רשעתיים) enemy from Aram-Naharaim in the distant north[17] and thus acted as a national hero, not only a regional one.[18]

Moreover, the description of Israel as having a cyclical history is a golden opportunity to highlight the repeated sinning of the northern tribes and the limited influence of their leaders. It also serves to justify the historical fate of the northern kingdom as a nation wallowing in sin. Thus, even if the population of the north was the original one, composed of the northern tribes and not a mixture of the deportees with the original population, it was preferable not to communicate with them.[19]

In the context of the northern kingdom, we cannot ignore the appearance of Shechem in the book of Judges. Abimelech, Gideon's son born to him by his concubine in Shechem (Judg 8:32), was enthroned in this city by all the citizens of Shechem after the murder of his brothers (9:1–7). Abimelech is depicted as a negative leader, symbolized by a thornbush (vv. 8–20, 22–57). Shechem is depicted as a city of mixed population that Abimelech and his army finally destroyed. Thus, God repaid the inhabitants of Shechem for all their wickedness. This negative attitude toward the city, which became central in the days of Jeroboam I, continued after the

---

17. The enemy's name in its present form is a kind of Hebraism. On the peculiarities of the phrasing "Cushan Rishathaim king of Aram Naharaim," see Amit, *Book of Judges*, 165.

18. On Othniel son of Kenaz as a source for formulaic statements and on the interpretation of the entire unit as a work of editing, see Amit, *Book of Judges*, 160–66. Bustanay Oded sees this episode as a pro-Judahite polemic and a hidden polemic against Benjamin and the house of Saul ("Cushan-Rishathaim [Judges 3:8-11]: An Implicit Polemic," in *Texts, Temples, and Traditions: A Tribute to Menahem Haran* [ed. Michael V. Fox et al.; Winona Lake, Ind.: Eisenbrauns, 1996], *89–*94 [Heb.]).

19. On the myth of the empty land, see Bustanay Oded, "Where Can the Myth of the Empty Land Be Found? History vs. Myth," in *Judah and the Judeans in the Neo-Babylonian Period* (ed. Oded Lipschits and Joseph Blenkinsopp; Winona Lake, Ind.: Eisenbrauns, 2003), 55–74. For a different approach, see Diana Edelman, "The 'Empty Land' as a Motif in City Laments," in *Ancient and Modern Historiography, L'historiograhie biblique, ancienne et modern* (ed. George J. Brooke and Thomas Römer; BETL 207; Leuven: Leuven University, 2007), 127–49.

exile, because the population of the north built a temple near Shechem on Mount Gerizim, which some archaeologists today are convinced was already active in the fifth century B.C.E.[20] In other words, the tone of the criticism of Shechem in the book of Judges has a supportive audience in the late Persian period.

THE PARADIGMATIC CHARACTER OF HISTORY

The book of Judges is characterized by a unique model of cyclical history, composed of five stages: sin, punishment, crying to God, deliverance and tranquility, repeated again and again.[21] This stern model highlights the existence of reward and of a direct correlation between the people's behavior and God's judgment.

This model was known to the editors of Kings, but they used it only once, in the description of the reign of Jehoahaz (2 Kgs 13:1–9). Thus, on the one hand, the description lost its cyclical character, and on the other hand, it shows that the editors of the book of Kings preferred not to use the sin-punishment-reward-model and to adopt a more flexible system in which there is no immediate reward. In a flexible reward system, the people may sin but the punishment comes after some generations. The advantage of the flexible system, where the reward can be remote, is that it does not force the author-editor to fit history to a specific model but enables him to fit the model to the historical data, as in the case of Hezekiah and the representatives of Merodach-Baladan king of Babylon (2 Kgs 20:12–19). Hezekiah was not punished because of this alliance but was told that his descendants would be punished. Actually, it happened after more than a hundred years.

Nevertheless, the Chronicler chose the strict, artificial model of reward similar to that of the book of Judges.[22] Thus, he created a new historical

---

20. See Yitzhak Magen, "The Dating of the First Phase of the Samaritan Temple on Mount Gerizim in Light of the Archaeological Evidence," in *Judah and the Judeans in the Fourth Century B.C.E.* (ed. Oded Lipschits and Joseph Blenkinsopp; Winona Lake, Ind.: Eisenbrauns, 2007), 157–211.

21. All the stages do not always appear, but when one or more of them is missing, the story or stories support enough details to understand it; see Amit, *Book of Judges*, 35–45, and the analysis of the stories throughout the book.

22. See Sara Japhet, *The Ideology of the Book of Chronicles and Its Place in Biblical Thought* (trans. A. Barber; BEATAJ 9; Frankfurt am Main: Lang, 1989), 150–76, and esp. 154 n. 452.

description of the period of the Kings that differs from his sources in many ways. His intention to focus on the House of David caused him to begin his history with the death of Saul and the transfer of the kingdom from the House of Saul to David (1 Chr 10).

The Chronicler does not ignore the period of the judges. In his "dynastic oracle" (1 Chr 17:1–15) the judges are mentioned explicitly twice. The first occurrence is connected to God's refusal to let David build him a temple. There, God asks: "Did I ever reproach any of the judges of Israel whom I appointed to care for my people Israel? Why have you not built Me a house of cedar?" (v. 6)? Although the version in the book of Samuel uses "the tribes of Israel" (2 Sam 7:7) instead of "the judges of Israel," I prefer the Chronicler's version, because it is natural that the appeal to build a temple would be submitted not to a general entity (tribes) but to a specific leader or leaders.[23]

The judges appear again in the same oracle, but this time in the context of the many wars they had to face: "Evil men shall not wear them down anymore as in the past, ever since I appointed judges over My people Israel. I will subdue all your enemies" (9b–10a). Here the period of the judges is characterized by wars and instability in contrast to the nation's future under the Davidic rule.

Many scholars find a hint of the times of the judges in Azariah's address to king Asa and his people (2 Chr 15:1–6). I will cite S. Japhet as a typical example: "The period which the Chronicler chooses as an example is not clearly defined, but its features imply the pre-monarchical age ... generally called (although not by the Chronicler) 'the period of the judges.'"[24] The connection with the period of the judges is based here on the stages of the

---

23. Compare, for example, Edward D. Curtis, and Albert A. Madsen, who claim the true text of 2 Sam 7:7, שבטי, is a clear case of a copyist's confusion of letters (*A Critical and Exegetical Commentary on the Books of Chronicles* [ICC 11; Edinburgh: T&T Clark, 1910], 228). Similar views are expressed by Hugh G. M. Williamson (*I and 2 Chronicles* [NCBS; Grand Rapids: Eerdmans, 1982], 135), Gary. N. Knoppers (*I Chronicles 10–29: A New Translation with Introduction and Commentary* [AB 12A; New York: Doubleday, 2004], 664, 668–69), and Ralph Klein (*1 Chronicles: A Commentary* [Hermeneia; Minneapolis: Fortress, 2006], 378). See also his commentary on v. 9 on 379, where he mentions "the various enemies who oppressed Israel during the period of the Judges."

24. See also, for example, Curtis and Madsen, *Chronicles,* 384; Jacob M. Myers, *II Chronicles* (AB 13; Garden City, N.Y.: Doubleday, 1965), 88; Klein, *1 Chronicles,* 378 n. 32.

cyclical model: sin, punishment, returning to God, and deliverance; and, much like in Judges, the sin is religious and the punishment is a confrontation with an enemy.[25]

To sum up: the Chronicler, who also was familiar with the book of Kings, still preferred the strict, artificial model of reward used in the book of Judges and even upgraded it by relating it to specific sinners, in this case King Asa and his followers.[26]

THE IDEA OF GOD'S KINGSHIP

The book of Judges is the first text containing the idea that God has to rule over Israel, as phrased in Gideon's saying: "I will not rule over you myself, nor shall my son rule over you; YHWH alone shall rule over you" (Judg 8:23). This idea, which appears again in Samuel's objection to appointing a king (1 Sam 8), has received two main directions of interpretation. The first is by J. Wellhausen, who argued that these texts reflect a later period, a period of theocracy when priests who were considered the representatives of God ruled over Israel.[27] The second comes from M. Buber, who described the tribes of Israel in the days of the judges in somewhat romantic colors as offering a realistic resistance to human rule and showing conscious preference for God's rule.[28] The idea of God's kingship appears in the book of Chronicles, too, but in a different way. Moreover, in this book we find for the first time the term/concept of "YHWH's kingship" accompanied by its explanation.[29] The later book of Chronicles raises the question of how the rule of God should be implemented. In other words: who

---

25. The stage of the sin (v. 3): "Israel has gone many days without the true God, without a priest to give instruction and without Teaching"; the stage of the punishment (only the beginning of v. 4): "But in distress"; the stage of returning to God (v. 4a+b1): "it returned to the Lord God of Israel, and sought Him"; the stage of deliverance (v. 4b2): "and He responded to them." See also vv. 5–6.

26. It is not surprising that a similar approach, based on personal reward, was developed by the exilic prophet Ezekiel; see, for example, Ezek 18.

27. See Julius Wellhausen, *Prolegomena to the History of Ancient Israel* (trans. A. Menzies and S. Black; New York: Meridian Books, 1957), 239–40, n. 1. This approach is accepted by most critical scholars; for details, see Frank Crüsemann, *Der Widerstand gegen das Konigtum* (WMANT 49; Neukirchen-Vluyn: Neukirchener Verlag, 1978).

28. See Martin Buber, *Kingship of God* (trans. R. Scheimann; New York: Harper & Row, 1967).

29. See 1 Chr 28:5; 2 Chr 13:8; and also 1 Chr 17:14; 29:23; 2 Chr 9:8.

should rule Israel, God or God through specific representatives? Examination of the occurrences of the term "YHWH's kingship" leads Japhet to conclude, "In these verses, we find the clearest biblical expression of the idea that Israel's monarchy—the actual political institution—is none other than divine kingship; the king is God's representative and executor of the functions of kingship."[30]

From the point of view of the Chronicler, the idea of God's kingship is fulfilled only when David's sons rule over Israel, as Abijah from the summit of Mount Zemaraim declared against Jeroboam's rebellion: "Now you are bent on opposing the kingdom of YHWH, which is in the charge of the sons of David" (2 Chr 13:8). The phrases "My house," "My kingdom" (1 Chr 17:14), "the throne of the kingdom of YHWH over Israel" (1 Chr 28:5), or "the throne of the Lord" (1 Chr 29:23; cf. 2 Chr 9:8) all actually refer to the kingdom of Israel, albeit under the reign of David, Solomon, and their sons.

Thus, we see that the Chronicler resolves the question of God's kingship in the books of Judges and Samuel. In the book of Chronicles, when David and his sons rule, there is no tension between human rule and God's rule. In the book of Judges we find the conclusion that Israel needs a king; otherwise, everyone does as they please. The Chronicler supports and strengthens this idea by emphasizing that, in order to be God's kingdom, it is not enough to have an earthly ruler; the ruler must be a descendant of the Davidic dynasty. The fulfillment of God's kingdom is the rule of David's House.[31]

The Anti-Saul Approach

The preference for the tribe of Judah and the anti-Saul approach are prominent in the opening and the ending of the book of Judges. The editors of Judges invested effort in describing Judah as a positive tribe in contrast

---

30. See Japhet, *Ideology of Chronicles*, 400.

31. I disagree with Japhet's conclusion in that "Saul's monarchy also implements YHWH's kingship" and that the Chronicler has a positive attitude toward Saul (*Ideology of Chronicles*, 409 n. 38). See Yairah Amit, "Saul in the Book of Chronicles," in *Shai le-Sara Japhet: Studies in the Bible, Its Exegesis and Its Language* (ed. Mosheh Bar-Asher et al.; Jerusalem: The Bialik Institute, 3–15 (Heb.); an English version is now available in my *In Praise of Editing in the Hebrew Bible: Collected Essays in Retrospect* (trans. B. S. Rozen; Sheffield: Sheffield Phoenix), 231–47.

to the northern tribes (Judg 1) and in depicting the only Judahite judge, Othniel son of Kenaz (Judg 3:7–11), as the first, successful judge who takes a national view and, therefore, fights against a northern enemy. Moreover, some editors added to this and concluded the book with an anti-Benjaminite and anti-Saulide document: the story of the concubine in Gibeah.[32] The editors, whenever they acted, would have known that the opening of a text influences the whole process of subsequent reading and its ending makes the final and lasting impression. Thus David, who embodies the hope of many texts in the Persian period implicitly or explicitly, first appears in an indirect way in the book of Judges by means of his tribe, Judah, and by means of his competitor Saul and his tribe, Benjamin, who are described as the "bad guys." The echo of these deliberate clues is heard in biblical books of the Persian period such as Haggai (2:20–23), Zechariah (3:8; 4; 6:12),[33] Ruth (4:17, 22) and in the entire book of Chronicles.

LEGITIMIZING FOREIGN WOMEN

Gideon the judge is not criticized for having a concubine in Shechem (Judg 8:31), and the judge Jephthah was possibly the son of a foreign woman (11:1–2), because sometimes foreign women are depicted as prostitutes (see, for example Prov 7), and Jephthah's brothers tell him that he is "the son of an outsider" (אשה אחרת). Similarly, Samson's parents, who are against his marriage to a Philistine woman, do not mention her being part of a heathen culture but relate to her different nationality that differs from his own kin or his people by asking: "Is there no one among the daughters of your own kinsmen and among all our [the Hebrew version: 'my'] people, that you must go and take a wife from the uncircumcised Philistines" (Judg 14:3)? With that, the foreign background of Yael the Kenite

---

32. On the one hand, I think this story is an editorial digression (Amit, *Book of Judges*, 337–57). On the other hand, it is a hidden polemic against Saul; see my chapter, "Criticism of Saul's Kingdom: A Formula for Character Assassination," in Amit, *Hidden Polemics*, 167–88. Cynthia Edenburg highlights how this story is mainly against the tribe of Benjamin. See her doctoral thesis, "The Story of the Outrage at Gibeah (Jdg. 19–21): Composition, Sources and Historical Context" (Ph.D. diss., Tel Aviv University, 2003) (Hebrew).

33. Zechariah's prophecies are sometimes nebulous and it is not totally clear if Zerubbabel is the governor of Judah, if he is from the Davidic line, or if he is the "son of Shealtiel at all." Even the use of the name צמח in Zech 3:8; 6:12 differs from its use in Jer 23:5; 33:15, where it is connected directly with the House of David.

does not prevent the national poet from describing her as "most blessed of women" (5:24). This open approach to foreign women, who are evaluated according to their deeds or their social status, reminds us of the attitude to Ruth the Moabite and of the Chronicler's attitude to non-Israelite women,[34] which runs counter to attitudes expressed in the books of Ezra and Nehemiah (Ezra 1:9–10; Neh 9:1, 13:1, 23–30; and in Mal 2:11–12).

Conclusion

The book of Judges was an authoritative book in the Persian and Hellenistic periods. The authors of the time referred to Judges because it covered an epoch of Israel's history and could also serve as an anchor and an appropriate historical background, as at the beginning of Ruth scroll: "In the days when the judges ruled" (1:1). Furthermore, the book was authoritative because it could be and was a source of inspiration and brainstorming regarding issues such as God's control over history, God's justice, earthly monarchy, divine kingship, the resistance to northern Israel, the promising Judahite leader and the anti-hero Saul, and even the willingness to legitimize foreign women.

Therefore, it is no exaggeration to say that the book of Judges was an important source for writers in the Persian and Hellenistic periods.

---

34. On the positive place of foreign women in Chronicles, see Japhet, *Ideology in Chronicles*, 334–51.

Memories Laid to Rest:
The Book of Judges in the Persian Period

Susanne Gillmayr-Bucher

"And the people of Israel did what was evil in the eyes of YHWH." This appraisal repeated again and again is the most striking evaluation of the era of judges. It is firmly established throughout the reign the judges before it is superseded in the final chapters by another evaluation: "Everyone did what was right in his own eyes". This quite pessimistic view of Israel, both as a people and as individuals, runs through the whole book. It offers a point of view that is contrasted by single stories of great heroes, of saviors, and of people who try to cope with a difficult situation as well as possible.

I will outline on the basis of two exemplary themes: the search for Israel's identity and the question of leadership, why the portrayal of such a heterogeneous era, as it is presented in the book of Judges, might become an attractive or even authoritative part of Israel's tradition during the Persian period.[1]

Who Is Israel?

The image of Israel the book of Judges portrays in the beginning is one of a distinct ethnicity.[2] Israel is vehemently distinguished from other peoples living in the same area. The separation between Israel and the other peo-

---

1. In this article I will focus on the final composition of the book of Judges and will not ask which parts might have been added or which editorial modifications of the text took place in the Persian period. For the history of the origins of the book, see, e.g., Philippe Guillaume, *Waiting for Josiah: The Judges* (JSOTSup 385; London: T&T Clark, 2004) and Walter Groß, *Richter* (HKAT; Freiburg: Herder, 2009), 82–94.

2. For an overview of different approaches defining Israelite identity, see Jon L. Berquist, "Constructions of Identity in Postcolonial Yehud," in *Judah and the Judeans*

ples and their deities is one of the demands the Israelites are reminded of by a prophet (Judg 6:8–10), a messenger (Judg 2:1–3; 6:11–21; 13:3–20), or YHWH himself (Judg 10:11–14). The repetition of this claim emphasizes its importance and points to the threat of mixture and the subsequent loss of Israel's uniqueness.

Closely connected to identity as ethnicity is the concept of identity as religion.[3] This aspect is especially emphasized in the schematic portrayal of the era at the beginning (Judg 2:11–13, 17,19–20; 3:7), the introduction to the story of Jephthah (Judg 10:10–16), and it is hinted at in the framework of the single stories. The common evaluation "evil in the eyes of YHWH" is explained as worship of the deities of the foreign nations several times.[4]

While the problem of other nations and foreign deities is emphasized at the beginning of the book in the single stories—with the exception of the Samson story—the importance of a distinction from other nations is undisputed and the borders seem to be well established. Regardless of the claim of a separation from other nations and their deities, however, the implementation is not satisfactory. Thus, this topic remains an ongoing question throughout the book.

Shifting the focus from exclusion to inclusion, the tribal structure of Israel gains attention. The book of Judges starts with a reference to the בני ישׂראל, but this unity is already differentiated in the first direct speech in v. 1. "The Israelites" clearly see themselves as a divided unity as they ask their deity: "Who shall go up first for us against the Canaanites?" Israel is presented as a unity that exists in a variety of different tribes. This concept runs through the entire book. Only the common scheme of the era (Judg 2:11–19) and the framework refer to Israel; the single narrations make the tribes the centre of attention.

Nevertheless, the relationship between Israel and the tribes is not without problems. The unity between the tribes is neither steadfast nor well defined. Different elements constituting unity are mentioned throughout the book: the area of settlement, the solidarity of the tribes as well as shared values, interests, and tasks. These elements are sufficient to evoke

---

in the Persian Period (ed. Oded Lipschits and Manfred Oeming; Winona Lake, Ind.: Eisenbrauns, 2006), 53–66 (54–56).

3. See Berquist, "Identity," 57–58.

4. See Judg 2:12–13; 10:11–14; see also the story of Gideon and the altar of Ba'al in Judg 6:25–32.

the image of the tribes; however, the differing emphasis they receive creates a new picture.

Israel and the Land

The first concept of Israel is as a unity structured by territorial distribution.[5] The conquest of the land in the first chapter outlines an image of the tribes located in adjoining areas of settlement.[6] Although the conquest of the land remains to a great extent wishful thinking, the tribes are presented according to their settlement areas, from south to north.

In the ensuing stories, the theme of conquest merges into a defense of the land. Each of the tribes holds its own position and defends it, thereby acting for the benefit of Israel.[7] The focus on the land highlights the theme of supremacy in the land. The urgent problem is the threat posed by hostile nations from outside, who threaten to control and dominate the land of one or several tribes. Israel is not in danger of losing the land or being driven out of it, but foreign nations oppress and exploit them.[8]

At the end of the book, the topic of the conquest is resumed (Judg 18). Dan, the most unsuccessful tribe (Judg 1), finally finds its own area of settlement. With this last act, the ongoing struggle for supremacy in the land comes to its end. At the beginning of Judg 20, Israel is again gathered as a territorial unity: "from Dan to Beersheba and all of Gilead" (v. 1) and at the end (Judg 21:24) all the sons of Israel return to their "property" (נחלה).[9] Thus, at the beginning and at the end of the book, the image of Israel includes the inheritance of all its tribes.

---

5. The book of Judges presents only a territorial organization of the tribes; a genealogical scheme not mentioned.

6. The basis for this territorial scheme can be found in the narratives about the apportionment of the land in the book of Joshua (Josh 13–19) and also in Josh 21:4–7, 9–38; Ezek 48:1–28; 1 Chr 6:39b–48, 50–66; 12:25–38. See Zecharia Kallai, "The Twelve-Tribe Systems of Israel," *VT* 47 (1997): 53–90 (57–77).

7. E.g. the suspense built up at the beginning of Jephthah's story uses the topographical concept. As the enemies draw closer, they threaten more and more tribes.

8. See 3:8, 14; 4:2–3, 6:2–6; 10:8.

9. See Josh 24:28; within the book of Judges, Judg 2:6 is fulfilled. The tribes seem to have taken possession of the land. The idea of a return to the "inheritance" can be found also in the context of hopes for return from the exile, e.g., Jer 12:15. Also, in Neh 11:20, order in the land is presented according to inheritance.

Israel and the Tribes

Although the image of Israel as a structured unity is maintained throughout the book, the number and identity of the tribes is not determined. The most comprehensive lists of tribes can be found in Judg 1, the summary of the conquest of the land, and the song of Deborah (Judg 5). Both lists name six tribes in common (Benjamin, Ephraim, Zebulun, Asher, Naphtali, Dan); Judg1 adds Judah, Simeon, Joseph, and Manasseh, while Judg 5 further mentions Issachar, Reuben, and Gilead.[10] Most of these tribes, however, are just mentioned but not given an exhaustive account.

Judah is the first of the tribes to take action. It begins to conquer the land and is quite successful. Although the conquest is presented in a general summary, some details are added emphasizing Judah's importance. In the short episode of king Adoni-bezek's capture (Judg 1:5–7), for example, Judah is portrayed to be an enemy of equal standing with this king, who had once captured and mutilated seventy kings himself. He, the mighty king, now accepts Judah as his superior (v. 7). Despite this high degree of attention at the beginning, Judah fades into the background in the rest of the book.[11] The stories of the two judges from the territory of Judah, Othniel and Ibzan, are not elaborated.

Joseph is the only tribe besides Judah that successfully conquers its share of the land (Judg 1:22–26). A short scene tells about the conquest of Bethel, and later Joseph is even able to subjugate the Amorites (Judg 1:35). The two tribes mark a successful beginning: Judah conquers the land in the south and Joseph the north. They show what might have been possible. In this way, they set expectations the other tribes are not able to meet. But like Judah, the tribe of Joseph fades from the story.[12]

Despite the prominent position of Judah and Joseph in Judg 1, more emphasis lies on the tribes of Benjamin (Judg 3:15 Ehud; Judg 20–21),[13]

---

10. The tribe of Gad is not mentioned in Judges.

11. However, YHWH's answer (Judg 20:18) refers back to Judg 1:2 and gives Judah a leading role that is not continued in the story.

12. According to Josh 17:12–18 the sons of Joseph, Manasseh, and Ephraim share the land. Manasseh gets the northern part of the Ephaimite hill country and Ephraim the southern part; see also Isa 17:14–18. So Heinz-Dieter Neef, *Ephraim: Studien zur Geschichte des Stammes Ephraim von der Landnahme bis zur frühen Königszeit* (BZAW 238; Berlin: de Gruyter, 1995), 304.

13. For a portrayal of Benjamin, see Philip R. Davies, "The Trouble with Benjamin," in *Reflection and Refraction: Studies in Biblical Historiography in Honour of A.*

Ephraim (Judg 8:1-2; 12:4-6),[14] and Dan (Judg 13:2; Samson's origins; Judg 18). Yet none of the three serve as a positive example; instead, they are portrayed in an ambiguous way. All the remaining tribes that are named complete the image of Israel as a unity of different tribes. Still, the book of Judges does not offer a systematic picture of Israel and its tribes; rather, it provides snapshots of seemingly "typical" situations, with their problems and solutions. The loose union of the tribes forms an important element in this depiction; tribal Israel is conceived of as a diverse unity.

Establishing a Self-Concept

The way the book of Judges establishes a self-concept of Israel includes several components. Besides the image of Israel as an ethnic group that is clearly distinguishable from other peoples, there are several elements of cohesion within Israel. One identity-forming aspect is linked to Israel's past, especially to the story of the group's origin in the liberation from Egypt.[15] This event is mentioned several times—in the context of a reprimand (Judg 2:1-2; 6:8-9; 10:11-13), in the question of Gideon (Judg 6:13), in the negotiation between Jephthah and the king of the Ammonites (Judg 11:13, 16)—always in relation to normative guidelines. Furthermore, the memory of this event stresses Israel's exclusive relation to its deity.

Another constituent element is the concept of solidarity. Commitment to the community of Israel is also considered to be an identity-forming element.[16] This aspect is unfolded in positive and negative examples, but

---

Graeme Auld (ed. Robert Rezetko, Timothy H. Lim, and W. Brian Aucker; VTSup 113; Leiden: Brill, 2007), 93-111. For Benjamin and its role in the Persian period, see Joseph Blenkinsopp, "Benjamin Traditions Read in the Early Persian Period," in *Judah and the Judeans in the Persian Period* (ed. Oded Lipschits and Manfred Oeming; Winona Lake, Ind.: Eisenbrauns, 2006), 629-45.

14. For a portrayal of Ephraim, see Neef, *Ephraim*.

15. This kind of self-concept corresponds to *traditionale Codierung* according to Bernhard Giesen. The group is united by common traditions and stories about their origin ("Codes Kollektiver Identität," in *Religion und Identität im Horizont des Pluralismus* [ed. Werner Gephart and Hans Waldenfels; STW1411; Frankfurt: Suhrkamp, 1999], 13-43 [25-34]).

16. This concept could be classified as an example of Bernhard Giesen's *universalistische Codierung*. The unity defines itself through common commitments (Giesen, "Codes," 34-43; Bernhard Giesen and Kay Junge, "Der Mythos des Universalismus," in *Mythos und Nation: Studien zur Entwicklung des kollektiven Bewusstseins in der Neuzeit*

the demand is not expressly declared. Solidarity becomes necessary when the tribes are endangered. Thus, most of the time, the call for solidarity has a military background. The first coalition is already shown in Judg 1, when Judah asks Simeon to cooperate in their fight against the Canaanites. And similarly, most of the judges call all or some tribes to arms. In the stories of Deborah and Gideon these tribes are explicitly named: Deborah and Barak call Naphtali and Zebulun to take action; Gideon asks the tribes of Manasseh, Asher, Zebulun, Naphtali, and Ephraim to pursue the enemy. The song of Deborah (Judg 5) offers the most elaborate presentation of the ideal of solidarity. With this song she sets an example and tries to win support for an attitude of solidarity. Deborah starts by praising Israel because the people voluntarily took action. Like a keynote, this praise sets the tone for the following song. In vv. 14–18 Deborah describes the different tribes of Israel and their participation in the war. She praises those who act cooperatively: Ephraim, Benjamin, Issachar, Zebulun, Naphtali, and the people from Machir, and she reprimands those who stayed away and did not take part: Reuben, Gilead, Dan, Asher, and the inhabitants of Meroz.

Similar to Judg 1, the Song of Deborah evaluates the tribes of Israel but uses different criteria. Solidarity rather than individual success is of prime importance. Another significant element in the song is the interaction between the leaders and the people. YHWH and Deborah call for action and the people's solidarity supports them. Thus, the song sets an example: when YHWH, the leaders, and Israel's tribes act together, common success ensues. With this message, the Song of Deborah forms the center of the positive image of Israel as sketched in the book of Judges. In her prophetic retrospective, an example of successful behavior is presented and set as a model for future actions. However, in the following stories Israel tends to ignore the principle of solidarity. Bit by bit, solidarity crumbles as individual tribes and single persons act only in their own interest.

The tribe of Ephraim starts this process in the story of Gideon, when it feels neglected and demands a larger share in the fight with the enemy (Judg 8:1–3). A quite similar demand by the Ephraimites escalates in the

---

3 [ed. Helmut Berding; STW 1246; Frankfurt: Suhrkamp, 1996], 34–64 [39–44]). For a summary and application of the concepts of traditional and universal encoding to biblical texts, see Klaus Bieberstein, "Grenzen definieren: Israels Ringen um Identität," in *Impuls oder Hindernis? Mit dem Alten Testament in multireligiöser Gesellschaft, Beiträge des Internationalen Bibel-Symposions Bayreuth, 27.–29. September 2002* (ed. Joachim Kügler; Bayreuther Forum Transit 1; Berlin: LIT, 2004), 59–72 (60–71).

conflict with Jephthah (Judg 12:1–6), resulting in bloodshed that cruelly reduces the people of Ephraim. Quarrels arise not only between tribes but judges and individuals also come into conflict with tribes. The men of Judah deliver Samson to the enemies, the Philistines; the Danites rob Micah, and the men of Gibeah turn against the Levite and his host and rape the Levite's concubine. The worst escalation of conflict within Israel, however, appears in the last chapters of the book. It is the battle of Israel against Benjamin. The conflict starts with Israel's attempt to act in solidarity with the Levite, who lost his concubine. "All Israelites" (כל־בני ישראל) gather at Mizpah (Judg 20:1) to hear the case and to discuss how to react to this crime and mete out punishment. They declare the act of violence as a severe violation of their ethical boundaries and set out to punish the people who are responsible. They act according to the law and even quote it: "to purge the evil from Israel" (Judg 20:13).[17] In their attempt to do so they start a war and in its course, the coalition of Israel suffers heavy losses, but Benjamin is almost wiped out. The joint action of Israel's tribes to establish themselves as a people, to enforce their ethical norms and so secure their community, failed completely. In the end, Israel is more endangered than ever. Thus, the book ends with the comment by the narrator's voice: "Everyone did what was right in his own eyes."

Parallel to the threat from outside enemies who seek supremacy over Israel, the book of Judges constructs an even more threatening idea: the loss of solidarity and the subsequent dissolution of Israel. In between these threats, Israel longs for a self-determined way of life in the land. However, this will only become possible if the process of identity formation succeeds.

Israel's Image in the Persian Era

The book of Judges clearly holds on to the image of Israel as a unity of tribes. Although this concept lacks a clear definition and although various problems with it are discussed, it is not abandoned. Israel ideally is a collection of tribes that embraces solidarity and acts on this principle.[18] This por-

---

17. See Deut 13:6; 17:7, 12; 19:19; 21:21, 22, 24; 24:7. Judg 20:13 is the only reference to an active effort to act according to the law and thus to define Israel according to this guideline.

18. Trent Butler points out that the editor of the book of Judg "has let each of the parts represent the whole. … No one individual part of Israel can claim leadership for

trayal continues the image of the people presented in the book of Joshua. The troubled image of the time of the judges contributes to the high esteem attached to tribal unity. Even if it can no longer be taken for granted, it still must be preserved, and, what is more, Israel is responsible for its unity. With the book of Judges, this responsibility becomes a memory. Already in the early times of the conquest of the land, the unity and identity of the people was a troubled one, but it could be maintained. This concept could gain interest in subsequent times when unity is challenged. In the Persian era, it could offer a critical voice that ran against attempts to focus only on Judah, as the books of Ezra and Nehemiah did. The book of Judges gives Judah a special role in so far as it does not emphasize problems with or within Judah. Nevertheless, Judah is not offered leadership, nor is it separated from the other tribes.[19] Throughout the book, Judah remains one of the tribes of Israel. From the point of view expressed in the book of Judges, the memory of Israel includes all the tribes.[20]

The reality of the Achaemenid era demands a critical debate on how the relationship between the people of Yehud and Samaria is to be constructed. Samaria was a well-established, populous, and flourishing province,[21] and close economic and cultural contacts were established between Samaria and Yehud.[22] Nevertheless, relations between the people in Yehud and the people in the north were strained.[23] From the perspective of Judges, this unity is troubled but, nonetheless, worth carrying on, at least in memory. Similarly, the pessimistic view of the people includes all of Israel. It is due to the failure of the people that Israel is in trouble and even on the verge of breaking up. Furthermore, the most eminent danger from outside, the loss

---

itself, nor can any one part separate itself from the rest" (*Judges* [WBC 8; Nashville: Thomas Nelson, 2009], lxxxiii).

19. Twice Judah is asked to "make the start" (תחלה): to initiate the conquest of the land (Judg 1:2) and to initiate the battle against Benjamin (Judg 20:18). Nevertheless, Judah is not asked to take the lead.

20. A similar view is presented in 1–2 Chronicles.

21. Gary N. Knoppers, "Revisiting the Samarian Question in the Persian Period," in *Judah and the Judeans in the Persian Period* (ed. Oded Lipschits and Manfred Oeming; Winona Lake, Ind.: Eisenbrauns, 2006), 265–89 (273).

22. Knoppers, "Revisiting," 279–80.

23. Reinhard Achenbach, "The Pentateuch, the Prophets, and the Torah in the Fifth and Fourth Centuries B.C.E.," in *Judah and the Judeans in the Fourth Century B.C.E.* (ed. Oded Lipschits, Gary N. Knoppers and Rainer Albertz; Winona Lake, Ind.: Eisenbrauns, 2007), 253–85 (255).

of sovereignty in the land, is also connected to Israel's misbehavior. Thus, both foreign sovereigns as well as the split-up of the land and the tribes are considered undesirable developments.

The book of Judges promotes trends that try to establish the idea of a larger unity. It supports those voices that hold on to or invent a pan-Israelite history that undergirds the integration of all tribes into a unity called "Israel."[24] Accordingly, the book of Judges does not enhance the more radical perspectives emerging at the end of the fifth century B.C.E. that considered only the returnees from Babylon to constitute Israel.[25]

Israel and Its Leaders

Another important issue in the book of Judges is Israel's leadership. The judges, who save Israel, appear side by side with the negative image of Israel, thus providing a positive contrast. But the reign of judges is just one concept of leadership. At the beginning and especially at the end of the book, the tribes fulfill this task without an appointed leader.[26]

Times without Leadership

The book of Judges starts with an image of Israel without a leader. It is the responsibility of the tribes to accomplish successful settlement and dwelling in the land. The situation, however, is portrayed very critically. The tribes do not fulfill expectations: they fail to conquer the land and they abandon their deity. As a result, the unity and continuity of Israel are not secure. This situation takes a turn for the worse in the last stories of the book. With an exaggerated reaction to an act of violence, the pro-

---

24. Looking for an era when Judah could understand itself as "Israel," Philip R. Davies points out that the Neo-Babylonian-Persian period is "a time in which an identity 'Israel' could be absorbed by a population that also saw itself as 'Judah'" (*The Origins of Biblical Israel* [LHBOT 485: London: T&T Clark, 2007], 8).

25. "Regardless of the reason, it appears that the latter part of the fifth century saw a religious reaction to many of the practices of the people and serious attempts to restrict its social and commercial relations with those outside a very narrowly defined community" (Lester L. Grabbe, *Yehud: A History of the Persian Province of Judah* [vol.1 of *A History of the Jews and Judaism in the Second Temple Period*; LSTS 47; London: T&T Clark International, 2004], 357).

26. The two concepts of leadership are not mutually dependent. No interdependence is pointed out in the book of Judges.

tagonist of Judg 19 forces Israel to take a close look at the situation in the land and assume responsibility. The action of dismembering the body of the concubine and sending her body parts all over Israel refers to Saul (1 Sam 11:1–11) and thus, this message makes a claim for leadership and asks for support and loyalty. Nevertheless, the Levite does not assume the lead; he rejects the role his act asked for and leaves it to the community. Again, leadership is missing. In the following narrative, the tribes act collectively. Although they are able to find a solution and restore peace, the unity of Israel barely survives.

The time without leadership is shown in all its ambiguity. The ideal image of every tribe living peacefully in its own heritage with the community as a corrective to control undesirable developments is still visible but cannot be realized. During the time without a leader, the stories focus on the community but also on individual persons. Similar to the evaluation of the scheme and framework: "And the sons of Israel did evil in the eyes of YHWH" throughout the reign of the judges, the stories at the end of the book offer another evaluation: "a man did what was right in his own eyes" (Judg 17:6; 21:25). Such an individual evaluation and orientation is suspicious at best. This attitude is not consistent with the ideals found in other parts of the Bible.[27] In the book of Proverbs, for example, an individual evaluation is viewed quite critically (Prov 12:15; 21:2). In the context of cult and ritual acts, self-determined actions are also highly problematic (e.g., Deut 12:8). Thus, what is right is not an individual decision. The story of Micah (Judg 17–18) points out this problem and strengthens a sceptical approach. The individual appraisal of a situation leads to actions that do not produce predictable results. Best intentions are no guarantee for success if they lack a confirmed guideline.

THE JUDGES

The narratives of the individual judges portray heroes who, with God's help, rescue their people from the oppression of fierce enemies. Although the tribal origin of a judge is usually mentioned, his or her actions are not limited to one tribe but affect the whole of Israel.[28] Despite a repeated

---

27. See Yairah Amit, "Hidden Polemic in the Conquest of Dan: Judges XVII–XVIII," *VT* 40 (1990): 4–20 (6).

28. The local heroes they once might have been vanish, and they act as representatives of Israel.

frame and a similar scheme, the stories of the judges, with the exception of Othniel, unfold individually. Ehud is a cunning assassin who successfully murders the king of the enemies and afterwards leads Israel into a victorious battle. Deborah acts as a judge; she is responsible for the people and is portrayed as a savior. In addition, she adds prophetic-charismatic aspects to the more common, martial image of a judge, transposing the image of a judge from a military leader to a prophetic, charismatic, and strategic leader.

The appointment of Gideon emphasizes the contrast between his origin from one of the smallest families of Israel and his mission for all of Israel. He and subsequently also his warriors are selected, hand-picked by the deity, to save Israel. Only after the main victory is won does the story focus on single incidents and conflicts with other tribes and towns. The image of Gideon as a savior for Israel dissolves into local quarrels. Finally, the men of Israel strive for a unitary perspective once more as they offer to make Gideon their king. But he does not accept this new appointment over Israel; he still adheres to YHWH as the driving force behind his success. The double appointment of Gideon to lead Israel—once by YHWH and once by the men of Israel—already shows part of the dynamics of the entire book. The men of Israel are portrayed to have limited insight. Although they desperately want Israel to be a secure entity, they are not able to act in a way that accomplishes that desire. Their perspective of the situation falls short of the expectations of the narrator's voice. For the first time, the Gideon story raises two alternatives: God saves Israel or Israel saves itself (Judg 7:2).

God's refusal to appoint another judge is the starting point for the ensuing story of Jephthah. The uncertainty as to whether Jephthah is God's chosen judge remains open until the רוח יהוה "the spirit of YHWH" is mentioned in Judg 11:29. This is the first evidence given to the readers that God is with Jephthah, although he did not raise him; the elders of Gilead appoint Jephthah. Although they seek him out for their local problems, Jephthah approaches the conflict from a pan-Israelite perspective. He argues with the king of the Ammonites as a representative of Israel and negotiates in a conflict between Israel, as a historical unity, and Ammon (Judg 11:15–26). Further on in the story, this phenomenon of acting locally within an all-Israelite perspective is repeated as the sacrifice of Jephthah's daughter, a family affair, is embedded in the memory of Israel (Judg 11:40). But it is not only the border between local and pan-Israelite, private and public that starts shifting. With this judge, the problem of leadership on the whole becomes more urgent. Although Jephthah is a successful military leader and argues like a learned scholar of Torah in his negotiation with the king of Ammon, Israel's unity deteriorates. Jephthah is not accepted as a leader by all the tribes, and his leadership becomes the reason for a bloody battle between two tribes. Whether Jephthah has really been God's chosen leader is not revealed. He remains a highly successful, although tragic hero. With this undecided role, God's intervention and military success are no longer irrefragably connected.

The process of dissolution escalates in the Samson story. He is introduced as a promised child who grows up to become a man of superhuman strength. In several conflicts, he is superior to the Philistines and can only be overwhelmed by treachery. The national dimension of this leader and savior is only alluded to, whereas his personal skirmishes fill most of the narrative. The story of Samson not only individualizes the portrait of a savior but also exaggerates and ridicules it. With the last of the judges, the role of "God's tool for his people," the scheme designed for a judge, collapses. Simultaneously, the whole concept of leadership becomes questionable.[29]

In the perspective of the entire book, the success of the judges undergoes critical evaluation. In contrast to the stories of the preceding great leaders, Moses and Joshua, the judges are shown over a long period of time. As a result, even their great achievements are diminished. Considering the whole period, the reign of a single judge does not make a difference. Their great victories and battles are just minor events while the behavior of the people remains the same; they do evil in the eyes of YHWH. The introduction in Judg 2:11–19 in particular disempowers the judges and reduces the great heroes to God's tools without any lasting improvement. A framework connects these stories and, together with the stories of the minor judges, helps to construct the image of an era. From this point of view, the book of judges portrays the dissolution of everything achieved under Joshua. The retrospect challenges the continuity of the people and their relationship to YHWH. The question arises, which is a pressing one, whether anybody will be able to guide Israel.

---

29. J. Cheryl Exum interprets the dissolving of the well-established narrative elements as a sign that the "cyclical pattern of punishment and deliverance has exhausted itself" ("The Centre Cannot Hold: Thematic and Textual Instabilities in Judges," *CBQ* 52 [1990]: 410–43 [413]).

Looking for an ideal leader, the stories do not present an example but, nevertheless, offer elements of an ideal image. The necessary characteristics of a leader are: cunning, courage, far-sightedness, initiative, but also trust in God and the ability to interpret current situations in the light of Israel's history. Thus, it is the image of a savior who intervenes in times of danger. The different portrayals of the judges nonetheless reveal individual images. Although the stories include repetitions of some elements, this only emphasizes the impossibility of a pattern. For example, the concept that an experienced warrior takes the lead is successfully told in the Othniel story. But it is viewed critically in the story of Jephthah. Gideon, who is explicitly chosen by YHWH, becomes a successful leader, but the same strategy is highly problematic in the Samson story. In a similar way, the solidarity of the tribes extolled in the Song of Deborah is not success in Judg 20.

The judges remain unique figures. They are remembered as heroes who are part of Israel's history. Furthermore, they prove that YHWH is with Israel. Nevertheless, they offer no role model. The scheme and framework stress this aspect even more by pointing out that the judges fail to guarantee Israel's commitment to YHWH and his commandments. Their leadership lacks permanence.[30] In this way, the era of the judges is shown as an interim period. Simultaneously, this kind of leadership is challenged: a judge does not prove to be the ideal form of leadership.

No King in Israel

In the last chapters of the book of Judges, the absence of a king (אין מלך בישראל) is mentioned four times (Judg 17:6; 18:1; 19:1; 21:25). Whether there is "not yet" a king or "not one any longer" is not explained. Neither does this comment indicate clearly whether a king is considered a solution to the shown problems. If it really is a king this comment is hoping for, it has to be an ideal king fulfilling many expectations (Deut 17:14–20), like the (Deuteronomic) "ideal of the king as a holy warrior, executor of inter-tribal covenant loyalty, supreme patron of the cult and arbiter of convenant justice."[31] From the retrospective of postmonarchical times, the hope for restoration of an ideal kingdom might appear as a solution to contem-

---

30. The perspective of the scheme comes close to the retrospect in Neh 9:26–31.
31. Andrew D. H. Mayes, "Deuteronomistic Royal Ideology in Judges 17–21," *BibInt* 9 (2001): 241–58 (246).

porary problems. But the statement, "there was no king in Israel," can also be a genuine part of the distorted world depicted in these stories.[32] The twisted world with its figures is only described, without providing a guideline or secure point of view for the readers. The combination of different aspects, maybe different traditions, is used to portray an overall image of the situation and the era. The whole situation is presented as a world turned upside-down. But it is not shown unfavorably—traces of sympathy for the twisted world belong to the persuasive strategy of the narrations. In this way the narrated world is more understandable, so that the rejection of this world not only reaffirms the readers but challenges their own attitudes. However, the stories only work if they are told knowing that the readers are familiar with religious and social principles that enable them to review the stories critically. The stories themselves do not construct such principles; rather, they assume the audience already shares them.

A solution that might overcome the described shortcomings first of all points to the essential necessity of a guideline. Although Torah is not mentioned, the implementation of Torah, especially the Deuteronomistic laws, is the most probable answer to this question. As long as Torah is not known and obeyed by everyone, the chaotic situation will remain. Consequently, the question of legitimate leadership also has to be considered from this perspective. The king is not a reliable solution per se, but if a king is able to implement the cultic and ethical requirements of the law,[33] then a king offers a solution. In this role a king might become a guarantee of identity.[34]

Jotham's speech (Judg 9:7-20) with its metaphoric tale of the trees (vv. 8-15) offers another critical element in this discussion. It provides a clear warning of excessive expectations and the over-hasty appointment of a king. In the beginning of the story, a group of trees head out urgently looking for a king.[35] The story depicts four attempts to find a

---

32. See, for example, Yairah Amit: "The explicit, sympathetic position, that sees the monarchy as an overall solution, a kind of wonderdrug for all the ills of society, is part of a polemic" (*Hidden Polemics in Biblical Narrative* [trans. J. Chipman; Leiden: Brill, 2000], 102).

33. See Mayes, "Deuteronomistic royal ideology," 255.

34. This underlying expectation alludes to the images of the exemplary kings like Josiah (2 Kgs 22–23) or Hezekiah (2 Kgs 18–20).

35. The *figura etymologica* הלוך הלכו puts a special emphasis on the trees' action: "Absolutely determined, the trees went out to anoint a king over them." In this way, a special focus lies on the attitude of the trees that go out to select a king. The verb is

king. Each time the trees follow the same procedure; three times they even choose quite a similar kind of tree, namely a fruit tree. When the trees approach a possible candidate they do not ask whether this tree is willing to become king; rather, they demand it (vv. 8, 10, 12, 14). The replies of the fruit trees, however, do not provide a clear answer. They neither accept nor explicitly reject the offer of becoming king; instead, they challenge the proposal of the other trees, polemically revealing their request to be futile and counterproductive. The elements of the dialogue do not create successful communication. From the first attempts onwards, the attitude of the trees that try to appoint a king is called into question. Three times their concept of a king, the fertile fruit tree, is ridiculed and compared to an aimlessly swaying tree.[36] Only in the last, seemingly senseless (or even self-destructive) approach to the thorn tree[37] does the candidate himself offer an appropriate concept. This metaphorical tale does not focus primarily on the concept of a king; rather, the attitude of those who offer the position of a king to other trees is the decisive element. With this focus, the story transgresses the world of the trees and addresses its audience. Similar to other stories, like the song of the vineyard (Isa 5) or Nathan's parable (2 Sam 12:1–4), Jotham uses the elements of a metaphorical tale for rhetoric purposes. In this way, the audience first adopts a neutral attitude as they follow the trees' dialogue. With the answer of the thorn tree, however, they are implicitly called on to act as judges and to decide whether the trees have acted באמת or not (v. 15). In retrospect, Jotham's metaphoric narration appears like a prophetic oracle, sketching a gloomy future.[38] Jotham's speech thus criticizes and foretells the consequences of the (wrong-) doing of the inhabitants of Shechem.[39] The concept of a king, however, is not rejected as a whole even though the dialogue of the trees

---

used to express the idea of "trembling or shaking with fear" or "straying or roaming without a destination" (Jer 14:10; Ps 59:16; Gen 4:14) like a drunk or blind person (Isa 24:20; [EV 29:9]; Ps 107:27); and "swaying like trees in the wind" (Isa 7:2). Thus, it is not a planned, controlled action but a reaction to some (uncontrollable) force.

36. The verb נוע refers to an uncontrolled or aimless movement that is in no way acceptable or even desirable, especially for a king.

37. The אטד is a thorn tree, Zizyphus spina Christi, rather than a thorn-bush, as noted by Silviu Tatu, "Jotham's Fable and the Crux Interpretum in Judges IX," VT 56 (2006): 105–24.

38. See 2 Sam 12:9; 1 Sam 13:13; 28:16, 18; 2 Kgs 1:3; Amos 4:1.

39. Karin Schöpflin, "Jotham's Speech and Fable as Prophetic Comment on Abimelech's Story: The Genesis of Judges 9," SJOT 18 (2004): 3–22 (11).

utters a severe warning: if it should (ever) succeed, it has to be approached with the utmost caution.

Still Looking for Ideal Leadership?

In the early fifth century B.C.E., attempts to reestablish a Davidic kingdom were rejected, and Cyrus was proclaimed messianic ruler of Israel (Isa 44:24–45:7).[40] However, this enthusiastic perspective does not offer a satisfactory solution on its own to the urgent questions of leadership and guiding principles in Israel. Furthermore, a transition from Israel's great past, the memories of an independent monarchy, to the present situation that integrates Israel into the Persian Empire has to be justified. In the book of Judges the literary device of periodization is used as a tool for reconstructing the past.[41] The final concept of this book portrays an era without a leader that is interrupted but not changed by a succession of judges. In this way, the urgency of a fundamental change is emphasized. Stories of trial and error offer an image of an era that barely succeeds in establishing Israel in the land.

The period of judges cannot serve as an example; rather, it shows possible dead ends. The fascination and admiration the great heroes evoke is a necessary part of the narrative strategy. The achievements are neither ignored nor denied, but they are put into perspective. In this way they can be kept in memory, but they no longer offer a role model. The challenge to find a better way to establish Israel is continued. With the critical view of the judges as leaders and a restrained and guarded view of kingship, this perspective does not easily embrace single rulers but rather, asks for a different basis of leadership. In the middle of a hoped-for future is Israel as a community of tribes living on its own land. But the future of Israel is not necessarily combined with the hope for a state of Israel.[42] Thus, the

---

40. Achenbach, "Pentateuch," 280.

41. Sara Japhet, "Periodization between History and Ideology II: Chronology and Ideology in Ezra-Nehemiah," in *Judah and the Judeans in the Persian Period* (ed. Oded Lipschits and Manfred Oeming; Winona Lake, Ind.: Eisenbrauns, 2006), 491–508 (505). Guillaume points out convincingly that the chronological place in the premonarchical period the book of Judges received is the invention of a late editing, probably the third century B.C.E. (*Josiah*, 251–52).

42. E. Axel Knauf, "Bethel: The Israelite Impact on Judean Language and Literature," in *Judah and the Judeans in the Persian Period* (ed. Oded Lipschits and Manfred Oeming; Winona Lake, Ind.: Eisenbrauns, 2006), 291–349 (320–21).

perspective of this book encourages a critical view not only of the era of the judges but also of the concepts of leadership in the book of Joshua and even more in the books of Samuel and Kings. Besides appointed governors, there is no room for great leaders in Israel during the Persian period.[43] In this regard, the book of Judges is a reflection of and a warning for its own time. As in the time of Nehemiah, cultic regulations did not exist in the book of Judges and the relations between the people in Yehud and their brothers in the north were problematic.[44]

The book of Judges offers a reserved view of both concepts: neither a leader nor the people on their own are presented as an ideal state of affairs. Still, the book makes it clear that a guideline is missing. The judges do not instruct the people (with the exception of Deborah), and the people, although they take the lead, have no authoritative foundation.[45] Reconstructing life in Judah following the guidelines of Deuteronomy, as is the aim in the books of Ezra-Nehemiah, is explicitly absent in the book of Judges.[46] Thus, the necessity to provide access to divine instructions and teachings is even more emphasized.[47]

The need for a written tradition became urgent during the Persian period, when "Judah was no longer a nation but functioned as a small distant province with the Persian Empire."[48] Although loyal to the Persian rulers, the colonial Judean society was developing a national ideology. In this process, the written form of the traditions that had been the repository

---

43. Ehud Ben Zvi, "What Is New in Yehud? Some Considerations," in *Yahwism after the Exile: Perspectives on Israelite Religion in the Persian Era* (ed. Rainer Albertz and Bob Becking; STAR 5; Assen: Royal Van Gorcum, 2003), 32–48 (41).

44. Achenbach, "Pentateuch," 255.

45. There is no memory of the giving of Torah as in Neh 9:13–15.

46. See Tamara C. Eskenazi, "The Missions of Ezra and Nehemiah," in *Judah and the Judeans in the Persian Period* (ed. Oded Lipschits and Manfred Oeming; Winona Lake, Ind.: Eisenbrauns, 2006), 509–29 (526).

47. Ben Zvi points out that an implicit concept of "weakening of generations" is perceptible in the discursive marginalisation of the writers and contemporary readers in the literature of Yehud. "The implications of this concept … strengthened the position of the later generations of literati." Only their literature carries the divine teachings and only they have access to these written texts ("New in Yehud," 41). The concept of "weakening of generations" can also be observed in Judges. The examples of capable leaders, successful communities or tribes disappear more and more, thus emphasizing the necessity of such literati.

48. Grabbe, *History*, 342.

of collective memory now became an important part of identity.[49] Access to these traditions and with it, to the divine knowledge found in the texts, lies in the hands of a scribal class. Only these literati are able to read and (re)write the texts and to pass them on.[50] The answer to the search for leadership does not lie in a monarch but rather, in the (cultic and social) law.[51] A leader who is able to personify these ideals would probably also be a man like Ezra: "skilled in the Torah of Moses that YHWH the God of Israel had given" (Ezra 7:6).[52] Nevertheless, it is not necessarily a leader Judges is hoping for but rather, the spreading of guidelines enabling the people to do what is right in the eyes of YHWH.

The book of Judges presents a very critical as well as a highly reflective retrospective view. It (re)constructs a glorious history but it also is aware that these memories offer no solution for current challenges. The time of the great charismatic leaders, chosen by God, is over and, simultaneously, people without guidance are endangered. Thus, the book offers a tradition that is aware of the need for change, but it does not anticipate a totally new beginning. Altogether, it is an inclusive point of view that embraces all of Israel in its memory, in order to (re)construct Israel. It reassures those who already know what is right and what is wrong and shows them different examples, thereby urging them to remember their past and at the same time to rise to the challenge to reinvent Israel.

---

49. Grabbe, *History*, 342.

50. Ben Zvi, "New in Yehud," 41–42.

51. See Philip R. Davies, *Scribes and Schools: The Canonization of the Hebrew Scriptures* (Library of Ancient Israel; Louisville: John Knox, 1998), 69.

52. The aim of Ezra is "to observe and to teach statute and custom in Israel" (Ezra 7:10). So Gary N. Knoppers, "Ethnicity, Genealogy, Geography, and Change: The Judean Communities of Babylon and Jerusalem in the Story of Ezra," in *Community Identity in Judean Historiography: Biblical and Comparative Perspectives* (ed. Gary N. Knoppers and Kenneth A. Ristau; Winona Lake, Ind.: Eisenbrauns, 2009), 142–72 (159).

1–2 Samuel and Jewish *Paideia* in the Persian and Hellenistic Periods

Thomas M. Bolin

To arrive at an answer to the question of who read 1–2 Samuel in the Persian and Hellenistic periods and what they saw as authoritative or important about these texts, we will be required to explore the social and cultural contexts of Israelite literacy and education in the fifth–third centuries B.C.E.[1] This will require recourse to archaeological and literary support for an elite class of readers in Persian and Hellenistic Palestine in order to clarify the social and institutional contexts of any potential readers of 1–2 Samuel. Our task is made more difficult, however, by the fact that, when looking for examples in surviving Persian and Hellenistic texts for how 1–2 Samuel was read, one is hard pressed to find evidence that very many people were reading it at all. Thus, we will also have to look for examples of how similar texts in similar cultural milieux were read, in order to allow construction of an analogous and hopefully plausible scenario for the reading 1–2 Samuel. This requires a brief but important examination of education in the ancient Levant, since being taught the nuts and bolts of how to read presupposes written material that is determined to be worth reading. In other words, learning "how to read" implies

---

1. For another recent attempt to answer this question, see Diana Edelman, "Did Saulide-Davidic Rivalry Resurface in Early Persian Yehud?" in *The Land That I Will Show You: Essays on the History and Archaeology of the Ancient Near East in Honor of J. Maxwell Miller* (ed. Andrew Dearman and Patrick Graham; JSOTSup 343; Sheffield: Sheffield Academic Press, 2001), 70–92. Robert Rezetko deals more with the redactional history of the text rather than how it would have been read ("What Happened to the Book of Samuel in the Persian Period and Beyond?" in *A Palimpsest: Rhetoric, Ideology, Stylistics, and Language Relating to Persian Israel* [ed. Ehud Ben Zvi and Diana Edelman; Piscataway, N.J.: Gorgias, 2009], 237–52).

much more than technical skill; it assumes an orientation into a literary and interpretive tradition in which "reading" means also "what to read" and "how to read it." After this investigation into ancient Near Eastern and Hellenistic pedagogies, it will remain to determine what kinds of educational processes and reading strategies would have been in use by postexilic readers of 1–2 Samuel. I am aware that these are well-plowed fields in biblical scholarship. However, I am equally mindful of S. Niditch's justified criticism of the scholarly reconstructions of the composition and redaction of the Bible which, as she rightly points out, fail to "describe the nitty-gritty world in which the collecting, copying, and incorporating takes place."[2] Thus, in order to get at "the nitty-gritty world" of postexilic readers in Yehud, it is necessary to go over these preliminary questions. By doing so, I hope to show that 1–2 Samuel played a role in the educational practice of Yehud in which the Jerusalem elites reading 1–2 Samuel were taught culturally normed interpretations intended to shape their own behavior and attitudes.

Archaeological Evidence for Elites in Yehud

For the past twenty years, the Persian period has been seen as a time for a great deal of literary activity in Yehud, and many scholars speak of the presence of intellectuals or literati in Persian Yehud as if this were a given.[3] However, some have argued that the archaeological data, including settlement numbers, site size, and distribution are such that there simply were not enough people and resources to support the kind of elite culture needed

---

2. Susan Niditch, *Oral World and Written Word: Ancient Israelite Literature* (Louisville: Westminster, 1996), 115.

3. E.g., Giovanni Garbini, "Hebrew Literature in the Persian Period," in *Second Temple Studies: 2. Temple Community in the Persian Period* (ed. Tamara C. Eskenazi and Kent H. Richards; JSOTSup 175; Sheffield: Sheffield Academic Press, 1994), 180–88; Philip R. Davies, *Scribes and Schools: The Canonization of the Hebrew Scriptures* (Louisville: John Knox, 1998), 65; Ehud Ben Zvi, *Signs of Jonah: Reading and Rereading in Ancient Yehud* (JSOTSup 367; Sheffield: Sheffield Academic Press, 2003); Ehud Ben Zvi, "Imagining Josiah's Book and the Implications of Imagining It in Early Persian Yehud," in *Berührungspunkte: Studien zur Sozial- und Religionsgeschichte Israels und seiner Umwelt. Festschrift für Rainer Albertz zu seinem 65. Geburtstag* (ed. Ingo Kottsieper, Rüdiger Schmitt, and Jakob Wöhrle; AOAT 350; Münster: Ugarit Verlag, 2008), 193–212.

to create and preserve literature.⁴ It is worth taking a little time to examine this issue. Regarding Jerusalem specifically, I. Finkelstein has argued that in the Persian period, Jerusalem was at best a "small community of several hundred inhabitants ... (that is, not many more than 100 adult men), with a depleted hinterland and no economic base."⁵ This estimate is a good deal lower than other recent investigations that place Jerusalem's population at circa 1,200–1,500 in the Persian period.⁶ However, there are some good reasons to believe that the extant Persian-period remains are not representative of Yehud's actual situation at that time, which casts doubt on Finkelstein's low population estimates. Many of the larger building projects from the late Hellenistic and Roman periods were sunk onto bedrock and would have destroyed any traces of prior occupation. In this regard, and in response to Finkelstein, O. Lipschits has provided a cogent argument for this being the case in Jerusalem, going on to argue that a narrow strip running ca. 350 meters along the ridge of the City of David

---

4. E.g., Niels Peter Lemche, "The Old Testament—A Hellenistic Book?" *SJOT* 7 (1993): 163–93; cf. Kenneth G. Hoglund, *Achaemenid Imperial Administration in Syria-Palestine and the Missions of Ezra and Nehemiah* (SBLDS 125; Atlanta: Scholars Press, 1992), 165–205. See other discussion in John Kessler, "Diaspora and Homeland in the Early Achaemenid Period: Community, Geography and Demography in Zechariah 1–8," in *Approaching Yehud: New Approaches to the Study of the Persian Period* (ed. Jon Berquist; Atlanta: Society of Biblical Literature, 2007), 137–66. According to Charles Carter's analysis, only Jerusalem, Ramat Raḥel and Mizpah were walled in the Persian period, and the entire province was smaller and poorer than it had been before the Babylonian invasion. Nevertheless, he maintains the possibility of texts being written and preserved during this time (*The Emergence of Yehud in the Persian Period: A Social and Demographic Study* [JSOTSup 294; Sheffield: Sheffield Academic Press, 1999], 215–47).

5. Israel Finkelstein, "Jerusalem in the Persian (and Early Hellenistic) Period and the Wall of Nehemiah," *JSOT* 32 (2008): 501–20 (510).

6. "The population of Jerusalem in the Persian II period was between 1250 and 1500, or between 6.0 and 7.3 per cent of the population of Yehud" (Carter, *Emergence of Yehud*, 20); compare Oded Lipschits: "The settled area of Jerusalem during the Persian period included the 28–30 dunams of the City of David plus the 20 dunams of the Ophel, which altogether amounts to about 50 dunams.... Calculating the population of Jerusalem according to the lower coefficient of 20 people per one built-up dunam brings the population estimate to about 1,000 people; and according to the higher coefficient of 25 people per one built-up dunam to about 1,250 people" ("Persian Period Finds from Jerusalem: Facts and Interpretations," *JHS* 9 [2009]: article 20; available online at http://www.jhsonline.org/Articles/article_122.pdf and in *Perspectives in Hebrew Scriptures VI: Comprising the Contents of Journal of Hebrew Scriptures, vol. 9* (ed. Ehud Ben Zvi; Piscataway, N.J.: Gorgias, 2010), 423–53.

was occupied during the Persian period, with inhabitants also occupying the Ophel just south of the Temple Mount.[7] The possibility that significant Persian and early Hellenistic remains were present in Yehud and were either destroyed or might lie as yet unexcavated is supported by the recent discovery of a massive early Hellenistic administrative building and residence erected over a similar Persian-period structure in Kedesh just north of Hazor. Over 2,000 square meters in area, this Hellenistic building contained dining facilities, a bath, a large storeroom, and an archive where over two thousand bullae were found.[8]

---

7. "However, this scarcity of building remains from the Persian period does not fully reflect the actual, admittedly poor, situation at that time … the Persian and early Hellenistic period occupation levels were severely damaged by intensive building activities conducted in the late Hellenistic, Roman, Byzantine, and even later periods.… It seems to me that the main destructive force in Jerusalem was the efforts, along many different periods, to build new structures and the need to clear the debris from earlier periods. Additionally, the topographical nature of the Southwestern Hill, which is very steep and narrow at the top, requires that buildings, especially the more prominent ones, be built on bedrock.… The Persian period in Jerusalem did not end suddenly with a violent destruction. One can assume that had this not been the case, we could have detected many more finds in the destruction level. However, when archaeologists are dealing with a period that ended in a long transition bridging the Persian and Hellenistic periods (the 4th and 3rd centuries B.C.E.), and adding the nature of this calm end to the nature of the poor and small settlement throughout the 6th to 3rd centuries B.C.E., and the nature of the later periods (late Hellenistic, Roman and Byzantine) characterized by huge building projects founded on the bedrock, we have a reasonable explanation for the absence of Persian period building remains in Jerusalem without taking this absence as a proof for the actual situation in the city throughout this period" (Lipschits, "Persian Period Finds," 5, 8–9).

8. See the detailed preliminary report in Sharon C. Herbert and Andrea M. Berlin, "A New Administrative Center for Persian and Hellenistic Galilee: Preliminary Report of the University of Michigan/University of Minnesota Excavations at Kedesh," *BASOR* 329 (2003): 13–59. See also the critique of Finkelstein's low estimates of Persian-period settlements in Ziony Zevit, "Is There an Archaeological Case for Phantom Settlements in the Persian Period?" *PEQ* 141 (2009): 124–37. Most recently, Finkelstein has acknowledged that more evidence for Persian-period Jerusalem most likely lies underneath the Temple Mount (Israel Finkelstein, Ido Koch, and Oded Lipschits, "The Mound on the Mount: A Possible Solution to the 'Problem with Jerusalem,'" *JHS* 11 [2011]: article 12 available online at http://www.jhsonline.org/Articles/article_159.pdf and in *Perspectives in Hebrew Scriptures VIII: Comprising the Contents of Journal of Hebrew Scriptures, vol. 11* [ed. Ehud Ben Zvi; Piscataway, N.J.: Gorgias, 2012], 317–39).

Other archaeological evidence, albeit of a modest nature, attests to the presence of elites in Persian and early Hellenistic Yehud. Persian period winepresses and grain storage facilities have been discovered at Khirbet er-Ras immediately southwest of Jerusalem, along with a number of other farming settlements immediately on the city's outskirts, which could have provided crops for the city's elites.[9] Imported pottery and a modest amount of coins have been found in and around Jerusalem, and at Jericho, 'Ein Gedi, Beth Zur, Ramat Raḥel, and Gezer.[10] By the mid-third century B.C.E., witnessed in both the archaeological record and Zenon papyri, there is evidence in Yehud for widespread organization and stability, efficient bureaucracy and security, greater use of money, and technological advancements in agriculture increasing both yields and crop specialization.[11] The modest evidence of luxury items in Yehud during both the Persian and early Hellenistic periods, combined with a plausible explanation for the absence of substantial architectural remains, allow for the assumption that the levels of urbanization[12] and economic prosperity meet the

---

9. Carter, *Emergence of Yehud*, 250.

10. Carter, *Emergence of Yehud*, 256–57. He singles out "the correlation of the pottery and material culture with the major centers of commerce" (257). Elsewhere, he states: "Trade with Greece, Egypt and Persia led not only to the exchange of goods but also to a lively local market in which imitations of foreign goods were produced. These goods—both foreign and domestic produced—are typically found in major market centers and within the context of a social elite" (285). On the question of international trade in Persian-period Jerusalem, see Diana Edelman, "Tyrian Trade in Yehud under Artaxerxes I: Real or Fictional? Independent or Crown Endorsed?" in *Judah and the Judeans in the Persian Period* (ed. Oded Lipschits and Manfred Oeming; Winona Lake, Ind.: Eisenbrauns, 2006), 207–46; and Benjamin J. Noonan, "Did Nehemiah Own Tyrian Goods? Trade Between Judea and Phoenicia during the Achaemenid Period," *JBL* 130 (2011): 281–98.

11. Rami Arav, *Hellenistic Palestine: Settlement Patterns and City Planning, 337–31 B.C.E.* (British Archaeological Reports International Series 485; Oxford: B.A.R., 1989), 127–33; Arav notes the presence of olive and grape presses even at small farms. Hans-Peter Kuhnen discusses the legal changes in the Hellenistic period changes that helped in the creation of large plantation farms ("Israel unmittelbar vor und nach Alexander dem Grossen," in *Die Griechen und das Antike Israel: interdisciplinäre Studien zur Religions-und Kulturgeschichte des Heiligen Landes* [ed. Stefan Alkier and Markus Witte; OBO 201; Fribourg: University Press, 2004], 1–27). One is also reminded of the statement in Neh 11:1 that only one-tenth of the *gōlâ* community moved into Jerusalem, while the remainder resided in neighboring cities (note the text's use of עָרִים).

12. On the necessary correlation between urbanization and the presence of literacy, see David Jamieson-Drake, *Scribes and Schools in Monarchic Judah: A Socio-*

minimum threshold required to support an elite class that would produce and read literary texts.[13]

Education of Elites in Yehud

Moving from the question of whether there would have been literate elites in Yehud, one must next deal with the issue of what kind of education would have been given to them. Although there has been a great deal of scholarly attention focused on writing and literacy in Iron Age Israel,[14] less

---

archeological Approach (JSOTSup 109; Sheffield: Sheffield Academic Press, 1991), 32–37; and William V. Harris, *Ancient Literacy* (Cambridge: Harvard University Press, 1989), 17–20. Arav's observation is perhaps significant: "An examination of the density of Hellenized cities in Palestine reveals that Palestine had more Hellenized cities per square km. than any other province outside Greece" (*Hellenistic Palestine*, 119). According to his analysis, Palestine averaged one city per 1,200 km², followed by northern Syria at one city per 3,150 km². Arav attributes the high number of cities in Palestine to the geographical and topographical variety of the region.

13. So Carter: "This question is really one of the size and nature of urban elites. In agrarian societies urban communities accounted for a relatively small proportion of the total population, usually less than 10 per cent, but were responsible for a wide variety of social, political and religious functions. In such urban communities craft specialization is ubiquitous; elites with different functions concentrated in these communities, supported in large measure by extracting surplus from agrarian peasants in the surrounding villages.... The population of Jerusalem in the Persian II period was between 1250 and 1500, or between 6.0 and 7.3 per cent of the population of Yehud; these figures are well within the 5 to 10 per cent average of urban centers in the preindustrial age. Thus, based on historical and sociological parallels cited here, the level of literary creativity traditionally attributed to the Persian period need not be questioned on the grounds either of a small province or a small Jerusalem" (*Emergence of Yehud*, 287–88). In his study of Greek literacy, Harris notes with reference specifically to the cities of Astypalaea and Mycalessus that "towns do not necessarily have to be large to encourage literacy" (*Ancient Literacy*, 65; cf. 49–50). Davies asserts that, because of Persian efforts to create wealth in Yehud, "the class of wealthy, relatively leisured people grew—literate, cosmopolitan and demanding education. The scribal class had no more monopoly of learning" (*Scribes and Schools*, 68). His view merits cautious acceptance, albeit while avoiding the danger of anachronistically envisioning these ancient Jewish elites as similar to their modern counterparts.

14. E.g., André Lemaire, *Les Écoles et la Formation de la Bible dans l'Ancien Israël* (OBO 39; Fribourg: University Press, 1981); Menahem Haran, "On the Diffusion of Literacy and Schools in Ancient Israel," in *Congress Volume: Jerusalem, 1986* (ed. John A. Emerton; VTSup 40; Leiden: Brill, 1988), 81–95; Graham I. Davies, "Were There Schools in Ancient Israel?" in *Wisdom in Ancient Israel: Essays in Honour of*

attention has been devoted to the phenomenon in the Persian and early Hellenistic periods. David Carr's monograph on the subject does much to rectify this situation.[15] Drawing on Greek pedagogical traditions and contemporaneous evidence from Egypt, Carr argues persuasively for an educational model in the fifth-third centuries whose purpose was to socialize and enculturate elite males into a world where their piety and behavior were modelled on a set of narratives that were eventually to become canonical. Carr's study reminds us of a significant point brought to light by recent examinations of education and literacy, namely, that there is an important distinction to be made between the purpose of education in Egypt and Mesopotamia, on the one hand, and Greece and Western Asia Minor, on the other.[16] In the older Near Eastern cultures, educational training was the domain mainly of palace or temple personnel. The purpose of education was to enable the student to master a set "canon" of normative texts, be they prayers, omens, or mythologies, and to use this knowledge in the ongoing service to both the king and the gods.[17] While character formation was a significant part of this educational process, the character to be cultivated was that of an industrious and loyal functionary for the palace or temple. In the Aegean, on the other hand, literacy was

---

J. A. Emerton (ed. John Day; Robert P. Gordon, and Hugh G. M. Williamson; Cambridge: Cambridge University Press, 1995), 199–211; James L. Crenshaw, *Education in Ancient Israel: Across the Deadening Silence* (New York: Doubleday, 1998); Ian Young, "Israelite Literacy: Interpreting the Evidence," *VT* 48 (1998): 239–53, 408–22; Michael D. Coogan, "Literacy and the Formation of Biblical Literature," in *Essays in Archaeology and Biblical Interpretation in Honor of Edward F. Campbell, Jr. at his Retirement* (ed. Prescott H. Williams and Theodore Hiebert; Scholars Press Homage Series 23; Atlanta: Scholars Press, 1999), 47–61; Ron E. Tappy et al., "An Abecedary of the Mid-Tenth Century B.C.E. from the Judaean Shephelah," *BASOR* 344 (2006): 5–46; Ryan Byrne, "The Refuge of Scribalism in Iron I Palestine," *BASOR* 345 (2007): 1–31; Christopher A. Rollston, *Writing and Literacy in the World of Ancient Israel: Epigraphic Evidence from the Iron Age* (Archaeology and Biblical Studies 11; Atlanta: Society of Biblical Literature, 2010). For the debate among scholars of classical Greece on exactly this question, despite the much greater amount of archaeological and literary data, see Harris, *Ancient Literacy*, 94 n. 134.

15. *Writing on the Tablet of the Heart: Origins of Scripture and Literature* (New York: Oxford University Press, 2005); see also Karel van der Toorn, *Scribal Culture and the Making of the Hebrew Bible* (Cambridge: Harvard University Press, 2007), 75–108.

16. John Baines, "Literacy and Ancient Egyptian Society," *Man* 18 (1983): 572–99; Harris, *Ancient Literacy*, 7; Carr, *Writing on Heart*, 108.

17. Description in van der Toorn, *Scribal Culture*, 51–74.

not exclusively for the practical purposes of political or cultic functionaries; rather, it helped train the next generation of elite males in the cultural norms of their forefathers.[18]

In looking at the educational influences in postexilic Yehud, Persian exemplars are logical candidates. Unfortunately, very little is known about Persian education, and what evidence there is must be inferred from written remains or comes from Greek writers whose motives and biases are difficult to distinguish from any factual information they may preserve.

Extant Persian texts point to an administrative class of scribes in the service of the crown in a manner consistent with centuries of Mesopotamian practice. From the Behistun inscription and the Fortification and Treasury texts from Persepolis, it is clear that Achaemenid scribes were trained to use cuneiform, which they used to write texts in Akkadian, Elamite, and Old Persian. They also made extensive use of Aramaic, and the presence of a single Fortification tablet in Greek (Fort. 1771) allows for the possibility that some Persian scribes were trained in that language as well.

Among the Greek descriptions of Persian education, Herodotus states that the boys of Persian elite families were educated only in hunting, archery and "truth-telling" (ἀληθίζεσθαι).[19] This is also stated by Xenophon in his well-known account of Persian education in Book 1 the *Cyropaedia*. Echoing Herodotus, Xenophon notes that the education of elite Persian males focuses mainly on hunting and warfare but also includes training in "justice" (δικαιοσύνην) and "self-control" (σωφροσύνην).[20] By "justice"

---

18. Harris, *Ancient Literacy*, 59–61. "The results of the new education were complex; they included, for instance, the paradoxical entrenchment in the minds of many ordinary Greeks of the heroic, militaristic and religious ideals of the *Iliad* and the *Odyssey*" (61). While Harris's observation concerns Greece in the fifth century, this pedagogical goal does not change in the Hellenistic period; if anything, it becomes more pronounced. This is not to say that there was no scribal class at all in Greece, particularly during the archaic period (Rosalind Thomas, *Literacy and Orality in Ancient Greece* [Cambridge: Cambridge University Press, 1992], 70).

19. παιδεύουσι δὲ τοὺς παῖδας ἀπὸ πενταέτεος ἀρξάμενοι μέχρι εἰκοσαέτεος τρία μοῦνα, ἱχνεύειν καὶ τοξεύειν καὶ ἀληθίζεσθαι (*Hist.* 1.136) = "They teach the boys, beginning at age five until the age of twenty, only three things: to ride, to shoot the bow, and to tell the truth."

20. οἱ μὲν δὴ παῖδες εἰς τὰ διδασκαλεῖα φοιτῶντες διάγουσι μανθάνοντες δικαιοσύνην … διδάσκουσι δὲ τοὺς παῖδας καὶ σωφροσύνην (*Cyr.* 1.2.6-8) = "The boys go to school and spend their time learning justice.... They also teach the boys self-control."

Xenophon envisions the ability to judge legal cases, as he goes on to state that the boys practice accusing one another and trying cases. This is as important, he notes, as the learning of literacy is in Greek education.[21]

The remaining description of Persian education in Greek literature comes some centuries later from Strabo, who is clearly aware of the accounts in both Herodotus and Xenophon, noting the emphasis in Persian education on riding, warfare, and justice. However, Strabo adds to this the statement that the young men are also taught the deeds of both gods and virtuous men by means of fables, either sung or recited.[22] This resembles the use of Homer in Greek education (discussed below) and should perhaps be taken with a grain of salt, as must Xenophon's description of Persian education, which is clearly influenced by Spartan pedagogy, which he greatly admired. Moreover, given Strabo's distance of more than three centuries from the Achaemenid kingdom and his evident reliance upon both Herodotus and Xenophon, his description of Persian boys learning the tales of gods and heroes is also most likely a projection of Greek pedagogy. The most we can say about Persian education is that it appears to have been indebted to the ancient Near Eastern scribal model.[23]

Before looking at Greek pedagogy, we must first ask how much Greek influence we may assume in Yehud during the late fifth to early fourth centuries B.C.E. Although ceramic finds show evidence of Greek imports, most notably the presence of Attic ware in several sites in the coastal areas, it is rash to claim, with E. Stern, that these finds demonstrate that, "about two hundred years before its actual conquest by Alexander's armies, Pal-

---

21. ὥσπερ παρ' ἡμῖν ὅτι γράμματα μαθησόμενοι (*Cyr.* 1.2.6) = "Just as our [boys] learn letters."

22. Ἀπὸ δὲ πέντε ἐτῶν ἕως τετάρτου καὶ εἰκοστοῦ παιδεύονται τοξεύειν καὶ ἀκοντίζειν καὶ ἱππάζεσθαι καὶ ἀληθεύειν, διδασκάλοις τε λόγων τοῖς σωφρονεστάτοις χρῶνται, οἳ καὶ τὸ μυθῶδες πρὸς τὸ συμφέρον ἀνάγοντες παραπλέκουσι, καὶ μέλους χωρὶς καὶ μετ' ᾠδῆς ἔργα θεῶν τε καὶ ἀνδρῶν τῶν ἀρίστων ἀναδιδόντες (*Geogr.* 15.3.18) = "From the ages of five to twenty-four they are taught to shoot the bow, throw the javelin, ride, and to speak the truth. They have very clever teachers who lecture, weaving myths and songs into their collected recitations—both with and without music—of the deeds of gods and of the best men."

23. Pierre Briant goes further in maintaining that elite youths in the Achaemenid period were taught "the oral traditions of their people" (*From Cyrus to Alexander: A History of the Persian Empire* [trans. P. T. Daniels; Winona Lake, Ind.: Eisenbrauns, 2002], 330).

estine was already under strong, direct Greek influence."[24] It makes too much of the evidence. Other scholars acknowledge a more modest Greek influence[25] based on numismatic rather than ceramic grounds, relying on the presence of both Greek coins and local coinage modelled on Greek exemplars dating from the early fifth century B.C.E. onward.[26] By the fourth century, local coinage with the Athenian owl can be found in Yehud[27] and, although evidence seems to point to the widespread presence of a money-based economy only under the Ptolemies, these coins attest to some contact with Greece as well as emulation of Greek cultural institutions by means of iconographic borrowing.[28] We may conclude, then, that there was some awareness of Greek culture in late fifth century Yehud, and as I will argue below, these archaeological data are supported by the portrayal of elites in Ezra-Nehemiah.

---

24. Ephraim Stern, *Archaeology of the Land of the Bible: The Assyrian, Babylonian and Persian Periods, 732-332 BCE* (ABRL; New York: Doubleday, 2001), 436–41, 518–19, 522. More cautious and methodologically sound are Jane Waldbaum's observations that the quantity of imported pottery as an absolute value is not as important as its relative value next to the quantity of local pottery, and that local pottery value is often underestimated, because the foreign ware is more thoroughly counted ("Greeks *in* the East or Greeks *and* the East? Problems in the Definition and Recognition of Presence," *BASOR* 305 [1997]: 1–17). For an inventory of Attic pottery in Palestine, see Robert Wenning, "Nachweis der attischen Keramik aus Palästina Aktualisierter Zwischenbericht," in *Die Griechen und das Antike Israel: Interdisziplinäre Studien zur Religions- und Kulturgeschichte des Heiligen Landes* (ed. Stefan Alkier and Markus Witte; OBO 201; Fribourg: University Press, 2004), 61–72.

25. E.g., Anselm C. Hagerdorn, "'Who Would Invite a Stranger from Abroad?' The Presence of Greeks in Palestine in Old Testament Times," in *The Old Testament in Its World* (ed. Robert P. Gordon and Johannes C. de Moor; OtSt 52; Leiden: Brill, 2005), 68–93; and Wenning, "Griechischer Einfluss," 29–60.

26. E.g., the Greek tetradrachma dated 450 B.C.E. found at Beth Zur (Stern, *Archaeology of Bible*, 437).

27. For a discussion of the numismatic evidence, see Leo Mildenburg, "Yehud: A Preliminary Study of the Provincial Coinage of Judea," in *Greek Numismatics and Archaeology: Essays in Honor of Margaret Thompson* (ed. Otto Mørkholm and Nancy M. Waggoner; Wetteren: Cultura, 1979), 183–96; Yaakov Meshorer, *Ancient Jewish Coinage* (2 vols.; Dix Hills, NY: Amphora, 1982), vol. 1; John Wilson Betlyon, "The Provincial Government of Persian Period Judah and the Yehud Coins," *JBL* 105 (1986): 633–42; and Carter, *Emergence of Yehud*, 259–81.

28. So Carter, *Emergence of Yehud*, 267–77; compare with Betylon's more expansive claim that "[t]he coin types reflect extensive interchange with the Greeks" ("Provincial Government," 641).

Like its ancient Near Eastern counterparts—but with different aims in mind—Greek pedagogy utilized the memorization of authoritative works that Carr designates "long duration texts,"[29] with the Homeric epics being preeminent.[30] By way of example, Xenophon has a character in one of his dialogues remark that when he was a boy, his father, "concerned that I become a good man, forced me to learn all of Homer; I am even now able to recite the entire *Iliad* and *Odyssey*."[31] Similarly, Plato has Protagoras tell Socrates that "the greatest part of a man's education is to be skilled in poetry."[32] In this understanding, literature is used to help form the habits and characters of young men, mainly through the process of μίμησις— imitation both of the qualities of the characters in the texts and of the language of the text itself.[33] Plato critiques this standard view of a "proper education" (τοὺς ὀρθῶς παιδευομένους) that required boys to become "much listened and much learned" in the poets (πολυηκόους … πολυμαθεῖς) on the assumption that their ability to memorize these works in their entirety would make them grow up to be good and wise.[34]

---

29. *Writing on the Tablet of the Heart*, 19.

30. Harris notes that the Homeric texts are an essential part of Greek education beginning in the archaic period (*Ancient Literacy*, 59). Indeed, in the Homeric corpus itself is the claim that poetry is used to teach: τὸν δὲ θεοὶ μὲν τεῦξαν, ἐπεκλώσαντο δ' ὄλεθρον, ἀνθρώποις, ἵνα ᾖσι καὶ ἐσσομένοισιν ἀοιδή = "The gods weave destruction for humanity, that it might be a song for those to come" (*Odyssey* 8.579–80).

31. Ὁ πατὴρ ὁ ἐπιμελούμενος ὅπως ἀνὴρ ἀγαθὸς γενοίμην ἠνάγκασέ με πάντα τὰ Ὁμήρου ἔπη μαθεῖν· καὶ νῦν δυναίμην ἂν Ἰλιάδα ὅλην καὶ Ὀδύσσειαν ἀπὸ στόματος εἰπεῖν (*Symp.* 3.5).

32. ὦ Σώκρατες, ἐγὼ ἀνδρὶ παιδείας μέγιστον μέρος εἶναι περὶ ἐπῶν δεινὸν εἶναι (*Protagoras* 338e–339a).

33. Henri I. Marrou refers to "the fundamental ideas of Homeric education: 'example' and 'imitation'—παράδειγμα, μίμησις" (*A History of Education in Antiquity* [trans. G. R. Lamb; New York: Sheed & Ward, 1956], 84).

34. λέγω μὴν ὅτι ποιηταί τε ἡμῖν εἰσίν τινες ἐπῶν ἑξαμέτρων πάμπολλοι καὶ τριμέτρων καὶ πάντων δὴ τῶν λεγομένων μέτρων, οἱ μὲν ἐπὶ σπουδήν, οἱ δ' ἐπὶ γέλωτα ὡρμηκότες, ἐν οἷς φασι δεῖν οἱ πολλάκις μυρίοι τοὺς ὀρθῶς παιδευομένους τῶν νέων τρέφειν καὶ διακορεῖς ποιεῖν, πολυηκόους τ' ἐν ταῖς ἀναγνώσεσιν ποιοῦντας καὶ πολυμαθεῖς, ὅλους ποιητὰς ἐκμανθάνοντας· οἱ δὲ ἐκ πάντων κεφάλαια ἐκλέξαντες καί τινας ὅλας ῥήσεις εἰς ταὐτὸν συναγαγόντες, ἐκμανθάνειν φασὶ δεῖν εἰς μνήμην τιθεμένους, εἰ μέλλει τις ἀγαθὸς ἡμῖν καὶ σοφὸς ἐκ πολυπειρίας καὶ πολυμαθίας γενέσθαι (*Laws* 810e–811a) = "I say that we have lots of poets, some of whom compose hexameters, or trimeters, or any other meter you can speak of. Some try to be serious, others funny, and of their writings, people by the thousands say we ought to raise young men on them if we are to teach them properly, making them listeners of long recitations and widely learned, memorizing

By the Hellenistic era, a more or less set curriculum had taken shape, having drawn on the practices of the previous decades.[35] Built throughout the educational process was continual exposure to long duration texts in increasingly larger excerpts. At the introductory phase, students—male offspring of elite families in cities throughout the Hellenistic world—learned language and grammar by means of proverbial sayings drawn from authoritative texts. As was the case in fifth century Athens, Homer was given pride of place.[36] Students were first given summaries or anthologies of the texts,[37] followed by excerpts for which they were required to master proper recitation, gloss any archaic or obscure words, and learn any necessary historical background.

As they progressed from the summaries and anthologies to the complete Homeric texts, students were taught established methods of interpretation. Here we should not think of the critical kind of textual analysis that typified the scholarly work at the library of Alexandria but rather, the allegorical and moral interpretations used most notably by the Stoics.[38] This kind of reading was necessary, given that the Homeric poems were not originally intended to function as normative, moral literature and consequently contained numerous instances of morally dubious behavior on the part of both human and divine characters. This was Plato's problem with

---

the complete works of poets. There are others who gather together the main points and assemble entire collections of sayings and say that a boy must memorize these if we care about having him become good and wise by means of a wide and varied education." Carr notes, "this often intimate education in Homer and other poetic classics was about much more than the learning of certain ethical principles or imitation of great heroes of the past. It was the induction of a student into an elite male culture where the poetic tradition served as a cultural text on multiple levels" (*Writing on the Tablet of the Heart*, 101).

35. The following description relies on Marrou, *History of Education*, 160–75 and Harris, *Ancient Literacy*, 129–39.

36. Dirk C. Hesseling notes a Roman era wax school table from Egypt in the Bodleian with the phrase: θεὸς οὐδ' ἄνθρωπος Ὅμηρος, "Homer is a god and not a man" ("On Waxen Tablets with Fables of Babrius," *The Journal of Hellenic Studies* 13 [1892–1893], 293–314 [296 n. 11]).

37. Plato (*Laws*, 811a) refers to these texts as κεφάλαια ("summaries" or "essential points"), while Plutarch (*Moralia* 14e) calls them τὰς ποιητικὰς ὑποθέσεις ('poetic themes').

38. Marrou, *History of Education*, 164; see more recently, John Van Seters, *The Edited Bible: The Curious History of the "Editor" in Biblical Criticism* (Winona Lake, Ind.: Eisenbrauns, 2006), 46–52.

the use of Homer in education and why he famously argues in the *Republic* that Homer ought either to be censored or banned in an ideal society. Indeed, in the citation from Plato's *Protagoras* quoted above, Protagoras goes on to describe the study of poetry as the ability "to understand in the words of the poets, what has been rightly composed or not, and to know how to distinguish between them."[39]

Five centuries later, Plutarch, in his essay "on how the young ought to read poetry" (Πῶς δεῖ τὸν νέον ποιημάτων ἀκούειν), echoes Protagoras— hardly surprising, given the conservative nature of Greek education[40]— and offers readers a variety of strategies for dealing with morally suspect passages in canonical texts.[41] For example, the reader should judge the portrayal of base deeds according to whether they are fitting to the characters, resolve any contradictory passages by choosing the one that advocates a moral path, and counter any morally repugnant statements with others that extol virtue. Throughout his discussion, Plutarch is careful never to impugn the integrity of the poet or the gods and so in dealing with the capricious nature of Zeus in Homer, Plutarch argues that sometimes the name, "Zeus" refers to the god, while at other times it refers to blind fate.[42] He also asserts that study of the Homeric epithets shows that, for Homer, people are worthy of praise or blame based upon their inner qualities, not upon their appearance, and that Homer will use an epithet that describes only a person's outer appearance when he is portraying that character negatively.[43]

Ultimately, Plutarch notes, the moral advantage of studying poetry is to make readers moderate in their blame of others' misfortune and resil-

---

39. ἔστιν δὲ τοῦτο τὰ ὑπὸ τῶν ποιητῶν λεγόμενα οἷόν τ' εἶναι συνιέναι ἅ τε ὀρθῶς πεποίηται καὶ ἃ μή, καὶ ἐπίστασθαι διελεῖν τε καὶ ἐρωτώμενον λόγον δοῦναι (*Protagoras* 339a). Marrou notes that the purpose of this activity was "ultimately moral, and he [the student] was thus in the main stream of the old tradition, with its search for heroic examples of 'human perfection' ... in the annals of the past" (*History of Education*, 169).

40. This is why, despite the fact that Plutarch is writing at a considerably later time than that being discussed in this essay, his description of reading strategies may be confidently placed in the Hellenistic period.

41. *Moralia* 17d–38a.

42. *Moralia* 23d.

43. *Moralia* 34f–35c; ψόγου γὰρ ἀποφαίνει καὶ λοιδορίας ἄξιον ᾧ μηδέν ἐστιν ἀγαθὸν εὐμορφίας κάλλον = "For he [Homer] sets forth as deserving of blame and abuse the one who has no other redeeming quality than good looks."

ient in the face of abuse on account of their own.[44] Mastery of these core cultural texts in the Greek pedagogical model was thus a means to an end, i.e., the cultivation of values and habits that distinguished one of the urban male elite.[45] This was to be demonstrated, not only in one's demeanor and bearing, but also in the creation of new texts on the part of the fully educated person. It is important to note, however, that in the oral-literate interface that characterized ancient Greece,[46] creation of a text did not necessarily mean putting something into writing. Rather, the interiorization of normative texts provided the educated person in the intensely intimate, often competitive, all-male elite world of a Hellenistic city with a repository of language and phrases to embroider his own speech and, in certain situations—most notably the symposium but also the law courts and the assembly—to compose extemporaneously both prose and poetry by adapting textual exemplars to a contemporary theme or situation.[47] In the Hellenistic intellectual world, then, the reading and interpretation of texts also implied the creation of new ones, albeit not always in writing.

What kind of educational practices would have been available to Persian period elites in Yehud? The descriptions of literacy in Ezra-Nehemiah are worth examination in order to see what evidence they provide. There is ample evidence of the ancient Near Eastern bureaucratic scribalism that

---

44. *Moralia* 35d.

45. In looking at what led to the spread of literacy in classical Greece, Harris notes "[t]he answer goes beyond the easiness of the Greek alphabet and beyond the economic success, based largely on colonization and on slavery, which gave some leisure to part of the free population in many cities.... writing gained general prestige and gradually came to be associated with the rights of the citizens [here Harris lists ostracism, the publication of laws, and recourse to the legal system]. Thus its use became, at least in Athens, a mark in theory of a proper citizen and in practice of the urban citizen with property. Such men now found literacy indispensable" (*Ancient Literacy*, 115).

46. See the thorough discussion in Thomas, *Literacy and Orality*.

47. Thus, Carr observes that memorization gave the student "a repertoire of themes, phrases, characters and plots that they could then incorporate into their oral and written speech" (*Writing on the Tablet of the Heart*, 102). "Literacy" is, therefore, not merely "having letters": rather, it is a demonstrated competence in the cultural world to which literacy is a prerequisite. See Dennis Smith for the cultural influence of the Greek symposium in Judaism (*From Symposium to Eucharist: The Banquet in the Early Christian World* [Minneapolis: Augsburg, 2003], 13–66) and Sir 31:31–32:13 for a Jewish description of a symposium, presumably from Jerusalem.

is also present in Persian written remains. In Ezra 4:8,[48] reference is made to the office of scribe (סָפְרָא) and to the royal functionary title of בְּעֵל־טְעֵם (translated as "royal deputy" in the NRSV). Administrative documents are also mentioned, namely, the memorandum (דִּכְרוֹנָה, Ezra 6:3) the letter (אִגֶּרֶת, Neh 2:7–8) and the command or report (טְעֵם, Ezra 5:5, 6:14). Archival documents are also referenced, specifically the two genealogical texts, the כְּתָבָם הַמִּתְיַחְשִׂים (Ezra 2:62) and the סֵפֶר הַיַּחַשׂ (Neh 7:5).

In addition, however, Ezra-Nehemiah refers to the memorization and interiorization of normative texts by elites in the manner that characterizes Greek pedagogical practice. In the first description of Ezra, the narrative notes that he had "dedicated his heart to the study of YHWH's teaching" (הֵכִין לְבָבוֹ לִדְרוֹשׁ אֶת־תּוֹרַת יְהוָה, Ezra 7:10). The *hiphil* of כּוּן with לֵב as an object has a range of meanings, including "dedicating oneself to something." In Prov 8:5 it refers to becoming wise or intellectually competent, i.e., dedicating oneself to wisdom.[49] In Ezra 7:10, Ezra the priest and scribe has dedicated his heart to the study of Torah. Since the *hiphil* of כּוּן also embraces the idea of "preparing something for a purpose" (e.g., 1 Chr 9:32, 22:10), another way of reading this phrase is that Ezra has prepared his heart for the study of Torah, i.e., he has memorized the text and now knows it thoroughly enough to expound upon it and teach it to others. Note that in the scene of the Torah's public reading in Neh 8, special measures are taken to make sure not only that the people hear the words of Torah, but that they see the scroll in which it is written.[50] In other words, Ezra's use of the scroll at the public reading need not be seen as necessary for him, since he already was a scribe "skilled in the Torah of Moses" (Ezra 8:6). Instead, its presence is there as a visual symbol to the people of the authority of Ezra's words.

The description of the Levites' actions in this scene also supports the idea of elite males educated in the content of a normative text, since we are told that they both read the text clearly and explained it to the people.[51] Indeed, it is the Levites who are the most visible of the literate elite in Persian period Yehud, and their roles as temple singers not only implies

---

48. Fittingly, this is the Aramaic portion of Ezra, it being a bureaucratic language of the era.
49. הָבִינוּ פְתָאיִם עָרְמָה וּכְסִילִים הָבִינוּ לֵב׃
50. וַיִּפְתַּח עֶזְרָא הַסֵּפֶר לְעֵינֵי כָל־הָעָם (Neh 8:5).
51. וְהַלְוִיִּם מְבִינִים אֶת־הָעָם לַתּוֹרָה וְהָעָם עַל־עָמְדָם וַיִּקְרְאוּ בַסֵּפֶר בְּתוֹרַת הָאֱלֹהִים מְפֹרָשׁ וְשׂוֹם שֶׂכֶל וַיָּבִינוּ בַּמִּקְרָא (Neh 8:7–8). For criticism of the traditional understanding

memorization of poetic texts but also the ability to recite them musically, a skill cultivated also by Greek elites in their mastering of Homer.

Moreover, this interaction with normative texts was not limited to temple or cultic personnel alone, as is still maintained by some scholars.⁵² In Neh 8:13, priests and Levites are joined by "the male heads of ancestral clans" (רָאשֵׁי הָאָבוֹת לְכָל־הָעָם) to study Torah under the tutelage of Ezra.⁵³ This is not a bureaucratic or administrative exercise, but rather the orientation of these elite, noncultic male individuals into the Torah. That is to say, they are to become competent in their knowledge of the text, just as Ezra and the Levites are.

This episode of textual study is then followed in Neh 9 by a lengthy oral recitation that summarizes the Torah and, in its divergences from details in the written text, does not demonstrate evidence of different and as yet nascent biblical traditions⁵⁴ but rather, the fluidity of an oral culture that has interiorized authoritative written texts. More than exclusively a continuation of the educational traditions of Mesopotamia and Egypt, the picture in Ezra-Nehemiah shows education in Yehud also to include aspects of the Greek model that are not limited to priestly or cultic functionaries.⁵⁵

---

that the Levites are translating the Hebrew text into Aramaic for the people, see Lester L. Grabbe, *Ezra-Nehemiah* (Old Testament Readings; London: Routledge, 1998), 53.

52. E.g., van der Toorn, *Scribal Culture*, 205–64; Christine Schams, *Jewish Scribes in the Second-Temple Period* (JSOTSup 291; Sheffield: Sheffield Academic Press, 1998), 309–12.

53. וּבַיּוֹם הַשֵּׁנִי נֶאֶסְפוּ רָאשֵׁי הָאָבוֹת לְכָל־הָעָם הַכֹּהֲנִים וְהַלְוִיִּם אֶל־עֶזְרָא הַסֹּפֵר וּלְהַשְׂכִּיל אֶל־דִּבְרֵי הַתּוֹרָה (Neh 8:13).

54. As I had mistakenly argued some fifteen years ago (Thomas Bolin, "When the End Is the Beginning—The Persian Period and the Origins of the Biblical Tradition," *SJOT* 10 [1996]: 3–15).

55. "As in the case of ancient Greece, the issue in Israel is not mastery of an esoteric sign system to achieve literacy but use of literacy to *help* enculturate, shape the behavior, and otherwise mentally separate an educated upper class from their noneducated peers" (Carr, *Writing on the Tablet of the Heart*, 119). "[I]t is not at all apparent that the temple was the primary site of education, even though the priests as part of educated elite may have continued to instruct the young in both Homer and the Torah" (John Van Seters, "The Origins of the Hebrew Bible: Some New Answers to Old Questions, Part Two," *Journal of Ancient Near Eastern Religions* 7 [2007]: 219–38 [232]).

1-2 Samuel in Persian and Early Hellenistic Yehud

Looking at 1–2 Samuel, we are in the position to answer the question why, among the preexilic traditions, the figures of Samuel, Saul, and David were preserved. This will require a good deal of speculation, given that we are faced with a paucity of evidence. First Chronicles parallels a portion of the narrative of 1–2 Samuel but offers a significantly different picture of David, portraying him as a royal dynast noted for his piety, musical skills, and martial prowess.[56] The majority of the remaining references to David in postexilic biblical literature are consonant with this portrayal in 1 Chronicles,[57] and concerning other significant figures in 1–2 Samuel—Samuel, Saul, Jonathan, Joab, Michal and Bathsheba—there are few, if any, references at all.[58] Consequently, apart from the partially parallel account

---

56. While it has become standard scholarly opinion that 1– 2 Chr uses the Dtr history as a source due to the work of Martin Noth (*The Chronicler's History* [trans. H. G. M. Williamson; JSOTSup 50; Sheffield: Sheffield Academic Press, 1987), for a much more nuanced example of this basic approach, see Steven L. McKenzie, *The Chronicler's Use of the Deuteronomistic History* [HSM 33; Atlanta: Scholars Press, 1985] and also compare the recent discussion of Ehud Ben Zvi, "Are There Any Bridges Out There? How Wide Was the Conceptual Gap between the Deuteronomistic History and Chronicles?" in *Community Identity in Judean Historiography: Biblical and Comparative Perspectives* [ed. Gary N. Knoppers and Ken A. Ristau; Winona Lake, Ind.: Eisenbrauns, 2009], 59–86). The textual instability of the Hebrew text of Sam-Kgs up through the Hellenistic period should cast doubt on this claim. See the criticisms of A. Graeme Auld, *Kings without Privilege: David and Moses in the Story of the Bible's Kings* [Edinburgh: T&T Clark, 1994]; John Van Seters, *The Biblical Saga of King David* [Winona Lake, Ind.: Eisenbrauns, 2009]; and Raymond F. Person, Jr., *The Deuteronomic History and the Book of Chronicles: Scribal Works in an Oral World* [SBLAIL 6; Atlanta: Society of Biblical Literature, 2010]).

57. This speaks against Carr's claim that 1–2 Chr played little role in Jewish education (*Writing on the Tablet of the Heart*, 155).

58. Outside of 1–2 Chr and the genealogical lists in Ezra-Neh, Samuel is mentioned in Jer 15:1 and Ps 99:6; Saul in the psalm superscriptions discussed below and in Isa 10:29 as part of a toponynm; Joab, Jonathan, Bathsheba and Michal are not mentioned at all. Among the few apocryphal and pseudepigraphical texts that refer to David as something other than a pious king and musician, Eupolemus (ca. mid-second century B.C.E.) focuses on David's military victories and repeats the tradition found both in 1 Kgs and 1 Chr in which David is forbidden to build the temple because of these martial exploits (*OTP* 2:866). Oblique reference to David's adultery with Bathsheba is also made in Sir 47:11 (Marko Marttila, "David in the Wisdom of Ben Sira," *SJOT* 25 [2011]: 29–48). The earliest detailed reference to narratives in 1–2 Sam

in 1 Chronicles, there is practically no evidence of the Samuel-Saul-David narrative complex of 1–2 Samuel having been read in postexilic Israel.

This is a significant feature in the Tanak that does not often receive much attention but, given the disproportionately large number of scholarly works published on 1–2 Samuel, perhaps it should. However, if we rely on the picture in Ezra-Nehemiah of an educational process for both cultic and noncultic male elites similar to the Greek model in which long duration texts were used for socialization, some cautious assumptions may be made.

Among the temple elites during the Persian and early Hellenistic periods, the priests would have seen the stories in 2 Sam 5–6 of David's having captured Jerusalem and moved the ark there to confirm the sanctity of the city and its temple. In contrast, David's first failed attempt to bring the ark into the city, thwarted by divine intervention, and God's rebuff of David's offer to build the temple may have been interpreted against the Persian monarchy's successful effort to build a temple in Jerusalem, as witnessed by the panegyric of Cyrus in Deutero-Isaiah (Isa 40–55) and its ongoing support of that temple as described in Ezra-Nehemiah. Alternatively, these texts, when put alongside the rejection of Saul after he offers sacrifice in Samuel's stead (1 Sam 13), might have been read by postexilic priests as affirmation of the authority and priority of cultic officials over the monarchy. Along these same lines, although Samuel is called both a "seer" (רֹאֶה) and a "prophet" (נָבִיא) in 1–2 Chronicles, his distinctly priestly functions in 1–2 Samuel (tending the ark, offering sacrifice) might have made Samuel a figure with whom postexilic priestly elites identified. Saul's order to destroy the entire priestly community at Nob would have been seen by these readers as justification for his demise and the eradication of his line.

With the Levites we may venture to be more specific, given their connection with music in the temple. This allows us to look at the Psalter, and doing so shows that the superscriptions of fourteen psalms refer to specific events in the life of David,[59] twelve of which are stories found in 1–2 Sam-

---

are in the writings of Pseudo-Philo, and his account breaks off with the death of Saul (*L.A.B.* 50–65 [*OTP* 2:364–77]). 1–2 Sam are preserved at Qumran, and the Hebrew manuscripts have done much to shed light on the fascinating textual history of the books, but there are no references to the lives of Samuel, Saul or David as recounted in 1–2 Sam in any of the other Qumran literature, with the exception of 11QPs[a].

59. With the exception of Ps 142, all of these psalms are included in one of the two so-called Davidic collections in the Psalter.

uel.⁶⁰ Of these twelve, nine refer in some fashion to David's conflict with Saul, i.e., before David assumed the kingship,⁶¹ while the remaining three refer to events that happened after David was king in Jerusalem: the revolt of Absalom, the affair with Bathsheba, and the victory over the Arameans.⁶² Of these twelve, ten are laments, while the remaining two are songs of thanksgiving.⁶³ Most scholarship on the psalms classifies these superscriptions as later additions inserted by someone other than the composers of the psalms, in order to give these poems a respectable, i.e., Davidic pedigree.⁶⁴ However, given our discussion of the kinds of pedagogy evidenced in both the Greek world and in Ezra-Nehemiah, one could see the process as running the other way. An advanced student, well-versed in the stock phrases of Hebrew poetry as well as the narratives of 1–2 Samuel, would compose a poem to fit the particular story about David. In part this would help the training of a Levite in the ability to produce poetic texts for worship in the temple,⁶⁵ but it would be also as much about character formation as it was a display of literary prowess on the student's part. Thus

---

60. "A psalm of David, when he fled from Absalom his son" (Ps 3:1; cf. 2 Sam 15:14); "Of David, who spoke the words of this song to YHWH on the day that YHWH had delivered him from all his enemies and from the hand of Saul" (Ps 18:1; cf. 2 Sam 22:1–51); "Of David, when he changed his demeanor before Abimelech, and he drove him out, and so he went away" (Ps 34:1; cf. 1 Sam 21:13); "A psalm of David, when Nathan the prophet came to him, after he had gone in to Bathsheba" (Ps 51:1–2; cf. 2 Sam 12:1–15); "A *maskil* of David, when Doeg the Edomite came and told Saul, saying to him, 'David has come to the house of Ahimelech'" (Ps 52:1–2; cf. 1 Sam 22:9); "A *maskil* of David, when the Ziphites came and said to Saul, 'Is not David hiding with us?'" (Ps 54:1–2; cf. 1 Sam 23:19); "A *miktam* of David, when the Philistines seized him in Gath" (Ps 56:1; cf. 1 Sam 21:10); "A *miktam* of David, when he ran from Saul in the cave" (Ps 57:1; cf. 1 Sam 24:3–7); "A *miktam* of David, when Saul sent and watched the house to kill him" (Ps 59:1; cf. 1 Sam 19:11); "A *miktam* of David, for teaching, when he battled Aram-naharaim and Aram-zobah, and when Joab returned and killed twelve thousand Edomites in the Valley of Salt. (Ps 60:1–2; cf. 2 Sam 8:13; 10:7–15); "A psalm of David, when he was in the wilderness of Judah" (Ps 63:1; cf. 2 Sam 15:23); "A *maskil* of David, when he was in the cave, a prayer (Ps 142:1; cf. 1 Sam 24:3–7). Of the remaining two, Ps 7:1 refers to the otherwise unknown "Cush the Benjaminite," and Ps 30:1 possibly refers to 1 Chr 29.

61. Pss 18; 34; 52; 54; 56; 57; 59; 63; 142.

62. Pss 3; 51; 60.

63. Lament: Pss 3; 51; 52; 54; 56; 57; 59; 60; 63; 142; thanksgiving: Pss 18; 34.

64. See the overview in James Limburg, "Psalms, Book of," *ABD* 5:522–36 (528).

65. Cf. Davies, *Scribes and Schools*, 131–34.

because the poem would serve to show the "correct" response one ought to offer to a given situation of good or bad fortune. The predominance of lament over thanksgiving poems in these psalms shows that priority was given to having the student demonstrate the ability to respond and behave properly in instances of calamity. As T. L. Thompson notes in his treatment of these superscriptions, the songs both help interpret events in David's life and challenge the reader to emulate the heroic king.[66] This is practically identical with the goal given by Plutarch for the study of Homer: "When we ourselves are met with ill-fortune, we will neither be humiliated or shaken, but bear meekly the mockery, abuse, and laughter."[67] Evidence to support this can be found in 1–2 Samuel itself, where poetic texts are included and sung by David at key points in the narrative.[68] Apocryphal psalms with similar superscriptions that are clearly from the same hand also support this scenario.[69]

As seen in the accounts of Ezra-Nehemiah, literacy with the aim of acquiring textually encoded cultural knowledge, with correspondingly modelled behavior, was not restricted to cultic personnel but encompassed the male elites designated as heads of families or clans. Texts were read, and perhaps produced, both inside and outside the temple.[70] What would these readers have made of 1–2 Samuel? Given the Persian policy of utilizing local elites to help maintain imperial oversight, these readers, as beneficiaries of Achaemenid rule, would perhaps not have longed for a

---

66. Thomas L. Thompson, *The Messiah Myth: The Near Eastern Roots of Jesus and David* (New York: Basic Books, 2005), 319.

67. χρησαμένους τύχαις μὴ ταπεινοῦσθαι μηδὲ ταράττεσθαι, φέρειν δὲ πράως καὶ σκώμματα καὶ λοιδορίας καὶ γέλωτας (*Moralia* 35d).

68. Indeed, the text of Ps 18 is duplicated in 2 Sam 22; see also 2 Sam 1:19–27; 3:33–34; 23:1–7, as well as the Song of Hannah in 1 Sam 2:1–10. Both Carr (*Writing on the Tablet of the Heart*, 159–60) and van der Toorn (*Scribal Culture*, 109–41) note how educational texts are revised and expanded as the curriculum moves through time. The poetry in 1–2 Samuel may be understood as an example of this phenomenon.

69. Pss 151–153 in the Syriac (5ApocSyrPs 1a–4) and 11QPs[a]; both in *OTP* 2:612–17.

70. Using the concept of hybridity from postcolonial theory, Carr argues for indigenous education in ancient Israel modeled on a Hellenistic curriculum as a form of resistance to Greek cultural dominance (*Writing on the Tablet of the Heart*, 177). Van Seters, however, is skeptical that anything like a fully-established curriculum containing a proto-canon of Hebrew texts existed ("The Origins of the Hebrew Bible," 235).

restoration of an indigenous monarchy and would have found the often negative portrayal of David justification for Persian rule in their own days. Their reading of 1–2 Samuel would have been different from other interpretive traditions, such as that which focused on David's piety, as is found in 1–2 Chronicles, or the one that built upon the divine promise of an eternal dynasty in 2 Sam 7 and blossomed into various messianic beliefs. If these Jerusalem elites had been brought up in educational practices similar to or even inspired by Greek pedagogy, there are several other themes in 1–2 Samuel they would have seized upon.[71] For example, the contrast in the Succession Narrative between Saul, the doomed king, and David, the chosen one, is also found throughout Greek literature, which often contrasts good and evil kings. It can be seen as early as in the stark difference between Agamemnon and Priam in the *Iliad*,[72] as well as in numerous other Greek texts, most notably tragedy and historiography.[73] Ancient

---

71. Klaus-Peter Adam has argued for the influence of Greek tragedy on the portrayal of Saul in 1 Sam 14, based both on formal elements and content, with Saul representing a tragic figure insofar as his downfall is due both to a complex combination of his own free choice and his destiny ("Saul as a Tragic Hero: Greek Drama and its Influence on Hebrew Scripture in 1 Samuel 14, 24–46 (10,8; 13,7–13A; 10,17–27)," in *For and Against David: Story and History in the Books of Samuel* [ed. Erik Eynikel and A. Graeme Auld; BETL 232; Leuven, Peeters, 2010], 123–83).

72. This contrast is highlighted by the parallel structures of Books 1 and 24, long noted by Homeric scholars. Some critics have noted parallels between David's cleverness and Odysseus's in the *Odyssey* (e.g., Robert Alter, *The David Story: A Translation and Commentary of 1 and 2 Samuel* [New York: W.W. Norton, 1999], 134, 172, 203). But recently, Paul Borgman has argued that David and Odysseus are really two very different characters, based on differences between Homeric and Israelite culture (*David, Saul, and God: Rediscovering an Ancient Story* [New York: Oxford University Press, 2008], 221–44). Unfortunately, Borgman's analysis is weakened by an overreliance on dated scholarship that makes too much of the Greek-Hebrew contrast and relies too much on an interpretive aesthetic that views biblical authors as the genius creators of literary masterpieces.

73. Note in particular Herodotus's treatment of Solon, Croesus, and Darius. Some argument has been made for the dependence of the Dtr history on Herodotus (Sara Mandel and David Noel Freedman, *The Relationship between Herodotus' History and Primary History* [South Florida Studies in the History of Judaism 60; Atlanta: Scholars Press, 1993]; Flemming Nielsen, *The Tragedy in History: Herodotus and the Deuteronomistic History* [JSOTSup 251; Sheffield: Sheffield Academic Press, 1997]; Jan-Wim Wesselius, *The Origin of the History of Israel: Herodotus' Histories as Blueprint for the First Books of the Bible* [JSOTSup 345; London: Sheffield Academic Press, 2002]). However, I am simply pointing out a similarity in the fact that both Herodotus and the

Yehudite readers of 1–2 Samuel may have focused on the differences between Saul and David and looked to discover what about Saul led him to be scorned by God while David retained God's favor, despite his moral failings.[74] Using reading strategies similar to those popular in Hellenistic pedagogy and illustrated by Plutarch's manual, such as the approach to the divine epithets in Homer, these ancient readers might have noticed that in Saul's first appearance in the story (1 Sam 9:2), he is described positively only by his outward appearance, whereas when David first appears in the narrative (1 Sam 16:7), his worth in clearly stated to be something beyond his outward good looks. This would immediately raise red flags for these readers about Saul's character or inner qualities, which would, in turn, play into how those readers interpreted his ultimately bitter demise. To take another example, in the same way that references to Zeus in Homer were interpreted depending on the kind of action performed by the deity, these readers might have understood God's rather capricious action in 2 Sam 24 in causing David to order a census, only to punish the kingdom for it subsequently, as a description more of blind fate than the will of YHWH. The fact that the parallel account in 1 Chr 21 attributes the census to Satan can perhaps be seen as evidence of this particular story being interpreted in a way analogous to Plutarch's suggested strategy.

---

entire complex of Sam-Kgs shape their portrayal of kings in order to have them serve as positive or negative models. For an analysis of the contrast between good and bad kings in the Tanakh, see Thompson, *Messiah Myth*, 259–83.

74. An analogous example of this kind of interpretation can be found in the rabbinic and midrashic debates on Gen 4 that sought to explain why God accepted Abel's offering but rejected Cain's. Cf. the alternative explanation provided by Edelman: "[t]he two interrelated themes of the kingship of YHWH in place of human kingship and divine unpredictability imply a social setting in which human kingship is no longer a viable option, on the one hand, and one in which YHWH has not lived up to national expectations, showing himself to be undependable or fickle, on the other. A date after the bitter experience of the exile would account well for the latter ideology, and one after 586 B.C.E. and the loss of status as an independent nation headed by a Davidide king is likely for the other. Combining both suggested dates, a more specific social setting can be proposed: a date in the latter part of the reign of Darius after the death of Zerubbabel, when the Persian administration decided to appoint loyal Persians to serve as governors in various provinces in place of puppet kings descended from former royal houses. Once the latter policy was put in place, leaders of the two main factions in Yehud may have effected a rapprochement, the issue of a Saulide vs. Davidide leader having become moot and Jerusalem having become the site of the capital, with its temple rebuilt" ("Did Rivalry Resurface?" 85).

A more specific example of how noncultic elites would have read 1–2 Samuel may be found in Qohelet, a text dated either to the late Persian or Hellenistic period. The author's assumption of Solomon's persona, named only by his Davidic patronymic, is one of the more intriguing features of the book, and scholars have seen in Qoh 1:16–2:10 an allusion to the fabulous wealth and opulence of Solomon recounted in 1 Kgs 4–11.[75] However, Qohelet makes numerous other references to seemingly historical or contemporary events, and exegetes have long puzzled over the exact nature of these references.[76] I would like to suggest that some of them are in fact allusions to portions of the narrative found also in 1–2 Samuel. As R. F. Person's careful analysis demonstrates, written texts in primarily oral environments allude to earlier traditions in a way not characterized by a slavish textual literalism.[77] Allusions to or even direct copying of a text need not require identical wording, nor are any deviations from the wording in a source text automatically to be attributed to deliberate, ideological intentions. Instead, written citations or allusions in the predominantly oral culture of ancient Israel would allow for both fluidity and multiformity.[78] For instance, the observation in Qoh 4:11–13 that one who sleeps alone cannot get warm, immediately followed by mention of "an old and foolish king" (מֶלֶךְ זָקֵן וּכְסִיל), seems like nothing other than an allusion to David's ignominious ending, bundled in bed with the young and lovely Abishag, who still cannot keep the old king warm.[79] Qohelet's advice in 5:1–2 to refrain from sacrifices and vows before God calls to mind the rashness of Saul, whose oaths in 1 Sam 14 and abrogation of sacrificial

---

75. E.g., Choon-Leong Seow, *Ecclesiastes: A New Translation with Introduction* (AB 18C; New York: Doubleday, 1997), 148–50.

76. Following the lead of other exegetes, Thomas Krüger looks for referents to these allusions in the political history of the Ptolemies (*Qoheleth: A Commentary* [trans. O. C. Dean, Jr.; Hermeneia; Minneapolis: Fortress, 2004], 20). More recently, Jennie Barbour has explored this in detail (*The Story of Israel in the Book of Qohelet: Ecclesiastes as Cultural Memory* [New York: Oxford University Press, 2012]). For the problem of looking for referents only in events contemporaneous with a biblical text's author, see Ferdinand Deist, "The Yehud Bible: A Belated Divine Miracle?" *JNSL* 23 (1997): 128–31.

77. Raymond F. Person Jr., "The Ancient Israelite Scribe as Performer," *JBL* 117 (1998): 601–8; Person, *Deuteronomic History*, 41–68.

78. Person, *Deuteronomic History*, 67.

79. While this occurs in 1 Kgs 1, I consider it to be a continuation of the narrative in 2 Samuel.

rites from Samuel in 1 Sam 13 help contribute to the revocation of his kingship. The claim in 6:3-5 that a dead infant is fortunate not to see all the suffering in the world calls to mind the nameless child of David and Bathsheba whose death is preordained even before his birth. Indeed, the use of verbs of motion for imagery in David's poignant remark after hearing of the baby's death, "I will go to him, but he will not return to me" (הֹלֵךְ אֲנִי אֵלָיו וְהוּא לֹא־יָשׁוּב אֵלָי, 2 Sam 12:23) is echoed in Qohelet's observation that the untimely birth "comes forth in emptiness and goes into darkness" (כִּי־בַהֶבֶל בָּא וּבַחֹשֶׁךְ יֵלֵךְ, Qoh 6:4).[80] The similarity here, as Person notes, is not in identical vocabulary but rather, in a fluid expression of similar ideas.

This may also be the case in Qohelet's reference to the small city in 9:14-15 that ends a long siege through the actions of a wise citizen. It is strikingly similar to the account of Joab's siege of Abel Beth Ma'acah in 2 Sam 4, which is finally lifted due to the initiative of a wise citizen. The fact that Qohelet refers to this wise person as a man, while in 2 Sam 4 the person is a woman, can be an example of the kind of variation that occurs in predominantly oral cultures when making textual allusions.[81]

Looking at these traces of postexilic reading of 1-2 Samuel in both the Psalter and Qohelet, it is significant that the majority are to episodes in which something terrible befalls the main character. With the case of the Psalms, we saw that the poetic texts were written by advanced students and served as demonstrations of the normative way for a faithful Yahwist to respond to catastrophe. However, Qohelet uses episodes from 1-2 Samuel not to show how one ought to remain faithful and pious but rather, to critique some of the very values extolled in the Psalms with Davidic superscriptions. This, of course, is consonant with Qohelet's critical attitude to much of the traditional religious teachings of his day, and Qohelet's ability to allude deftly to a variety of culturally normative texts can also be seen as evidence of his position as a teacher in Jerusalem, and hence, someone

---

80. There is a striking parallel to Qoh 6:4 in a quotation from a lost play of Euripides preserved in Plutarch (*Moralia* 36f): "To lament the newborn as he comes into evil, but to carry out of the house with joy and reverence the man who has died and has ceased his toil" (τὸν φύντα θρηνεῖν εἰς ὅσ' ἔρχεται κακά, τὸν δ' αὖ θανόντα καὶ πόνων πεπαυμένον χαίροντας εὐφημοῦντας ἐκπέμπειν δόμων).

81. In this particular instance, given Qohelet's negative statement about women in 7:26, this might be an example of a conscious, ideologically motivated alteration.

thoroughly familiar with a literary corpus.[82] We can thus begin to see the outlines of an educational system at work in Yehud during the Persian and early Hellenistic periods through the use of 1–2 Samuel in the Psalms and Qohelet, with the former illustrating text creation by advanced students on their way to full interiorization of the texts and the values inculcated through them, and with the latter providing a rare glimpse of a fully socialized member of the educated class looking back on the tradition with a critical eye.

Conclusion

Let us return to Niditch's criterion mentioned at the outset of this essay, namely that historical reconstructions of how texts were used in ancient Israel should be as concrete and specific as possible. To that end, I offer the following observations, which also provide an answer to the questions of who read 1–2 Samuel in the Persian and Hellenistic periods: in fifth-century Jerusalem, both cultic and noncultic elites read 1–2 Samuel, a text with ancient cultic and monarchical traditions, through the lenses of their own social location. In their roles as functionaries in the Persian imperial bureaucracy, normative texts that extolled the sacredness of Jerusalem were given special attention and emphasis, as were those traditions that critiqued the defunct indigenous monarchs, whether Saulide or Davidic.

Focusing on the negative portrayals of David in 1–2 Samuel, Levitical elites generated poetic texts for use in the cult and for pedagogical purposes. Moving into the fourth century B.C.E., with more exposure to Greek culture, we may venture a more specific scenario: elite boys, of both priestly and nonpriestly families, set forth on an educational process in the home of a teacher that involved learning the somewhat archaic Hebrew of the Pentateuch and the Deuteronomistic History. Memorization would begin with small units of text,[83] progressing to larger and larger portions as the boys grew older. As texts are introduced to students, methods of interpretation are also taught, especially for passages that seem to contradict cultural norms. After a good deal of the normative texts have been thus introduced and committed to memory, the students, now adolescents

---

82. On the similarities between Qohelet and Genesis, and the possibility of allusions between the two texts, see Thomas M. Bolin, "Rivalry and Resignation: Girard on Qoheleth and the Divine-Human Relationship," *Bib* 86 (2005): 245–59.

83. The *shema*? Von Rad's *kleine geschichtliche Credo*? The Ten Commandments?

or young men, are set to generating texts—by recitation, rather than written composition—in order to demonstrate that they have fully incorporated the content and values of their previous years of study. In order to make this as challenging as possible, the generated texts must be given as a response to a morally or theologically problematic episode in the literature. Particularly excellent samples of these student recitations were written down and collected or even incorporated into the normative text on which they were commenting.

Presiding over these recitations, and sitting in judgment of them, would be a grown man, himself the product of the same educational process. His ability to cite, allude to, and comment on texts would have been honed by years of study and teaching. Although most of the men who reached this station in life may have lacked the self-awareness to stand back from their own cultural moorings to do so, occasionally, one of these teachers would have the skill needed to use the tradition to critique itself. The thoughts of at least one such individual have been preserved, and in both the student compositions of the Psalter and the songs inserted into 1–2 Samuel as well as the master's analysis in Qohelet, we are provided a glimpse of how some of the more thorny passages from 1–2 Samuel were being turned over and thought through in early Hellenistic Yehud.

What Made the Books of Samuel Authoritative in the Discourses of the Persian Period? Reflections on the Legal Discourse in 2 Samuel 14

Klaus-Peter Adam

Were the books of Samuel relevant for Second Temple Judaism under Achaemenid rule? Thematically, the books of Samuel are largely set up as strings of loosely connected episodes about the origin of the Israelite and Judahite monarchies. Situated at and around the royal court, partially written in a unique style with plots that feature the emerging administration of Israel and Judah, their main emphasis seems to be the theme of royal authority. How can the accounts of the kings of Israel and Judah in this setting be relevant for Judeans in the Persian period and how were they authoritative? A main aspect that helps elucidate the authority of the books of Samuel and considers segments of Jewish identity that the books may have shaped are the sources that potentially originated in Persian times. All uncertainties of absolute dates left aside, for primarily three reasons we can assume that at least parts of Samuel developed in Yehud in the Persian era: text-critical witnesses provide evidence for the growth of traditions through the Achaemenid period;[1] the Deuteronomistic language arguably continued to develop gradually during this time period,[2] and the

---

1. For 1 Sam, see among others, Anneli Aejmelaeus, "The Septuagint of 1 Samuel," in *On the Trail of the Septuagint Translators: Collected Essays* (rev. and expanded ed.; Contributions to Biblical Exegesis & Theology 50; Leuven: Peeters, 2006), 123–42 and for individual texts, see for instance, Ralph W. Klein, *1 Samuel* (WBC 10; Waco Tex.: Word, 1983), xxvi-xxviii; P. Kyle McCarter Jr., *I Samuel* (AB 8; Garden City N.Y.: Doubleday, 1980), 5–11; along with the LXX L edition of Natalio Fernández Marcos and José Ramón Busto Saiz, *El texto antioqueno de la biblia griega I, 1–2 Samuel* (Madrid: Instituto de Filologia, 1989).

2. On the history of source-critical scholarship, see, among others, Thomas

narratives' characters were constantly revised.³ Besides these three aspects

---

Römer, *The So-Called Deuteronomistic History: A Sociological, Historical, and Literary Introduction* (London: T&T Clark, 2005), 165–83, esp. 177. Römer suggests three main interests of the Deuteronomistic History edition in Persian time: segregation, monotheism, and integration of Golah concerns. Generally speaking, in a model of successive literary layers of reworking by a Dtr H, P, and N editor, the latest layer would tentatively be placed in late exilic or Achaemenid times. Another suggestion is to label these additions as a collective of "late Deuteronomists/Dtr S" and to date them to postexilic time. See, for instance, Hans-Christoph Schmitt, "Das spätdeuteronomistische Geschichtswerk Genesis I–2 Regum XXV und seine theologische Intention," in *Congress Volume: Cambridge, 1995* (ed. John A. Emerton; VTSup 66; Leiden: Brill, 1997), 261–79. Themes that were identified in an analysis of the speeches in Josh 1, 23–24, 1 Sam 12, and 1 Kgs 8 are, for example, Israel's sinfulness, the merciful care of YHWH that is substantiated in giving the land, in establishing the Davidic kingship, and in the temple, and YHWH's demand to observe Torah. For a detailed discussion, see Jochen Nentel, *Trägerschaft und Intentionen des deuteronomistischen Geschichtswerks: Untersuchungen zu den Reflexionsreden Jos 1; 23; 24; 1Sam 12 und 1Kön 8* (BZAW 297; Berlin: de Gruyter, 2000), 274–300.

3. For instance, Samuel's passion for Saul's tragedy in 1 Sam 14:23–46, for messianism (in 1 Sam), and for the legal interpretation of the strife between David and Saul apparently mark areas of interest in Achaemenid time. Also, the forms of narratives were either elaborated or freshly introduced—both forms of growth are in line with the books' expansion over a long time. The specific claim of authority can more distinctly be grasped when comparing the historiography in Sam and Kgs with that in Chr. Many differences between the historiographic versions of Sam–Kgs and of the Chronicler highlight their specific intentions. While both ultimately root in the genre of synchronistic Mesopotamian chronicles of neighboring states, their current forms have moved far away from such chronistic literature. The Deuteronomists have ornately enlarged the history of the kings toward their origins. Besides adding their Dtr version of the Moses-Torah, they have inscribed in their historiography their immense interest in Josiah's installation of this Moses-Torah; see David Carr, "Empirische Perspektiven auf das Deuteronomistische Geschichtswerk," in *Die Deuteronomistischen Geschichtswerke, Redaktions- und Religionsge-schichtliche Perspektiven zur Deuteronomismus-Diskussion, in Tora und Vorderen Propheten* (ed. M. Witte et. al., BZAW 365; Berlin: de Gruyter, 2006), 1–17 (14). See also Carr's reference on 4 n. 5 to Norbert Peters, who has proposed that Israel's historiographic tradition is to be seen in the context of education (*Unsere Bibel: Die Lebensquellen der Heiligen Schrift* [Katholische Lebenswerte 12; Paderborn: Bonifacius, 1929], 208–10) and to Hubert Cancik (*Grundzüge der hethitischen und alttestamentlichen Geschichtsschreibung* [Abhandlungen des Deutschen Palästinavereins; Wiesbaden: Harrasowitz, 1976], 54–64). In line with this interest in the law is reflection over legal aspects in Sam, like the concept of kingship in Israel in 1 Sam 8*, 12*. Another distinctive feature of the development of the books and their claim of authority are various

of textual development that point to the origin of some traditions in Persian times, factors that determine the books' authority are: (1) their typical modes of reception and (2) their thematic content, which led to additions being made in either the Neo-Babylonian or Persian periods.[4]

---

plot expansions. Probably not earlier than the Achaemenid period, Samuel presents David as a character in an elaborate *Vita* that includes episodes about him as a young man. See, for instance, the additions about David's youth in 1 Sam 17:1–18:5 MT. Many details, such as the names of the brothers of David, do not appear elsewhere and most likely are added as elements of David's early years. Another plot and character development in Sam is the feud-like quarrel between the protagonists Saul and David in 1 Sam 18–27*. This episodic strand follows its own themes. While this is not definitive proof of their postexilic origin, it is noteworthy that the strand is lacking in Chr, as is a reception history of these narratives in the HB with the exception of the headings in the David-Psalter.

4. For instance, the divinatory technique of casting lots is mentioned in what are most likely postexilic passages (1 Sam 14:40–42; cf. Josh 7:14–18). Achan's theft in Josh 7 has been interpreted as (post) exilic by Timo Veijola, "Das Klagegebet in Literatur und Leben der Exilsgeneration am Beispiel einiger Prosatexte," in *Moses Erben: Studien zum Dekalog, zum Deuteronomismus und zum Schriftgelehrtentum* (BWANT 149; Kohlhammer: Stuttgart, 2000), 176–91, esp. 189 n. 79. Veijola partly substantiates his dating on the basis of the inclusion of the wrath of YHWH that was kindled against the Israelites and YHWH's refrain from anger in 7:1, 26a. The dating of the entire narrative cannot be reconsidered in this context. Another theme that probably did not play an important role before the Persian period is the fundamental solidarity of the living with the dead, which includes the care of the living for the deceased and keeping corpses away from exposure to scavengers (1 Sam 17:44, 46; 2 Sam 21:1–14). The fascination with heroic scenes of single combat (1 Sam 17; 2 Sam 23:9–12, 20–23) along with the Greek tradition of lists of heroes (2 Sam 23:24–39), the superiority of prophet over king (e.g.1 Sam 19:18–24), and the tragic character of Saul all are likely themes that reflect cultural contact with Greek tradition in Persian times. The universal historian Leopold von Ranke called Saul "the first tragic personage in the history of the world" (*Universal History: The Oldest Historical Group of Nations and the Greeks* [ed. George W. Prothero; New York: Harper & Brothers, 1885], 43). Saul's tragedy can be seen in many episodes. For example, 1 Sam 14:24–46 describes how Saul fails to pursue the Philistines and, instead of accepting his limits, is determined to cast lots to find out who has broken an oath he had sworn. His rash vow leads to the sacrifice of his son. The episode's anticipatory character points to Saul's tragic nature: he would have ended his dynasty prematurely by himself, without having obviously villainous intentions. Furthermore, the hasty oath that was intended to secure future military success in an uncertain situation results in a much more severe loss; in this case, his heir, which is a typically tragic motif. The tragic character can also be seen in the manner in which Saul interacts with the people like the king in a Greek drama, as acknowledged by Gerhard

Homicide Law, Plot Chains, and Character Formation

The following remarks focus on the content and the narrative genre of legal traditions in Samuel and from this vantage point, reflect Samuel's contribution to law and to legal debates in Persian times. With clear relations to discourses in law collections, a number of narratives in Samuel comment in great detail on decision making, on legal authority, legal procedure, and on the content of laws. Across the breadth of legal traditions, remarkably few passages ponder themes like marriage law or the specifics of the rights of the king (2 Sam 8:10–22; 2 Sam 7*), while private acts of violence are much more prominently featured. Violence between individuals is a topic in 1 Sam 18–27* and 2 Sam 1–4*, where the protagonists are seen not so much as functionaries of the respective political elites but rather, as individuals who are involved in a kinship feud. Notably, an everyday legal aspect of ancient society stands out: the narratives demonstrate how the dynamic of violence can potentially result in homicide and can trigger endless bloody acts of revenge. Numerous plots of the books discuss the role of judicial authorities when they focus thematically on feud and revenge.[5] Saul's bloody revenge against the priests of Nob, executed merely because they helped his enemy David, is a typical example (1 Sam 22:6–19).[6] By the same token, David's self-restraint from taking revenge on Nabal (1 Sam 25) reflects on the default mechanisms of revenge that inform homicide law.

Beyond the individual storylines, the narratives even flesh out entire characters around the themes of enmity, homicide and revenge. Prominent examples are Asahel, Joab, and Abner. Abner dies at Joab's hand (2 Sam 3:26–27), while Ishbaal (2 Sam 4:7) and Absalom (2 Sam 18:11–17)

---

von Rad when commenting on 1 Sam 14:24–46: "Israel never again gave birth to a poetic production which in certain of its features has such close affinity with the spirit of Greek tragedy" (*Old Testament Theology* [trans. D. M. G. Stalker; 2 vols.; New York: Harper & Row, 1962], 1:325). I have proposed that a "tragic" layer inspired by Greek tragedy has been added to the Saul narratives, which is visible in 1 Sam 10:8; 13:7–13a; 10:17–27; 14:24–46; 26*; 28* and 1 Sam 31*.

5. Homicide and revenge are idiosyncratic themes in the plots of 1 Sam 18–27* and 2 Sam 15–1 Kgs 2*; see, for instance, Pamela Barmash, "The Narrative Quandary: Cases of Law in Literature," *VT* 54 (2004): 1–16. For reflections on the development in homicide law reflected in legal cases in Samuel, see, for instance, Henry McKeating, "The Development of the Law on Homicide in Ancient Israel," *VT* 25 (1975): 46–68.

6. We can only tentatively assume an origin of this narrative in Yehud in the Persian period.

are killed during revolts. The biography of Absalom in his early years in 2 Sam 13–14* provides another example.[7] It recounts the spiteful revenge of Absalom for his brother's rape of Tamar 2 Sam 13:23–29. This episode reflects on justice among kin and on the idea of just retribution. His intentional homicide out of revenge leads to Absalom's three-year exile in Geshur (2 Sam 13:37–38).[8] In a related thread, 2 Sam 11 presents David's violation of marriage law (vv. 2–5) intertwined with the killing of the deceived husband (vv. 14–17). This episode equally picks up themes of justice and of just retribution with the death of Bathsheba's firstborn. One is tempted to understand the infant's death in 12:15b–24a as retribution for the killing of the deceived husband Uriah.

The cases of David's killing of Uriah (2 Sam 11:14–17; 2 Sam 12) and Absalom's revenge on Amnon (2 Sam 14) are thematically interrelated. In addition, they were both the subject of source-critical considerations. Called melodramatic by literary critics,[9] the parable in 2 Sam 12:1–5 makes

---

7. An in-depth source criticism of 2 Sam 13–14 is beyond the scope of this paper. One reason to date parts of 2 Sam 13–14 after the exile is that, from a form-critical perspective, the episodes about the young Absalom are likely to be later than the episodes that feature him in his mature years as a usurper in public rebellion. For a parallel, see the form-critical analysis of the synoptic gospels with its corresponding biographic pattern that explains the literary development of the traditions in Helmut Koester, "Gospel II. Genre 2e. Legend," *Religion Past and Present* (ed. Hans Dieter Betz et al.; 13 vols.; Boston: Brill, 2005–2013), 5:528–31. Compare Walter Radl, "Kindheitsgeschichten," *Religion in Geschichte und Gegenwart* (ed. Kurt Galling; 7 vols.; 4th ed.; Tübingen: Mohr Siebeck, 1998–2005), 4:993–94. Previously, Leonhard Rost, *Die Überlieferung von der Thronnachfolge Davids* (BWANT 42; Stuttgart: Kohlhammer, 1926), 104, had seen the plot emerging in two strands of episodes of background stories before the actual succession in 1 Kgs 1–2: the first, 2 Sam 10–12, told the story of the person of the successor and, the second, 2 Sam 9 together with 2 Sam 13:1–20:22, was the background story to the process of the succession.

8. On the relation of Absalom's exile to the asylum regulations in Deut 19:1–12 (and Num 35), see below, 174–75.

9. See, for instance, the interpretation of the episode with relation to David's character in Stuart Lasine, "Melodrama as Parable: The Story of the Poor Man's Ewe Lamb and the Unmasking of David's Topsy-Turvy Emotions," *HTR* 8 (1984): 101–24. Based on its peculiar forms of presentation, Lasine interprets the parable to be filled with stereotypical contrasts, such as "rich/poor." 2 Sam 12 contributes to this emotional portrait of David and the emotional aspects of David as listener. While rejecting any common points between David's response and Aristotelian tragedy, Lasine sees his response as the appropriate reaction to melodrama, not tragedy. The melodramatic response of David corresponds to the "extremely unrealistic nature of the tale which

a bold legal comment on David's killing of Uriah.[10] Three typical source-critical scenarios can be distinguished: 12:1–7a was added,[11] 12:1–15a is secondary,[12] or 2 Sam 11:27a was originally followed by 12:24bβ, which would indicate that 11:27b–12:24abα was an addition.[13] Beyond similar source-critical explanations of 2 Sam 12 and 14, they consider the same theme of homicide, and formally both are examples of the genre of the judicial parable.[14] The parables in 12:1–5 and in 14:2–22 are told in scenes that place the audience within the story in the role of the judge. They are

obscures any connection between the fictional events and David's actual crimes" (Lasine, "Melodrama," 110).

10. The secondary character of this episode is well established; see already Stanley A. Cook, "Notes on the Composition of 2 Samuel," *American Journal of Semitic Languags* 16 (1899–1900): 156–57; compare Elias Auerbach, *Wüste und Gelobtes Land* (2 vols.; 2nd ed.; Berlin: Schocken, 1938), 1:228 n. 1. Ernst Würthwein, *Die Erzählung von der Thronfolge Davids: Theologische oder Politische Geschichtsschreibung?* (Theologische Studien 115; Zurich: Theologischer Verlag, 1974), 32. Würthwein suggests a secondary origin of the passage for two reasons. First, the story is not carried through to the end: the naming of the first child is missing. Secondly, the narrative of Solomon's birth summarizes what follows after a long period of time, while the first child dies after the short span of seven days, and the entire episode supposedly happens during a siege of Rabbah of Ammon. See further source-critical positions in Walter Dietrich and Thomas Naumann, *Die Samuelbücher* (Erträge der Forschung 287; Darmstadt: Wissenschaftliche Buchgesellschaft, 1995) 250–51.

11. As opposed to Rost (*Thronnachfolge*, 96), who still assumed vv. 1–7a to be part of the Succession Narrative, while the words of threat in vv. 11–12 and 7b–10 are later additions.

12. So, e.g. Karl Budde, *Die Bücher Samuel* (KHC 8; Tübingen: Mohr, 1902), 255. Walter Dietrich suggests DtrP was an original source and a redactional stratum in vv. 6, 7b, 9b, 10b–14 (*David, Saul und die Propheten: das Verhältnis von Religion und Politik nach den prophetischen Überlieferungen vom frühesten Königtum in Israel* [2d ed.; BWANT 122; Stuttgart: Kohlhammer, 1992], 28–29).

13.The secondary character of 2 Sam 12:15b–24 has been asserted strongly by Timo Veijola, "Solomon: Bathsheba's Firstborn. Dedicated to the memory of Uriah the Hittite," in: *Reconsidering Israel and Judah: Recent Studies on the Deuteronomistic History* (ed. Gary N. Knoppers and J. Gordon McConville; Winona Lake, Ind.: Eisenbrauns, 2000), 340–57; quoted from the reprint in idem, *Leben nach der Weisung: Exegetisch-historische Studien zum Alten Testament* (ed. Walter Dietrich and Marko Martilla; FRLANT 224; Göttingen: Vandenhoeck & Ruprecht, 2008), 101–17, esp. 101. On the source-criticism of 2 Sam 14, see below, 170–72.

14. This category was introduced by Uriel Simon, "The Poor Man's Ewe Lamb," *Bib* 48 (1967): 207–42, esp. 221. He mentions five examples: 2 Sam 11:1–14; 14:1–20; 1 Kgs 20:35–43; Isa 5:1–7; Jer 3:1–5. The parable's relevance as legal source has recently

set in a communicative situation in which the fictive audience, King David, has to decide, and they both urge the audience to pass a clear-cut sentence. As a literary genre, such parables are known beyond the Hebrew Bible. For instance, in Greek drama, they feature

> a realistic story about a violation of the law, related to someone who had committed a similar offence with the purpose of leading the unsuspecting hearer to pass judgment on himself. The offender may only be caught in the trap that is set for him if he truly believes that the story that is told to him actually has happened, and only if he does not prematurely detect the similarity between the offence in the story and the one he has himself committed.[15]

The narrative context of 2 Sam 11–12 is a case in point: David has just broken up Uriah's marriage and commanded his death. In this situation, the case narrative in 2 Sam 12:1–5 confronts David with a rich man's robbery of his neighbor's ewe lamb. In 1 Kgs 3:16–28, two women present their dispute before the king and urge him to decide. The handling of the case, the legal reasoning and the king's individual decisions vary. In 2 Sam 12, without further investigation, David decides in favor of the poor man; 1 Kgs 3 presents Solomon as a wise judge who renders a fair verdict in a difficult case. The books of Samuel contribute to a legal discourse in which homicide and revenge is a dominant theme. Another example showcasing the form and the content of the legal discourse is the fratricidal case of the woman from Tekoa. It is set in an audience scene with the king that presents David as a knowledgeable expert in law, and it builds on the expectation that, as judge, the king is able to solve the dispute. Thus, it corresponds with the expectations of Deut 17:14–20* that the king will "observe the law" (שמר מצות/מצוה; Deut 17:19).[16] The idiom "YHWH's commandment/s" (מצות/מצוה יהוה)[17] as used 1 Sam 13:13b also has parallels in (late) layers

---

been affirmed by Raymond Westbrook and Bruce Wells, *Everyday Law in Biblical Israel: An Introduction* (Louisville: Westminster John Knox, 2008), 14.

15. Simon, "Ewe Lamb," 220–21.

16. See this idiom and variations of it among others in Deut 4:2//10:13; 4:40; 5:10, 26, 6:17; 7:9, 11; 8:6, 11; 11:22; 13:19; 15:5; 26:17–18; 27:1; 28:1,15, 45; 30:10, 16; Josh 22:5; 1 Kgs 2:3; 6:12; 8:58, 61; 11:34; 13:21; 14:8; 2 Kgs 17:19; 23:3; Ps 119:60; 1 Chr 29:19; 2 Chr 34:31; Neh 10:30.

17. See its use, for example, in Lev 4:2,13, 22; 5:17; Num 15:39; Deut 4:2; 6:17; 8:6;

of Deuteronomic-Deuteronomistic writings and in Leviticus.[18] Given the emphasis on royal competence in law, we can, generally speaking, assume that the case narrative in 2 Sam 14 indeed mirrors current legal practice in Yehud in the Persian period, when it was written.[19]

The reason for the emphasis on a seemingly extreme case of homicide and revenge in Samuel requires an explanation. As is the case in law collections, legal rules typically cover extreme forms of violence and of blood feud. By presenting examples of these extreme cases, the books of Samuel underscore their very nature as key themes of legislation. Homicide and revenge are, indeed, key themes in kinship-based societies that lack law enforcement. Blood feud functions as a rule-based mechanism to ensure just retaliation, on the one hand, and to limit the use of uncontrolled violence, on the other hand.[20] Both just retaliation and the limitation of uncontrolled violence are critical for any society, including Persian-period Yehud. The books of Samuel deal with the subject matter of law in their narrative material. In the debate over the authority of the books of Samuel, the reflection in 2 Sam 14 over homicide law is relevant not only as an isolated episode but also when seen against the backdrop of other narratives on homicide. The characters of the short, dramatic case narrative closely relate to other characters that are notorious for their bloody activities, especially Joab. The relevance of these characters in Samuel and the emphasis on them is best explained when their metonymic understanding as legal comments on homicide and revenge are acknowledged. The plot in 2 Sam 14:1–24 about revenge and persecution is embedded in a larger nar-

---

10:13; 11:27–28; 28:9, 13; Josh 22:3; Judg 2:17; 3:4; 1 Kgs 18:18; 2 Kgs 17:16, 19; Ezek 7:11; Neh 10:30; 1 Chr 28:8; 2 Chr 24:20; Ps 19:9.

18. Determining the absolute date of origin of this idiom poses a problem; a good number of references point in this direction and allow for a date in the Persian era.

19. The king's role in the application of Israelite Law has been been assessed differently, depending on one's understanding of source-critical and dating issues. See, for instance, Keith W. Whitelam (*The Just King: Monarchical Judicial Authority in Ancient Israel* [JSOTSup 12; Sheffield: JSOT Press, 1979], 123–25) versus Georg Christian Macholz, who argued that 2 Sam 14 presupposes David's authority over the city-state of Jerusalem, which would have claimed judicial authority over the case ("Die Stellung des Königs in der israelitischen Gerichtsverfassung," *ZAW* 84 [1972]: 157–82, esp. 165–66).

20. For the relevance of feud and revenge in homicide law, see Pamela Barmash, *Homicide in the Biblical World* (Cambridge: Cambridge University Press, 2005), 23 n. 7.

rative context in which each character pursues his own interest in a typical homicide-revenge-feud. In revenge for his brother, Joab kills Abner. More complex than this, Joab himself is involved in the killing of Uriah on behalf of David in 2 Sam 11:14–25 and, as a just consequence, Solomon executes Joab in revenge for his killing of Abner and Amasa (1 Kgs 2:5–6, 28–34). Absalom is as complex a personality as Joab. Having been permitted to return to Judah, Absalom puts pressure on Joab by burning his fields in order to get an audience at the court (14:27–29).

The strong opposition between the characters and their interactions from a legal point of view are the core interest of the framing narrative. Since the larger source-critical contexts of this framing narrative are not the focus, I will only discuss two aspects. First, from a literary compositional point of view, i.e., from the perspective of a final-form reading, in light of the actual revolt of Absalom in 2 Sam 15–19*, the episodes in 2 Sam 13–14* function as a "prenarrative" about Absalom's early years.[21] This prenarrative elaborates on homicide law and revenge. Later, the storyline of the Absalom narrative picks up on both themes: at the climax of Absalom's revolt, Joab himself, against the king's explicit request, kills Absalom (2 Sam 18:14). Joab's homicide is motivated by the previous scenes and arises from his anger against Absalom.

Second, when considering the two protagonists, Joab and Absalom, in light of what ensues in 2 Sam 15–18, the narrator's intention is to render in detail the mechanisms of a private enmity that both are acting out in their relationships. The account of Absalom's killing of his brother Amnon in revenge for the rape of his sister Tamar and the resulting exile of Absalom and his forced reentry into the city is typical of private controversies between two individuals. In 2 Sam 14, the king takes up the role of a superior judge with the authority to judge between the enemies, yet he is incapable of establishing fair retaliation in this particular case. That said, the judicial reasoning with the king as authority is set in a literary frame that demonstrates that as a superior institution, the king lacks the capacity to solve the problem of the extreme of fratricide. As a consequence of the legal quandary, the petitioner succeeds in her intent to manipulate him, and the king authorizes Joab to bring Absalom back from his exile. The legal problem of an equitable retaliation for Absalom remains a dilemma, as 2 Sam 14 demonstrates.

---

21. Rost, *Thronnachfolge*, 104.

Divine Retribution in 2 Samuel 12

The secondary character of 2 Sam 14:2–22 draws attention to a number of parallels with the judicial parable in 2 Sam 12, including the death of the second child as a form of divine retribution for David's homicide. This dimension of divine sanction is best explained against the backdrop of the narrative as a form of law-based reasoning. We can read 12:15b–24 as a rebuttal to any claim of Solomon's dishonorable origin. This explains the passage's peculiarities[22] and what this insertion adds to the story's earlier version. When 12:15b–24 recounts the first child's death, it aims at removing Solomon's potential guilt as heir to a murderous father. The child's death counts as blood spilled in retributive justice for his father's guilt. The divinely imposed "revenge" outweighs the human bloodguilt. The child's death is presented as divinely arranged justice. The introductory comment on the infant's death in 2 Sam 12:15b sets up the interpretation of the entire episode: "YHWH struck the child ... and it became sick." In parallel instances in Chronicles, YHWH's act of reprisal (נגף *qal*) is targeted at disobedient kings. As a form of immediate punishment,[23] such divine intervention is conceptually nuanced, and it is different from the guilt that is accumulated over generations in the "Deuteronomistic" historiographic model presented in the book of Kings.[24]

The notion of divine retaliatory punishment as a means to prevent human revenge has three parallels in the David narratives in Samuel. First,

---

22. For instance, the fact that David mourns for exactly seven days but then stops once the child is dead (vv. 18b–24a). Seven days are the length of time a woman remains impure after giving birth to a son. Here, the notice of Bathsheba's purification is placed before the seven days (11:4), after which she could again be touched (Lev 5:19–24; 18:19; 20:18; the same held for a mother who gave birth to a son Lev 12:2). This then motivates the narrator to have David come to her after this time period so that the second child, Solomon, would be conceived in purity; see Veijola, "Solomon," 111–12.

23. See, for instance, 2 Chr 13:15, 20. The reasons for the defeat of Jeroboam are (1) that he rose up against his Judahite lord, gathered scoundrels around him, and defied Rehoboam (vv. 6–7); (2) he made the golden calves (v. 8); and (3) he expelled the priests of YHWH (v. 9). See also נגף *qal* in 2 Chr 21:18 with Jehoram as object, who is accused of having built high places in Judah, having led the Judahites into "whoredom," and caused Judah to be thrust out (21:11).

24. Ralph W. Klein, *1 Chronicles: A Commentary* (Hermeneia; Minneapolis: Fortress, 2006), 46–47.

1 Sam 25:38 states that YHWH slew Abigail's husband, Nabal, who then dies as the narrative explicitly points out, within a very short span of time, ten days after Abigail has talked to David and has convinced him to refrain from a revenge killing of Nabal.[25] Intentional violence that causes death is also at stake in 1 Sam 26:10 when, instead of engaging in a fight against Saul, David refrains from revenge in the hope of divine retribution. The third episode is 2 Sam 12:15b, in which YHWH slays David's firstborn. Obviously, the theme of God exercising justice by "slaying" a person rather than individuals exercising their physical revenge is in the background of the narrative.[26]

This concept of immediate individual reward and punishment has close parallels with the Chronicler's historiography that highlights the idea of the punishment of individual kings instead of working with the notion of guilt inherited by later royal generations. The concept of retributive justice develops on legal grounds and privileges the individual over corporate kinship identity. When Nathan approaches David, he is far from reflecting on the specifically royal position of his opponent; instead, he is pointing out David's murderous nature as a private individual. This further buttresses the passage's tentative origin in the Persian period, when this debate has parallels in the books of Samuel that relate to this time.[27] Also,

---

25. In the current text, the comment interprets the explanation for Nabal's death given in 25:37: "and his heart died within him and he turned to stone." Placed after this description v. 37, the comment adds the notion of a divinely imposed punishment and subsequent death.

26. See the motif of YHWH slaying the Egyptians through the plagues in Exod 7:27; 12:23a,b, 27.

27. Retributive justice through violent acts is equally a topic in 1 Sam 25, as cross-references to this narrative point out. The words "on me and my house will be the guilt" (cf. עון, 2 Sam 14:32) finds their only exact parallel in 1 Sam 25:24. In her address to David, Abigail takes the "guilt" that Nabal caused in rejecting David's men, which then provoked his feeling for revenge, upon herself. This guilt would be transferred to David should he choose to take revenge and put Nabal to death. This guilt would be upon Absalom or upon the surviving brother should the king not prevent the avenger of blood from taking revenge. The woman (and her father's house) offer to take over the guilt vicariously. Both of these confessions of guilt are uttered in the context of a plea to a king not to exercise nor allow revenge. And they both intend the prevention of an individual from "going into blood guilt" (1 Sam 25:34). In 2 Sam 14:9 the woman uses the expression when she points to David's potential guilt should he allow the blood avenger to kill her remaining son. In a different understanding, Jean Hoftijzer finds the parallel between the vicarious confession of guilt in 2 Sam 14:9 and 1 Sam

the connection between homicide and punitive death can be seen against the backdrop of the debate over immediate retribution that is the basis of the Chronicler's historiography. As a consequence, we can hardly date the Nathan parable before the late sixth century B.C.E.; that is, it most likely originated in Persian times.

Human Leniency and Entrapment in 2 Sam 14

Rooted in the debate about immediate individual punishment and in the discourses about homicide law and revenge, 2 Sam 14:1–24 is also a parable and, as such, represents a specific form of legal reasoning. This will become apparent in more detail when we examine the episode's outline and form. It consists of a prologue (vv. 1–4), in which Joab instructs a woman to disguise herself as mourner when she presents her fictitious case to the king, and a scene of a royal audience granted to the woman. The core episode is the audience scene in vv. 5–20 that contains a dialogue between the woman and the king. The closing scene in vv. 21–22 transitions into the king's audience with Joab, which leads to Absalom's return in vv. 23–24. Although the king responds to Joab's request and Absalom can be brought back from asylum, he remains banned from the royal palace (v. 24). By narrativizing the petitioner's legal appeal, 2 Sam 14 presents legal reasoning in a dramatic description of litigation. The core audience scene is structured as follows:

5a	the king invites the woman to speak
5b–7	the woman's case description
8	the king's first answer
9	the woman's offer to take potential guilt upon her
10	the king's prompt to adduce a potential plaintiff
11a	the woman's repeated concern about the avenger of blood
11b	the king's reassurance for safety of woman's son
12	renewed invitation to the woman to speak

25:24 to derive from the similar purpose of both supplications. The women are taking upon themselves the responsibility for guilt with the intention to plead that they might not be punished or plead mitigating circumstances ("David and the Tekoite Woman," *VT* 20 [1970]: 419–44 [424–27]).

13–17   the woman pleads for the return of the exiled; she blesses the king
18   the king's request for honesty, the woman reopens her speech
19a   the king's suspicion about Joab's involvement
19b–20 the woman's confession and her blessing

Four markers indicate the passage has been secondarily inserted, with diverse and distinct undertones and, possibly, additions to an earlier form.[28] (1) The episodic character of 2 Sam 14:2–22 suggests expansion. Verses 1 and 23 connect perfectly: Joab has brought Absalom home from Geshur without consulting with the king, and, as a consequence, the king refuses

---

28. To mention some source-critical solutions, Budde takes vv. 25–27 out and sees v. 26 as a later addition (*Samuel*, 264). Timo Veijola tentatively suggests vv. 4–20 were added (*Die ewige Dynastie: David und die Entstehung seiner Dynastie nach der deuteronomistischen Darstellung* [STTSB 193; Helsinki: Suomalainen Tiedakatemie, 1975], 47 n. 3). Würthwein argues that three reasons qualify vv. 2–22 as an insertion influenced by what he generally labels as wisdom thought: (1) 2 Sam 13:39 already states David's change of mind. If so, the presentation of a convincing plot in a case narrative is superfluous. (2) The insertion of vv. 2–22 has the function of blaming Joab for the fact that Absalom could reenter the court. It increases Joab's responsibility in the matter. (3) The episode presents the return for opposite reasons than a supposedly earlier stratum. The woman's case suggests that Joab's interest was primarily directed toward the son. Instead, 13:39 is pointing to David's interest in bringing Absalom back to the court (*Thronfolge Davids*, 46–47). The source critical reflections, paired with *Tendenzkritik*, have been refined without being more convincing. See, for example, Rainer Bickert, who has suggested a detailed source-critical model of a pre-Deuteronomistic wisdom anecdote embedded between vv. 1 and 23* (vv. 2–3, 4aαb*, 5, 6, 7aα, 10, 11b*, 12aα, 13b, 15, 18, 19, 20, 21) ("Die List Joabs und der Sinneswandel Davids: Eine dtr bearbeitete Einschaltung in die Thronfolgeerzählung: 2 Sam. XIV 2–22," in *Studies in the Historical Books of the Old Testament* (ed. John A. Emerton; VTSup 30; Leiden: Brill, 1979), 30–51). He argues that two commentators reworked this layer: (1) a commentator unrelated to Dtr, who added doublets that tentatively converted the son into David's heir, describing him as the inheritance of YHWH (vv. 13a, 14), who also added further comments that introduced a dynastic element and an allusion to the people of God in vv. 13a, 16; and (2) a Dtr-related commentator, who intensified the tone of the court and idealized David (vv. 4aβ, 8–9, 12aβb, 22) (Bickert, "List Joabs," 49). This same commentator also inserted the urge that the king should change his mind for the sake of the people as a collective, arguing with respect to the people of God and the relevance for David. Bickert assumes these comments to be later than DtrN ("List Joabs," 51).

to give Absalom access to the palace. 2 Samuel 14:1 and 23 would offer a more plausible plot without vv. 2–22. In addition, a change in David's attitude between 13:39 and 14:1 is apparent, which may well be the main reason for the insertion of the episode. While 2 Sam 14:1 states the heart of the king was "against Absalom" (על־אבשלום), 13:39 refers to the case with an ambivalent undertone,[29] using כלה piel to describe how "David gave up pursuing (לצאת) Absalom, because he relented from Amnon, because he was dead." (2) The use of generic designations for the protagonists typifies inserted case narrative. (3) The narrative about the wise woman is never referred to otherwise, as is also the case with Abigail in 1 Sam 25. (4) The narrative considers legal aspects of Absalom's return. The short plot is an excursus on a closely related theme of relevance for key characters in the books of Samuel.

Given its character as an inserted excursus, its specific form in comparison with other narratives becomes relevant. As has already been mentioned, the arrangement of 2 Sam 14, its presentation of the legal case, and its theme are closely related to Nathan's parable in 2 Sam 12. A formal parallel is that not only is Joab confronting the king as the superior judge who decides a fictitious case, but Nathan's parable of the man's ewe lamb in 2 Sam 12:1–4 also functions as a literary device for highlighting David's guilt. Compared with 2 Sam 14, Nathan's parable exhibits a more pointed version of the dramatic case narrative that criticizes the king more blatantly and which demonstrates his misdemeanor in more detail. The case narrative intentionally culminates in a self-induced verdict of guilty (v. 7). Similar to the use of the lawsuit in 2 Sam 14, 2 Sam 12:1–4 is invented to reveal the legal liability resting on David for Uriah's death. In comparison with 2 Sam 12, Joab challenges the king's decision by presenting a fictitious case in 2 Sam 14.

---

29. Larry L. Lyke sees this description as "quite vague" (*King David with the Wise Woman of Tekoa: The Resonance of Tradition in Parabolic Narrative* [JSOTSup 255; Sheffield: Sheffield Academic Press, 1997] 161), while Georg Hentschel suggests that this is a negative attitude of David toward Absalom, in contrast to 13:39 ("Die weise Frau von Tekoa (2Sam 14, 1–24)," in *Auf den Spuren der schriftgelehrten Weisen: Festschrift für Johannes Marböck anlässlich seiner Emeritierung* [ed. Irmtraud Fischer, Ursula Rapp, and Johannes Schiller; BZAW 331; Berlin: de Gruyter, 2003], 63–75 [68–69]). According to Hentschel, this contrast between the two vv. hints that 14:1 can be seen to begin the separate narrative in 14:1–22.

On the basis of the comparison with 2 Sam 12, some specifics of 2 Sam 14 become apparent. The case's nuanced nomenclature evinces its indebtedness to homicide legislation. In the biblical discourse about homicide law, 2 Sam 14 hardly represents an early stage; rather, when it mentions the execution of revenge by a kin member, the so-called "avenger of blood" (v. 11), the narrative seems to presuppose later stages in the law collections.[30] This prominent term suggests that the case law in its current form in 2 Sam 14 dates no earlier than Persian times. This date is buttressed by idioms or phrases without earlier parallels, such as the "people of God," עַם אלהים.[31] In 2 Sam 14:13, the adjective "guilty" (אָשֵׁם) specifies the guilt of the people in the context of the killing, i.e., with reference to the refusal to bring Absalom back. It also appears in the decision of the woman's suit that in the case of a fratricide, the remaining brother should not be exposed to blood revenge (vv. 10–11). The adjective "guilty" is rarely used otherwise. It is found (in retrospect) for the guilt when carrying out an assault on a kin member with the potential intent of a homicide in Gen 42:21.[32] The idiom in v. 14, "to surround (turn) the

---

30. Absent in the older homicide law in Exod 21:12–14*, this terminology is typical for later stages, such as Deut 19:1–11*. The avenger of blood first appears in Deut 19:6 in a short case narrative, then in the regulation for the implementation in Deut 19:12 and, increasingly, in the late text, Num 35:19, 21, 24, 25, 37 (2x) and in Josh 20:5, 9. Deuteronomy 19 is in itself source-critically complex; see, for instance, Jan Christian Gertz, who suggests a basic layer in Deut 19:2a, 3b, 4, 5b, 6, 11–12 (*Die Gerichtsorganisation Israels im deuteronomischen Gesetz* [FRLANT 165; Göttingen: Vandenhoeck & Ruprecht 1994] 118–26).

31. This construct is only used in Judg 20:2; on its meaning, see Eduard Lipiński, "עַם," *ThWAT* 6:177–94 (192).

32. A further reference of the adjective and the noun is Ezra 10:19. The noun's meaning can be "trespass offering," see Lev 5; 6:10; 7:14; 19:21–22, as well as Num 5:6–7; 6:12; 18:9; Ezek 40:39, 42:13, 44:29, 46:20. The bulk of the further references of the root suggests it did not originate earlier than Persian time. See Lev 14; Num 6:12; Lev 8:23; cf. in Samuel the Philistines' אָשָׁם of golden mice and tumors (1 Sam 6:3, 4, 8, 17) and in 2 Kgs 12:17 an אָשָׁם of money was given to the priests. In the Song of the Servant (Isa 53:10) it is an isolated cultic term. The servant offers himself as an אָשָׁם in compensation for the sins of the people. The notion of wrongdoing and guilt are associated with the feminine noun אַשְׁמָה. See Lev 22:16 and Ezra 10:10 as well as Lev 5:24 in the case of restitution; cf. Ps 69:6; Ezra 9:6, 7, 13, 15, with the notion of "becoming guilty" in 1 Chr 21:3, Ezra 10:10, 10:19; see also Lev 4:3; Amos 8:14, or the reference to the "bringing of a trespass-offering" in Lev 5:24. For a dating in Persian time and later, see Diether Kellermann, "אָשָׁם," *ThWAT* 1:463–72 (469).

'appearance' (פנה) of the matter," is a variation of idioms such as "turn the face."[33] In particular, the nuanced usage of the categories for guilt in 2 Sam 14 points to an origin in Persian times.

In many respects, 2 Sam 14 is a stylized case narrative. The law case describes a homicide between (half-) brothers, and it mirrors Absalom's revenge for the rape of his sister Tamar. In the framing narrative, Absalom is forced into asylum with a relative in the hope of later being granted permission to return (2 Sam 13:38). In this way, the narrative modifies the themes of homicide, asylum, and revenge as expressed in the law collections. For instance, Deut 19:5–6,[34] 11–12 clarifies the circumstances under which it is possible to request exile for a killer in an asylum city after his nonintentional homicide. The assailant is denied asylum if he intentionally killed his victim.[35]

That Absalom was forced into exile after a homicide (נדה *niphal*) is taken up in a second round of clarifications in 2 Sam 14:13–14. Some questions arise when comparing the granting of city asylum for homicide to the case that the woman adduces. Absalom's exile in Geshur was a remedy to avoid David's revenge. His intention to return from exile is seemingly based on the assumption of having spent enough time in asylum. If so, Absalom's return is based on legal assumptions divergent from those in Deut 19. And, this divergence from Deut 19 is also apparent when looking at the fact that Absalom killed intentionally and, hence, would not have been eligible for city asylum according to Deut 19. We would need to assume extenuating circumstances if we would insinuate a connection between the basic assumptions of the case of Absalom and of Deut 19. We might look in two directions to find the reason for the difference in the legal understanding of asylum and the extenuating circumstances that would have allowed Absalom to enjoy asylum in a city, as well as the reason for his request to return despite having intentionally killed his brother. One

---

33. Cf. this object in Judg 18:23; 1 Kgs 8:14//2 Chr 6:3; 1 Kgs 21:4; 2 Kgs 20:2; Isa 38:2; Ezek 7:22; 2 Chr 29:6; 35:22 (*hiphil*). See Diether Kellermann, "סבל," *ThWAT* 5:730–44 (734).

34. Deuteronomy 19:5 provides a semantic link to "exile/being impelled" (נדה) when it describes that the iron blade accidentally "is impelled" from the hand when using the axe when cutting wood.

35. City asylum is unknown in Exod 21:13–14; see however in Deut 19:1–11*; more elaborately Num 35 and Josh 20, which both assume that the killer could stay for a longer period of time in the asylum city.

possibility of explaining the difference between Absalom's asylum after his intentional killing of Amnon (2 Sam 13:23–29) and the asylum rules could be that his case reflects an everyday case while Deut 19:1–11 reflects a more theoretical understanding of asylum. Another possibility is that 2 Sam 14 differs from homicide law as represented in law collections due to the extenuating fact that Absalom is seeking refuge at a relative's house.

Another peculiarity of the case narrative relates to the king's theoretical entitlement to grant Absalom's return from exile. The case narrative suggests exactly this possibility, and it clearly highlights the complexity of this matter. At the center of the debate to which the fictitious case speaks is the king's leeway in decision-making. Second Samuel 14 debates the king's decision and his competence to handle revenge killings under procedural law.

In this debate about legal decision-making, 2 Sam 14 portrays the king as being highly concerned about the bloodshed among his kin, yet the episode also portrays the king as highly reluctant to prosecute a family member who has carried out a revenge killing. The king's reluctance to punish Absalom is a character trait that echoes his reticence to penalize Amnon for his rape of Tamar (2 Sam 13:21). Within the larger plot of the David narratives, 2 Sam 14 offers a counter case to the way in which the king handles the revenge killings of Joab. David requests that Solomon execute Joab (1 Kgs 2:5–6; 28–34). The macro context juxtaposes two contrasting images of David. One shows him as a mellow king, while the other, at the end of his rule in 1 Kgs 1–2, portrays him as a law-abiding hardliner who defers the execution of justice to his successor. Within the storyline before 1 Kgs 1–2, the king's reluctance to punish Absalom and his decision in favor of Absalom's return appear as a prerequisite to the son's possible rebellion.

Beyond the aforementioned peculiarities of the case, the narrative's very form is highly stylized. In light of the judicial aspects of 2 Sam 14, we can call it a "judicial parable."[36] While it reports a unique case and not a norm,[37] and even though the judicial aspect of the parable seems to be

---

36. The judicial relevance of 2 Sam 14 becomes more apparent when compared with 2 Sam 12. See Simon, "Ewe-Lamb," 224–25. The "functioning" of this genre in ancient Israel's judicial practice was rejected by, for instance, Whitelam, *Just King*, 135–36. Whitelam rightly favors an interpretation as "literary constructions" that relied on the theoretical aspects of monarchical authority.

37. Whitelam, *Just King*, 125.

problematic if understood to have a practical function,[38] 2 Sam 14 clearly discusses the king's institutional "judicial authority," for instance, whether the king has the authority of a supreme court.[39] Even though the episode reflects on the king's role and even though it is written in an elaborate style, it mainly is a deliberation in the field of Israelite law.[40]

The reason to interpret 2 Sam 14 as a judicial parable is, more specifically, its function as a trap for the offender. The trap springs shut in the moment when the respondent realizes how the story relates to his own case and that he himself has committed the offense.[41] David responds and interprets the parable in exactly this way within the formation of the characters as defendant and judge. This stylization finds expression in three aspects. Second Samuel 14 abstracts from individuals and refers to the generic titles of the king and the maid instead of names. Second, in the speech of the woman, the plot is entirely made up to illustrate an extreme legal case and, finally, the short scene is kept in a dramatic tone.

In what follows we shall adduce further evidence for the stylized nature of the narrative and for its dramatic tone. First, the use of generic titles instead of names is typical of the corresponding genre of prophetic narratives in the book of Kings.[42] While the name "David" does not occur once in ch. 14, the generic title "the king" appears forty times. Joab is named directly in the introduction and conclusion (vv. 1–3, 19–23). It stands to reason that the character of Joab is introduced on purpose with the meaningful epithet, "the son of Zeruiah." Within the books of Samuel, this character description at the outset of the narrative in 2 Sam 14:1 sets a particular tone for the episode as a reflection on violence against humans and, more specifically, homicide.[43]

---

38. Whitelam, *Just King*, 127.

39. See Macholz, "Stellung des Königs," 166–68; Whitelam, *Just King*, 124.

40. The dating and the exact understanding of the theme vary. See, for instance, the interpretation of kinship law and the understanding of Israel as an acephalous entity in which David is understood as chief who establishes his rule in Elizabeth Bellefontaine, "Customary Law and Chieftainship: Judicial Aspects of 2 Samuel 14.4–21," *JSOT* 38 (1987): 47–72.

41. Simon, "Ewe-Lamb," 221.

42. See, for instance, Alexander Rofé, *The Prophetical Stories: The Narratives about the Prophets in the Hebrew Bible, Their Literary Types and History* (Jerusalem: Magnes, 1988).

43. Most of the twenty references in which the epithet "son of Zeruiah" is found use it metonymically for violence, homicide and revenge (1 Sam 26:6; 2 Sam 2:13, 18;

Other features in this genre of stylized narratives need to be attributed to the streamlining of the form of the narrative, such as the woman's attention to royal etiquette when she communicates with the king. Clearly, the woman's mission in the narrative highlights her subservience to the king. Her repeated self-reference as שפחה adds a tone of humbleness to her self-predication.[44] In a formalized conversation between the king/judge and the petitionary 2 Sam 14:1–21, this contributes to the authentic atmosphere that a recipient could expect in any royal audience. The woman first humbly asks for permission to speak.

The formalized conversation correlates with the case's fictitious nature. From the beginning, the reader is aware that Joab crafted the woman's case in order to be in line with the king's own experience: The woman mimics a parent who mourns her son at a point in time when David himself is mourning the loss of Amnon and of his other son Absalom in exile. The formalized character is clearest as the woman introduces her parable about a fratricide and about its tragic consequences of punishment and revenge within the clan. Another aspect of the stylization of the narrative is the woman's intention to influence the king in his decision concerning Absalom. Its artistic style, the fictitious nature and, most importantly, its setting in a dramatic scene all contribute to a particularly stylized legal debate.

Second, the narrative is artistically composed. It artfully arranges the flow of the speech of the woman: After a first answer of the king, v. 11b, the woman asks for further consideration of the case. With her request in vv. 13–17, the woman meanders away from the actual case of the revenge of a fratricide, and she juxtaposes this case with the other case.

Third, one of the narrative's peculiarities that may be instrumental when pointing out its teaching agenda is its dramatic tone that is also

---

3:39; 14:1; 16:9–10 and 19:20–21); 2 Kgs 2:5, 22 condemn Joab's killings by explicitly quoting the royal authority; a further reference is his association with the party that supports the usurpation of Adonijah in 1 Kgs 1:7. The association of Joab with violent killing may have led secondarily to Joab's function as David's military commander in 2 Sam 8:16; 18:2. It is compelling that "son of Zeruiah" in 18:2 alludes to Absalom's intentional homicide later in the war narrative in 2 Sam 18:18. Further references to "son of Zeruiah" include Joab's description as a warrior (2 Sam 21:26) and a hero among the thirty (2 Sam 23:37) and a genealogical note (2 Sam 17:25). In Chronicles, it appears in genealogies (1 Chr 2:16; 11:39), designates the chief commander (2 Chr 11:6, 39), and is used further in 2 Chr 26:28; 27:24.

44. 2 Sam 14:6, 7, 12, 15, 17, 19. אמה is used in vv. 15–16. On the aspect of subservience, see Eleonore Reuter, "שׁפחה," ThWAT 8:403–8 (406).

found in other narratives in 2 Samuel. The so-called "Succession Narrative" is thoroughly soaked in an elaborate, dramatic style. L. Rost has drawn attention to the numerous dramatic episodes and dramatic forms of 2 Samuel that served as stylistic markers to delineate the "Succession Narrative" as a literary unity from surrounding parts: the use of metaphors,[45] the use of frequent inclusions, like the repetition of an introductory phrase in the closing of a speech,[46] and the preeminent literary device of the messenger speeches,[47] which create a typical overlap between scenes. It is especially this overlap between two scenes that creates a smooth transition and that presents the plot in the form of a screenplay that can be performed on stage.

This typical cross-fade of scenes can be more fully grasped in the spatial arrangement of an on-stage performance of the dramatic narrative. First Kings 1 showcases the dramatic effect: At the delicate moment of Solomon's royal installment through anointing, the shouts of joy from his followers and their noise from pipes and trumpets reach the assembly of those who, earlier on this day, have gathered in celebration of Adonijah's enthronement (1 Kgs 1:40–50). The concurrent, ongoing scenes could not be more theatrical. The narrator specifically highlights this performance aspect of two concurrent scenes: He lets the reader know Adonijah has heard the noise of Solomon's enthronement assembly as Adonijah was just about to finish feasting. In the very moment in which Joab, who is among the revelers, still publicly wonders about the reason for the noise and assumes there is an uproar in the city, a messenger arrives. To add historical credibility to his narrative, the author mentions him by name, Jona-

---

45. According to Rost, Meribaal refers to himself as a dead dog (2 Sam 9:8); Amnon acts like a fool (13:13); the woman from Tekoa compares humans with water spilled on the ground (2 Sam 14:14); Ahitophel wants to lead the people to Absalom like a bride to her husband (2 Sam 17:3); and a warrior has a heart like a lion (2 Sam 17:10) (*Thronnachfolge*, 113).

46. Rost refers to the figure of speech of the so-called πλοκή, ploce, the repetition of a word; cf. the rhetorical figure ἀντανάκλασις, antanaclasis, a repetition of a word or phrase. When in 2 Sam 11:20–21 Joab asks: "Why have you been going so close to the wall of the city with your fight?" he continues to refer to the killing of Abimelech ben Jerubaal. "Has he not been killed by a woman who threw a millstone at him?" Joab repeats: "Why have you been going so close to the wall of the city with your fight?" Hushai's speech in 2 Sam 17:8–10 has a thought that is then framed by the description of the current situation in 17:11–13.

47. See further, 2 Sam 18:19–33; 17:15–22; 15:13.

than ben Abiathar, and introduces him when he appears on stage for his announcement. When Jonathan has informed Adonijah's assembly about Solomon's installation, Adonijah's enthronement festivities end abruptly. Rost used these stylistic features of "artistic prose"[48] as relevant source-critical markers that delineate the extent of the Succession Narrative and its alleged sub-sources.

Entrapment

As has been pointed out, the narrative in 2 Sam 14 is a fictitious, highly stylized, dramatic case narrative that is well embedded in the legal discourses in Samuel. Its precise, carefully nuanced dramatic scenes are told with a clear-cut purpose. The specific intent that the stylistic features of 2 Sam 14 serve becomes apparent when considering the episode as a form of dramatic reflection on a legal matter. The woman's use of the case narrative in 2 Sam 14 points to comparable uses of case narratives, first in 2 Sam 12 but also to the use of case narratives either in the courtroom or in an artificial courtroom in classical drama. As a matter of fact, 2 Sam 14 varies two literary techniques. First, it uses a case narrative to influence the king's decision. This is reminiscent of entrapment, a well-known form in quarrels in antiquity. In modern contexts, entrapment is the effort by an official or an undercover representative from the judicial system to tempt an individual to commit a wrongful deed. Unlike in many contemporary societies, the judicial system in antiquity for the most part did not know of public prosecution. In classical Athens, for instance, no law would proscribe such conduct by a representative of the legal system.[49] Typically, individuals who were at enmity with each other used entrapment as a strategy to tempt an opponent. The victim of the entrapment could have been convicted of having committed a previous crime or could have offended someone directly.[50]

In contemporary British and American detective fiction, another technique associated with entrapment, "framing," "often refers to the act of devising evidence in order to convict a person of a crime that someone else

---

48. Rost, *Thronnachfolge*, 115.
49. Adele C. Scafuro, *The Forensic Stage: Settling Disputes in Graeco-Roman New Comedy* (Cambridge: Cambridge University Press, 1997), 329.
50. Scafuro, *Stage*, 329.

has committed or that has not been committed at all."[51] An offender's ability to prove he had been framed and demonstrate he had been the victim of a fraudulent plot would not necessarily alleviate the case against him, but in cases of adultery or fornication,[52] such proof was crucial in rendering the final decision. Thus, the woman's use of entrapment in 2 Sam 14 refers to a common element of tempting an offender in a form of a trial. It is telling to adduce examples of entrapment of which enemies made use in private disputes.

Cases of entrapment and framing can be found in the Greek orators. In Lysias I, the defendant, Euphiletos, is a cuckolded husband who has killed the adulterer, Eratosthenes, *in actu* in bed with his wife. He then faces accusations by the relatives of the victim. They charge him with having sent the housemaid to the adulterer to have him come to the house. This would mean Euphiletos had acted viciously in a feud-like quarrel against his long-term foe, a judicially relevant circumstance in this case. Euphiletos needs to refute such an accusation that he has entraped a long-term enemy.[53] His strategy in his defense speech is to demonstrate to the jury Eratosthenes' history of adultery. His point is: Eratosthenes has long been an adulterer; therefore, Euphiletos did not entice him to act this way. Euphiletos refutes the accusation he might have entrapped Eratosthenes.

In Demosthenes 53 Nikostratos likewise mentions an entrapment scenario. Arethousios seeks to entice his enemy Apollodorus to commit a violent act. First, he and Nikostratos vandalize Apollodorus' house at night. On the following day, they provoke their enemy even more by sending a young slave to pluck his rose garden and further destroy his property before his very eyes. In his defense, Apollodorus expounds that he did not fetter nor strike the slave, knowing well that this would have entitled his opponent to indict him of having acted out of *hubris* towards a slave. Then Apollodorus would have lost his ability to proceed with a formal indictment that he had set up against his enemy.[54] Aware of his enemies' attempt

---

51. Scafuro, *Stage*, 330.

52. Greek *moikheia*. The term *moikhos* "adulterer" is used in Lysias 1.30 and in the context of other self-help remedies in Lysias 1.29, 49 (Scafuro, *Stage*, 196 nn. 9 and 10).

53. Lysias 1.37: "Please consider, gentlemen: my opponents accuse me of having ordered my slave girl on the night in question to fetch the young man" (*Lysias* [trans. S. C. Todd; Oratory of Classical Greece 2; Austin: University of Texas Press, 2000], 22).

54. *Graphe pseudokleteias*, Demosthenes 54,14–15, i.e., an "indictment for fraudulently testifying to a summons" (Scafuro, *Stage*, 334).

to entrap him, Apollodorus' self-control in the quarrel with his neighbors proved to be critical. He demonstrates in his speech that he acted against their obvious plot, and his reference to the fact that he refrained from a violent attack is critical to preserve his ability to move forward with his own accusation against his opponent.

Such mechanisms of criminal entrapment and of framing are also found in New Comedy. Entrapment scenarios exhibit four hallmark features:

> (1) A plot is devised to entice an individual into committing a crime. Successful execution of the plot entails that the crime be committed and that witnesses be present who could later testify to its commission.
> (2) The script entails a mistake in status.
> (3) The plot presupposes a rehearsal. In this case, the free Athenian is to be instructed on what to do and how to act as a slave; presumably, witnesses for the plotters are to be instructed where to be present and what to observe.
> (4) The motive for the entrapment is to settle a dispute. Here, it is to intimidate Apollodorus into dropping his case against Arethousios.[55]

A parallel to Greek drama in its actual form, 2 Sam 14 varies these hallmark features: (1) A plot of entrapment: Joab seeks to bring Absalom back into the city and to the royal court. Making up a similar fictitious case, he presents it through the woman of Tekoa. (2) The script entails a mistake in status: The woman pretends to be a mourning widow who has lost her son. (3) Joab rehearses the plot with the wise woman. (4) The main motive for the "entrapment" of David is only partly the intent to settle a dispute between two parties who are at enmity with each other. In its current context, the entrapment of the king seeks to criticize his understanding of the legal necessity of exile for his son. The case narrative's intent is to reflect on the plausibility of revenge for the homicide of a kin member.

Outlook

We have seen that the woman's fictional case in 2 Sam 14 speaks to two distinct legal discourses. In the foreground, she adduces the language of

---

55. Scafuro, *Stage*, 336.

homicide laws and she fosters a debate about this topic. This discourse on revenge in 2 Sam 14:2–22 presents as parallels the prehistory of Absalom and, indirectly, Joab. Both have killed, and both will therefore lose their lives. In its narrative form, 2 Sam 14 comments on just retribution for those who aspire to rule as a king in Judah. Ultimately, Absalom is punished for his bloodshed, and, in retrospect, David appears as too lenient a king. The parables in 2 Sam 12 and 14 seemingly were set under David in order to emphasize the king's traditional role as a legal expert. At the same time, they portray David as a prototypical king who fails to live up to the ideal of legal expertise. The books of Samuel question the authority of the Davidic king, and they bring out David's shortcomings as a lawful ruler. In doing so, they in theory affirm the king's authority, yet they confront this ideal with the way in which David exercises his actual kingship.

As has become apparent, the books of Samuel also reflect over the principle of immediate individual retribution in the case of homicide. In the guise of a legal matter, Samuel speaks authoritatively to individual retribution as a matter of principle. Consider, for instance, the prophet's announcement of the divine retribution and the death of the first child of Bathsheba and David in 2 Sam 12. Also, the expected recipients of the judicial parables offer an important clarification about the narrative's main intention and its claims of authority.

Hidden from this case, in the background, the wise woman in 2 Sam 14 is speaking. The undertones of this second discourse on legal procedure are seemingly subtle, yet when seen against the backdrop of common legal procedure at the time, they become more apparent. For instance, the woman requests that the king apply the same law to all cases. Along with the narrative, the petitioner's parable artistically insinuates entrapment and framing. The woman gradually achieves her goal of luring the king and confronting him with a difficult decision and the very procedure she uses can be seen as a comment on legal practice at the time. This is even more important as the woman pressures the king to exercise his authority.

When the narrative pairs the killing of Amnon with an extreme form of fratricide, it explicates the feud-like character of the controversy at the Judean court[56] and comments on legal administration. The narrative pres-

---

56. These feud-like aspects of the narrative have long been seen to be central to 2 Sam 14 (Bellefontaine, "Customary Law," 47–72).

ents the king as involved in solving the quarrels of feud-like structures. Set at the time of the early monarchy in Judah, the parable reflects the private quarrels and power structures in the Judean kin-based society at the time of its origin, as suggested, in Persian times.

While this episode is set in the royal sphere, other narratives in the books of Samuel set in priestly contexts may offer complementary perspectives on the legal reality in Yehud. Historically, Yehud's character as a temple-community, like many others in the Persian Empire, would imply the sanctuary's use as an administrative center with its own (priestly) control, with its collection of revenues that are, in the understanding of the narratives, ultimately operating under the monarch's supreme authority.[57] The assumption of a Judean temple state may well explain the prominence of the controversies about priestly lineages[58] and about the general "assimilation of prophetic-divinatory functions into the priesthood,"[59] all of which are thought to be typical of the Persian era.

The criticism of priestly roles in Samuel contributes in some ways to a discussion about authority in legal matters. An example is the legitimacy of the Elides in 1 Sam 1–3*, which forms part of a discussion about religious authority. The books of Samuel also discuss the authority of Samuel himself, a character who serves as a foil for reflecting on prophetic, priestly and royal authority, especially in three speeches in 1 Sam 8–12* (1 Sam 8; 10:17–27; 12). In 1 Sam 8:1, 3–5 the book takes a stand, for instance, against corrupt judges and is leading a discourse about the constitution. The etiology of the installment of the first king derives from the corruption of judges. Traditionally, the entire chapter is attributed to the Dtr,[60]

---

57. Joseph Blenkinsopp, *A History of Prophecy in Israel* (rev. and enl. ed.; Louisville: Westminster John Knox, 1996), 195–97; cf. earlier Albrecht Alt, "Die Rolle Samarias bei der Entstehung des Judentums," in *Kleine Schriften zur Geschichte des Volkes Israel* (3 vols.; Munich: Beck, 1964), 2:316–34 (331–37).

58. See, for instance, Ezra 2:59–63. Blenkinsopp, *History of Prophecy*, 199.

59. Blenkinsopp, *History of Prophecy*, 199.

60. In the wake of what was partly considered an anti-monarchic context in 1 Sam 7–12* (J. Wellhausen), see M. Noth, *Überlieferungsgeschichtliche Studien: Die sammelnden und bearbeitenden Geschichtswerke im Alten Testament* (Königsberg: Königsberger Gelehrte Gesellschaft, 1943; repr., Darmstadt: Wissenschaftliche Buchgesellschaft, 1967), 56–57. Timo Veijola's redaction-critical study suggested vv. 6–22 were an anti-monarchic tradition (*Das Königtum in der Beurteilung der deuteronomistischen Historiographie: Eine redaktionsgeschichtliche Untersuchung* [STTSB 198; Helsinki, Suomalainen Tiedeakatemia, 1977], 55).

while its stratum with a generally positive attitude toward kingship in 8:1, 3–5, 22b has been suggested to have originated in the Persian era:

> 1 And it happened, when Samuel was old, he installed his sons as judges for Israel.
> 3 But his sons did not walk in his ways[61] and they bent after the (unjust) gain, and they took the bribe, and they bent the law.
> 4 Then all the elders of Israel gathered and went to Samuel to Ramah.
> 5 They said to him: "See you are old, and your sons do not walk in your ways. Now install a king over us, so that he may judge us, as in all the nations."

Samuel installs his sons as judges who then go after "gain," take bribes, and lose their integrity to establish justice.[62] In its earliest layers, 1 Sam 8*[63] does not criticize the installation of a king per se as a negative act. At the same time, the critical remarks about the judges' failures reveal potential problems as they became apparent in this institution, as a consequence of which kingship emerges, according to this etiology.[64] When 1 Sam 8:3

---

61. Read plural with many Hebrew manuscripts, Peshitta, Targum, Vulgate.

62. Hating "unjust gain" is a criterion for judges (Exod 18:21). בצע is originally a technical term that refers to a weaver cutting off a piece of cloth from the warp, leaving only a thrum; literally, it means "to cut; cut off material." See Eli D. Fisher, "Violence, Tradition and Ideology: A Story of the Hebrew Terms BṢʿ, ḤMS and ŠDD" (PhD diss., Vanderbilt Divinity School, 1998), 79–120, esp. 80. The root can convey a neutral sense; the noun often carries an underlying negative bias, which leads to the derived meaning "unjustly made gain." In part, בצע specifically refers to gain that is made through the use of physical violence against individuals. In this meaning, the term is attested in passages dating to the postexilic/Persian period; see the context of homicide in Gen 37:26: no "gain" from homicide. Compare Ezek 22:13 in parallelism with "bribes" (שחד) for bloodshed; 22:27 for physical destruction; Jer 22:17 in the critique of Jehoiakim in vv. 13–19. Cf. also with less specific undertones of physical violence: Exod 18:21 those who hate "unjust gain"; Ezek 33:31; Isa 33:15; 56:11 said of the appetite of dogs as images for violent enemies; 57:17; Jer 6:13; 8:10; Mic 4:13; Hab 2:9; Mal 3:14; Ps 119:36. Cf. also Ps 30:10; Job 22:3; Prov 1:19, cf. also Prov 15:27. See Diether Kellermann, "בצע," ThWAT 1:731–36. LXX L translates *pleonexia*; LXX B translates *synteleia*. 1 Sam 8:1–3 reflects on the misuse of the judges' authority; cf. Tikva Frymer-Kenski, "Israel," in *A History of Ancient Near Eastern Law* (ed. Raymond Westbrook; 2 vols.; Handbuch der Orientalistik 72; Leiden: Brill, 2003), 2:975–1046 (993).

63. Compare the close literary relation between 1 Sam 8* and Deut 17:13–14.

64. Reinhard Müller, *Königtum und Gottesherrschaft: Untersuchungen zur alttestamentlichen Monarchiekritik* (FAT 2/3; Tübingen: Mohr Siebeck, 2004), 120–46.

criticizes bribes and gains that prevent fair conflict settlement, this is thematically related to the discourse on feud-like quarrels that are set at the royal court in 2 Sam 12 and 14.

These considerations intend to clarify the authority of the books of Samuel in the Persian period. We exposed a discourse on homicide and revenge and a discourse on the king's ability as judge, as well as the criticism of corruption. We also elucidated their authority by pointing out their nature as a judicial narrative in dramatic form. The narrative's authority is based on its dramatic form, with its prevalent use of direct speech and its elaborate literary style developed in a short, dramatic scene. This sheds new light on the narrative's supposed reception in the Persian era.[65] Its formal and thematic paralleling of lawsuits that include entrapment, found also in Greek drama, hints that oral presentation might have been a potentially genuine *Sitz im Leben*. Which other narratives on legal topics in Samuel and elsewhere in the Hebrew Bible were based on the literary style of predominantly direct speech and were orally performed requires further study.[66] Based on the form and the content of the legal narrative

---

65. Dtr texts from the Persian era allude to education and to the teaching of texts, for instance, to the learning of the Torah through reading or "mumbling" (Josh 1:8) for an educational purpose. Narratives recount semi-public readings of the Torah in front of the king (2 Kgs 22:10) or the public at large (2 Kgs 23:1–3; Neh 8:1–5). The sermons that summarize the "saving history" (*Heilsgeschichte*) in Josh 23–24, for instance, show a comparable emphasis on learning and teaching. While the dating of passages within these Deuteronomistic summaries to the Persian period may be disputed, their use in this era is most plausible. On the role of orality in education in the HB, see David Carr, *Writing on the Tablet of the Heart: Origins of Scripture and Literature* (Oxford: Oxford University Press, 2005), 111–73.

66. A number of legal narratives that portray the character of Moses assuming the role of a legal authority rendering current legal interpretation equally consist predominantly of direct speech. See, for instance, Lev 24:10–23, Num 9:6–14; 15:32–36; 27:1–11 and 36:1–12, which have been interpreted to reflect the institution of a supreme court. A Persian origin of some of the narratives was suggested by Matthias Millard, "Mündlichkeit nach der Schriftlichkeit," in *Freiheit und Recht: Festschrift für Frank Crüsemann zum 65. Geburtstag* (ed. Christof Hardmeier, Rainer Kessler, and Andreas Ruwe; Gütersloh: Kaiser, 2003), 277–89 (281) in relation to Frank Crüsemann, *Die Tora: Theologie und Sozialgeschichte des alttestamentlichen Gesetzes* (Munich: Kaiser 1992), 276–82. Crüsemann based his assumptions largely on Ludwig Köhler's 1931 article, "Die hebräische Rechtsgemeinde"; repr. in *Der hebräische Mensch: Eine Skizze; Mit einem Anhang: Die hebräische Rechtsgemeinde (Zehn Gastvorlesungen)* (ed. Ludwig Köhler; Tübingen: Mohr, 1953), 143–71, and dates the concept of Moses as an allusion

in 2 Sam 14, we suggest that these parts of the books of Samuel targeted an audience that was acquainted with such forms of legal discourse in a dramatic style. The socio-historical, the religious, and the cultural worlds of readings and of performances of these short scenes about preeminent aspects of Jewish law illuminate the circles of Persian time Yehud among which the books of Samuel have claimed authority. What made the books of Samuel authoritative in the discourses of Persian time Yehud was, among other things, their contribution to Jewish law in their distinctive, performable shape.

---

to the supreme court to the period of the monarchy. Millard suggests an Achaemenid origin ("Mündlichkeit," 281). The curse against the name in Lev 24:11 combines the problem of being a foreigner and of a making a curse in a unique way. It suggests a patrilinear understanding of Judaism that it applies to the "foreigner" (גר) as well as to the "native" (אזרח, v.16b). Historically, this poses a problem in Achaemenid times. If this is correct, these reflections on the authority in law took place at a time in which successive stages of the consolidation of laws as forms of reorganization and restoration were carried out under Darius I and Artaxerxes I. See, for instance, Joseph Blenkinsopp, "Was the Pentateuch the Constitution of the Jewish Ethnos?" in *Persia and Torah: The Theory of Imperial Authorization of the Pentateuch* (ed. James W. Watts; Atlanta: Society of Biblical Literature, 2001), 41–62 (61) and his earlier comments in *The Pentateuch: An Introduction to the First Five Books of the Bible* (New Haven: Yale University Press, 1992), 239–42. This assumption of an outside pressure that led to the combination of the Priestly composition "KP" and the Deuteronomistic composition "KD" no later than the reign of Darius I was also taken up by, among others, Erhard Blum (*Studien zur Komposition des Pentateuch* [BZAW 189; Berlin: de Gruyter 1990], 333–60).

The Case of the Book of Kings

Thomas Römer

Introduction: How Authoritative Was the Book of Kings in the Persian and Early Hellenistic Periods?

What is the book of Kings about? Is it about monarchy, about good kings and bad kings? And which idea about kingship does this book want to promote? Or, is Kings rather about prophets? Half of the book of Kings is, in fact, dedicated to stories about prophets. Or is the book about YHWH's wrath against Israel and Judah, since the book ends with the collapse of Samaria and Jerusalem?

Should we speak of one or two books of Kings? The division between 1 Kings and 2 Kings is indeed somewhat artificial since it splits up the stories of the Israelite king Ahaziah and those of the prophet Elijah. Nevertheless, this division is already presupposed in the Greek version of Kings, which, however, counts the two books of Kings as 3 and 4 Reigns. This indicates that for the Greek translators, Kings should not be separated from the book of Samuel, called in Greek 1 and 2 Reigns. And indeed, there is no clear break between these books because they narrate the story of the Israelite and Judahite monarchy from its beginning until its end. 1 Kings opens with the last days and the death of David, whose story is told in the books of Samuel. One may therefore ask whether the book of Kings ever was intended to be read on its own or always in connection with Samuel.

The authority of Kings in the Persian period was not "canonical" in the sense that the book would already have reached a definite form. The important differences between the Greek and the Masoretic texts of Kings are probably best explained by the assumption that the Greek text depends in many cases on a Hebrew *Vorlage* different from the Masoretic text. According to the work of A. Schenker and others, the Hebrew text that underlies the LXX in many cases preserves an older textual tradition than the Masoretic version of Kings.[1] It is not necessary for our topic to decide whether the Masoretic text is a new edition of the *Vorlage* used by the Greek in order to integrate theological corrections into the older text, as argued by Schenker, or whether the LXX and MT constitute two competing textual traditions during the Persian period.[2] It is obvious in any case that during the Persian and early Hellenistic periods there was no "fixed" edition of Kings. The fixing did not take place earlier than the Hasmonean period: according to LXX 3 Reigns 2:35, the king has the power to establish the "first" or high priest ("as for Zadok the priest, the king appointed him to be high priest in the room of Abiathar"), whereas in 2 Kgs 2:35, the king can only replace a priest with another priest ("and the king put the priest Zadok in the place of Abiathar.") This diminution of the king's prerogative may reflect the situation of Simon Maccabeus who, after having been appointed high priest by King Demetrius, was then established in this charge by the assembly of the people and the priests (according to 1 Macc 14:41–49 this happened in 140 B.C.E.).[3]

The ongoing revision of the text of Kings points to an ambiguous status of authority: on the one hand, the story of the monarchy was considered an important tradition to be kept and transmitted; on the other hand, the story itself remained open to different interpretations. This is also shown by the fact that during the end of the Persian period or the beginning of the Hellenistic era, an alternative account of the history of the monarchy was published in the book of Chronicles. It is an account that transforms the Judahite kings into founders of the cult and liturgical chiefs and which reinterprets theologically "difficult" texts of Samuel

---

1. Adrian Schenker, *Septante et texte massorétique dans l'histoire la plus ancienne du texte de 1 Rois 2–14* (CahRB 48; Paris: Gabalda, 2000); see also Philippe Hugo, *Les deux visages d'Elie: texte massorétique et Septante dans l'histoire la plus ancienne du texte de 1 Rois 17–18* (OBO 217; Fribourg: Academic Press; Göttingen: Vandenhoeck & Ruprecht, 2006).

2. Frank H. Polak, "The Septuagint Account of Solomon's Reign: Revision and Ancient Recension," in *Xth Congress of the International Organization for Septuagint and Cognate Studies, Oslo 1998* (ed. Bernard A. Taylor; SCSS 51; Atlanta: Society of Biblical Literature, 2001), 139–64; Jobst Bösenecker, "Text und Redaktion: Untersuchungen zum hebräischen und griechischen Text von 1 Könige 1–11" (Th.D. diss; University of Rostock, 2000); Percy S. F. Van Keulen, *Two Versions of the Solomon Narrative: An Inquiry into the Relationship between MT 1 Kgs. 2–11 and LXX 3 Reg. 2–11* (VTSup 104; Leiden: Brill, 2005).

3. Schenker, *Septante*, 146–47.

and Kings, like the long reign of the bad king Manasseh, for example. The Chronicler did not draw on the present MT of Samuel-Kings but on an earlier textual tradition dealing with the history of the Israelite and Judahite monarchies. I will not enter into the complicated discussion about the relationship between Samuel-Kings and Chronicles.[4] Suffice it to point out that the existence of an alternative history that, contrary to Kings, does not end with the fall of Jerusalem and exile but with an appeal by the Persian king to rebuild the temple and to go up to Jerusalem indicates a "relative" authority for the Book of Kings.

Another point in which the authority of Kings is restricted is the fact that Kings (as well as Samuel) constructs a purely Judean discourse. Contrary to the books of the Pentateuch, and in a certain way also to the book of Joshua, Samuel-Kings excludes the "Samaritans" from the "true Israel." The focus on Jerusalem as the only legitimate place of sacrificial worship and the very negative account of the foundation of Yahwistic sanctuaries in the north provides the book of Kings with a polemical, anti-northern perspective. Even if most of the narrative material in Kings predates the construction of the Gerizim sanctuary, there is no doubt that 1 Kgs 12 and other condemnations of the northern cult are meant in the context of a Judean audience in the Persian period to allude to the competing sanctuary in the province of Samaria.[5] The existence of Gerizim seems to be presupposed by the MT, which, contrary to LXX, introduces in 1 Kgs 12:31 the strange

---

4. Even if the thesis of A. Graeme Auld (*Kings Without Privilege: David and Moses in the Story of the Bible's Kings* [Edinburgh: T&T Clark, 1994]) about a shared common text from which the authors of Kings and Chronicles drew has not found many followers, there is a growing awareness that the Chronicler's source was not the present book of Kings. See David M. Carr, "Empirische Perspektiven auf das Deuteronomistische Geschichtswerk," in *Die deuteronomistischen Geschichtswerke. Redaktions- und religionsgeschichtliche Perspektiven zur "Deuteronomismus"-Diskussion in Tora und Vorderen Propheten* (ed. Markus Witte et al.; BZAW 365; Berlin: de Gruyter, 2006), 1–17; and Gary N. Knoppers, *1 Chronicles 10–29* (AB 12A; New York: Doubleday, 2004). Auld's proposal has been adopted, for example, by Raymond Person (*The Deuteronomistic History and the Books of Chronicles: Scribal Works in an Oral World* [SBLAIL 6; Atlanta: Society of Biblical Literature, 2010]).

5. Contrary to the commonly held view that this sanctuary was built around 300 B.C.E., recent archaeological evidence points to its existence in the Persian period. For details, see Ephraim Stern and Yitzhak Magen, "Archaeological Evidence for the First Stage of the Samaritan Temple on Mount Gerizim," *IEJ* 52 (2002): 49–57.

expression בית במות,[6] "the house of the high places" or "a house (as bad) as high places," which may well contain an allusion to the Gerizim sanctuary.[7]

These introductory remarks show that the authority of Kings is restricted and partial: it restricts its discourse to Judeans in Yehud and in Babylonia. But even for these addressees its authority is limited: the text of Kings is not fixed yet, and there is an alternative account of the monarchy in Chronicles. Let us see now how the book constructs authoritative discourses.

An Authoritative Discourse …

The story of Joseph in Gen 37–50 constitutes an open theological discourse. With the exception of Gen 39, which may constitute a late insertion, the narrator gives no information about the divine project or intervention. God only appears in the speeches of the story's protagonists (Joseph, his brothers, the king of Egypt …). The reader is, therefore, free to decide whether he agrees with these statements or whether he prefers to understand the story differently. The reader finds nothing of the sort in Kings. Here, the addressees are confronted with a narrator who knows everything about YHWH. He knows which king offended his god and which king's behavior pleased the deity. The narrator constructs a discourse about divine anger that begins with Solomon and culminates in the destruction of Jerusalem. The narrator knows that it was YHWH who had sent Solomon's enemies (1 Kgs 11:9–25) and that the fall of Samaria and Jerusalem resulted from YHWH's anger: "Therefore YHWH was very angry with Israel and removed them out of his sight" (2 Kgs 17:15); "Indeed, Jerusalem and Judah so angered YHWH that he expelled them from his presence" (2 Kgs 24:20). Using this narrative strategy, the "omniscient" narrator establishes his authority over the audience, which has no choice but to understand the events as presented and interpreted. The only places where some freedom is left to the reader involve traditional material, like the court intrigue at the beginning of the book in which YHWH does not intervene directly (1 Kgs 1) or some of the Elisha stories that lack theological comments. One can also include the end of Kings, where the narrator becomes astonishingly silent.

---

6. LXX: "he made houses on the high places."
7. Schenker, *Septante*, 103–6.

... But a Book with an Open Beginning and an Open End

As mentioned already, the book of Kings opens with what is properly an ending, since 1 Kgs 1–2 concludes the account of the succession to David that begins in 2 Samuel. Even if, in Kings, David is the founder of the divinely favored dynasty and the one with whom all his successors are compared, he first appears in Kings as old and lacking vigor. The book begins with a weak and dying David and ends with the last Davidic king living comfortably in Babylonian exile. This framework, which is made up of two kings who depend on others (David on his servants, Jehoiachin on the Babylonian king), creates an ambiguous depiction of the Davidic dynasty. The concluding passage in 2 Kgs 25:27–30 allows different and contradictory interpretations,[8] as is shown by the ongoing discussion of these verses. Was Jehoiachin's "rehabilitation" the last event known by the author, who had no specific purpose when reporting this fact from about 562 B.C.E., as argued by M. Noth: "this event—even though of little interest to the story as such—is still part of the description of the destiny of the Judean kings?"[9] Or, was his intention to underline that the Davidic dynasty had come to an end? Or, to the contrary, was this passage added to foster messianic expectation about the restoration of the Davidic dynasty?[10]

---

8. See, among others, Thomas Römer, "La fin du livre de la Genèse et la fin des livres des Rois: ouvertures vers la Diaspora. Quelques remarques sur le Pentateuque, l'Hexateuque et l'Ennéateuque," in *L'Ecrit et l'Esprit: Etudes d'histoire du texte et de théologie biblique en hommage à Adrian Schenker* (ed. Dieter Böhler, Innocent Himbaza and Philippe Hugo; OBO 214; Fribourg: Academic Press; Göttingen: Vandenhoeck & Ruprecht, 2005), 285–94; Ronald E. Clements, "A Royal Privilege: Dining in the Presence of the Great King," in *Reflection and Refraction: Studies in Biblical Historiography in Honour of A. Graeme Auld* (ed. Robert Rezetko, Timothy H. Lim, and W. Brian Aucker; VTSup 113; Leiden: Brill, 2007), 49–66; Serge Frolov, "Evil-Merodach and the Deuteronomists: the Sociohistorical Setting of Dtr in the Light of 2 Kgs 25,27–30," *Bib* 88 (2007): 174–90.

9. Martin Noth, *Überlieferungsgeschichtliche Studien* (Halle: Niemeyer, 1943; 3rd ed.; Darmstadt: Wissenschaftliche Buchgesellschaft, 1967), 87; ET = *The Deuteronomistic History* (JSOTSup 15; 2nd ed.; Sheffield: Sheffield Academic Press, 1991), 117.

10. Gerhard von Rad, "Die deuteronomistische Geschichtstheologie in den Königsbüchern (1947)," in *Gesammelte Studien zum Alten Testament* (TB 8; Munich: Kaiser, 1958), 189–204; Erich Zenger, "Die deuteronomistische Interpretation der Rehabilitierung Jojachins," *BZ* NS 12 (1968): 16–30. According to Jakob Wöhrle, the text wants to rehabilitate Jehoiachin and to legitimate Zerubbabel as the continuation of the Davidic dynasty ("Die Rehabilitierung Jojachins. Zur Entstehung und Intention

The interpretation of these verses depends very much on how one reads the book of Kings. If one reads 2 Kgs 25 as the ending of an Enneateuch, one would probably see it in a negative light: from the exile out of Eden to the exile out of the land.[11] If one takes into account that Kings has become part of the Nevi'im (Prophets), then one should not read 2 Kgs 25 as an absolute ending but more as a transition to the prophetic oracles concerning an ideal king in Isaiah or the idea of a new David in Ezekiel. According to this view, 2 Kgs 25:27–30 had been conceived not as an end but as a transition to the prophetic corpus.[12] This alternative also raises the important question whether the book of Kings was really conceived as an independent book or whether it was part of a larger library presupposing knowledge of the surrounding books on the shelf. If one tries to read 2 Kgs 25:27–30 as the conclusion to the book of Kings solely, then one may understand it to endorse acceptance of the situation of the Exile, or even of the Diaspora.[13] As I have argued elsewhere, the fate of Jehoiachin recalls the ascension of "Diaspora-heroes" such as Joseph, Daniel, and Mordecai.[14] The book of Kings concludes, then, with the acceptance of the loss of political autonomy and of a foreign power that may treat the Judeans well. Such a Diaspora perspective is also visible in Solomon's inauguration prayer in 1 Kgs 8, where the temple is assigned the function of a *kiblah* for those living outside the land. Nevertheless, the book of Kings is also very much concerned with the question of monarchy.

---

von 2 Kön 24,17–25,30," in *Berührungspunkte: Studien zur Sozial- und Religionsgeschichte Israels und seiner Umwelt. Festschrift für Rainer Albertz zu seinem 65. Geburtstag* [ed. Ingo Kottsieper, Rüdiger Schmitt, and Jakob Wöhrle; AOAT 350; Münster: Ugarit-Verlag, 2008], 213–38).

11. Bernard Gosse, "L'inclusion de l'ensemble Genèse–II Rois, entre la perte du jardin d'Eden et celle de Jérusalem," *ZAW* 114 (2002): 189–211.

12. Konrad Schmid, "Une grande historiographie allant de Genèse à 2 Rois a-t-elle un jour existé?" in *Les dernières rédactions du Pentateuque, de l'Hexateuque et de l'Ennéateuque* (ed. Thomas Römer and Konrad Schmid; BETL 203; Leuven: Peeters, 2007), 35–46 (42–43).

13. Donald F. Murray, "Of All Years the Hope-or Fears? Jehoiachin in Babylon (2 Kings 25:27–30)," *JBL* 120 (2001): 245–65; Jeremy Schipper, "'Significant Resonances' With Mephiboshet in 2 Kings 25:27–30: A Response to Donald F. Murray," *JBL* 124 (2005): 521–29.

14. Thomas Römer, "Transformations in Deuteronomistic and Biblical Historiography: On 'Book-Finding' and Other Literary Strategies," *ZAW* 109 (1997): 1–11.

A Discourse about Good Kings and Bad Kings and the Limitation of Royal Authority

The book of Kings begins with the picture of a "united kingdom" under Solomon and David, a Judahite united monarchy, with Jerusalem as the capital and the place of the only legitimate sanctuary. The "schism" that occurs after Solomon's death is presented as divine punishment for Solomon's behavior. Despite this punishment, the Jerusalemite temple remains the only legitimate sanctuary, and the foundation of Yahwistic sanctuaries by Jeroboam (1 Kgs 12) is presented as the original sin of the north. In the context of the end of the Persian period, this story about the splitting away of the northern tribes was certainly understood as a means of depreciating the legitimacy of the competing sanctuaries in Samaria.

At the very beginning of the book, the figure of King Solomon combines the positive and the negative behavior of Israelite and Judahite kings. These two perspectives are bookmarked by two divine manifestations in 1 Kgs 3 and 9. First Kings 3–8 presents the positive part of Solomon's reign: his wisdom and especially, the construction of the temple in Jerusalem. YHWH's second speech to Solomon evokes the possibility of his drifting away from YHWH's commandments. In fact, 1 Kgs 9:10–11:43 views Solomon negatively: he integrates many foreign women in his harem and builds sanctuaries for their divinities. Even if the story of the Queen of Sheba was originally written to enhance Solomon's glory, the context in which it now stands transforms the narrative into an example of Solomon's mingling with foreign women. Through the story of Solomon, Kings constructs a segregationist ideology that compares with some texts in Ezra and Deuteronomy (see the prohibition of mixed marriages in Deut 7; 12:2–7; Ezra 9–10). Apparently, this ideology reflects a social option in the Persian period: to construct the identity of nascent Judaism through segregation. Solomon appears as a negative example, showing the consequences of the nonrespect of segregation: Solomon's misbehavior provokes YHWH's anger and introduces a series of divine punishments, the final outcome of which is the destruction of Samaria and Jerusalem. According to Kings, kingship is in crisis from its very beginning.

After Solomon's death and the splitting up of his empire, the accounts of the reigns of the northern and Judahite kings are constructed stereotypically. The book affirms the authority of the narrator over all the kings; he is able to pronounce theological judgments on every king. Kings is not much interested in the political achievements of various rulers. For that it refers to a range of annals, which the audience is theoretically able to consult.

All kings are judged on two criteria, which are taken over from the book of Deuteronomy: the acceptance of the Jerusalemite temple as the only legitimate temple and the exclusive veneration of YHWH. From this perspective, all northern kings are systematically blamed (although with some differentiation)[15] for pursuing "Jeroboam's sins," that is, the royal Yahwistic sanctuaries in the north. The southern kings are judged according to their conformity to David's behavior; they are "to do what is right in YHWH's eyes like David." YHWH is often labeled David's "father." Interestingly, in the context of Kings it is not quite clear in which sense David is to be taken as a model. The basis of emulation is only indirectly stated in David's testament to Solomon, where he exhorts his son to respect the *tōrâ* of Moses, and in Solomon's speeches in 1 Kgs 3 and 8 in which he praises David's exemplary loyalty towards YHWH. Even if some Judahite kings receive pass-marks, none conforms to the Davidic standard except Hezekiah (2 Kgs 18:3-6) and Josiah (2 Kgs 22:2). The others are accused of tolerating Yahwistic sanctuaries outside Jerusalem, which are called "high places" in the narrative. Despite Hezekiah's very positive image, there are some discrete criticisms in the account of his reign: he submitted to the Assyrian king and plundered the Jerusalemite temple in order to pay his tribute (18:13-16). The somewhat strange story about a Babylonian embassy (20:12-19) includes a prophetic oracle to Hezekiah that announces the exile of the royal family and the transfer of the temple's treasures to Babylon. Therefore, Josiah remains the best of all Judahite kings, not because of major military achievements but because of his submission to the book of the Law, as we will see later. In contrast to some good kings, the book of Kings also constructs very bad kings, the worst of all being Manasseh, who appears in some texts as the king solely responsible for Jerusalem's fall (2 Kgs 21:10-15; 24:34).

By constructing a cultic history of the Israelite and Judahite monarchy in which all kings are submitted to theological evaluation, the editors of Kings claim authority to judge all kings and kingship in general. There is no coherent discourse about the main actor responsible for the end of Israel and of Judah; some texts blame the people, others the kings

---

15. For details, see Thomas Römer, *The So-Called Deuteronomistic History: A Sociological, Historical and Literary Introduction* (London: T&T Clark, 2005), 155-57.

in general, and still others Manasseh. Even so, the book of Kings argues that kingship finally failed and that another authority is needed. This discourse fits well in the second half of the Persian period, when the leading economic and intellectual forces of nascent Judaism accepted the loss of political autonomy.

The Authority of the Prophets

At least in the Hellenistic period, Kings (as well as with Joshua, Judges, and Samuel) was considered to be a "prophetic" book, since it was integrated into the collection of the Nevi'im. The book of Kings contains an important number of passages mentioning prophets and also lengthy prophetic stories. It is even framed by stories about prophets. First Kings 1 mentions the prophet Nathan, who plays a major part in Solomon's ascension to the throne, and the final destruction of Judah is introduced with a reference to YHWH's servants, the prophets, who had announced the divine judgment (2 Kgs 24:2). Prophetic appearances have different functions.

(a) Some prophets pronounce divine oracles, usually oracles of punishment, and their fulfillment is expressly stated (e.g., Ahijah's oracle against Jeroboam's house is fulfilled in Baasha's revolt, 1 Kgs 15:27–29). Through this pattern of oracle/fulfillment, the editors of Kings demonstrate that YHWH's words always come to pass.

(b) The appearance of the prophet Isaiah in 2 Kgs 18–20 creates a cross-reference with the scroll of (Proto-) Isaiah, since Isa 36–39 contains a parallel account of the prophet's activity under Hezekiah. The same holds true for the book of Jeremiah: 2 Kgs 24–25 have a parallel in Jer 52, even if Jeremiah is not mentioned in these chapters. The Talmud considers Jeremiah to be the author of the book of Kings. These cross-references make the book of Kings a forerunner to the books of Isaiah and of Jeremiah and indicate they all belong together in the "prophetic library."

(c) Most prophetic narratives were integrated in the book of Kings during the Persian period to foster the prophetic character of the book. These stories often have a prophet confront a king and claim that prophetic authority stands above royal authority. Prophetic authority culminates in the figure of Elijah, who is constructed as a second Moses: he travels forty days and nights to Horeb, the mountain of God (1 Kgs 19), and like Moses in Exod 33, he is granted a private theophany. This theophany in 1 Kgs 19 criticizes or corrects the Mosaic one (and also the one of 1 Kgs 18): contrary to the Sinai theophany, YHWH does not appear accompanied by thunder, lightning, and earthquake but in "a sound of sheer silence" (19:12). In the end, Elijah surpasses Moses. The latter's death (Deut 34) is more than remarkable since he is buried by YHWH himself and his grave remains unknown. Elijah, however, does not experience death but ascends to heaven in a whirlwind (2 Kgs 2). The importance given to Elijah in the book of Kings prepares for the idea of his return, which is expressed at the end of the prophetic collection in Mal 3:22–24.

(d) In the last chapters of the book an anonymous group of prophets appears, who are characterized as YHWH's servants.[16] Their function is to exhort the people to obey YHWH's law: "Yet YHWH warned Israel and Judah by every prophet and every seer, saying, 'Turn from your evil ways and keep my commandments and my statutes, in accordance with all the law that I commanded your fathers and that I sent to you by my servants the prophets'" (2 Kgs 17:13). They announce the imminent fall of Israel and Judah due to the failure of the people and the kings to respect *tōrâ* (2 Kgs 17:23; 21:10–12; 24:2). These passages prepare for the idea of YHWH's continuous sending of prophets, who are rejected by his people, an idea that can be traced from the book of Jeremiah (Jer 7:25–26; 25:4; 26:5; 29:19; 35:15; 44:4) into the New Testament (especially in Luke).[17] Most of these passages transform the prophets from messengers of doom into preachers of the law, whose aim is to exhort the audience to change their behavior to avoid divine punishment. In the context of the Persian period, this new function given to the prophets can be understood as an attempt to redefine prophetic activity after the events of 587 B.C.E., which were understood as accomplishments of the prophecies of doom and which raised the question of the function of the prophets.

The book of Kings constructs a prophetic authority that is ranked above royal authority. Prophetic authority, however, is also relative and depends on the final authority of Moses and the Torah.

---

16. As a collective, the expression occurs for the first time in the book in 2 Kgs 9:7. Individually, the title "servant" is attributed to Ahijah (1 Kgs 14:18), Elijah (18:36), and Jonah (2 Kgs 14:25).

17. Odil Hannes Steck, *Israel und das gewaltsame Geschick der Propheten: Untersuchungen zur Überlieferung des deuteronomistischen Geschichtsbildes im Alten Testament, Spätjudentum und Urchristentum* (WMANT 23; Neukirchen-Vluyn: Neukirchener, 1967).

The Authority of Moses and the (Book) of the Torah

David's testament to Solomon, which opens the history of kingship in Kings, provides criteria by which the reader is to evaluate the history of the two kingdoms: "keep the charge of YHWH your God, walking in his ways and keeping his statutes, his commandments, his ordinances, and his testimonies, as it is written in the law of Moses, so that you may prosper in all that you do and wherever you turn" (2 Kgs 2:2).

In the book of Kings, Moses is mentioned ten times;[18] in six of these passages Moses appears as the mediator of the law, three other mentions in 1 Kgs 8 relate to the Horeb covenant (v. 9: stone tablets; vv. 53 and 56: Israel's adoption as YHWH's people), and a final one mentions a bronze serpent made by Moses (2 Kgs 18:4). The first king who explicitly respects the Mosaic book of the law is Amaziah,[19] who "did not put to death the children of the murderers; according to what is written in the book of the law of Moses, where the Lord commanded, 'The parents shall not be put to death for the children, or the children be put to death for the parents; but all shall be put to death for their own sins'" (2 Kgs 14:6). Although this passage contains a quotation from Deut 24:16, this does not necessarily mean in the context of the late Persian period that the תורת משה was considered to be only the book of Deuteronomy; it already could allude to some kind of Pentateuch. The next king who respects the Law of Moses more fully is Hezekiah: "he was loyal to YHWH; he did not depart from following him but kept the commandments that YHWH had commanded Moses" (2 Kgs 18:6). In contrast, the fall of Samaria that took place during his reign happened because the Israelites "did not listen to the voice of YHWH their God but transgressed his covenant, all that Moses, YHWH's servant, had commanded; they neither listened nor acted (conformingly)" (18:12).

In order to underline Manasseh's infamous behavior, the editors inserted a "quotation" of a YHWH-speech to David and Solomon that does not exist in the book of Kings and appears to be a summary of a sampling of topics from Solomon's speech on the occasion of the inaugu-

---

18. See also Philip Davies, who comments on the different uses of Moses in Kgs and Chr ("Moses in the Book of Kings," in *La construction de la figure de Moïse - The Construction of the Figure of Moses* [ed. Thomas Römer; TransSup 13; Paris: Gabalda, 2007], 77–87).

19. Amaziah belongs among the kings who were not too bad but who tolerated the high places (14:3–4).

ration of the temple:[20] " '...I will not cause the feet of Israel to wander any more out of the land that I gave to their fathers, if only they will be careful to do according to all that I have commanded them, and according to all the law that my servant Moses commanded them.' But they did not listen; Manasseh misled them to do more evil than the nations had done that the Lord destroyed before the people of Israel" (21:8–9).

This passage prepares, in contrast, for the final appreciation of King Josiah: "Before him there was no king like him, who returned to YHWH with all his heart, with all his soul, and with all his might, according to all the law of Moses; nor did any like him arise after him" (2 Kgs 23:25). This is the final mention of Moses and the Torah in the book of Kings, and Josiah is the only king who conforms to the *whole Torah* of Moses. Indeed, the entire account of Josiah's reign is about the discovery and the installation of the "book of the law" in the temple in Jerusalem. Interestingly, this book of is not explicitly identified as the Mosaic Torah; this equation occurs only in the final comment about Josiah's achievements.

Josiah is also the only king who is portrayed to fulfill the loyalty prescription of Deut 6:4–5 literally: 2 Kgs 23:25 is the only exact parallel to Deut 6:5 in the Hebrew Bible:

Deut 6:5   וְאָהַבְתָּ אֵת יְהוָה אֱלֹהֶיךָ בְּכָל־לְבָבְךָ וּבְכָל־נַפְשְׁךָ וּבְכָל־מְאֹדֶךָ

2 Kgs 23:25   אֲשֶׁר־שָׁב אֶל־יְהוָה בְּכָל־לְבָבוֹ וּבְכָל־נַפְשׁוֹ וּבְכָל־מְאֹדוֹ

For centuries, the book found in the temple has been identified with the book of Deuteronomy. The cultic reforms undertaken by the king correspond to the Deuteronomic laws of centralization, the prohibition of foreign cults, and of YHWH worship outside Jerusalem. This equation of Deuteronomy with the book of the law may have been the intention of the first version of the book-finding account. In a Persian period setting, however, one may ask, as does E. Ben Zvi, whether the identification with the book of Deuteronomy is the only possibility.[21]

---

20. Thomas Römer, *Israels Väter: Untersuchungen zur Väterthematik im Deuteronomium und in der deuteronomistischen Tradition* (OBO 99; Fribourg: Universitätsverlag ; Göttingen: Vandenhoeck & Ruprecht, 1990), 370–71.

21. Ehud Ben Zvi, "Imagining Josiah's Book and the Implications of Imaging It in Early Persian Yehud," in *Berührungspunkte. Studien zur Sozial- und Religionsgeschichte*

In the narrative context, the finding of the law book is somewhat astonishing since there is no story in Kings or elsewhere that tells how this book had been lost. This could be an indication that the book of the law comprises more than the book of Deuteronomy—probably the entire Pentateuch or a "proto-Pentateuch." The following observations support this idea: Josiah's public reading of the book parallels Ezra's public reading of the Law. The eradication of the cult of Molech (23:10) is not based on a law in Deuteronomy but on prohibitions in the book of Leviticus (18:21; 20:2–5). Equally, the *tĕrāpîm* (23:24) are not mentioned in Deuteronomy but appear as "pagan idols" in Genesis (31:19, 34–35). The expression "the book of the covenant"[22] appears in Exod 24:7 but not in Deuteronomy. Thus, the discovery appears to be a new invention: the Pentateuch, which, in the second half of the Persian period, becomes the real foundation of nascent Judaism, at least in the view of the intelligentsia in Babylon and in Yehud.

This new foundation replaces the traditional markers of religious identity: temple, prophet, and king. In fact, 2 Kgs 22 transforms the literary *topos* of the discovery of the temple's foundation stone that is largely attested in royal inscriptions. In 2 Kgs 22 the foundation stone is replaced by the book, which has become the "true" foundation of YHWH's cult. In 2 Kgs 23 Josiah purifies the temple of all cultic symbols and transforms it into a proto-synagogue, a place where the book of the Law is being read to the people. The replacement of the traditional sacrificial cult by the reading of the Torah in 2 Kgs 22–23 constitutes a strategy underlining the importance of the written scroll. The editors of Josiah's reform prepare for the transformation of Judaism into a "religion of the book." Second Kings 22–23 in its final form is about the disappearance of the king in favor of the book. As F. Smyth has said, "The kingship accomplished through the rigor of the Torah of YHWH has no other future but the lasting peace of the tombs. ... There remains the scribe, the true servant of the book to be read."[23]

Israels und seiner Umwelt: Festschrift für Rainer Albertz zu seinem 65. Geburtstag (ed. Ingo Kottsieper, Rüdiger Schmitt and Jakob Wöhrle; AOAT 350; Münster: Ugarit-Verlag, 2008), 193–212.

22. The MT reads "this book of the covenant" and suggests an identification of "the book of the covenant" with "the book of the law." The LXX and Vulgate (and a Hebrew manuscript) read, however, "the book of this covenant."

23. Françoise Smyth, "When Josiah Has Done His Work or the King Is Properly Buried: A Synchronic Reading of 2 Kings 22.1–23.28," in *Israel Constructs Its His-*

The strange oracle of Huldah announcing that Josiah will die *běšālôm*, which seems to be contradicted by the account of Pharaoh killing him at Megiddo, has surprised many an exegete. An audience in the late Persian or early Hellenistic periods could have understood this oracle in the sense that the pious Josiah was spared seeing the destruction of Jerusalem (22:20b). However, they could equally have understood it to indicate that, after the introduction of the book of *tôrâ*, kingship was no longer necessary and could vanish "peacefully." After creating room in the temple for the reading of the book, the king, who was the traditional mediator between God and humans, became dispensable. Josiah's death is accompanied by a caesura that compares with the caesura after Moses' death:

Deut 34:10   וְלֹא־קָם נָבִיא עוֹד בְּיִשְׂרָאֵל כְּמֹשֶׁה

2 Kgs 23:25   וְאַחֲרָיו לֹא־קָם (מֶלֶךְ) כָּמֹהוּ

With Josiah, kingship disappears and gives way to the Mosaic Torah that becomes the new authority, to which not only kingship but also prophecy must submit. Why would the officials of the king seek the prophetess Huldah when the king has already understood the meaning of the book? When a king wants to ask his God about war or other affairs, he usually consults a prophet directly (see, e.g., 1 Kgs 22). But here a prophetess is asked to comment on the meaning of the book to Josiah. Huldah appears in this passage and in the parallel one in 2 Chr 34 as the interpreter of the book and not as an independent prophetess. The passage apparently makes the prophet dependent on a book; the same thing happens to Jeremiah in Jer 36.

This evolution makes sense in the context of the Persian period, during which Judaism was confronted by eschatological hopes. Many prophets of salvation heralded the restoration of the Davidic kingship and, in the mind of the lay people and priests who accepted integration into the Persian Empire, threatened the peace of the province of Yehud. To fight against these movements, they tried to limit prophecy to the one transmitted by

---

tory: *Deuteronomistic Historiography in Recent Research* (ed. Albert de Pury, Thomas Römer, and Jean-Daniel Macchi; JSOTSup 306; Sheffield: Sheffield Academic Press, 2000), 343–58.

the book. This is how the idea arose that prophecy came to an end in the Persian period. The Talmud contains the following idea: "since the day the temple was destroyed, divine inspiration has been taken from the prophets and given to the sages" (*Baba Bathra* 12b).

The editors of Kings were close to those who began to constitute a prophetic collection in order to limit prophecy to written prophecy, a collection that later would become the Nevi'im. However, the main authority that Kings constructs is the book of the Law of Moses, the Pentateuch, or a forerunner to it.

Conclusion: The "Deuterocanonical" Authority of the Book of Kings

The narrative strategy of the book of Kings leaves very few spaces open to interpretation and so constructs a strong sense of authority for the book. The narrator or the editors know about YHWH's will and plans that finally lead to the fall of Samaria and Judah. In the context of the Persian or early Hellenistic period, the authority of Kings is, nevertheless, limited: the text is not yet fixed, and there is a competing history in the book of Chronicles. It is not at all clear if Kings was ever meant to be read separately or only conjoined in a sequence with Samuel or some of the prophetic scrolls.

Kings constructs a hierarchy of authority: the kings are judged according to their cultic behavior, which must conform to dominant Deuteronomic themes like cult centralization and the exclusive worship of YHWH or more generally to the *tōrâ* commanded by Moses. The prophets are depicted as standing above the kings and at the end of the book, become "preachers of the law." Prophetic authority is also limited by the book: prophecy can only be commentary on and actualization of the book of the law. The report of Josiah's reform shows that the main authority is the book of Mosaic Law, which, at the end of the Persian period, probably represents the Pentateuch. By submitting kings and prophets to the Mosaic Law, the book of Kings constructs itself as a "deutero-canonical" authority, a book that reads the story of the monarchy with the authority of the "canonical" or "proto-canonical" Torah.

On the Authority of Dead Kings

James R. Linville

For God's sake, let us sit upon the ground
And tell sad stories of the death of kings.
Richard II 3.2:155–156

Always remember that the crowd that applauds your coronation is the same crowd that will applaud your beheading. People like a show.[1]

The book of Kings tells a story that has all the makings of a great show. It begins with the pathetic end of Israel's most celebrated king and the rather scandalous rise to power of his successor. Solomon is celebrated as the legitimate and wise king, only to have his glorious empire dismembered because of his own religious failings. The following tale of the divided kingdom ends with the destruction of both halves, despite the radical reformation and cultic purge of Josiah only decades before the ultimate fall. It is a story of power, intrigue, clashing dynasties, and war set against a theme of divine judgment. Although a bit shy on explicit descriptions of scandalous sexual encounters, the book has its share of seemingly gratuitous violence. Besides the sheer entertainment value of Kings that lies in letting the reader voyeuristically share a god's eye view on the rise and fall of a number dynasties, empires, prophets, monarchs, tyrants, and charlatans, what did the ancient readers find in it that it commanded enough respect on significant social matters to be copied and recopied over the centuries? As E. Ben Zvi does regarding the Chronicler, we might reword that question to ask what would make a Persian or early Hellenistic Judean reader of Kings regard the book and/or its implied author "godly" and,

---

1. Terry Pratchett, *Going Postal* (new ed.; London: Corgi, 2005), 382.

therefore, expressing views and providing information that we might label as authoritative for that readership?[2]

The concept of authoritative texts is very nebulous but in the least, it does not point to inherent qualities or features of a book, regardless of what the readers who ascribe authority to it themselves may think. Rather, it speaks of a socially constructed interpretative framework into which a readership places certain documents. This marks these texts as embodying truths or insights considered to be necessary or valuable resources for public discourse on socially significant topics such as matters of religious practice, belief, the symbolic boundaries of society, and social order. Little can be known definitively concerning the authoritative status of Kings in the Persian and early Hellenistic periods. There is insufficient data about how the book was used in the historical discourses and in policy-making in Judean society in these centuries. Still, some things seem clear. In the very least, Kings was part of the library of the relatively small scribal community in Jerusalem whose members were associated with the temple administration. The scribes served as mediators between YHWH and the general population through the act of transmitting, producing, and publicizing the contents of books said to contain or discuss divine words and public and personal obligations towards the god.[3] Accepted wisdom says that through the Second Temple period, the religions and society of Yehud tended to place increasing importance on selected books, eventually resulting in something of a fluid canon. We must not assume that, at an early stage in its history, Kings was more important than any other narrative of Israel's monarchic past, or that its place in any future collection of classics, let alone a canon, was inevitable or planned.[4]

---

2. Ehud Ben Zvi, "One Size Does Not Fit All: Observations on the Different Ways That Chronicles Dealt with the Authoritative Literature of Its Time," in *What Was Authoritative for Chronicles?* (ed. Ehud Ben Zvi and Diana V. Edelman; Winona Lake, Ind.: Eisenbrauns, 2010), 14, 17.

3. Ehud Ben Zvi offers a brief but very good discussion on the great diversity of the now-biblical literature as the product of such a small group of literati. He also highlights some of the social contexts in which the scribes worked and the impact of their efforts ("Towards an Integrative Study of the Production of Authoritative Books in Ancient Israel," in *The Production of Prophecy: Constructing Prophecy and Prophets in Yehud* [ed. Diana V. Edelman and Ehud Ben Zvi; London: Equinox, 2009], 15–28).

4. Scholars sometimes have an oversimplified view of the development of the rabbinic/Masoretic canon, assuming that the trajectory to the extant canon was a linear phenomenon. See Philip R. Davies, "Loose Canons," *JHS* 1 (1997), article 5; available

It might seem more intuitive to view the authority of a book about past events to lie in the perceived veracity of its story, but this can only take us so far in understanding the interpretative frameworks in which Kings was placed in the first half of the Second Temple period. While comparative evidence suggests that the presentation of events in Kings would hardly have been discounted, it was not the only presentation that could have won an audience. This essay will view the presence of contrasting histories as part of a social discourse that is always flexible and open-ended; Kings found its favorable reception amongst other documents that also earned a readership. In my opinion, the authority of Kings lies in its utility for constructing relevant meanings rather than its inscription of ideological points validated by the population as a whole or the powers that be to the exclusion of other points of view. Part of this utility derives from its capitalization on ritual episodes and prototypical events in a myth-making enterprise that allows readers to reflect on the differences between their lives and the various social constructions found in Kings and other texts. Highlighting a few of these essentially mythic, provocative episodes will be the purpose of this essay.

Myth at least implies some level of a narrative, but it is best to avoid any kind of form-critical or genre definition of the term.[5] B. Mack writes, "The study of myths as religious phenomena has not found a way to say when a story is a myth and not some other kind of narrative."[6] Rather, the term should be used of those narratives (explicitly told, implied or alluded to) that are employed in the course of social formation and expression. R. McCutcheon cautions against the view of W. Doniger that myths are those stories in which a society *finds* its deepest meaning, writing, "[m]ight it not be that a group of people *fabricate* their most important meanings *by means* of myth?"[7] He describes myth as a form of social argu-

---

at http://www.jhsonline.org/Articles/article5.pdf and in *Perspectives in Hebrew Scriptures: Comprising the Contents of Journal of Hebrew Scriptures, Volumes 1–4* (ed. Ehud Ben Zvi; Piscataway, N.J.: Gorgias, 2006), 57–72.

5. As I argued briefly in James R. Linville, *Amos and the Cosmic Imagination* (SOTSMS; Aldershot: Ashgate, 2008), 28–29.

6. Burton L. Mack, *Myth and the Christian Nation: A Social Theory of Religion* (Religion in Culture: Studies in Social Contest and Construction; London: Equinox, 2008), 48.

7. Russell McCutcheon, "Myth," in *Guide to the Study of Religion* (ed. Willli Braun and Russell T. McCutcheon; London: Cassell, 2000), 199, referring to Wendy Doniger, *The Implied Spider: Politics and Theology in Myth* (New York: Columbia University

mentation that casts created meanings as self-evident.[8] As some researchers have noticed, tradition can include alternative models of and for society; alternative ways of negotiating social boundaries and conceptions.[9] This is probably behind the diversity of materials that now make up the Hebrew Bible. They loosely hang together but provide a myriad of opportunities for rethinking society and its norms. Perfect consistency and coherence in the tradition would actually be counter-productive as it leaves less room for creativity. In this sense, Kings might be deemed authoritative because it is part of the whole matrix and can sometimes be relied on for a purportedly "final" word in particular matters by some readers, and as a starting point for further discussions that lead to the production of new meanings by others or the same readers on different occasions. I. Pyysiäinen observes that writing not only preserves various ideas not otherwise memorable but also allows for their systematic exploration. In sacred writings, "both intuitive and *radically* counter-intuitive ideas become stored and thus can be taken up for comment and analysis in different occasions." She continues by saying that "written text makes it possible to store ideas that people can read about even when they do not (fully) understand them." [10] It is easy to see how the effort by religious specialists on behalf of the general population to understand such enigmas or disjunctions between different texts, traditions, or lived experience can become an important social activity, not to mention ploy for and marker of authority and status.

Press, 1998), 2. She uses a similar language of "finding" meaning but quickly qualifies this by writing that myths are paradigms for modeling meaning and meanings are products of interpretation (Wendy Doniger O'Flaherty, *Other Peoples' Myths: The Cave of Echoes* [New York: Macmillan, 1995], 31–35).

8. McCutcheon, "Myth," 200–202.

9. Philip C. Salzman, "Culture as Enhabilmentis," in *The Structure of Folk Models* (ed. Ladislav Holy and Milan Stuchlik; Association of Social Anthropology Monographs 20; London: Academic Press, 1981), 233–56; followed by M. Elaine Combs-Schilling, "Family and Friend in a Moroccan Boom Town: The Segmentary Debate Reconsidered," *American Ethnologist* 12 (1985): 659–75 (663); Kristen Borré, "Seal Blood, Inuit Blood, and Diet: A Biocultural Model of Physiology and Cultural Identity," *Medical Anthropology Quarterly* 5 (1991): 48–62 (52).

10. Ilkka Pyysiäinen, "Holy Book—A Treasury of the Incomprehensible: The Invention of Writing and Religious Cognition," *Numen* 46 (1999): 269–90 (281). Pyysiäinen also argues that scripturalization gives birth to ultimately unsuccessful attempts at systematization.

As Doniger O'Flaherty notes, a myth is always a part of a mythology.[11] Mythologies are also embedded in a wider matrix of social life and action, including ritual. The key to understanding Kings, then, is in its comparison with and use of other myths of Israel's identity and history, from the patriarchs to the exodus and especially, the exile, since that is where the story ends. Justifying the exile is a major theme in the book. Kings also offers descriptions of other important social products and properties, including other books. As J. W. Watts points out, the rising status of books in early Jewish religion was the exception, not the norm, in the ancient Near East, and it is difficult to understand how this came about. Written law codes were not typically cited as authorities, even though the "idea of law functioned as a pervasive social ideal."[12] Treaties were significant, but the newest, not the oldest, were most important. Watts also notes that it is hard to defend divinatory interpretation of prophetic texts as the start of Jewish conceptions of scripture, as Torah seems to have attained a high status prior to the oracular books. Watts finds the solution to the enigma in the fact that, when ancient Near Eastern societies marked some texts as authoritative, more often than not those compositions were ritual texts.[13]

Key episodes in Kings surround ritual and ritual spaces and items, but Kings does not provide a set of instructions for what rituals must be performed and how to do them. As Watts illustrates, however, the stories of Josiah in Kings and Chronicles and of Ezra's reading of the Book of the Law in Neh 8 imply "that ritual books were conventionally associated with claims for reestablishing discontinued festivals."[14] Building on this, episodes of ritual in Kings should play an important role in understanding the social standing of the book in the Persian and Hellenistic eras. As myths about the performance and efficacy of rituals, the episodes of the temple dedication and YHWH's threatening response (1 Kgs 8:1–9:9) and Josiah's cultic purge that was accompanied by covenant renewal and Passover (2 Kgs 22–23) do more than simply legitimize the kind of temple service preferred by the writers. They give the reader an opportunity to

---

11. Doniger O'Flaherty, *Other Peoples' Myths*, 31, 56. Following Lévi-Strauss, she also notes how a myth may preserve only a fragment of an "inexpressible truth."
12. James W. Watts, "Ritual Legitimacy and Scriptural Authority," *JBL* 124 (2005): 401–17 (403).
13. Watts, "Ritual Legitimacy," 402–4.
14. Watts, "Ritual Legitimacy," 406.

reflect upon the meaning and nature of those rituals and their importance to social formulations.

According to Mack, myth works by offering a juxtaposition of an imagined world with experience that evokes further thought. Mack writes that people "usually gain advantage from the familiar in order to make the unfamiliar comprehensible. In the case of religion, it is the unknown and unfamiliar as a fantastic construction upon the known and familiar that is used to defamiliarize the customary and invite its mediation."[15] That Kings leaves the Judeans in exile would have raised questions about the status of Second Temple Jerusalem. Moreover, Kings' two major ritual texts construe a unified people willingly bound to a covenant, with YHWH enjoying ideal social harmony and unity of activity that is unlike what must have persisted in those centuries. The book simply assumes that the reader acknowledges the narrator's omniscience about the nature of this covenant and the makeup of the Israelite people. Yet, the notion of the covenant and the nature of the surviving Israelite nation would have been one of the cultural landmarks that were constantly open to reinterpretation and reformulation.

The story of Josiah and his discovery of the law book in 2 Kgs 22–23 is the lynchpin for most scholarly attempts to reconstruct the origins and intent of Kings. The majority view is that this episode refers to some form of Deuteronomy.[16] According to this view, the Deuteronomistic History was subsequently updated after the eventual fall of Judah with a brief presentation of the death of Josiah and subsequent events leading up to the exile with various additions made to justify and explain these events at earlier points in the original story.[17] Others see Kings as essentially a post-monarchic product that upholds Deuteronomy as the appropriate basis for Judean society.[18] There is no point in rehearsing these debates in any detail

---

15. Mack, *Myth and the Christian Nation*, 40.

16. Lauren A. S. Monroe finds the closest parallel to some of the deeds attributed to Josiah to be in the Holiness Code of Lev 17–26 and not Deuteronomy ("A Pre-exilic 'Holiness' Substratum in the Deuteronomistic Account of Josiah's Reform," in *Scribes Before and After 587 BCE: A Conversation*," ed. Mark Leuchter *JHS* 7 [2007], article 10, 42–53, available online at http://www.jhsonline.org/Articles/article_71.pdf and in *Perspectives in Hebrew Scriptures IV: Comprising the Contents of Journal of Hebrew Scriptures, Vol. 7* (ed. Ehud Ben Zvi; Piscataway, N.J.: Gorgias, 2008), 293–307.

17. Richard D. Nelson defends the majority view ("The Double Redaction of the Deuteronomistic History: The Case Is Still Compelling," *JSOT* 29 [2005]: 319–37).

18. E.g., Thomas Römer, *The So-Called Deuteronomistic History: A Sociological,*

but a few points need to be made. For my part, I agree with E. A. Knauf when he writes:

> There is no better way to misunderstand the legend of the "discovery of the book" completely than to take it as factual history. What is discovered in 2 Kings 22–23 is the Torah of the Second Temple, laying the foundation for its cult by both condemning the historical practice of the First Temple and, at the same time, claiming continuity and identity between the two.[19]

In my earlier work, *Israel in the Book of Kings*, I express great uncertainty over the applicability of conceptions of the "Deuteronomistic History" to Kings or any of the other books allegedly included, and monarchic-era dates for an early edition of Kings are less than certain.[20] To my mind, Kings is probably not an "exilic" text in terms of the date of composition or final redaction. Arguing for a Persian compositional date is well beyond the purpose of this essay, but it suffices to say I find none of the arguments for a "preexilic" composition and "exilic-era" completion of Kings persuasive.[21] Clearly, Kings was transmitted through the Hellenistic age without the "return from exile" or fall of Persia appended to the text, despite other

---

Historical and Literary Introduction (London: T&T Clark, 2007). See the four reviews by Richard D. Nelson, Steven L. McKenzie, Eckart Otto, Yariah Amit, and Römer's response, in Raymond F. Person, ed., "In Conversation with Thomas Römer, *The So-Called Deuteronomistic History: A Sociological, Historical and Literary Introduction* (London: T&T Clark, 2005) *JHS* 9 (2009), article 17, available at http://www.jhsonline.org/Articles/article_119.pdf and in *Perspectives in Hebrew Scriptures VI: Comprising the Contents of Journal of Hebrew Scriptures, Vol. 9* (ed. Ehud Ben Zvi; Piscataway, N.J.: Gorgias, 2010), 333–86.

19. Axel Knauf, "Kings among Prophets," in *The Production of Prophecy: Constructing Prophecy and Prophets in Yehud* (ed. Diana V. Edelman and Ehud Ben Zvi; BibleWorld; London: Equinox, 2009), 131–49 (141–42).

20. James R. Linville, *Israel in the Book of Kings: The Past as a Project of Social Identity* (JSOTSup 272; Sheffield: Sheffield Academic Press, 1998), 46–73. See also James R. Linville, "Rethinking the 'Exilic' Book of Kings," *JSOT* 75 (1997): 21–42.

21. See Linville, "Rethinking." More significantly, I find the arguments that constrain the dating of the book to the Neo-Babylonian period to be particularly weak. Moreover, the historical periodization schema of preexilic/exilic/postexilic should be abandoned. Without simply taking Ezra and Nehemiah at face value, no clear end to the exile can be found. That Kings ends without resolving the political/theological issue of the "exile" and without the more optimistic outlook purportedly characteristic of postexilic writings can hardly constrain the composition or redacting of the text to

changes that resulted in the different MT and LXX readings, not to mention the production of Chronicles. The burden of proof lies with those who hold that scribes in the Persian or Hellenistic eras could not have composed or completed a history of the monarchy without telling the end of the "exile," itself a mythologization of events in the aftermath of Jerusalem's fall. The actual events and aftermath of the deportations in the Neo-Babylonian period must be differentiated from the literary representation of those events in religious and political writings. This is not to say that such writings are devoid of historical referents. Yet, no representation is without distortion, and the idea of the exile as a religious/religious state of being marks much of the Old Testament.[22] As a result, no uniformity can be expected. J. L. Wright writes:

> It is not surprising that the exaggerated, tendentious depiction of complete destruction in the final passages of Kings prompted some of its readers to "set the record straight" by composing counter-histories that avoid the implication of radical discontinuity in Judahite history. Such "historical revisionism" may be found already in the final paragraphs of Kings (2 Kgs 25:22–30), which affirms a *royal-dynastic* continuity to the former branch of the Davidic line, which survived the Babylonian deportations.[23]

---

the so-called "exilic" period. It is absurd to expect that scribes would necessarily bring their history of the monarchy up to date.

22. I am particularly influenced in this regard by Robert P. Carroll, "Exile! What Exile? Deportation and Discourses of Diaspora," in *Leading Captivity Captive: "The Exile" as History and Ideology* (ed. Lester L. Grabbe; JSOTSup 278; Sheffield: Sheffield Academic Press, 1998), 62–79. See also the rest of the essays in that volume, especially Philip R. Davies, "Exile? What Exile? Whose Exile?" 128–38, and Knud Jeppesen, "Exile a Period—Exile a Myth," 139–44. More recently, see Niels Peter Lemche, "'Because They Have Cast Away the Law of the Lord of Hosts'—Or: 'We and the Rest of the World': The Authors Who 'Wrote' the Old Testament," *SJOT* 17 (2003): 268–90 (273–76).

23. Jacob L. Wright, "The Deportation of Jerusalem's Wealth and the Demise of Native Sovereignty in the Book of Kings," in *Interpreting Exile: Displacement and Deportation in Biblical and Modern Contexts* (ed. Brad E. Kelle, Frank Ritchel Ames, and Jacob L. Wright; Ancient Israel and Its Literature 10; Atlanta: Society of Biblical Literature), 105–34. This volume offers a comprehensive set of essays on the deportations and the idea of exile and contains many valuable contributions.

The exile marks Kings profoundly. More importantly, however, one must notice how Kings marks the exile. The book is a deeply "exilicist" text, even if it is not "exilic" in date. By this I mean that the book espouses a view of Israelite/Judean identity that is characterized by states of estrangement: from God, from the past, and even from the land, or at least, social integrity and completeness in the land.[24] As I imagine it, exilicism is not a singular ideological phenomenon but rather an ancient Judean mode of thought about the past and present that embraces considerable variation. As I have argued in a recent essay, the exilicism of Kings is rather different from that of the emotion-laden Lamentations. Moreover, it is not entirely exclusive of the "restorationism" of Chronicles and Ezra-Nehemiah. Rather, each provides a different set of resources for thinking about the basis of society.[25] Exilicism was not the only lens for thinking about and relating the history of the Judean monarchy in the Second Temple period, as Chronicles casts the exile as a Sabbath that has come to an end (2 Chr 36:20–21). As will become clear below, it is interesting that Chronicles labels the period of deportations as a religious ritual.

Ben Zvi notes how the Chronicler, despite introducing many changes, still adopted large sections of Kings with little emendation, there being some key points that were held to be unalterable, such as the length of reigns. In the places where the Chronicler changed his sources, he most likely was reflecting what he understood to be the meaning of his sources.[26] Even so, some of the changes are noteworthy. Josiah's death in Chronicles differs not only in some added details but also in its apparent evaluation of the king's religious standing vis-à-vis YHWH (compare 2 Kgs 23: 29–30 and 2 Chr 35:20–25). Manasseh's end is also substantially different. Chronicles makes the archetypal villain in Kings into the model penitent (2 Kgs 21:10–12; 24:3; 2 Chr 33:10–19). On the one hand, when Chronicles

---

24. Linville, "Rethinking." See also Ehud Ben Zvi, who labels Genesis–2 Kings an incomplete or truncated creation myth, in that the "social/cultural/theological entity is still not established (or fully established) within the world of the story" ("Looking at the Primary (Hi)story and the Prophetic Books as Literary/Theological Units within the Frame of the Early Second Temple: Some Considerations," *SJOT* 12 [1998]: 26–43 [30]).

25. James R. Linville, "Lest We Forget Our Sins: Lamentations, Exilicism and the Sanctification of Disjunction," in *Remembering and Forgetting in Early Second Temple Judah* (ed. Ehud Ben Zvi and Christoph Levin; FAT 85; Tübingen: Mohr Siebeck, 2012), 315–27 (316–17).

26. Ben Zvi "One Size Does Not Fit All," 18–19.

repeats the frequent notice found in Kings that additional information can be found in other documents, it sometimes changes the names of those documents. For example, 1 Kgs 11:41 has the Book of the Acts of Solomon while 2 Chr 9:29 refers to the Chronicles of the Prophet Shemaiah and Iddo the Seer. The Annals of the Kings of Judah in 1 Kgs 15:7 becomes the document of the Prophet Iddo in 2 Chr 13:22. On the other hand, 2 Chr 16:11 and 28:26 mention a book of Kings of Judah and Israel while 2 Chr 32:32 refers to a book of the visions of Isaiah and (or "in") the Book of the Kings of Judah and Israel (cf. 2 Kgs 20:20, Matters of the Days of the Kings of Judah).[27] As D. Edelman and L. Mitchell point out, these three passages, along with 2 Chr 27:7; 35:27; 36:8, all of which have "Kings of Israel and Judah," may be references to some form of Kings.[28] All of this suggests that the world in which Kings was read was one of multiple perspectives on what constituted the past and what it "really" meant. Thus, "authority" is a dynamic product of discourse and perhaps sharp disagreement. It is also plausible that the Chronicler had alternative (written or oral) sources of history he regarded to be of equal, if not superior, authenticity and authority to Kings.

The same situation prevails when we look at Kings and the prophetic traditions. As is well known, of the prophets to whom books are attributed in the Hebrew Bible, only Isaiah and Jonah are named in Kings.[29] The flow of monarchic history reported in Kings may have helped form the historical frame work into which the various components of the Latter Prophets were slotted via the addition of superscriptions and sequencing of the books, but a king-list may also have existed outside of Kings. While parts

---

27. Ben Zvi ("One Size Does Not Fit All," 33 n. 67) and Joseph Blenkinsopp (*Isaiah 1–39: A New Translation with Introduction and Commentary* [AB 19; New York: Doubleday, 2000], 74) find a reference to an independent book of Isaiah, while Steven J. Schweitzer translates Chr 32:32 to indicate the visions of Isaiah "in" the book of the Kings ("Judging a Book by Its Citations: Sources and Authority in Chronicles," in *What Was Authoritative for Chronicles?* [ed. Ehud Ben Zvi and Diana V. Edelman; Winona Lake, Ind.: Eisenbrauns, 2010], 37–65 [64]).

28. Diana Edelman and Lynette Mitchell, "Chronicles and Local Greek Histories," in *What Was Authoritative for Chronicles?* [ed. Ehud Ben Zvi and Diana V. Edelman; Winona Lake, Ind.: Eisenbrauns, 2010], 229–52 (239).

29. Karel van der Toorn argues that the reference to Micaiah in 1 Kgs 22:28 is a reference to the book of Micah, based on the similarity of wording with Mic 1:2 (*Scribal Culture and the Making of the Hebrew Bible* [Cambridge: Harvard University Press, 2007], 174).

of Kings reappear in Isaiah and Jeremiah, the scope of the reproduced text is limited. J. Blenkinsopp notes that, while most scholars are right in seeing Isa 36–39 to be an adoption of most of 2 Kgs 18:13–20:19, the shared passages reflect the influence of Isa 1–35 and even 40–48. Blenkinsopp explains this to have arisen because the producers of Kings were aware of some early Isaianic legendary material.[30] However, this may simply indicate the high status of the legends of the prophet and convenience rather than the authoritativeness of Kings in its entirety. The reproduction of the last chapter of Kings in Jer 52 is notable but again, it does not really offer enough to clarify the issue of Kings' status as the arbiter of debates on the history of the monarchy and its fall. Kings places great emphasis on Josiah's exemplary reformation despite the decision to exile Judah for the sins of Manasseh (2 Kgs 21:10–12; 24:3). Jeremiah knows of Manasseh's sin (Jer 15:4) and Jer 22:15–16 acknowledges that Josiah was a just king. Jeremiah 25:3–11 predicts destruction and exile for sins despite consistent prophetic warning from the thirteenth year of Josiah that judgment was imminent. No mention of his cultic purge is made. According to 2 Kgs 22:3, the reform was inspired by events in Josiah's eighteenth year and there is no episode in Kings of his backsliding during his life.

This inconsistency again suggests that regardless of how much of a framework was provided by Kings for situating the components of the prophetic corpus, the two bodies of writing could take quite different views on some important points about the past. Ben Zvi observes that, in view of Deut 17:18–19, the framework of Kings, along with those of Joshua and Judges, imply a Deuteronomistic historiographical perspective that placed comparatively little importance on prophets and prophecy.[31] Jeroboam II does evil in the eyes of YHWH (2 Kgs 14:24), but in the very next verse his political and military successes as predicted by Jonah are noted. In 2 Kgs 14: 26–27, however, the successes are due to YHWH seeing the dire situation of Israel, not to the prophecy. Ben Zvi notes that while the role of the prophet might have been very highly regarded in the received tradition, it is undermined in redactional notes in Kings, thus setting limits on the role

---

30. Blenkinsopp, *Isaiah 1–39*, 458–63. He notes, however, that the majority position is not without difficulty as the shared passages reflect influence of passages now in Isa 1–35 and even 40–48.

31. Ben Zvi, "Prophets in I–II Kings," 336; he calls Gen–2 Kgs and the Latter Prophets two different kinds of discourse or genres of writing shared by the same social group ("Primary (Hi)story," 39).

of the prophet that cohere with the redactor's Deuteronomistic point of view.[32] What is important for us is how received tradition that is authoritative in the sense that its inclusion is deemed necessary can still be subject to qualifying or limiting interpretation on the grounds of other ideological perspectives.

At least, if not more important for our purposes than the relationship between Kings and other specific texts set in the monarchic period are the employment of key religious ideas and concepts, i.e., myths and rituals, in Kings itself. In the attempt to ground Second Temple Torah in a monarchic-era prototype, Kings attempts to legitimize and authorize, but in so doing, it gains legitimacy itself. E. Conrad notes how the mention of books in the Hebrew Bible is a strategy for establishing authority. Nothing is heard of the Book of the Law in the Former Prophets between its references in Joshua and 2 Kgs 14:6 (Amaziah's reign). The narrator knows the content of the book but the reader does not.[33]

By making general and even specific reference to a document that has been lost and found, and for the readers lost again, the narrator's voice has been empowered and given authority. The narrative voice suggests that it is knowledgeable about what the readers can only imagine, the lost ספר התורה/ספר הברית. This rhetorical technique also has the effect of empowering the narrative. The narrative gains authority because it reports the stories of the document's origins, including the words and actions of Moses, who received "the law" (התורה) from God and mediated a "covenant" (ברית) between Israel and the LORD.[34]

On the one hand, by recognizing the authority of Moses, Kings gains authority itself. On the other, it produces a new myth that is at odds with some aspects of the old and provokes new ways of imagining society. Doniger O'Flaherty has used the term "metamyth" to discuss myths about myths and/or rituals, and it seems apt in regards to Kings. Such metamyths allow for innovation and the preservation of received tradition.[35] Indeed, Kings (and the whole Former Prophets) can be viewed as a myth about the myth of Torah revelation and how its covenant curses came true. But

---

32. Ehud Ben Zvi, "Prophets and Prophecy in the Compositional and Redactional Notes in 1–11 Kings," *ZAW* 105 (1993): 331–53 (340–41).

33. Edgar W. Conrad, "Heard but Not Seen: The Representation of 'Books' in the Old Testament," *JSOT* 54 (1992): 45–59 (47–48, 52–53).

34. Conrad, "Heard but Not Seen," 52–53.

35. Doniger O'Flaherty, *Other People's Myths*, 31, 38, 113.

more than just highlight the law's "truth," Kings also provides a way to think beyond the destruction promised in the Torah myth, back to the initial moment of its revelation on Sinai after the flight from Egypt. Its innovation lies in its turning the exile myth into the exodus myth without allowing for its dénouement in a new, and successful, conquest.[36]

For its part, Chronicles offers a different way of thinking about the monarchic period. Schweitzer's comments on Chronicles are apt. He notes how Chronicles does not seek to supplant, complement, or dismiss Samuel-Kings but also sees no need to repeat it verbatim.[37] Rather:

> The Chronicler constructs a different history, a *better alternative reality* that sometimes affirms and often contradicts both the Pentateuch and Samuel-Kings as well as the society of his own time. The same tension between continuity and innovation that is characteristic of prophecy, speeches and authority in Chronicles is manifested in the Chronicler's vision of the future, which is presented as a utopian history.[38]

Similarly, in some people's opinion, Kings might have produced a "better alternative reality" than other contemporary texts, resulting in its transmission that, in turn, influenced subsequent thinking and rethinking, including that expressed in Chronicles. But rather than just a better alternative to other texts, Kings provided a useful, alternative reality with which to affirm, question, and perhaps subvert the *status quo* and projected social/political agendas.[39] This is ultimately the role of myth as a part of a living tradition.

First Kings 8 certainly invites a comparison between the Second Temple services and its paradigm instituted by Solomon and, by extension, also a comparison with the prototype of the First Temple, the wilderness

---

36. See Josh 5:13-15 where, after the circumcision and Passover in Canaan, Joshua sees the chief of the divine hosts, who declares himself neither friend nor foe.
37. Schweitzer, "Judging a Book," 61-62.
38. Schweitzer, "Judging a Book," 62.
39. Standard wisdom has Chronicles written with Samuel-Kings as a source, but see A. Graeme Auld, who argues that they used a common source (*Kings without Privilege: David and Moses in the Story of the Bible's Kings* [Edinburgh: T&T Clark, 1994]). Auld's interest in seeing both Kings and Chronicles as commentaries on earlier texts is welcome. In a related vein, see Raymond F. Person Jr., "The Deuteronomistic History and the Book of Chronicles: Contemporary Competing Historiographies," in *Reflection and Refraction: Studies in Biblical Historiography in Honour of A. Graeme Auld* (ed. Robert Rezetko, Timothy H. Lim, and W. Brian Aucker; VTSup 113; Leiden: Brill, 2007), 315-36.

tabernacle. We can well imagine a great concern in the Second Temple period for the legitimacy of the cult. But the day-to-day operations of the temple would invariably elicit concerns over its adherence to proper ritual and purity requirements (cf. Mal 1:6–2:9 for a prophetic complaint about the Second Temple priesthood). Moreover, the community would have had its own share of less-than-ideal situations with which to deal, from crime and corruption to economic and environmental hardships. Ideological debate and discussions of practical matters would also have been at times pointed and sharp, and some of these disagreements may have concerned the status of the Judean/Jewish groups displaced from Judah and alleged non-Israelites in Judah and the northern regions (cf. 2 Kgs 17:24–41 and Ezra 4:1–3). What is most interesting about 1 Kgs 8:1–9:9, then, is how it imagines the ideal temple and its relation to the people to be fundamentally different from what must have been the reality in Persian Jerusalem. The episode is one of perfect harmony and unity.

In 1 Kgs 8:3–6 the ritual specialists, the priests and Levites, are given the task of moving the ark and sacred vessels and ministering in the sanctuary (from which they are driven by the deity's glory in 8:10–11), but it is actually Solomon and the people themselves who offer the sacrifices (8:5, 63–64). While recognizing something of the religious stratification of the monarchic temple and hence, the Second Temple, and the special prerogative of the priests and Levites to handle sacred items, the text stops short of acknowledging their role in the actual sacrifices, something that would have been a feature of actual Second Temple services. Moreover, it is interesting that the passage never names any priest (albeit see 1 Kgs 4:2, 4, which name Azariah, Zadok and Abiathar). Nor does it mention any of the other administrative officials listed in 1 Kgs 4:2–19. The secular administration of Israel appears immaterial to the dedication rites or to the imagined collective identity of Israel. Solomon's own family and the heir-apparent do not get a look in either. The writers of the story do not seem interested in the royal line as the proper political power in the time setting of the story but rather, show interest in the larger, trans-historical conception of the dynasty and assimilating it to the notion of the covenant and the Israelite collective imagined as the premonarchic, ancestral body. The movement of the ark is done in the presence of all the tribal heads (1 Kgs 8:1). In the next verse, "all the men of Israel" gather before the king.[40]

---

40. See my longer study of this in Linville, *Israel in the Book of Kings*, 278–82.

Yet, in making these associations, the text is left open to the question of whether the vanquished royal line is representative of the people being left without hope. Thus, the passage describes Solomon's greatest moment as king. His own series of petitions concerning divine responses to a penitent people has no space for a restoration of monarchy but makes considerable pleas on behalf of a penitent people (1 Kgs 8:27–53).

Similarly, the petitions never ask YHWH to acknowledge atoning sacrifices but rather, prayers. In his final petition (vv. 46–51), Solomon calls on God to recognize the prayers of exiles. It is interesting that v. 48 does not speak of prayer towards the temple per se but in the "direction" of land, city, and "the house which I have built," an ambiguity that leaves open the question of whether the temple still exists in the hypothetical exilic situation. Solomon's final petition invokes not only the myth of exile but also of the exodus.[41] The passage is interesting in that it does not specifically ask for the return of exiles but merely that their captors show them mercy (v. 50). The summation of the prayer (vv. 52–53) likewise refers to the exile and how Israel has been set apart from the nations. How might this have been read in Persian or Hellenistic Jerusalem, when foreign imperial power could not have been ignored? The passage also might have evoked the question whether the temple is necessary at all—certainly a proposition that would have raised eyebrows among Jerusalem's religious conservatives. Despite the reports that an uncountable number of sacrifices were offered by the king and whole community (v. 5) and that Solomon's sacrifices were too numerous for the altar to accommodate (vv. 63–64), the actual prayers that look ahead to the future say nothing of sacrifices at all. Framing the whole are references to the collective body of Israelites celebrating the weeklong feast of the seventh month, i.e., Sukkoth (vv. 2, 65).[42] Sukkoth, of course, celebrates the wilderness wanderings of the whole nation of Israel, and hence, reinforces the references to the exodus in the chapter and suggests that the inauguration of the temple is the proper end of that long journey.[43] Even so, the association of Sukkot with homeless-

---

41. "Land you gave to their fathers" in v. 48 may also be evoking the patriarchs.

42. Mordechai Cogan, *1 Kings: A New Translation with Introduction and Commentary* (AB 10; New York: Doubleday, 2000), 278, 290. He explains the twice seven-day celebration as a secondary addition inspired by 2 Chr 30:23.

43. 1 Kgs 6:1 MT puts the start of construction a symbolically important 480 years after the Israelites left Egypt; LXX makes it 440 years.

ness and the final petition's exilic references allows the reader to associate the temple itself with displacement.

The accent on an idealized community around a prototypical temple and the god's threatening response is enough in my mind to render 1 Kgs 8:1–9:9 a text of potentially mythical import. On the one hand, its purview is the idealization of Israel and the fundamental gap between the teaching that the temple is the seat of divine power and that YHWH resides in heaven, although even heaven cannot contain him (1 Kgs 8:27–28). The speech itself creates a comparison between the transcendent and earthly realities as much as it invites a comparison between the paradigmatic Solomonic Temple, the wilderness tabernacle, and Second Temple realities on the one hand, and, on the other, between the exodus Israelites, the Diaspora and the "restoration" community.[44] As noted by J. Z. Smith, ritual serves as a "focusing lens" in which nothing is accidental; everything is accorded significance and everything is paradigmatic.[45] Even the representation in text of ritual can serve this function. Smith writes:

> Within its [the temple's] arbitrarily demarcated boundaries, each transaction was the focus of all transactions; each transaction was capable of endless formal replication. In short, the Temple was a synchronic structure. The place could be replicated in a system of differences transferred to another realm or locale (for example Mishnah). For it is not the terms but the relations that mattered.[46]

The temple dedication episode in the book of Kings is one of those systems of differences, a myth that, among other things, begs for comparison between the "real" and the ever-malleable world of imagined social

---

44. In an important paper, Gerald A. Klingbeil emphasizes the importance of descriptive ritual texts in the HB and treating the social dimension of their ideology, not just their political aspects ("'Momentaufnamen' of Israelite Religion: The Importance of the Communal Meal in Narrative Texts in 1/II Regum and their Ritual Dimensions," *ZAW* 118 [2006]: 22–45). He builds his study of ritual meals around the thirteen dimensions of ritual posited by Jan Platvoet, of which the most important for our purposes is the "*traditionalizing innovation dimension*, recognizing the conventions and rules that govern rituals, but that posits ritual at the same time as innovative as well" (26).

45. Jonathan Z. Smith, "The Bare Facts of Ritual," *History of Religions* 20 (1980): 112–27 (113–14).

46. Jonathan Z. Smith, *To Take Place: Toward Theory in Ritual* (Chicago: University of Chicago Press, 1987), 86.

boundaries that allows for, among other things, postmonarchic Judah to find its "true" identity as part of the larger "Israel." In a sense, the episode reflects not what once was, but rather, a becoming.

First Kings 8:1–9:9 might be viewed as a liminal rite of passage of the whole nation of Israel, moving from the "wilderness" mode of existence to its "settled" mode represented by YHWH's residence in his "house" and the reinforcement of the Pentateuch's covenantal curses in the opening verses of I Kgs 9. V. Turner famously observed how in rites of passage there is a loss of individuality and loss of status in the neophytes.[47] He notes that secular distinctions of neophytes may disappear or become homogenized, writing:

> It is as though there are here two major "models" for human interrelatedness, juxtaposed and alternating. The first is of society as a structured, differentiated, and often hierarchical system of politico-legal-economic positions with many types of evaluation, separating men in terms of "more" or "less." The second, which emerges recognizably in the liminal period, is of society as an unstructured or rudimentarily structured and relatively undifferentiated *comitatus*, community, or even communion of equal individuals who submit themselves together to the general authority of the ritual elders.[48]

In Solomon's story, there are no neophytes, but a whole nation is assembled to adopt a new kind of religious life. It is easy to find the sense of "communitas" here.[49] The monarchy in this passage appears not as a political but religious institution in the chapter. First Kings 8:15–22 deals with Solomon's succession after David, but the real accent seems to be not so much on their political rule but on the divine promise that David's heir would finally build a house for the deity and install the ark of the covenant. Both 1 Kgs 8:9 and 8:21 emphasize the contents of the ark, the tablets of Moses. In 8:24–26 Solomon mentions his succession of David again and the eternal promise of a Davidic king but acknowledges that this can only be if the heir follows in David's pious footsteps. The last part of Solomon's petitions again reinforces the sense that Israel is the people of the exodus

---

47. Victor Turner, *The Ritual Process: Structure and Anti-Structure* (Chicago: Aldine, 1969; repr., New York: Aldine de Gruyter, 1995), 95.

48. Turner, *Ritual Process*, 96.

49. Turner replaces *comitatus* with this term, preferring it to "community" (*Ritual Process*, 96–97).

(vv. 51–53). Moses receives additional mention in v. 56, as does the law in vv. 58, 61. It is only after YHWH gives his warnings to Solomon in 1 Kgs 9 that the text returns to the idea that Israel has social/economic divisions, although it places Israelites in positions of authority over non-Israelite labor conscripts. By 11:28, however, Jeroboam is over the forced labor from Joseph.

If we wish to push the idea of 1 Kgs 8:1–9:9 signifying a rite of passage, we might see Solomon as the neophyte, since the conditions of the new status as king over a temple-society apply particularly to him. As a myth about ritual, however, the real neophyte may well be the ideal reader who identifies with the Israelites and their king and is hence assimilated to the textualized temple exchange system between Israel and God, and by extension, the "exilic" reality spoken of by Solomon in his petitions, the foreshadowing of the temple's dissolution, and most importantly, the efficacy of prayer.

Many myths, along with rituals, art, and other symbolic forms, are formulated in periods of liminality and structural inferiority. More than providing a mere reclassification system for social realities, they provoke thought and action of a multivocal nature.[50] The episode about the inauguration of the temple provides many such opportunities for thought. In particular, the emphasis on Israelite unity, distinctiveness, and independence must have provoked some thought in the Persian and Hellenistic periods, when Jerusalem was but a provincial center in someone else's empire and Judeans/Jews were spread far and wide across it. Rather than simply oppose reality, however, the passage provides some tools for thinking through the problem and arriving at a variety of solutions. Prayer becomes a popular-level surrogate for sacrifice, exile does not mean execution or exclusion from communion with the divine, and Israel is greater than just Judah. The divine law survived, even if it was not always obeyed, symbolized by the poles of the ark that are still there "to this day" (1 Kgs 8:8) even though the temple was vanquished. And yet, divine judgment has been harsh and can be again. It is in the episode's provocative disjunctions and the opportunity for meaningful social exchange fostered in the context of a large repertoire of texts and tradition that we might find a clue to Kings' significance in the Second Temple period.

---

50. Turner, *Ritual Process*, 128–29.

The same can be said of Josiah's episode in 2 Kgs 22–23. The story stands out from the surrounding narrative and despite its apparent importance to the writer, it plays little role in how the actual fall of Jerusalem is reported to have taken place. By the time the story of Josiah's successor is reached (2 Kgs 23:31–32), it is as if the two chapters dedicated to Josiah simply do not matter. The discovery of the law book introduces a new theme in Kings, as there is no record of it being lost. After Josiah, there is likewise no mention of it. Josiah's reign is a sacred, liminal "time-out-of-time" in which an ideal restoration interrupts an inevitable fall. It is transitory, temporary, and yet paradigmatic and eternal. It symbolically prepares the ideal reader to participate in the exile; not as a sinner under punishment but as a member of a community formed under a renewed covenant under the protection of the Passover rite. As a "focusing lens," it brings readers into a state in which they can experience and reshape themselves to be part of Josiah's community of celebrants. T. Prosic takes a structuralist approach to Passover, saying that the rite mediates oppositions such as death/life, freedom/slavery, want/abundance, and temporary/permanent sanctuary.[51] On this final opposition, it can be noted that Josiah's Passover reflects the loss of the ostensibly permanent sanctuary to another "wilderness quest." Following Leach's view concerning myth's mediation of opposed conditions and the "middle ground" that is the focus of taboos, Prosic regards Pesach as a rite of passage marking the transition from one state to another. She observes how, in the Hebrew Bible, Passover is not accompanied by contradictory figures, except perhaps in the juxtaposition of the Destroyer and preserved life.[52] In my view, however, the Josiah of 2 Kings is quite an ambivalent figure who is a good counterpart to the exodus Destroyer. He has the heterodox priesthood killed (2 Kgs 23:20) and sets in motion a reaffirmation of the covenant and the Passover. He is himself a contradiction, a penitent who cannot avert the death of exile. As a result, he provides a significant idealization of the postmonarchic person: one who accepts divine fate while preserving the integrity of the people around obedience to the covenant. And yet, Josiah comes to a violent end. Where is the "peace" that was promised him (2 Kgs 22:20)?

Again, one can see *communitas* highlighted in the Passover and covenant renewal ceremony. While some official positions are mentioned,

---

51. Tamara Prosic, "Passover in Biblical Narratives," *JSOT* 82 (1999): 45–55 (51).
52. Prosic, "Passover," 52.

2 Kgs 23:1–3 has all of the people, young and old, convene to hear the king read the book of the covenant, and "all the people" ratify it. Similarly, in v. 21, all the people offer the Passover. With Josiah's death, the liminal period seems to end, and there is a return to profane time. Yet, in another sense, the liminality continues beyond the end of Kings, forcing readers to explore the idea of whether the "exile" is truly over and what more they could or should do, while giving them a direction forward via obedience to the Torah and community reestablishment via key rituals.[53] Second Kings 23:21–23 invites readers/hearers to reconsider the original Passover narrative, and by extension, the first Passover mentioned and the one that celebrated the entry to the land in Joshua (5:10). The Josiah narrative casts the Passover as a rite of covenant formation in spite of the upcoming exile. It becomes a way of "passing over," if you will, the exile.

As myth, Kings does not prescribe rituals, nor is there evidence that a public recitation of parts of it ever occurred in ancient Judah. In its myths of ancient ritual, however, Kings both authorizes their contemporary counterparts and gains authority as a contributor to primary discourses on the boundaries, integrity, and characteristic actions and features of society. It provides models for conceptualizing and understanding both Sukkot and Passover, not to mention the meaning of the regular temple rituals. In a sense, it asks its readers to compare themselves to the various Israels of the past. In the end, Kings became part of the central repertoire of tools for conceptualizing key collective rituals of Judean/Israelite identity.

---

53. For a longer analysis of this passage along similar lines, see Linville, *Israel in the Book of Kings*, 235–53.

Contributors

Klaus-Peter Adam
Lutheran School of Theology, Chicago, Illinois, U.S.A.

Yairah Amit
Tel Aviv University, Israel (emeritus)

Thomas M. Bolin
St. Norbert College, Wisconsin, U.S.A.

Philip R. Davies
University of Sheffield, U.K. (emeritus)

Diana V. Edelman
Research Associate, Department of Near and Middle Eastern Studies
Trinity College, Dublin, Ireland

Serge Frolov
Southern Methodist University, Texas, U.S.A.

Susanne Gilmayr-Bucher
Catholic-Theological Private University of Linz, Austria

E. Axel Knauf
University of Bern, Switzerland

Christoph Levin
Ludwig Maximilian University, Munich, Germany

James R. Linville
University of Lethbridge, Canada

224 DEUTERONOMY–KINGS AS EMERGING AUTHORITATIVE BOOKS

Thomas Römer
University of Lausanne, Switzerland, and
Collège de France, France

Bibliography

Achenbach, Reinhard. "The Pentateuch, the Prophets, and the Torah in the Fifth and Fourth Centuries B.C.E." Pages 253–85 in *Judah and the Judeans in the Fourth Century B.C.E.* Edited by Oded Lipschits, Gary N. Knoppers, and Rainer Albertz. Winona Lake, Ind.: Eisenbrauns, 2007.

Adam, Klaus-Peter. "Saul as a Tragic Hero: Greek Drama and Its Influence on Hebrew Scripture in 1 Samuel 14,24–46 (10,8; 13,7–13A; 10,17–27." Pages 123–83 in *For and against David: Story and History in the Books of Samuel.* Edited by Erik Eynikel and A. Graeme Auld. Bibliotheca ephemeridum theologicarum lovaniensium 232. Leuven: Peeters, 2010.

Aejmelaeus, Anneli. "The Septuagint of 1 Samuel." Pages 123–42 in *On the Trail of the Septuagint Translators: Collected Essays.* Revised and expanded ed. Contributions to Biblical Exegesis and Theology 50. Leuven: Peeters, 2006.

Albertz, Rainer. "Why a Reform Like Josiah's Must Have Happened." Pages 27–46 in *Good Kings and Bad Kings: Kingdom of Judah in the Seventh Century.* Edited by Lester L. Grabbe. European Seminar on Methodology in Israel's History 5 and Library of Hebrew Bible/Old Testament Studies 393. London: T&T Clark, 2005.

Alt, Albrecht. "Die Heimat des Deuteronomiums." Pages 250–75 in vol. 2 of *Kleine Schriften zur Geschichte des Volkes Israel.* 3 vols. Munich: Beck, 1953–1959.

———. "Die Rolle Samarias bei der Entstehung des Judentums." Pages 316–34 in vol. 2 of *Kleine Schriften zur Geschichte des Volkes Israel.* 3 vols. Munich: Beck, 1964.

Alter, Robert. *The David Story: A Translation and Commentary of 1 and 2 Samuel.* New York: W. W. Norton, 1999.

Altmann, Peter. *Festive Meals in Ancient Israel: Deuteronomy's Identity Politics in Their Ancient Near Eastern Context.* Beihefte zur Zeitschrift für die alttestamentliche Wissenschaft 424. Berlin: de Gruyter, 2011.

Amit, Yairah. "Endings: Especially Reversal Endings." *Scriptura* 87 (2004): 213–26.

———. "Hidden Polemic in the Conquest of Dan: Judges XVII—XVIII." *Vetus Testamentum* 40 (1990): 4–20.

———. *Hidden Polemics in Biblical Narrative*. Translated by J. Chipman. Leiden: Brill, 2000.

———. *Reading Biblical Narratives: Literary Criticism and the Hebrew Bible*. Translated by Y. Lotan. Rev. and annotated ed. Minneapolis: Fortress, 2001.

———. "The Art of Composition in the Book of Judges." Ph.D. diss., Tel Aviv University, 1984 (Hebrew).

———. "The Book of Judges—Dating and Meaning." Pages 297–322 in *Homeland and Exile: Biblical and Ancient Near Eastern Studies in Honour of Bustenay Oded*. Edited by Gershom Galil, Mark Geller, and Alan Millard. Supplements to Vetus Testamentum 130. Leiden: Brill, 2009.

———. *The Book of Judges: The Art of Editing*. Translated by J. Chipman. Leiden: Brill, 1999.

———. "The Samaritans: Biblical Positions in the Service of Modern Politics." Pages 247–66 in *Samaritans: Past and Present. Current Studies*. Edited by Menachem Mor and Friedrich V. Reiterer. Studia Judaica 53. Studia Samaritana 5. Berlin: de Gruyter, 2010.

———. "Saul in the Book of Chronicles." Pages 3–15 in *Shai le-Sara Japhet: Studies in the Bible, Its Exegesis and Its Language*. Edited by Mosheh Bar-Asher et al. Jerusalem: The Bialik Institute, 2007 (Heb.). An English version is available as pages 231–47 in *In Praise of Editing in the Hebrew Bible—Collected Essays in Retrospect*. Translated by B. S. Rozen. Sheffield: Sheffield Phoenix, 2012).

———. "Saul Polemic in the Persian Period." Pages 47–61 in *Judah and the Judeans in the Persian Period*. Edited by Oded Lipschits and Manfred Oeming. Winona Lake, Ind.: Eisenbrauns, 2006.

Anderson, Robert T. and Terry Giles. *Tradition Kept: The Literature of the Samaritans*. Peabody: Hendrickson, 2005.

Arav, Rami. *Hellenistic Palestine: Settlement Patterns and City Planning, 337–31 B.C.E*. British Archaeological Reports, International Series 485. Oxford: B.A.R., 1989.

Assmann, Jan. *Religion and Culture Memory: Ten Studies*. Translated by R. Livingstone. Cultural Memory in the Present. Stanford, Calif.: Stanford University Press, 2006.

Auerbach, Elias. *Wüste und Gelobtes Land*. 2 vols. 2d ed. Berlin: Schocken, 1938.
Auld, A. Graeme. *Joshua, Moses and the Land: Tetrateuch-Pentateuch-Hexateuch in a Generation Since 1938*. Edinburgh: T&T Clark, 1980.
———. *Kings Without Privilege: David and Moses in the Story of the Bible's Kings*. Edinburgh: T&T Clark, 1994.
Baines, John. "Literacy and Ancient Egyptian Society." *Man* 18 (1983): 572–99.
Baltzer, Klaus. *The Covenant Formulary in Old Testament, Jewish, and Early Christian Writings*. Translated by D. E. Green. Philadelphia: Fortress, 1971.
Barmash, Pamela. *Homicide in the Biblical World*. Cambridge: Cambridge University Press, 2005.
———. "The Narrative Quandary: Cases of Law in Literature." *Vetus Testamentum* 54 (2004): 1–16.
Batten, Loring W. *A Critical and Exegetical Commentary on Ezra and Nehemiah*. International Critical Commentary 12. Edinburgh: T&T Clark, 1913.
Bellefontaine, Elizabeth. "Customary Law and Chieftainship: Judicial Aspects of 2 Samuel 14.4-21." *Journal for the Study of the Old Testament* 38 (1987): 47–72.
Ben Zvi, Ehud. "Are There Any Bridges Out There? How Wide Was the Conceptual Gap between the Deuteronomistic History and Chronicles?" Pages 59–86 in *Community Identity in Judean Historiography: Biblical and Comparative Perspectives*. Edited by Gary N. Knoppers and Kenneth A. Ristau. Winona Lake, Ind.: Eisenbrauns, 2009.
———. "Imagining Josiah's Book and the Implications of Imaging It in Early Persian Yehud." Pages 193–212 in *Berührungspunkte : Studien zur Sozial- und Religionsgeschichte Israels und seiner Umwelt. Festschrift für Rainer Albertz zu seinem 65. Geburtstag*. Edited by Ingo Kottsieper, Rüdiger Schmitt, and Jakob Wöhrle. Alter Orient und Altes Testament 350. Muenster: Ugarit-Verlag, 2008.
———. "Looking at the Primary (Hi)story and the Prophetic Books as Literary/Theological Units Within the Frame of the Early Second Temple: Some Considerations." *Scandinavian Journal of the Old Testament* 12 (1998): 26–43.
———. "One Size Does Not Fit All: Observations on the Different Ways That Chronicles Dealt with the Authoritative Literature of Its Time." Pages 13–35 in *What Was Authoritative for Chronicles?* Edited by

Ehud Ben Zvi and Diana V. Edelman. Winona Lake Ind.: Eisenbrauns, 2010.

———. "Prophets and Prophecy in the Compositional and Redactional Notes in I–II Kings." *Zeitschrift für die alttestamentliche Wissenschaft* 105 (1993): 331–53.

———. "Reconstructing the Intellectual Discourse of Ancient Yehud." *Studies in Religion/Sciences Religieuses* 39 (2010): 7–23.

———. *Signs of Jonah: Reading and Rereading in Ancient Yehud.* Journal for the Study of the Old Testament Supplement Series 367. Sheffield: Sheffield Academic Press, 2003.

———. "The Concept of Prophetic Books and Its Historical Setting." Pages 73–95 in *The Production of Prophecy: Constructing Prophets and Prophecy in Yehud.* Edited by Diana V. Edelman and Ehud Ben Zvi. BibleWorld. London: Equinox, 2009.

———. "Towards an Integrative Study of the Production of Authoritative Books in Ancient Israel." Pages 15–28 in *The Production of Prophecy: Constructing Prophecy and Prophets in Yehud.* Edited by Diana V. Edelman and Ehud Ben Zvi. BibleWorld. London: Equinox, 2009.

———. "What is New in Yehud?: Some Considerations." Pages 32–48 in *Yahwism after the Exile: Perspectives on Israelite Religion in the Persian Era.* Edited by Rainer Albertz and Bob Becking. Studies in Theology and Religion 5. Assen: Van Gorcum, 2003.

Berge, Kåre. "Literacy, Utopia and Memory: Is There a Public Teaching in Deuteronomy?" *Journal of Hebrew Studies* 12 (2012): article 3. Online: http://www.jhsonline.org/Articles/article_165.pdf.

Berquist, Jon L. "Constructions of Identity in Postcolonial Yehud." Pages 53–66 in *Judah and the Judeans in the Persian Period.* Edited by Oded Lipschits and Manfred Oeming. Winona Lake, Ind.: Eisenbrauns, 2006.

Bertholet, Alfred. *Deuteronomium.* Kurzer Hand-Commentar zum Alten Testament 5. Freiburg: Mohr Siebeck, 1899.

Betlyon, John Wilson. "The Provincial Government of Persian Period Judah and the Yehud Coins." *Journal of Biblical Literature* 105 (1986): 633–42.

Beyerlin, Walter. "Die Paranäse im Bundesbuch und ihre Herkunft." Pages 9–29 in *Gottes Wort und Gottes Land: Hans-Wilhelm Hertzberg zum 70. Geburtstag am 16 Januar 1965 dargebracht.* Edited by Henning G. Reventlow. Göttingen: Vandenhoeck & Ruprecht, 1965.

Bickert, Rainer. "Die List Joabs und der Sinneswandel Davids: Eine dtr bearbeitete Einschaltung in die Thronfolgeerzählung: 2Sam. XIV 2–22." Pages 30–51 in *Studies in the Historical Books of the Old Testament*. Edited by John A. Emerton. Supplements to Vetus Testamentum 30. Leiden: Brill 1979.
Bieberstein, Klaus. "Grenzen definieren: Israels Ringen um Identität." Pages 59–72 in *Impuls oder Hindernis? Mit dem Alten Testament in multireligiöser Gesellschaft, Beiträge des Internationalen Bibel-Symposions Bayreuth, 27.-29. September 2002*. Edited by Joachim Kügler. Bayreuther Forum Transit 1. Berlin: LIT, 2004.
Black, Jeremy, Andrew George, and Nicholas Postgate. *A Concise Dictionary of Akkadian*. Santag: Arbeiten und Untersuchungen zur Keilschriftkunde 5. 2d corrected printing. Wiesbaden: Harrassowitz, 2000.
Blenkinsopp, Joseph. *A History of Prophecy in Israel*. Rev. and enlarged ed. Louisville: Westminster John Knox, 1996.
———. "Benjamin Traditions Read in the Early Persian Period." Pages 629–45 in *Judah and the Judeans in the Persian Period*. Edited by Oded Lipschits and Manfred Oeming. Winona Lake, Ind.: Eisenbrauns, 2006.
———. *Ezra-Nehemiah: A Commentary*. Old Testament Library. Philadelphia: Westminster, 1988.
———. *Isaiah 1–39: A New Translation with Introduction and Commentary*. Anchor Bible 19. New York: Doubleday, 2000.
———. *The Pentateuch: An Introduction to the First Five Books of the Bible*. New Haven: Yale University Press, 1992.
———. "Was the Pentateuch the Constitution of the Jewish Ethnos?" Pages 41–62 in *Persia and Torah: The Theory of Imperial Authorization of the Pentateuch*. Edited by James W. Watts. Atlanta: Society of Biblical Literature, 2001.
Blum, Erhard. *Studien zur Komposition des Pentateuch*. Beihefte zur Zeitschrift für die alttestamentliche Wissenschaft 189. Berlin: de Gruyter 1990.
Bolin, Thomas M. "Rivalry and Resignation: Girard on Qoheleth and the Divine-Human Relationship." *Biblica* 86 (2005): 245–59.
———. "When the End Is the Beginning—The Persian Period and the Origins of the Biblical Tradition." *Scandinavian Journal of the Old Testament* 10 (1996): 3–15.

Borgman, Paul. *David, Saul, and God: Rediscovering an Ancient Story*. New York: Oxford University Press, 2008.

Borré, Kristen. "Seal Blood, Inuit Blood, and Diet: A Biocultural Model of Physiology and Cultural Identity." *Medical Anthropology Quarterly* 5 (1991): 48–62.

Bösenecker, Jobst. "Text und Redaktion: Untersuchungen zum hebräischen und griechischen Text von 1 Könige 1-11." Th.D. diss., University of Rostock, 2000.

Botterweck, G. Johannes and Helmer Ringgren, eds. *Theologishes Wörterbuch zum Alten Testament*. 15 vols. Stuttgart: Kohlhammer, 1970–2006.

Boyer, Pascal. *Religion Explained: The Human Instincts that Fashion Gods, Spirits, and Ancestors*. London: Vintage Books, 2002.

Braulik, Georg. "Das Deuteronomium und die Geburt des Monotheismus." Pages 115–59 in *Gott, der einzige: Zur Entstehung des Monotheismus in Israel*. Edited by George Braulik et al. Quaestiones disputatae 104. Freiburg: Herder, 1985.

Briant, Pierre. *From Cyrus to Alexander: A History of the Persian Empire*. Translated by P. T. Daniels. Winona Lake, Ind.: Eisenbrauns, 2002.

Brockington, Leonard H. *Ezra, Nehemiah and Esther*. New Century Bible Series. London: Thomas Nelson and Sons, 1969.

Buber, Martin, *Kingship of God*. Translated by R. Scheimann. New York: Harper & Row, 1967.

Budde, Karl. *Die Bücher Samuel*. Kurzer Hand-Commentar zum Alten Testament 8. Tübingen: Mohr, 1902.

Butler, Trent. *Judges*. Word Biblical Commentary 8. Nashville: Thomas Nelson, 2009.

Byrne, Ryan. "The Refuge of Scribalism in Iron I Palestine." *Bulletin of the American Schools of Oriental Research* 345 (2007): 1–31.

Campbell, Jonathan G. "4QMMT and the Tripartite Canon." *Journal of Jewish Studies* 51 (2000): 181–90.

Cancik, Hubert. *Grundzüge der hethitischen und alttestamentlichen Geschichtsschreibung*. Abhandlungen des Deutschen Palästinavereins. Wiesbaden: Harrassowitz, 1976.

Carr, David M. "Empirische Perspektiven auf das Deuteronomistische Geschichtswer." Pages 1–17 in *Die deuteronomistischen Geschichtswerke: Redaktions- und religionsgeschichtliche Perspektiven zur "Deuteronomismus"-Diskussion in Tora und Vorderen Propheten*. Edited by Markus Witte et al. Beihefte zur Zeitschrift für die alttestamentliche Wissenschaft 365. Berlin: de Gruyter, 2006.

———. *Writing on the Tablet of the Heart: Origins of Scripture and Literature.* New York: Oxford University Press, 2005.

Carroll, Robert P. "Exile! What Exile? Deportation and Discourses of Diaspora." Pages 62–79 in *Leading Captivity Captive: "The Exile" as History and Ideology.* Edited by Lester L. Grabbe. Journal for the Study of the Old Testament Supplement Series 278. Sheffield: Sheffield Academic Press, 1998.

Carter, Charles. *The Emergence of Yehud in the Persian Period: A Social and Demographic Study.* Journal for the Study of the Old Testament Supplement Series 294. Sheffield: Sheffield Academic Press, 1999.

Charlesworth, James H., ed. *Old Testament Pseudepigrapha.* 2 vols. New York: Doubleday, 1983–1985.

Choi, Soo Hang. "Communicative Socialization Processes: Korea and Canada." Pages 103–22 in *Innovations in Cross-Cultural Psychology: Selected Papers from the Tenth International Conference of the International Association for Cross-Cultural Psychology.* Edited by Saburo Iwawaki, Yoshihisa Kashima and Kwok Leung. Amsterdam: Swets & Zeitlinger, 1992.

Clements, Ronald E. "A Royal Privilege: Dining in the Presence of the Great King." Pages 49–66 in *Reflection and Refraction: Studies in Biblical Historiography in Honour of A. Graeme Auld.* Edited by Robert Rezetko, Timothy H. Lim, and W. Brian Aucker. Vetus Testamentum Supplements 113. Leiden: Brill, 2007.

Cogan, Mordechai. *1 Kings: A New Translation with Introduction and Commentary.* Anchor Bible 10. New York: Doubleday, 2000.

Combs-Schilling, M. Elaine. "Family and Friend in a Moroccan Boom Town: The Segmentary Debate Reconsidered." *American Ethnologist* 12 (1985): 659–75.

Connerton, Paul. *How Societies Remember.* Themes in the Social Sciences. Cambridge: Cambridge University Press, 1989.

Conrad, Edgar W. "Heard But Not Seen: The Representation of 'Books' in the Old Testament." *Journal for the Study of the Old Testament* 54 (1992): 45–59.

———. *Reading Isaiah.* Minneapolis: Fortress, 1991.

Coogan, Michael D. "Literacy and the Formation of Biblical Literature." Pages 47–61 in *Realia Dei: Essays in Archaeology and Biblical Interpretation in Honor of Edward F. Campbell, Jr. at His Retirement.* Edited by Prescott H. Williams and Theodore Hiebert. Scholars Press Homage Series 23. Atlanta: Scholars Press, 1999.

Cook, Stanley A. "Notes on the Composition of 2 Samuel." *American Journal of Semitic Languages and Literature* 16 (1899–1900): 156–57.
Cortese, Enzo. *Josua 13-21: Ein priesterschriftlicher Abschnitt im deuteronomistischen Geschichtswerk*. Orbis biblicus et orientalis 94. Freiburg: University Press, 1990.
Crenshaw, James L. *Education in Ancient Israel: Across the Deadening Silence*. New York: Doubleday, 1998.
Crüsemann, Frank. *Der Widerstand gegen das Konigtum*. Wissenschaftliche Monographien zum Alten und Neuen Testament 49. Neukirchen-Vluyn: Neukirchener Verlag, 1978.
———. *Die Tora: Theologie und Sozialgeschichte des alttestamentlichen Gesetzes*. Munich: Kaiser, 1992.
Curtis, Edward D. and Madsen, Albert A. *A Critical and Exegetical Commentary on the Books of Chronicles*. International Critical Commentary 11. Edinburgh: T&T Clark, 1910.
Davies, Graham I. "Were There Schools in Ancient Israel?" Pages 199–211 in *Wisdom in Ancient Israel: Essays in Honour of J.A. Emerton*. Edited by John Day, Robert P. Gordon, and Hugh G. M. Williamson. Cambridge: Cambridge University Press, 1995.
Davies, Philip R. "Exile? What Exile? Whose Exile?" Pages 128–38 in *Leading Captivity Captive: "The Exile" as History and Ideology*. Edited by Lester L. Grabbe. Journal for the Study of the Old Testament Supplement Series 278. Sheffield: Sheffield Academic Press, 1998.
———. "Josiah and the Law Book." Pages 65–77 in *Good Kings and Bad Kings: The Kingdom of Judah in the Seventh Century*. Edited by Lester L. Grabbe. European Seminar on Methodology in Israel's History 5/ Library of Hebrew Bible/Old Testament Studies 393. London: T&T Clark, 2005.
———. "Loose Canons," *Journal of Hebrew Scriptures* 1 (1997): article 5. Online: http://www.jhsonline.org/Articles/article_5.pdf
———. "M*n*th**sm." Paper presented at the SBL International Meeting. London, July 6, 2011.
———. "Moses in the Book of Kings." Pages 77–87 in *La construction de la figure de Moïse - The Construction of the Figure of Moses*. Edited by Thomas Römer. Supplements to *Transeuphratène* 13. Paris: Gabalda, 2007.
———. "Scenes from the Early History of Judaism." Pages 145–82 in *The Triumph of Elohim: From Yahwisms to Judaisms*. Edited by Diana

V. Edelman. Contributions to Biblical Exegesis and Theology 13. Kampen: Kok Pharos, 1995.

———. *Scribes and Schools: The Canonization of the Hebrew Scriptures.* Library of Ancient Israel. Louisville: John Knox, 1998.

———. "The Origin of Biblical Israel." *Journal of Hebrew Scriptures* 5 (2005): article 17. Online: http://www.jhsonline.org/Articles/article_47.pdf.

———. *The Origins of Biblical Israel.* Library of Hebrew Bible/Old Testament Studies 485. London: T&T Clark, 2007.

———. "The Trouble with Benjamin." Pages 93–111 in *Reflection and Refraction: Studies in Biblical Historiography in Honour of A. Graeme Auld.* Edited by Robert Rezetko, Timothy H. Lim, and W. Brian Aucker. Supplements to Vetus Testamentum 113. Leiden: Brill, 2007.

Deist, Ferdinand. "The Yehud Bible: A Belated Divine Miracle?" *Journal of Northwest Semitic Languages* 23 (1997): 128–31.

Dietrich, Walter. *David, Saul und die Propheten: das Verhältnis von Religion und Politik nach den prophetischen Überlierungen vom frühesten Königtum in Israel.* 2d ed. Beiträge zur Wissenschaft vom Alten (und Neuen) Testament 122. Stuttgart: Kohlhammer, 1992.

Dietrich, Walter, and Thomas Naumann. *Die Samuelbücher.* Erträge der Forschung 287. Darmstadt: Wissenschaftliche Buchgesellschaft, 1995.

Doniger O'Flaherty, Wendy. *Other Peoples' Myths: The Cave of Echoes.* New York: Macmillan, 1995.

Dozeman, Thomas B., Thomas Römer and Konrad Schmid, eds. *Pentateuch, Hexateuch, or Enneateuch? Identifying Literary Works in Genesis through Kings.* Ancient Israel and Its Literature 8. Atlanta: Society of Biblical Literature, 2011.

Driver, Samuel R. *A Critical and Exegetical Commentary on Deuteronomy.* International Critical Commentary. 3d edition. Edinburgh: T&T Clark, 1902.

Edelman, Diana. "Did Saulide-Davidic Rivalry Resurface in Early Persian Yehud?" Pages 70–92 in *The Land That I Will Show You: Essays on the History and Archaeology of the Ancient Near East in Honor of J. Maxwell Miller.* Edited by Andrew Dearman and Patrick Graham. Journal for the Study of the Old Testament Supplement Series 343. Sheffield: Sheffield Academic Press, 2001.

———. "The 'Empty Land' as a Motif in City Laments." Pages 127–49 in *Ancient and Modern Historiography, L'historiograhie biblique, ancienne et modern.* Edited by George J. Brooke and Thomas Römer. Bibliotheca ephemeridum theologicarum lovaniensium 207. Leuven: Leuven University, 2007.

———. "Tyrian Trade in Yehud under Artaxerxes I: Real or Fictional? Independent or Crown Endorsed?" Pages 207–46 in *Judah and the Judeans in the Persian Period*. Edited by Oded Lipschits and Manfred Oeming. Winona Lake, Ind.: Eisenbrauns, 2006.

Edelman, Diana and Lynette Mitchell. "Chronicles and Local Greek Histories." Pages 229–52 in *What Was Authoritative for Chronicles?* Edited by Ehud Ben Zvi and Diana V. Edelman. Winona Lake, Ind.: Eisenbrauns, 2010.

Edelman, Diana, et al. *The Books of Moses: Opening the Books*. BibleWorld. Durham: Acumen, 2012.

Edenburg, Cynthia. "The Story of the Outrage at Gibeah (Jdg. 19–21): Composition, Sources and Historical Context." Ph.D. diss., Tel Aviv University, 2003 (Hebrew).

Erll, Astrid. *Memory in Culture*. Translated by S. B. Young. Palgrave Macmillan Memory Studies. New York: Palgrave Macmillan, 2011.

Eskenazi, Tamara Cohn. "The Missions of Ezra and Nehemiah." Pages 509–29 in *Judah and the Judeans in the Persian Period*. Edited by Oded Lipschits and Manfred Oeming. Winona Lake, Ind.: Eisenbrauns, 2006.

Exum, J. Cheryl. "The Centre Cannot Hold: Thematic and Textual Instabilities in Judges." *Catholic Biblical Quarterly* 52 (1990): 410–43.

Fabry, Heinz-Josef. "Deuteronomium 15: Gedanken zur Geschwister-Ethik im Alten Testament." *Zeitschrift für Altorientalische und Biblische Rechtsgeschichte* 3 (1997): 92–111.

Fensham, F. Charles, *The Books of Ezra and Nehemiah*. New International Commentary on the Old Testament. Grand Rapids, Mich.: Eerdmans, 1982.

Fenton, Steve. *Ethnicity*. 2nd revised and updated edition. Key Concepts in the Social Sciences. Cambridge, UK: Polity, 2013.

Fentress, James and Chris Wickham. *Social Memory*. New Perspectives on the Past. Oxford: Blackwell, 1992.

Fernández Marcos, Natalio and José Ramón Busto Saiz, *El texto antioqueno de la biblia griega I, 1-2 Samuel*. Madrid: Instituto de Filologia, 1989.

Finkelstein, Israel. "Jerusalem in the Persian (and Early Hellenistic) Period and the Wall of Nehemiah," *Journal for the Study of the Old Testament* 32 (2008): 501–20.

———. "Persian Period Finds from Jerusalem: Facts and Interpretations." *Journal of Hebrew Scriptures* 4 (2009): article 20.

———. "Rehoboam's Fortified Cities (II Chr 11,5–12): A Hasmonean Reality?" *Zeitschrift für die alltestamentliche Wissenschaft* 123 (2011): 92–107.

Finkelstein, Israel, Ido Koch, and Oded Lipschits. "The Mound on the Mount: A Possible Solution to the 'Problem with Jerusalem.'" *Journal of Hebrew Scriptures* 11 (2011): article 12.

Fisher, Eli D. "Violence, Tradition and Ideology: A Story of the Hebrew Terms BṢ, ḤMS and ŠDD." PhD diss., Vanderbilt Divinity School, 1998.

Floyd, Michael H. *Minor Prophets, Part 2*. Forms of Old Testament Literature 22. Grand Rapids, Mich. Eerdmans, 2000.

Fohrer, Georg. *Introduction to the Old Testament*. Translated by D. Green. Nashville: Abingdon, 1968.

Frevel, Christian. "Deuteronomistisches Geschichtswerk oder Gechichtswerke? Die Thesen Martin Noths zwischen Tetrateuch, Hexateuch und Enneateuch." Pages 60–94 in *Martin Noth—aus der Sicht heutiger Forschung*. Edited by Udo Rüterswörden. Biblisch-theologische Studien 58. Neukirchen-Vluyn: Neukirchener Verlag, 2004.

Frolov, Serge. "Evil-Merodach and the Deuteronomist: The Sociohistorical Setting of Dtr in the Light of 2 Kgs 25,27-30." *Biblica* 88 (2007): 174–90.

———. "Fire, Smoke, and Judah in Judges: A Response to Gregory Wong." *Scandinavian Journal of the Old Testament* 21 (2007): 127–38.

———. "Joshua's Double Demise (Josh. xxiv 28-31; Judg. ii 6-9): Making Sense of a Repetition." *Vetus Testamentum* 58 (2008): 315–23.

———. *Judges*. Forms of Old Testament Literature 6B. Grand Rapids: Eerdmans, forthcoming.

———. "Rethinking Judges." *Catholic Biblical Quarterly* 71 (2009): 24–41.

———. "Succession Narrative: A 'Document' or a Phantom?" *Journal of Biblical Literature* 121 (2002): 81–104.

———. *The Turn of the Cycle: 1 Samuel 1–8 in Synchronic and Diachronic Perspectives*. Beihefte zur Zeitschrift für die alttestamentliche Wissenschaft 342. Berlin: de Gruyter, 2004.

Frymer-Kenski, Tikva. "Israel." Pages 975–1046 in vol. 2 of *A History of Ancient Near Eastern Law*. Edited by Raymond Westbrook. 2 vols. Handbuch der Orientalistik 72. Leiden: Brill, 2003.

Garbini, Giovannni. "Hebrew Literature in the Persian Period." Pages 180–88 in *Second Temple Studies: 2. Temple Community in the Persian Period*. Edited by Tamara C. Eskenazi and Kent H. Richards. Journal for the Study of the Old Testament Supplement Series 175. Sheffield: Sheffield Academic Press, 1994.

Gaster, Moses. "On the Newly Discovered Samaritan Book of Joshua." *Journal of the Royal Asiatic Society* (New Series) 40 (1908): 795–809.

———. "The Samaritan Hebrew Sources of The Arabic Book of Joshua," *Journal of the Royal Asiatic Society* (New Series) 62 (1930): 597–99.

Geertz, Clifford. *The Interpretation of Cultures: Selected Essays by Clifford Geertz.* New York: Basic Books, 1973.

Gertz, Jan Christian. *Die Gerichtsorganisation Israels im deuteronomischen Gesetz.* Forschungen zur Religion und Literatur des Alten und Neuen Testament 165. Göttingen: Vandenhoeck & Ruprecht, 1994.

Giesen, Bernhard. "Codes Kollektiver Identität." Pages 13–43 in *Religion und Identität im Horizont des Pluralismus.* Edited by Werner Gephart and Hans Waldenfels. Suhrkamp Taschenbuch Wissenschaft 1411. Frankfurt: Suhrkamp, 1999.

Giesen, Bernhard and Kay Junge. "Der Mythos des Universalismus." Pages 34–64 in *Mythos und Nation: Studien zur Entwicklung des kollektiven Bewusstseins in der Neuzeit 3.* Edited by Helmut Berding. Suhrkamp Taschenbuch Wissenschaft 1246. Frankfurt: Suhrkamp, 1996.

Gosse, Bernard. "L' inclusion de l'ensemble Genèse-II Rois, entre la perte du jardin d'Eden et celle de Jérusalem." *Zeitschrift für die alttestamentliche Wissenschaft* 114 (2002): 189–211.

Grabbe, Lester L. *Ezra-Nehemiah.* Old Testament Readings. London: Routledge, 1998.

———. *Yehud: A History of the Persian Province of Judah.* Vol.1 of *A History of the Jews and Judaism in the Second Temple Period.* Library of Second Temple Studies 47. London: T&T Clark International, 2004.

Groß, Walter. *Richter.* Herders theologischer Kommentar zum Alten Testament. Freiburg: Herder, 2009.

Guillaume, Philippe. *Land and Calendar: The Priestly Document from Genesis 1 to Joshua 18.* Library of Hebrew Bible/Old Testament Studies 391. New York: T&T Clark, 2009.

———. *Land, Credit and Crisis: Agrarian Finance in the Hebrew Bible.* BibleWorld. Sheffield: Equinox, 2011.

———. *Waiting for Josiah: The Judges.* Journal for the Study of the Old Testament Supplement Series 385. London: T&T Clark, 2004.

Hagerdorn, Anselm C. " 'Who Would Invite a Stranger from Abroad?' The Presence of Greeks in Palestine in Old Testament Times." Pages 68–93 in *The Old Testament in Its World.* Edited by Robert P. Gordon and

Johannes C. de Moor. *Oudtestamentische Studiën* 52. Leiden: Brill, 2005.

Handy, Lowell K. "The Role of Huldah in Josiah's Cult Reform." *Zeitschrift für die alttestamentliche Wissenschaft* 106 (1994): 46–52.

Haran, Menahem. "On the Diffusion of Literacy and Schools in Ancient Israel." Pages 81–95 in *Congress Volume, Jerusalem 1986*. Edited by John A. Emerton. Supplements to Vetus Testamentum 40. Leiden: Brill, 1988.

Harris, William V. *Ancient Literacy*. Cambridge: Harvard University Press, 1989.

Heine, Heinrich. "Geständnisse." Pages 97–179 in vol. 1 of *Vermischte Schriften*. 14 vols. Sämmtliche Werke. Hamburg: Hoffmann und Campe, 1854–1976.

Hempel, Johannes. *Die Schichten des Deuteronomiums: Ein Beitrag zur israelitischen Literatur- und Rechtsgeschichte*. Leipzig: Voigtländer, 1914.

Henige, David. "In Good Company: Problematic Sources and Biblical Historicity." *Journal for the Study of the Old Testament* 30 (2005): 29–47.

Hentschel, Georg. "Die weise Frau von Tekoa (2Sam 14,1-24)." Pages 63–75 in *Auf den Spuren der schriftgelehrten Weisen: Festschrift für Johannes Marböck anlässlich seiner Emeritierung*. Edited by Irmtraud Fischer, Ursula Rapp and Johannes Schiller. Beihefte zur Zeitschrift für die alttestamentliche Wissenschaft 331. Berlin: de Gruyter, 2003.

Herbert, Sharon C. and Andrea M. Berlin. "A New Administrative Center for Persian and Hellenistic Galilee: Preliminary Report of the University of Michigan/University of Minnesota Excavations at Kedesh." *Bulletin of the American Schools of Oriental Research* 329 (2003): 13–59.

Hesseling, Dirk C. "On Waxen Tablets with Fables of Babrius." *The Journal of Hellenic Studies* 13 (1892–1893): 293–314.

Hoftijzer, Jean. "David and the Tekoite Woman." *Vetus Testamentum* 20 (1970): 419–44.

Hoglund, Kenneth G. *Achaemenid Imperial Administration in Syria-Palestine and the Missions of Ezra and Nehemiah*. Society of Biblical Literature Dissertation Series 125. Atlanta: Scholars Press, 1992.

Holland, Martin. *Das Buch Josua erklärt*. Wuppertaler Studienbibel. Wuppertal: Brockhaus, 1997.

Hölscher, Gustav. "Komposition und Ursprung des Deuteronomiums." *Zeitschrift für die alttestamentliche Wissenschaft* 40 (1923): 161–255.

Horton, Robin. ""African Traditional Thought and Western Science: Part 1: From Tradition to Science." *Africa* 37 (1967): 50–71.

———. "African Traditional Thought and Western Science: Part 2: The Closed and Open Predicaments." *Africa* 37 (1967): 155–87.

Hugo, Philippe. *Les deux visages d'Elie: texte massorétique et Septante dans l'histoire la plus ancienne du texte de 1 Rois 17–18*. Orbis biblicus et orientalis 217. Göttingen: Vandenhoeck & Ruprecht, 2006.

Jacobson-Widding, Anita, ed. *Identity: Personal and Socio-Cultural*. Acta Universitatis Upsaliensis Uppsala Studies in Cultural Anthropology 5. Stockholm: Almqvist & Wicksell, 1983.

Jamieson-Drake, David. *Scribes and Schools in Monarchic Judah: A Socio-Archeological Approach*. Journal for the Study of the Old Testament Supplement Series 109. Sheffield: Sheffield Academic Press, 1991.

Janzen, David. "The 'Mission' of Ezra and the Persian-Period Temple Community." *Journal of Biblical Literature* 119 (2000): 619–43.

Japhet, Sara. "Periodization between History and Ideology II: Chronology and Ideology in Ezra-Nehemiah." Pages 491–508 in *Judah and the Judeans in the Persian Period*. Edited by Oded Lipschits and Manfred Oeming. Winona Lake, Ind.: Eisenbrauns, 2006.

———. *The Ideology of the Book of Chronicles and Its Place in Biblical Thought*. Translated by A. Barber. Beiträge zur Erforschung des Alten Testaments und des antiken Judentums 9. Frankfurt am Main: Peter Lang, 1989.

Jeppesen, Knud. "Exile a Period—Exile a Myth." Pages 139–44 in *Leading Captivity Captive: "The Exile" as History and Ideology*. Edited by Lester L. Grabbe. Journal for the Study of the Old Testament Supplement Series 278. Sheffield: Sheffield Academic Press, 1998.

Jobling, David. *1 Samuel*. Berit Olam. Collegeville: Liturgical Press, 1998.

Kallai, Zecharia."The Twelve-Tribe Systems of Israel." *Vetus Testamentum* 47 (1997): 53–90.

Kautzsch, Emil, ed. *Gesenius' Hebrew Grammar*. Translated by A. E. Cowley. 2d. ed. Oxford: Oxford University Press, 1910.

Keel, Othmar and Silvia Schroer. *Schöpfung: Biblische Theologien im Kontext altorientalischer Religionen*. Freiburg: University Press, 2002.

Kessler, John. "Diaspora and Homeland in the Early Achaemenid Period: Community, Geography and Demography in Zechariah 1–8." Pages 137–66 in *Approaching Yehud: New Approaches to the Study of the Persian Period*. Edited by Jon Berquist. Atlanta: Society of Biblical Literature, 2007.

Kissane, Edward J. *The Book of Psalms*. Dublin: Browne and Nolan, 1964.

Klein, Ralph W. *1 Chronicles: A Commentary*. Hermeneia. Minneapolis: Fortress, 2006.
———. *1 Samuel*. Word Biblical Commentary 10. Waco Tex.: Word, 1983.
———. "The Books of Ezra and Nehemiah." Pages 671–851 in vol. 3 of *The New Interpreter's Bible*. Edited by Leander Keck et al. 12 vols. Nashville: Abingdon, 1999.
Klingbeil, Gerald A. "'Momentaufnamen' of Israelite Religion: The Importance of the Communal Meal in Narrative Texts in 1/II Regum and their Ritual Dimensions." *Zeitschrift für die alttestamentliche Wissenschaft* 118 (2006): 22–45.
Klostermann, August. *Der Pentateuch: Beiträge zu seinem Verständnis und seiner Entstehungsgeschichte*. 2nd ed. Leipzig: Deichert, 1907.
Knauf, Ernst Axel. "Bethel: The Israelite Impact on Judean Language and Literature." Pages 291–349 in *Judah and the Judeans in the Persian Period*. Edited by Oded Lipschits and Manfred Oeming. Winona Lake, Ind.: Eisenbrauns, 2006.
———. "Biblical References to Judean Settlement in Eretz Israel (and Beyond) in the Late Persian and Early Hellenistic Periods." Pages 175–93 in *The Historian and the Bible: Essays in Honour of Lester L. Grabbe*. Edited by Philip R. Davies and Diana V. Edelman. Library of Hebrew Bible/Old Testament Studies 530. New York: T&T Clark, 2010.
———. "Does 'Deuteronomistic Historiography' Exist?" Pages 388–98 in *Israel Constructs its History: Deuteronomistic History in Recent Research*. Edited by Albert de Pury, Thomas Römer, and Jean-Daniel Macchi. Journal for the Study of the Old Testament Supplement Series 306. Sheffield: Sheffield Academic Press, 2000.
———. "History in Joshua." Pages 130–39 in *Israel in Transition: From Late Bronze II to Iron IIa (c. 1250-850 b.c.e.), Volume 2. The Texts*. Edited by Lester L. Grabbe. Library of Hebrew Bible/Old Testament Studies 521 and European Seminar on Historical Methodology 8. New York: T&T Clark, 2010.
———. "Inside the Walls of Nehemiah's Jerusalem: Naboth's Vineyard." Pages 185–94 in *The Fire Signals of Lachish: Studies in the Archaeology and History of Israel in the Late Bronze Age, Iron Age, and Persian Period in Honor of David Ussishkin*. Edited by Israel Finkelstein and Nadav Na'aman. Winona Lake, Ind.: Eisenbrauns, 2011.
———. *Josua*. Zürcher Bibelkommentare Altes Testament 6. Zürich: TVZ, 2008.

———. "Kings among Prophets." Pages 131–49 in *The Production of Prophecy: Constructing Prophecy and Prophets in Yehud*. Edited by Diana V. Edelman and Ehud Ben Zvi. BibleWorld. London: Equinox, 2009.

———. "L'Historiographie Deutéronomiste' (DtrG) existe-t-elle?" Pages 409–18 in *Israël construit son histoire: L'historiographie deutéronomiste à la lumière des recherches récentes*. Edited by Albert de Pury, Thomas Römer, and Jean-Daniel Macchi. Le monde de la Bible 34. Genève: Labor et fides, 1996.

———. "Observations on Judah's Social and Economic History and the Dating of the Laws In Deuteronomy." *Journal of Hebrew Studies* 9 (2009): article 18.

Knight, Douglas A. "Deuteronomy and the Deuteronomists." Pages 61–79 in *Old Testament Inerpretation Past, Present, and Future: Essays in Honour of Gene M. Tucker*. Edited by James L. Mays, David L. Petersen and Kent H. Richards. Edinburgh: T&T Clark, 1995.

Knoppers, Gary N. *I Chronicles 10–29: A New Translation with Introduction and Commentary*. Anchor Bible 12A. New York: Doubleday, 2004.

———. "Ethnicity, Genealogy, Geography, and Change: the Judean Communities of Babylon and Jerusalem in the Story of Ezra." Pages 142–72 in *Community Identity in Judean Historiography: Biblical and Comparative Perspectives*. Edited by Gary N. Knoppers and Kenneth A. Ristau. Winona Lake, Ind.: Eisenbrauns, 2009.

———. "Revisiting the Samarian Question in the Persian Period." Pages 265–89 in *Judah and the Judeans in the Persian Period*. Edited by Oded Lipschits and Manfred Oeming.Winona Lake, Ind.: Eisenbrauns, 2006.

Koester, Helmut. "Gospel II. Genre 2e. Legend." Pages 528–31 in vol. 5 of *Religion Past & Present*. Edited by Hans Dieter Betz et al. 6 vols. Boston: Brill, 2005.

Köhler, Ludwig. "Die hebräische Rechtsgemeinde." Pages 143–71 in *Der hebräische Mensch*. Edited by Ludwig Köhler. Tübingen: Mohr Siebeck, 1953.

Kokkinos, Nikos. *The Herodian Dynasty: Origins, Role in Society and Eclipse*. Journal for the Study of the Pseudepigrapha: Supplement Series 30. Sheffield: Sheffield Academic Press, 1998.

Kratz, Reinhard G. *The Composition of the Narrative Books of the Bible*. Translated by J. Bowden. New York: T&T Clark, International, 2000.

Kraus, Hans-J. *Psalms 60–150: A Commentary*. Translated by H. C. Oswald. Minneapolis: Augsburg, 1989.

Krüger, Thomas. *Qoheleth: A Commentary*. Edited by Klaus Baltzer. Translated by O. C. Dean Jr. Hermeneia. Minneapolis: Fortress, 2004.
Kuhnen, Hans-Peter. "Israel unmittelbar vor und nach Alexander dem Grossen." Pages 1–27 in *Die Griechen und das Antike Israel: interdisciplinäre Studien zur Religions-und Kulturgeschichte des Heiligen Landes*. Edited by Stefan Alkier and Markus Witte. Orbis biblicus et orientalis 201. Fribourg: Academic Press, 2004.
Labuschagne, Casper J. "The Literary and Theological Function of Divine Speech in the Pentateuch." Pages 154–73 in *Congress Volume Salamanca*. Edited by John A. Emerton. Supplements to Vetus Testamentum 36. Leiden: Brill, 1985.
Lasine, Stuart. "Melodrama as Parable: The Story of the Poor Man's Ewe Lamb and the Unmasking of David's Topsy-Turvy Emotions." *Harvard Theological Review* 8 (1984): 101–24.
Leith, Mary Joan Winn. "Israel among the Nations: The Persian Period." Pages 367–419 in *The Oxford History of the Biblical World*. Edited by Michael D. Coogan. New York: Oxford University Press, 1998.
Lemaire, André. *Les Écoles et la Formation de la Bible dans l'Ancien Israël*. Orbis biblicus et orientalis 39. Fribourg: University Press, 1981.
———. "New Aramaic Ostraca from Idumea and Their Historical Interpretation." Pages 413–56 in *Judah and the Judeans in the Persian Period*. Edited by Oded Lipschits and Manfred Oeming. Winona Lake, Ind.: Eisenbrauns, 2006.
Lemche, Niels Peter. "'Because They Have Cast Away the Law of the Lord of Hosts' — Or: 'We and the Rest of the World': the Authors Who 'Wrote' the Old Testament." *Scandinavian Journal of the Old Testament* 17 (2003): 268–90.
———. "Did a Reform Like Josiah's Happen"? Pages 11–19 in *The Historian and the Bible: Essays in Honour of Lester L. Grabbe*. Edited by Philip R. Davies and Diana V. Edelman. Library of Hebrew Bible/Old Testament Studies 530. London: T&T Clark, 2010.
———. "The Old Testament—A Hellenistic Book?" *Scandinavian Journal of the Old Testament* 7 (1993): 163–93.
Lenchak, Timothy A. *Choose Life! A Rhetorical-Critical Investigation of Deuteronomy 28,69–30,20*. Analecta Biblica 129. Rome: Pontifical Biblical Institute, 1993.
Leuchter, Mark. "Coming to Terms with Ezra's Many Identities in Ezra-Nehemiah." Pages 41–63 in *Historiography and Identity (Re)formulation in Second Temple Historiographical Literature*. Edited by Louis

Jonker. Library of Hebrew Bible/Old Testament Studies 534. London: T&T Clark, 2010.

———. "The Levite in Your Gates: The Deuteronomic Redefinition of Levitical Authority." *Journal of Biblical Literature* 126 (2007): 417–36.

Levin, Christoph. "Das Deuteronomium und der Jahwist." Pages 96–110 in *Fortschreibungen: Gesammelte Studien zum Alten Testament*. Beihefte zur Zeitschrift für die alttestamentliche Wissenschaft 316. Berlin: de Gruyter, 2003.

———. "Joschija im deuteronmistischen Geschichtswerk." *Zeitschrift für die alttestamentliche Wissenschaft* 96 (1984): 351–71.

———. "The Poor in the Old Testament: Some Observations." Pages 322–38 in *Fortschreibungen: Gesammelte Studien zum Alten Testament*. Beihefte zur Zeitschrift für die alttestamentliche Wissenschaft 316. Berlin: de Gruyter, 2003.

Levinson, Bernard M. *Deuteronomy and the Hermeneutics of Legal Innovation*. New York: Oxford University Press, 1998.

L'Hour, Jean. "Une législation criminelle dans le Deutéronome." *Biblica* 44 (1963): 1–28.

Limburg, James. "Psalms, Book of," Pages 522–36 in vol. 5 of *The Anchor Bible Dictionary*. Edited by David Noel Freedman et al. 6 vols. Garden City, N.Y.: Doubleday, 1992.

Linville, James R. *Amos and the Cosmic Imagination*. Society for Old Testament Studies Monograph Series. Aldershot: Ashgate, 2008.

———. *Israel in the Book of Kings: The Past as a Project of Social Identity*. Journal for the Study of the Old Testament Supplement Series 272. Sheffield: Sheffield Academic Press, 1998.

———. "Lest We Forget Our Sins: Lamentations, Exilicism and the Sanctification of Disjunction." Pages 315–27 in *Remembering and Forgetting in Early Second Temple Judah*. Edited by Ehud Ben Zvi and Christoph Levin. Forschungen zum Alten Testament. Tübingen: Mohr Siebeck, 2012.

———. "Rethinking the 'Exilic' Book of Kings." *Journal for the Study of the Old Testament* 75 (1997): 21–42.

Lohfink, Norbert. "Das deuteronomische Gesetz in der Endgestalt—Entwurf einer Gesellschaft ohne marginale Gruppen." Pages 205–18 in vol. 3 of *Studien zum Deuteronomium und zur deuteronomistischen Literatur*. 3 vols. Stuttgarter biblische Aufsatzbände, Altes Testament 20. Stuttgart: Katholisches Bibelwerk, 1995.

———. *Das Hauptgebot: eine Untersuchung literarischer Einleitungsfragen zu Dtn 5–11*. Analecta biblica 20. Rome: Pontifical Biblical Institute, 1963.

———. "Die Schichten des Pentateuch und der Krieg." Pages 51–110 in *Gewalt und Gewaltlosigkeit im Alten Testament*. Edited by Ernst Haag et al. Quaestiones disputatae 96. Freiburg: Herder, 1983. Reprinted as pages 255–315 in *Studien zum Pentateuch*. Stuttgarter biblische Aufsatzbände, Altes Testament 4. Stuttgart: Katholisches Bibelwerk, 1988.

———. "Fortschreibung? Zur Technik der Rechtsrevisionen im deuteronomischen Bereich, erörtert an Deuteronomium 12, Ex 21,2–11 und Dtn 15,12–18." Pages 127–71 in *Das Deuteronomium und seine Querbeziehungen*. Edited by Timo Veijola. Schriften der Finnischen Exegetischen Gesellschaft 62. Helsinki: Finnische Exegetische Gesellschaft and Göttingen: Vandenhoeck & Ruprecht.

———. "Zur neueren Diskussion über 2 Kön 22–23." Pages 24–48 in *Das Deuteronomium: Entstehung, Gestalt und Botschaft*. Edited by Norbert Lohfink. Bibliotheca ephemeridum theologicarum lovaniensium 68. Leuven: Leuven University Press, 1985.

Lyke, Larry L. *King David with the Wise Woman of Tekoa: The Resonance of Tradition in Parabolic Narrative*. Journal for the Study of the Old Testament Supplement Series 255. Sheffield: Sheffield Academic Press, 1997.

Lysias. Translated by S. C. Todd. Oratory of Classical Greece 2. Austin: University of Texas, 2000.

MacDonald, Nathan. *Deuteronomy and the Meaning of "Monotheism."* Forschungen zum Alten Testament 2.1. Tübingen: Mohr Siebeck, 2003.

Macholz, Georg Christian. "Die Stellung des Königs in der israelitischen Gerichtsverfassung." *Zeitschrift für die alttestamentliche Wissenschaft* 84 (1972): 157–82.

Mack, Burton L. *Myth and the Christian Nation: A Social Theory of Religion*. Religion in Culture: Studies in Social Contest and Construction. London: Equinox, 2008.

Magen, Yitzhak. "The Dating of the First Phase of the Samaritan Temple on Mount Gerizim in Light of the Archaeological Evidence." Pages 157–211 in *Judah and the Judeans in the Fourth Century B.C.E.* Edited by Oded Lipschits, Gary N. Knoppers, and Rainer Albertz. Winona Lake, Ind: Eisenbrauns, 2007.

Mandel, Sara and David Noel Freedman. *The Relationship between Herodotus' "History" and Primary History.* South Florida Studies in the History of Judaism 60. Atlanta: Scholars Press, 1993.

Marrou, Henri I. *A History of Education in Antiquity.* Translated by G. R. Lamb. New York: Sheed and Ward, 1956.

Marti, Karl. *Das fünfte Buch Mose oder Deuteronomium.* Die Heilige Schrift des Alten Testaments 1. 4th ed. Tübingen: Mohr Siebeck, 1922.

Marttila, Marko. "David in the Wisdom of Ben Sira." *Scandinavian Journal of the Old Testament* 25 (2011): 29–48.

Mathys, Hans-Peter. "Anmerkungen zu Mal 3,22-24." Pages 30–40 in *Vom Anfang und vom Ende: Fünf alttestamentliche Studien.* Beiträge zur Erforschung des Alten Testaments und des antiken Judentums 47. Frankfurt am Main: Peter Lang, 2000.

———. "Bücheranfänge und -schlüsse." Pages 1–29 in *Vom Anfang und vom Ende: Fünf alttestamentliche Studien.* Beiträge zur Erforschung des Alten Testaments und des antiken Judentums 47. Frankfurt am Main: Peter Lang, 2000.

Mayes, Andrew D. H. "Deuteronomistic Royal Ideology in Judges 17–21."*Biblical Interpretation* 9 (2001): 241–58.

———. *Deuteronomy.* New Century Bible Commentary. London: Oliphants, 1979.

McCarter, P. Kyle, Jr., *I Samuel.* Anchor Bible 8. Garden City, N.Y.: Doubleday, 1980.

McCarthy, Dennis J. *Treaty and Covenant: A Study in Form in Ancient Oriental Documents and in the Old Testament.* Analecta biblica 21. Rome: Pontifical Biblical Institute, 1963.

McConville, J. Gordon. "Singular Address in the Deuteronomic Law and the Politics of Legal Administration." *Journal for the Study of the Old Testament* 26 (2002): 19–36.

McCutcheon, Russell T. "Myth." Pages 190–208 in *Guide to the Study of Religion.* Edited by Willli Braun and Russell T. McCutcheon. London: Cassell, 2000.

McKeating, Henry. "The Development of the Law on Homicide in Ancient Israel." *Vetus Testamentum* 25 (1975): 46–68.

McKenzie, Stephen L. *The Chronicler's Use of the Deuteronomistic History.* Harvard Semitic Monographs 33. Atlanta: Scholars Press, 1985.

Mendenhall, George E. "Covenant Forms in Israelite Tradition." *Biblical Archaeologist* 17 (1954): 49–76.

Mendenhall, George E. and Gary Herion. "Covenant." Pages 1179–1202 in vol. 1 of *Anchor Bible Dictionary*. Edited by David N. Freedman et al. 6 vols. New York: Doubleday, 1992.

Merendino, Rosario P. *Das deuteronomische Gesetz: Eine literarkritische, gattungs-und überlieferungsgeschichtliche Untersuchung zu Dt 12–26*. Bonner biblische Beiträge 31. Bonn: Hanstein, 1969.

Meshorer, Yaakov. *Ancient Jewish Coinage* (2 vols. Dix Hills, NY: Amphora, 1982).

Mildenburg, Leo. "Yehud: A Preliminary Study of the Provincial Coinage of Judea." Pages 183–96 in *Greek Numismatics and Archaeology: Essays in Honor of Margaret Thompson*. Edited by Otto Mørkholm and Nancy M. Waggoner. Wetteren: Cultura, 1979.

Millard, Matthias. "Mündlichkeit nach der Schriftlichkeit." Pages 277–89 in *Freiheit und Recht: Festschrift für Frank Crüsemann zum 65. Geburtstag*. Edited by Christof Hardmeier, Rainer Kessler, and Andreas Ruwe. Gütersloh: Kaiser, 2003.

Monroe, Lauren A. S. "A Pre-Exilic 'Holiness' Substratum in the Deuteronomistic Account of Josiah's Reform." Pages 42–53 in "Scribes Before and after 587 BCE: A Conversation." *Journal of Hebrew Studies* 7 (2007). Online: http://www.jhsonline.org/Articles/article_71.pdf.

Müller, Reinhard. *Königtum und Gottesherrschaft: Untersuchungen zur alttestamentlichen Monarchiekritik*. Forschungen zum Alten Testament 2/3. Tübingen: Mohr Siebeck, 2004.

Murray, Donald F. "Of All Years the Hope-or Fears? Jehoiachin in Babylon (2 Kings 25:27–30)." *Journal of Biblical Literature* 120 (2001): 245–65.

Myers, Jacob M. *II Chronicles*. Anchor Bible 13. Garden City, N.Y.: Doubleday, 1965.

Na'aman, Nadav. "Sojourners and Levites in the Kingdom of Judah in the Seventh Century BCE." *Zeitschrift für altorientalische und biblische Rechtsgeschichte* 14 (2008): 237–79.

———. "The 'Discovered Book' and the Legitimation of Josiah's Reform." *Journal of Biblical Literature* 130 (2011): 47–62.

Neef, Heinz-Dieter. *Ephraim: Studien zur Geschichte des Stammes Ephraim von der Landnahme bis zur frühen Königszeit*. Beihefte zur Zeitschrift für die alttestamentliche Wissenschaft 238. Berlin: de Gruyter, 1995.

Nelson, Richard D. "The Double Redaction of the Deuteronomistic History: The Case Is Still Compelling." *Journal for the Study of the Old Testament* 29 (2005): 319–37.

———. *The Historical Books*. Interpreting Biblical Texts. Nashville: Abingdon, 1998.

———. *Joshua: A Commentary*. Old Testament Library. Louisville: Westminster John Knox, 1997.

Nentel, Jochen. *Trägerschaft und Intentionen des deuteronomistischen Geschichtswerks: Untersuchungen zu den Reflexionsreden Jos 1; 23; 24; 1 Sam 12 und 1 Kön 8*. Beihefte zur Zeitschrift für die alttestamentliche Wissenschaft 297. Berlin: de Gruyter, 2000.

Niccacci, Alviero. *The Syntax of the Verb in Classical Hebrew Prose*. Journal for the Study of the Old Testament Supplement Series 86. Sheffield: Sheffield Academic Press, 1990.

Nicholson, Ernest W. *Deuteronomy and Tradition*. Oxford: Blackwell, 1967.

Niditch, Susan. *Oral World and Written Word: Ancient Israelite Literature*. Louisville: Westminster/John Knox, 1996.

Nielsen, Flemming. *The Tragedy in History: Herodotus and the Deuteronomistic History*. Journal for the Study of the Old Testament Supplement Series 251. Sheffield: Sheffield Academic Press, 1997.

Noonan, Benjamin J. "Did Nehemiah Own Tyrian Goods? Trade Between Judea and Phoenicia during the Achaemenid Period." *Journal of Biblical Literature* 130 (2011): 281–98.

Noth, Martin. *The Chronicler's History*. Translated by H. G. M. Williamson. Journal for the Study of the Old Testament Supplement Series 50. Sheffield: Sheffield Academic Press, 1987

———. *Überlieferungsgeschichtliche Studien*. Halle: Niemeyer, 1943. Pages 1–110 translated as *The Deuteronomistic History*. Journal for the Study of the Old Testament Supplement Series 15. Sheffield: JSOT Press, 1981.

Oded, Bustanay. "Cushan-Rishathaim [Judges 3:8-11]: An Implicit Polemic." Pages *89–*94 [Heb.] in *Texts, Temples, and Traditions—A Tribute to Menahem Haran*. Edited by Michael V. Fox et al. Winona Lake, Ind.: Eisenbrauns, 1996.

———. "Where Can the Myth of the Empty Land Be Found? History vs. Myth." Pages 55–74 in *Judah and the Judeans in the Neo-Babylonian Period*. Edited by Oded Lipschitz and Joseph Blenkinsopp. Winona Lake, Ind.: Eisenbrauns, 2003.

Otto, Eckart. *Das Deuteronomium: Politische Theologie und Rechtsreform in Juda und Assyrien*. Beihefte zur Zeitschrift für die alttestamentliche Wissenschaft 284. Berlin: de Gruyter, 1999.

———. *Gottes Recht als Menschenrecht: Rechts- und literaturhistorische Studien zum Deuteronomium*. Beihefte zur Zeitschrift für Altorientalische und Biblische Rechtsgeschichte 2. Wiesbaden: Harrassowitz, 2002.
Otto, Eckhard and Reinhard Achenbach, eds. *Das Deuteronomium zwischen Pentateuch und deuteronomistischem Geschichtswerk*. Forschungen zur Religion und Literatur des Alten und Neuen Testaments 206. Göttingen: Vandenhoeck & Ruprecht, 2004.
Parpola, Simo and Kazuko Watanabe, eds. *Neo-Assyrian Treaties and Loyalty Oaths*. State Archives of Assyria 2. Helsinki: Helsinki University Press, 1988.
Perlitt, Lothar. " 'Ein einzig Volk von Brüdern': Zur deuteronomischen Herkunft der biblischen Bezeichnung 'Bruder.' " Pages 50–73 in *Deuteronomium-Studien*. Forschungen zum Alten Testaments 8. Tübingen: Mohr Siebeck, 1994.
Person, Raymond F., Jr. "In Conversation with Thomas Römer, *The So-Called Deuteronomistic History: A Sociological, Historical and Literary Introduction* (London: T&T Clark, 2005)." *Journal of Hebrew Studies* 9 (2009): 1–49. Online: http://www.jhsonline.org/Articles/article_119.pdf.
———. "The Ancient Israelite Scribe as Performer." *Journal of Biblical Literature* 117 (1998): 601–608.
———. *The Deuteronomic History and the Book of Chronicles: Scribal Works in an Oral World*. Society of Biblical Literature Ancient Israel and Its Literature 6. Atlanta: Society of Biblical Literature, 2010.
———. "The Deuteronomistic History and the Book of Chronicles: Contemporary Competing Historiographies." Pages 315–36 in *Reflection and Refraction: Studies in Biblical Historiography in Honour of A. Graeme Auld*. Edited by Robert Rezetko, Timothy H. Lim, and W. Brian Aucker. Supplements to Vetus Testamentum 113. Leiden: Brill, 2007.
Peters, Norbert. *Unsere Bibel: Die Lebensquellen der Heiligen Schrift*. Katholische Lebenswerte 12. Paderborn: Bonifacius, 1929.
Polak, Frank H. "The Septuagint Account of Salomon's Reign: Revision and Ancient Recension." Pages 139–64 in *Xth Congress of the International Organization for Septuagint and Cognate Studies, Oslo 1998*. Edited by Bernard A. Taylor. Septuagint and Cognate Studies 51. Atlanta: Scholars Press, 2001.
Prosic, Tamara. "Passover in Biblical Narratives." *Journal for the Study of the Old Testament* 82 (1999): 45–55.

Pury, Albert de, Thomas Römer, and Jean-Daniel Macchi, eds. *Israel Constructs its History: Deuteronomistic History in Recent Research*. Journal for the Study of the Old Testament Supplement Series 306. Sheffield: Sheffield Academic Press, 2000.

Pyysiäinen, Ilkka. "Holy Book—A Treasury of the Incomprehensible: The Invention of Writing and Religious Cognition." *Numen* 46 (1999): 269–90.

Rad, Gerhard von. "Die deuteronomistische Geschichtstheologie in den Königsbüchern (1947)." Pages 189–204 in *Gesammelte Studien zum Alten Testament*. Theologishe Bücherei 8. Munich: C. Kaiser, 1958.

———. *Old Testament Theology*. Translated by D. M. G. Stalker. 2 vols. New York: Harper & Row, 1962.

———. *Studies in Deuteronomy*. Translated by D. M. G. Stalker. Studies in Biblical Theology 9. London: SCM, 1953.

Radl, Walter. "Kindheitsgeschichten." Pages 993–94 in vol. 4 of *Religion in Geschichte und Gegenwart*. Edited by Kurt Galling. 7 vols. 4th ed. Tübingen: Mohr Siebeck, 1998–2005.

Ranke, Leopold von. *Universal History: The Oldest Historical Group of Nations and the Greeks*. Edited by George W. Prothero. New York: Harper & Brothers, 1885.

Rezetko, Robert. "What Happened to the Book of Samuel in the Persian Period and Beyond?" Pages 237–52 in *A Palimpsest: Rhetoric, Ideology, Stylistics, and Language Relating to Persian Israel*. Edited by Ehud Ben Zvi and Diana Edelman. Piscataway, N.J.: Gorgias, 2009.

Richter, Wolfgang. *Exegese als Literaturwissenschaft: Entwurf einer alttestamentlichen Literaturtheorie und Methodologie*. Göttingen: Vandenhoeck & Ruprecht, 1971.

Rollston, Christopher A. *Writing and Literacy in the World of Ancient Israel: Epigraphic Evidence from the Iron Age*. Archaeology and Biblical Studies 11. Atlanta: Society of Biblical Literature, 2010.

Römer, Thomas. "Doppelte Ende des Josuabuches." *Zeitschrift für die alttestamentlich Wissenschaft* 118 (2006): 523–48.

———. "La fin du livre de la Genèse et la fin des livres des Rois: Ouvertures vers la Diaspora. Quelques remarques sur le Pentateuque, l'Hexateuque et l'Ennéateuque." Pages 285–94 in *L'Ecrit et l'Esprit: Etudes d'histoire du texte et de théologie biblique en hommage à Adrian Schenker*. Edited by Dieter Böhler, Innocent Himbaza, and Philippe Hugo. Orbis biblicus et orientalis 214. Fribourg: Academic Press; Göttingen: Vandenhoeck & Ruprecht, 2005.

———. "From Prophet to Scribe: Jeremiah, Huldah and the Invention of the Book." Pages 86–96 in *Writing the Bible: Scribes and Scribalism in Ancient Judah*. Edited by Philip R. Davies and Thomas Römer. Bible-World. Durham: Acumen, 2013.

———. *Israels Väter: Untersuchungen zur Väterthematik im Deuteronomium und in der deuteronomistischen Tradition*. Orbis biblicus et orientalis 99. Göttingen: Vandenhoeck & Ruprecht, 1990.

———. "Moses Outside the Torah and the Construction of a Diaspora Identity." *Journal of Hebrew Studies* 8 (2008): article 15. Online: http://www.jhsonline.org/ Articles/ article_92.pdf

———. *The So-Called Deuteronomistic History: A Sociological, Historical and Literary Introduction*. London: T&T Clark, 2007.

———. "Transformations in Deuteronomistic and Biblical Historiography: On 'Book-Finding' and Other Literary Strategies." *Zeitschrift für die alttestamentliche Wissenschaft* 109 (1997): 1–11.

Römer, Thomas and Albert de Pury. "Deuteronomistic Historiography (DH): History of Research and Debated Issues." Pages 24–141 in *Israel Constructs its History: Deuteronomistic History in Recent Research*. Edited by Albert de Pury, Thomas Römer, and Jean-Daniel Macchi. Journal for the Study of the Old Testament Supplement Series 306. Sheffield: Sheffield Academic Press, 2000.

Rofé, Alexander. *The Prophetical Stories: The Narratives about the Prophets in the Hebrew Bible, their Literary Types and History*. Jerusalem: Magnes, 1988.

Rost, Leonhard. *Die Überlieferung von der Thronnachfolge Davids*. Beiträge zur Wissenschaft vom Alten (und Neuen) Testament 26. Stuttgart: Kohlhammer, 1926.

Roth, Martha T. *Law Collections from Mesopotamia and Asia Minor*. Writings from the Ancient World 6. Atlanta: Society of Biblical Literature, 1995.

Ryle, Herbert E. *The Books of Ezra and Nehemiah with introduction, notes, and maps*. Smaller Cambridge Bible for Schools. Cambridge: Cambridge University Press, 1893.

Salzman, Philip C. "Culture as Enhabilmentis." Pages 233–56 in *The Structure of Folk Models*. Edited by Ladislav Holy and Milan Stuchlik. Association of Social Anthropology Monographs 20. London: Academic Press, 1981.

Sanders, James A. "Canon as Dialogue." Pages 7–26 in *The Bible at Qumran: Text, Shape, and Interpretation*. Edited by Peter W. Flint. Studies in the

Dead Sea Scrolls and Related Literature. Grand Rapids, Mich.: Eerdmans, 2001.

———. "Intertextuality and Canon." Pages 316–33 in *On the Way to Nineveh: Studies in Honor of George M. Landes*. Edited by Stephen L. Cook and Sarah C. Winter; Atlanta: Scholars Press, 1999.

Scafuro, Adele C. *The Forensic Stage: Settling Disputes in Graeco-Roman New Comedy*. Cambridge: Cambridge University Press, 1997.

Schams, Christine. *Jewish Scribes in the Second-Temple Period*. Journal for the Study of the Old Testament Supplement Series 291. Sheffield: Sheffield Academic Press, 1998.

Schaper, Joachim. *Priester und Leviten in achämenidischen Juda: Studien zur Kult- und Sozialgeschichte Israels in persischer Zeit*. Forschungen zum Alten Testament 2/31. Tübingen: Mohr Siebeck, 2000.

Schenker, Adrian. *Septante et texte massorétique dans l'histoire la plus ancienne du texte de 1 Rois 2–14*. Cahiers de la Revue biblique 48. Paris: Gabalda, 2000.

Schipper, Jeremy. "'Significant Resonances' With Mephiboshet in 2 Kings 25:27–30: A Response to Donald F. Murray." *Journal of Biblical Literature* 124 (2005): 521–29.

Schmid, Konrad. *Erzväter und Exodus: Untersuchungen zur doppelten Begründung der Ursprünge Israels innerhalb der Geschichtsbücher des Alten Testaments*. Wissenschaftliche Monographien zum Alten und Neuen Testament 81. Neukirchen-Vluyn: Neukirchener Verlag, 1999.

———. *Literaturgeschichte des Alten Testaments: Eine Einführung*. Darmstadt: Wissenschaftliche Buchgesellschaft, 2008.

———. "Une grande historiographie allant de Genèse à 2 Rois a-t-elle un jour existé"? Pages 35–46 in *Les dernières rédactions du Pentateuque, de l'Hexateuque et de l'Ennéateuque*. Edited by Thomas Römer and Konrad Schmid. Bibliotheca ephemeridum theologicarum lovaniensium 203. Leuven: Peeters, 2007.

Schmid, Konrad and Raymond F. Person, Jr. eds. *Deuteronomy in the Pentateuch, Hexateuch, and the Deuteronomistic History*. Forschungen zum Alten Testament 2/56. Tübingen: Mohr Siebeck, 2012.

Schmitt, Hans-Christoph. "Das spätdeuteronomistische Geschichtswerk Genesis I–2 Regum XXV und seine theologische Intention." Pages 261–79 in *Congress Volume, Cambridge 1995*. Edited by John A. Emerton. Vetus Testament Supplements 66. Leiden: Brill, 1997.

Schöpflin, Karin. "Jotham's Speech and Fable as Prophetic Comment on

Abimelech's Story: The Genesis of Judges 9." *Scandinavian Journal of the Old Testament* 18 (2004): 3–22.

Schweitzer, Steven J. "Judging a Book by its Citations: Sources and Authority in Chronicles." Pages 37–65 in *What Was Authoritative for Chronicles?* Edited by Ehud Ben Zvi and Diana V. Edelman. Winona Lake, Ind.: Eisenbrauns, 2010.

Seitz, Christopher R. "Isaiah, the Book of [First Isaiah]." Pages 472–88 in vol. 3 of *Anchor Bible Dictionary*. Edited by David N. Freedman. 6 vols. Garden City, N.Y.: Doubleday, 1992.

Seitz, Gottfried. *Redaktionsgeschichtliche Studien zum Deuteronomium*. Beiträge zur Wissenschaft vom Alten (und Neuen) Testament 93. Stuttgart: Kohlhammer, 1971.

Seow, Choon Leong. *Ecclesiastes: A New Translation with Introduction*. Anchor Bible 18C. New York: Doubleday, 1997.

Simon, Uriel. "The Poor Man's Ewe Lamb." *Biblica* 48 (1967): 207–42.

Sinha, Jai B. P. "Collectivism, Social Energy, and Development in India." Pages 109–19 in *From a Different Perspective: Studies of Behavior Across Cultures*. Edited by Isabel Reyes Lagunes and Ype H. Poortinga. Lisse: Swets & Zeitlinger, 1985.

Smith, Anthony D. "Culture, community, and territory: the politics of ethnicity and nationalism." *International Affairs* 72/3 (1996): 445–58.

Smith, Dennis. *From Symposium to Eucharist: The Banquet in the Early Christian World*. Minneapolis: Augsburg, 2003.

Smith, Jonathan Z. "The Bare Facts of Ritual." *History of Religions* 20 (1980): 112–27.

———. *To Take Place: Toward Theory in Ritual*. Chicago: University of Chicago Press, 1987.

Smyth, Françoise. "When Josiah Has Done his Work or the King Is Properly Buried: A Synchronic Reading of 2 Kings 22.1–23.28. " Pages 343–58 in *Israel Constructs its History: Deuteronomistic Historiography in Recent Research*. Edited by Albert de Pury, Thomas Römer, and Jean-Daniel Macchi. Journal for the Study of the Old Testament Supplement Series 306. Sheffield: Sheffield Academic Press, 2000.

Soggin, J. Alberto. *Joshua: A Commentary*. Old Testament Library. Philadelphia: Westminster, 1972.

Steck, Odil Hannes. *Israel und das gewaltsame Geschick der Propheten: Untersuchungen zur Überlieferung des deuteronomistischen Geschichtsbildes im Alten Testament, Spätjudentum und Urchristentum.* Wissenschaftliche Monographien zum Alten und Neuen Testament 23. Neukirchen-Vluyn: Neukirchener Verlag, 1967.

Steiner, Richard C. "The *mbqr* at Qumran, the *episkopos* in the Athenian Empire, and the Meaning of *lbqr'* in Ezra 7:14: On the Relation of Ezra's Mission to the Persian Legal Project." *Journal of Biblical Literature* 120 (2001): 623–46.

Stern, Ephraim. *Archaeology of the Land of the Bible: The Assyrian, Babylonian and Persian Periods, 732–332 bce*. Anchor Bible Reference Library. New York: Doubleday, 2001.

Stern, Ephraim and Yitzhak Magen. "Archaeological Evidence for the First Stage of the Samaritan Temple on Mount Gerizim." *Israel Exploration Journal* 52 (2002): 49–57.

Stern, Menahem, ed. *Greek and Latin Authors on Jews and Judaism*. 3 vols. Jerusalem: Israel Academy of Sciences and Humanities, 1974–1984.

Steuernagel, Carl. *Das Deuteronomium*. 2d ed. Handkommentar zum Alten Testament series 1, 3/1. Göttingen: Vandenhoeck & Ruprecht, 1923.

Stott, Kathryn. "Finding the Lost Book of the Law: Re-reading the Story of 'The Book of the Law' (Deuteronomy–2 Kings) in Light of Classical Literature." *Journal for the Study of the Old Testament* 30 (2005): 153–69.

Sweeney, Marvin A. "Davidic Polemics in the Book of Judges." *Vetus Testamentum* 47 (1997): 517–29.

———. "Form Criticism." Pages 58–89 in *To Each Its Own Meaning: An Introduction to Biblical Criticisms and Their Application*. Edited by Steven L. McKenzie and Stephen R. Haynes. 2d ed. Louisville: Westminster John Knox, 1999.

———. *King Josiah, the Lost Messiah of Israel*. New York: Oxford University Press, 2001.

Tappy, Ron E. et al. "An Abecedary of the Mid-Tenth Century B.C.E. from the Judaean Shephelah." *Bulletin of the American Schools of Oriental Research* 344 (2006): 5–46.

Tatu, Silviu. "Jotham's Fable and the Crux Interpretum in Judges IX." *Vetus Testamentum* 56 (2006): 105–24.

Thomas, Rosalind. *Literacy and Orality in Ancient Greece*. Cambridge: Cambridge University Press, 1992.

Thompson, Thomas L. *The Messiah Myth: The Near Eastern Roots of Jesus and David*. New York: Basic Books, 2005.

Toorn, Karel van der. *Scribal Culture and the Making of the Hebrew Bible.* Cambridge: Harvard University Press, 2007.
Triandis, Harry C. "Theoretical and Methodological Approaches to the Study of Collectivism and Individualism." Pages 41–51 in *Individualism and Collectivism: Theory, Method, and Applications.* Edited by Uichol Kim et al. Cross-Cultural Research and Methodology Series 18. London: Sage, 1994.
Turner, Victor. *The Ritual Process: Structure and Anti-Structure.* Chicago: Aldine, 1969. Repr. New York: Aldine de Gruyter, 1995.
Ulrich, Eugene. "The Non-Attestation of a Tripartite Canon in 4QMMT." *Catholic Biblical Quarterly* 65 (2003): 202–14.
Van Keulen, Percy S. F. *Two Versions of the Solomon Narrative: An Inquiry into the Relationship between MT 1 Kgs. 2-11 and LXX 3 Reg. 2-11.* Supplements to Vetus Testamentum 104. Leiden: Brill, 2005.
Van Seters, John. *A Law Book for the Diaspora: Revision in the Study of the Covenant Code.* Oxford: Oxford University Press, 2003.
———. *The Biblical Saga of King David.* Winona Lake, Ind: Eisenbrauns, 2009.
———. *The Edited Bible: The Curious History of the "Editor" in Biblical Criticism.* Winona Lake, Ind.: Eisenbrauns, 2006.
———. "The Origins of the Hebrew Bible: Some New Answers to Old Questions, Part Two." *Journal of Ancient Near Eastern Religions* 7 (2007): 219–38.
Veijola, Timo. "Bundestheologische Redaktion im Deuteronomium." Pages 153–75 in *Moses Erben: Studien zum Dekalog, zum Deuteronomismus und zum Schriftgelehrtentum.* Beiträge zur Wissenschaft vom Alten (und Neuen) Testament 149. Stuttgart: Kohlhammer, 2000.
———. *Das 5. Buch Mose: Deuteronomium Kapitel 1,1–16,17.* Das Alte Testament Deutsch 8,1. Göttingen: Vandenhoeck & Ruprecht, 2004.
———. "Das Klagegebet in Literatur und Leben der Exilsgeneration am Beispiel einiger Prosatexte." Pages 176–91 in *Moses Erben: Studien zum Dekalog, zum Deuteronomismus und zum Schriftgelehrtentum.* Beiträge zur Wissenschaft vom Alten (und Neuen) Testament 149. Kohlhammer: Stuttgart, 2000.
———. *Das Königtum in der Beurteilung der deuteronomistischen Historiographie: Eine redaktionsgeschichtliche Untersuchung.* Suomalainen Tiedakatemie Toimituksia, Sarja B. 198. Helsinki: Suomalainen Tiedakatemie, 1977.

———. *Die ewige Dynastie: David und die Entstehung seiner Dynastie nach der deuteronomistischen Darstellung.* Suomalainen Tiedakatemie Toimituksia, Sarja B. 193; Helsinki: Suomalainen Tiedakatemie, 1975.

———. *Leben nach der Weisung: Exegetisch-historische Studien zum Alten Testament.* Edited by Walter Dietrich and Marko Martilla. Forschungen zur Religion und Literatur des Alten und Neuen Testament 224. Göttingen: Vandenhoeck & Ruprecht, 2008.

———. "Solomon: Bathsheba's Firstborn: Dedicated to the memory of Uriah the Hittite." Pages 340–57 in *Reconsidering Israel and Judah: Recent Studies on the Deuteronomistic History.* Edited by Gary N. Knoppers and J. Gordon McConville. Winona Lake, Ind.: Eisenbrauns 2000.

Waldbaum, Jane. "Greeks *in* the East or Greeks *and* the East? Problems in the Definition and Recognition of Presence." *Bulletin of the American Schools of Oriental Research* 305 (1997): 1–17.

Watts, James W., ed. *Persia and Torah: The Theory of Imperial Authorization of the Pentateuch.* Society of Biblical Literature Symposium Series 17. Atlanta: Society of Biblical Literature, 2001.

———. Ritual Legitimacy and Scriptural Authority." *Journal of Biblical Literature* 124 (2005): 401–17.

Weinfeld, Moshe. *Deuteronomy 1–11: A New Translation with Introduction and Commentary.* Anchor Bible 5. New York: Doubleday, 1991.

———. *Deuteronomy and the Deuteronomic School.* Oxford: Clarendon Press, 1972.

Weinreich, Peter. "The Operationalization of Ethnic Identity." Pages 149–68 in *Ethnic Psychology: Research and Practice with Immigrants, Refugees, Native Peoples, Ethnic Groups and Sojourners.* Edited by John W. Berry and Robert C. Annis. Amsterdam: Swets & Zeitlinger, 1988.

Weippert, Manfred. *Historisches Textbuch zum Alten Testament.* Grundrisse zum Alten Testament 10. Göttingen: Vandenhoeck & Ruprecht, 2010.

Welch, Adam C. *The Code of Deuteronomy: A New Theory of Its Origin.* London: J. Clarke, 1924.

Wellhausen, Julius. *Prolegomena to the History of Ancient Israel.* Translated by A. Menzies & S. Black. New York: Meridian Books, 1957.

Wenning, Robert. "Nachweis der attischen Keramik aus Palästina Aktualisierter Zwischenbericht." Pages 61–72 in *Die Griechen und das Antike Israel: Interdisziplinäre Studien zur Religions- und Kulturgeschichte*

des Heiligen Landes. Edited by Stefan Alkier and Markus Witte. Orbis biblicus et orientalis 201. Fribourg: University Press, 2004.
Wesselius, Jan-Wim. *The Origin of the History of Israel: Herodotus' Histories as Blueprint for the First Books of the Bible*. Journal for the Study of the Old Testament Supplement Series 345. London: Sheffield Academic Press, 2002.
Westbrook, Raymond and Bruce Wells. *Everyday Law in Biblical Israel: An Introduction*. Louisville: Westminster John Knox, 2008.
Westermann, Claus. *Die Geschichtsbücher des Alten Testaments: gab es ein deuteronomistisches Geschichtswerk?* Theologische Bücherei 87. Gütersloh: Kaiser, 1994.
Wette, Wilhelm Martin Leberecht de, "Dissertatio critica-exegetica qua Deuteronomium a prioribus Pentateuchi libris diversum alius cuiusdam recentioris auctoris opus esse monstratur" (Ph.D. diss., University of Jena, 1805). Repr. in *Opuscula theologica*. Berlin: Reimer, 1830.
Whitelam, Keith W. *The Just King: Monarchical Judicial Authority in Ancient Israel*. Journal for the Study of the Old Testament Supplement Series 12. Sheffield: JSOT Press, 1979.
Widengren, Geo. "The Persian Period." Pages 489–538 in *Israelite and Judaean History*. Edited by John H. Hayes and J. Maxwell Miller. Philadelphia: Westminster, 1977.
Williamson, Hugh G. M. *1 and 2 Chronicles*. New Century Bible Series. Grand Rapids, Mich.: Eerdmans, 1982.
Witte, Markus et al., eds. *Die deuteronomistischen Geschichtswerk: redaktions- und religionsgesichtliche Perspektiven zur "Deuteronomismus"-Diskussion in Tora und Vorderen Propheten*. Beihefte zur Zeitschrift für die alttestamentliche Wissenschaft 365. Berlin: de Gruyter, 2006.
Wöhrle, Jakob. "Die Rehabilitierung Jojachins: Zur Entstehung und Intention von 2 Kön 24,17-25,30." Pages 213–38 in *Berührungspunkte: Studien zur Sozial- und Religionsgeschichte Israels und seiner Umwelt. Festschrift für Rainer Albertz zu seinem 65. Geburtstag*. Edited by Ingo Kottsieper, Rüdiger Schmitt and Jakob Wöhrle. Alter Orient und Altes Testament 350. Muenster: Ugarit-Verlag, 2008.
Wright, G. Ernest. "Deuteronomy." Pages 311–30 in vol. 2 of *The Interpreter's Bible*. Edited by Leander Keck et al. 12 vols. Nashville: Abingdon, 1953.
Wright, Jacob L. "The Deportation of Jerusalem's Wealth and the Demise of Native Sovereignty in the Book of Kings." Pages 105–34 in *Interpreting Exile: Displacement and Deportation in Biblical and Modern*

Contexts. Edited by Brad E. Kelle, Frank Ritchel Ames, and Jacob L. Wright. Ancient Israel and its Literature 10. Atlanta: Society of Biblical Literature, 2011.

Würthwein, Ernst. *Die Erzählung von der Thronfolge Davids: Theologische oder Politische Geschichtsschreibung?* Theologische Studien 115. Zürich: Theologischer Verlag, 1974.

———. "Die josianische Reform und das Deuteronomium." *Zeitschrift für Theologie und Kirche* 73 (1976): 395–423.

Young, Ian. "Israelite Literacy: Interpreting the Evidence." *Vetus Testamentum* 48 (1998): 239–53, 408–22.

Zenger, Erich. "Die deuteronomistische Interpretation der Rehabilitierung Jojachins." *Biblische Zeitschrift NF* 12 (1968): 16–30.

Zevit, Ziony. "Is There An Archaeological Case for Phantom Settlements in the Persian Period?" *Palestine Exploration Quarterly* 141 (2009): 124–37.

Primary Sources Index

Genesis	4, 5, 74, 90, 157	20–Num 36	90
Genesis–Numbers	1, 5, 45	20–Deut 34	15, 91
Genesis–Deuteronomy	4, 45, 92, 93, 100, 156, 189, 197, 201	20:16	62
		20:22–23:19	50
Genesis–Joshua	91	20:22–23:33	31
Genesis–Kings	4, 5, 15, 16, 86, 89, 91–96, 98, 99, 100, 101, 213	21:1–3	64
		21:1–11	54
1	75	21:2–6	51
1–11	91	21:6–8	64
1–Exod 19	15, 90	21:12–14	173
4	154	21:13–14	174
4:14	129	21:16	65
7:27	169	21:23–24	60
12–36	92	22:24	71
12–Exod 19	91	22:25–26	67
12:23	169	23:1	60, 71
12:27	169	23:4–5	63
31:19	199	23:6	71
31:34–35	199	23:7	71
37–50	92, 190	23:10–11	54
37:26	184	23:11	71
39	190	24	16
42:21	173	24:7	199
49:3–27	91	31:10	35
		33	16, 195
Exodus	1, 4, 14, 50	40:13	35
Exodus–Deuteronomy	4, 92		
1	75	Leviticus	1, 4, 35, 166
1–19	90	4:2	165
13:14	78	4:3	173
15–Deut	34	4:13	165
14, 74		4:22	165
17	16, 80	5	173
18:21	184	5:17	165
20–Lev 27	90	5:19–24	168

5:24	173	32:12	80
6:10	173	34:1–12	74, 81
7:14	173	34:10	200
8:23	173	34:13–29	74
12:2	168	35	163, 174
14	173	35:19	173
17–26	36, 208	35:21	173
18:19	168	35:24	173
18:21	199	35:37	173
19	50	36:1–12	185
19:21–22	173		
20:2–5	199	Deuteronomy	1, 3–4, 6–7, 12–14, 23,
20:18	168		27–47, 49–71, 87, 89, 9, 131, 194, 197,
22:16	173		198, 199, 208
24:10–23	185	Deuteronomy–2 Kings	3, 5, 86, 87,
24:11	186		156, 208, 209
24:16	186	1–3	45
25:23	80	1–4	45
25:25	71	1–11	30
25:35–55	71	1–33	90
26:3–39	15, 91	1:1	27, 31, 92
		1:13	27
Numbers	1, 4, 35, 45, 74, 93	1:15	27
1–36	90	1:38	16, 80
5:6–7	173	3:21	16
6:12	173	3:21–22	80
9:6–14	185	3:28	16, 80
11	16	4:2	165
13	16	4:40	165
13–14	92	4:44–45	41
13:8	92	5	70
13:22	93	5:1	41
14	16	5:1–5	45
14:30	80	5:10	165
14:38	80	5:15	56
15:32–36	185	5:23	27
15:39	165	5:26	165
17–26	50	6:4–5	70, 198
18:9	173	6:5	198
22:1	82	6:17	165
26:65	80	6:20	78
27:1–11	185	7	193
27:15–23	80	7:1	64
27:18–22	16	7:6	58
32	92	7:9	165

7:11	165	15:9	59, 68, 71
7:14–16	58	15:10	56, 57, 70
7:16	61	15:11	57, 58, 59, 70, 71
8:6	165	15:12	57, 70
8:11	165	15:12–17	54,
9:20	35	15:12–18	13, 50, 52, 54
10:13	165, 166	15:13–14	57, 70
11:10	64	15:15	56, 70
11:22	165	15:16	55
11:27–28	166	15:17	56, 70
11:29	64, 80	15:18	56, 70
12–26	30, 49, 64	16:11	35
12:2–7	193	16:12	56
12:5	27	16:18	27, 37
12:8	124	17:2–5	61
12:12	35	17:4	61
12:14	27	17:7	61, 121
12:18	35	17:8–10	35
13	12, 41, 61	17:9	34
13:2–19	61	17:12	61, 121
13:6	61, 62, 121	17:13	62
13:9	61	17:13–14	184
13:12	62	17:14–20	12, 33, 34, 98, 127, 165
13:15	61	17:15	70
13:19	165	17:18	34
14:2	58	17:18–19	30, 213
14:21	70	17:19	165
14:27	35	17:24–41	34
14:29	64	18	35
15	52, 58, 59	18:1	34
15:1	52, 54, 55	18:5	27
15:1–2	59	18:15–18	77
15:1–3	50	19	173, 174
15:1–6	13, 52	19:1–11	174, 175
15:2	55, 56, 70	19:1–12	163
15:2–11	53	19:2	173
15:3	56, 58, 70	19:3	173
15:4	55, 58, 70	19:4	173
15:4–6	58	19:5	173, 174
15:5	55, 56, 58, 70, 165	19:5–6	174
15:6	58	19:6	173
15:7	55, 57, 58, 70	19:11–12	173, 174
15:7–8	55, 57	19:12	173
15:7–11	13, 50, 52, 58	19:13	61
15:8	57, 70	19:16–21	13, 60

Deuteronomy (cont.)

19:16	60, 61	25:1	68, 71
19:17	34, 60, 61, 62, 70	25:1–3	13, 68
19:18	61, 62, 70	25:2	68, 69
19:18–19	70	25:3	69, 70
19:19	61, 62, 65, 70, 121	25:13	61
19:20	70	26:3	61
19:21	60, 61, 70	26:11	35
21:5	34	26:12	35
21:9	61	26:17–18	56, 70, 165
21:10	21, 63	27	28
21:14	66	27:1	165
21:21	61, 62, 121	27:1–8	80
21:22	121	27:9	34
21:22–23	63	27:11–13	80
21:24	121	28	70
22	64	28:1	55, 165
22:1	63	28:1–68	15, 91
22:1–4	13, 62, 63, 70	28:9	166
22:2	63	28:13	166
22:3	63	28:15	165
22:4	63	28:21	64
22:5–12	63	28:45	165
22:13–23:1	63	28:63	64
22:21	61	29:1	41
22:22	61	29:21	40
23:7	79	30:10	40, 165
23:8	79	30:16	64, 165
23:20	64, 70	31–34	14, 74
23:20–21	64, 65	31:3	16
23:20–22	13	31:7	16, 80
23:21	64, 70	31:9	34, 35
24:7	13, 61, 65, 66, 70, 121	31:9–24	42
24:8	34	31:11	32
24:8–9	65	31:14	16
24:10–11	67	31:14–23	92
24:10–13	13, 65, 66, 68	31:23	16, 80, 92
24:12–13	67, 71	31:25	35
24:14	57, 67, 70, 71	31:26	40
24:14–15	13, 65, 66, 67, 68	32:1–43	91
24:15	59, 71	33:2–29	91
24:16	43, 197	34	14, 75, 88
24:18	56	34–2	Kgs
24:19	64	25	90
24:22	56	34:9	16, 74, 76, 92
		34:10	41

34:10–12	76, 77	13:32	82
		14–17	79, 81
Joshua	1, 3, 4, 5, 7, 14, 15, 16, 18, 73–84, 85–101, 189, 213, 214	14–21	83
		14:1–18:1	79
Joshua–Kings	4, 15, 45, 74, 89, 91	14:6	93
1–9	90	14:6–15	79
1–11	83, 90, 97	14:7–8	93
1–12	81, 97	14:9–12	93
1:1	15, 78, 88, 89	15–19	89
1:1–5	76	15:1	90
1:1–9	80	15:8	83
1:2–9	92	15:13–19	79
1:5–7	92	15:20–62	82
1:6–8	77	15:63	83, 93, 107
1:6–9	76, 77, 78	16:1	90
1:7	88	16:10	93
1:8	77, 185	17:1	90
1:9	77	17:12–13	93
1:12–15	92	17:12–18	118
2	97	18–19	81
4:6	78	18:1	81, 84
5:1–7	78	18:10–19:48	81
5:10	222	18:11	90
5:13–15	215	18:11–28	79
6–10	82	18:21–28	82
7	78, 161	18:28	83
7:1	161	19:1	90
7:2	161	19:5	81
7:14–18	161	19:10	90
8:30–35	78, 80	19:17	90
8:33	80	19:24	90
10–11	90	19:32	90
10:12–14	78	19:40	90
10:28–39	81	20	174
10:40–42	81	20:5	173
11:23	83	20:9	173
12	97	21:41	93
12–21	90, 97	21:42	95
12:1–5	97	21:43	83
12:7–24	97	21:43–45	97
12:9–24	83	22	83, 90, 97
12:10	83	22–24	81, 83
13	81	22:3	166
13–21	81, 97	22:5	165
13:2–6	100	23	91

Joshua (cont.)

23–24	90, 91, 97, 185	3:14	96, 117
24	75, 91	3:15	118
24:1	79, 80	4:2–3	117
24:26	78	4:3	96
24:28	117	5	118, 120
24:29	88	5:14–18	120
24:29–32	92	5:24	114
24:31	93	6:2–6	117
		6:8–9	119
		6:8–10	116
Judges	1, 3, 4, 5, 7, 15, 17, 18, 73, 74, 83, 84, 87, 90, 92, 93, 95, 96, 103–109,	6:11–21	116
		6:13	119
Judges–Kings	5, 15, 90, 91, 92, 111–14, 115–32, 213	6:24	104
		6:25–32	116
1	17, 75, 93, 113, 117, 118, 120	6:26–32	104
1:1	15, 88, 89, 114, 116	7:2	125
1:1–20	107	8:1–2	119
1:1–26	90	8:1–3	120
1:2	118	8:14	174
1:5–7	118	8:23	111
1:7	118	8:31	113
1:8	107	8:32	108
1:21	107	9:1–7	108
1:21–36	107	9:7–20	128
1:22–26	107, 118	9:8	129
1:27–35	93	9:8–15	128
1:27–36	90	9:8–20	108
1:35	118	9:10	129
2:1	107	9:12	129
2:1–2	119	9:14	129
2:1–3	116	9:15	129
2:1–5	107	9:22–57	108
2:6	117	10:8	96, 117
2:7	93	10:10–16	116
2:10–13	93	10:11–13	119
2:11–13	116	10:11–14	116
2:11–19	18, 116, 126	11:1–2	113
2:12–13	116	11:13	119
2:17	116, 166	11:15–26	125
2:19–20	116	11:16	119
3:1–6	90	11:29	125
3:4	166	11:40	125
3:7	116	12:1–6	121
3:7–11	108, 113	12:4–6	119
3:8	96, 117	13–19	117

13:2	119	8:1	183, 184
13:3–20	116	8:1–3	184
13:19–20	104	8:1–5	184
14:3	113	8:3	184
17–18	124	8:3–5	183, 184
17–21	18	8:6–22	183
17:6	124, 127	8:7–8	99
18	117, 119	8:14–15	82
18–19	17	8:22	184
18:1	127	9:2	154
19	124	9:14–15	156
19–21	17, 19	10:8	20, 162
19:1	127	10:17–27	20, 162, 183
20–21	118	11:1–11	124
20:1	117, 121	12	20, 160, 183
20:2	173	12:6–17	91
20:13	121	12:20–25	91
20:17–23	107	13	150, 156
20:18	118, 122	13:7–13	20, 162
20:26	107	13:13	129, 165
21:2	107	14	153, 155
21:4–7	117	14:22–26	162
21:9–38	117	14:23–46	20, 160
21:24	117	14:24–46	20, 160, 162
21:25	124, 127	14:40–42	161
		16:7	154
1 Samuel	159, 160	17	20, 161
1–2 Samuel	1, 3, 4, 5, 7, 19, 20, 21, 22, 25, 74, 84, 88, 90, 96, 112, 131, 133–34, 149–58, 159, 160, 162, 165, 166, 182, 185, 186, 187	17:1–18:5	20, 161
		17:44	20, 161
		17:46	20, 161
		18–27	20, 161, 162
1 Samuel–2 Kings	22, 25, 149, 154, 160, 187, 189, 215	19:11	151
		19:18–24	20, 161
1–3	183	21:10	151
1–8	99, 101	22:6–19	162
2:1–10	152	22:9	151
6:3	173	23:19	151
6:3–5	156	24:3–7	151
6:4	173	25	162, 169, 172
6:8	173	25:24	169, 170
6:17	173	25:34	169
7	99	25:37	169
7–12	183	25:38	169
8	111, 160, 183, 184	26:6	176
8–12	92, 183	26	20, 162

1 Samuel (cont.)		12:11–12	164
26:10	169	12:15	168, 169
28	20, 162	12:15–24	20, 164, 168
28:16	129	12:18–24	168
28:18	129	12:23	156
31	20, 162	12:24	164
		13–14	163, 167
2 Samuel	92, 98, 178, 191	13:1–20:22	163
1–4	20, 162	13:13	178
1:1	15, 89	13:21	175
1:19–27	152	13:23–29	175
2:13	176	13:38	174
2:18	176	13:39	20, 171, 172
3:26–27	162	14	20, 21, 159, 164, 166, 167, 170, 172, 176, 179, 180, 181, 182, 183, 185, 186
3:33–34	152		
3:39	177		
4	156	14:1	20, 171, 172, 176, 177
4:7	162	14:1–3	176
5–6	150	14:1–4	170
7	20, 153, 162	14:1–20	164
7:7	110	14:1–21	177
8:1–14	90	14:1–22	172
8:10–22	20, 162	14:1–24	166, 170
8:13	151	14:2–3	171
8:16	177	14:2–22	20, 164, 168, 171, 172, 182
9	163	14:4	171
9:8	178	14:4–20	171
10:7–15	151	14:5	171
10–12	101, 163	14:5–12	170
10:1–19	90	14:5–20	170
11–12	165	14:6	171, 177
11–14	20, 164	14:7	171, 172, 177
11:4	168	14:8–9	171
11:14–25	167	14:9	169
11:20–21	178	14:10	171
11:27	164	14:10–11	173
11:27–12:24	164	14:11	171, 172, 177
12	20, 163, 164, 165, 168, 172, 173, 175, 179, 182, 185	14:12	171, 177
		14:13	171, 172
12:1–4	20, 129, 172	14:13–14	174
12:1–5	164, 165	14:13–17	177
12:1–7	164	14:13–20	171
12:1–15	151, 164	14:14	171, 172, 178
12:7–10	164	14:15	171, 177
12:9	129	14:15–16	177

14:16	171	24	154
14:17	177		
14:18	171	1 Kings	149, 187
14:19	171, 177	1–2 Kings	1, 3, 4, 5, 7, 12, 15, 18, 21, 22, 23, 25, 42, 43, 44, 74, 90, 95, 111, 131, 160, 168, 187–201, 203–22
14:19–23	176		
14:20	171		
14:21	171	1	155, 190, 195
14:21–22	170	1–2	21, 163, 175, 191
14:22	171	1:7	177
14:23	171, 172	1:40–50	178
14:23–24	170	2:3	165
14:24	170	2:5–6	167, 175
14:25–27	171	2:28–34	167, 175
14:26	171	2:35	188
14:27–29	167	3	165, 193, 194
14:32	169	3–8	193
15–1 Kgs 2	162	3:16–28	165
15–18	167	4–11	155
15–19	167	4:2	216
15:13	178	4:2–19	216
15:23	151	4:4	216
16:9–10	177	6:1	217
17:3	178	6:12	165
17:8–10	178	8	192, 194, 215
17:10	178	8–9	24
17:11–13	178	8:1	216
17:15–22	178	8:1–9:9	207, 216, 218, 219, 220
17:25	177	8:2	217
18:2	177	8:3–6	216
18:11–17	162	8:5	216, 217
18:14	167	8:8	220
18:18	177	8:9	219
18:19–33	178	8:10–11	216
19:20–21	177	8:15–22	219
21:1–14	20, 161	8:21	219
21:13	151	8:24–26	219
21:26	177	8:27–28	218
22	152, 168	8:27–53	217
22:1–51	151	8:46–51	217
22:2–51	91	8:48	217
23:1–7	152	8:50	217
23:2–7	91	8:51–53	220
23:9–12	161	8:52–53	217
23:24–39	20, 161	8:56	220
23:37	177	8:58	165, 220

1 Kings (cont.)		14:6	43, 197, 214
8:61	165, 220	14:24	213
8:63–64	216, 217	14:25	196
8:6	217	14:26–27	213
9	193, 219, 220	17	92
9:3–9	91	17:7–23	91
9:10–11:43	193	17:13	196
11:9–25	190	17:15	190
11:28	220	17:16	166
11:34	165	17:19	165, 166
11:41	212	17:23	196
12	189, 193	17:24–41	216
12–15:8	105	17:27–28	39
12:27	78	18–20	128, 195
12:31	189	18–23	44
13:21	165	18:3–6	194
14:8	165	18:4	43, 197
14:18	196	18:6	43, 197
15:7	212	18:12	43, 197
15:27–29	195	18:13–20:19	213
16:34	75	20:2	174
18	195	20:12–19	109, 194
18:18	166	20:20	212
18:36	196	21:8	43
19	195	21:8–9	198
19:12	196	21:10–12	196, 211, 213
20:35–43	164	21:10–15	194
21:4	174	22	27, 33, 40, 43, 44, 49, 199
22	200	22–23	23, 24, 39, 41, 44, 49, 128, 199, 207, 208, 209, 221
22:28	212		
		22:3	213
2 Kings	44, 109, 187, 221	22:10	185
1:1	15, 89	22:17	40
1:3	129	22:20	200, 221
2	196	25:27–30	22
2:2	197	23	44, 199
2:5	177	23:1–3	185, 222
2:22	177	23:3	165
8	197	23:10	199
8:9	197	23:20	221
9:7	196	23:21	222
12:17	173	23:21–23	222
13:1–9	109	23:22	43
13:5	105	23:24	199
14:3–4	197	23:25	43, 198, 200

23:29–30	211	15:4	213
23:31–32	221	22:3	213
24–25	195	22:13–19	184
24:2	195, 196	22:15–16	213
24:3	211, 213	22:17	184
24:20	190	23:5	113
24:34	194	25:3–11	213
25	192	25:4	196
25:22–30	210	26:5	196
25:27–30	99, 191, 192	28:16	62
		19:19	196
Isaiah	74, 192, 212	29:32	62
1–35	213	33:15	113
1:1	88	35:15	196
1:5	62	36	200
5	129	44:4	196
5:1–7	164	47:3	78
7:2	129	52	195, 213
10:1–19	104		
10:29	149	Ezekiel	74, 192
17:14–18	118	5:10	78
24:20	129	7:11	166
29:9	129	7:22	174
31:6	62	18	111
33:15	184	20:18	78
36–39	195, 213	22:13	184
38:2	174	22:27	184
40–48	213	33:31	184
40–55	150	40:39	173
44:24–45:7	101, 130	42:13	173
53	101	44:29	173
53:10	173	46:20	173
56:11	184	48:1–28	117
57:15	184		
59:13	61	Amos	
		4:1	129
Jeremiah	29, 45, 74, 195, 196	8:14	173
1:1–2	88		
3:1–5	164	Micah	212
6:13	184	1:2	212
7:25–26	196	4:13	184
8:10	184		
12:15	117	Habbakuk	
14:10	129	2:9	184
15:1	149		

Jonah	101	52	151
		52:1–2	151
Zephaniah		54	151
2:2–3	59	54:1–2	151
3:8	59	56	151
3:12	59	56:1	151
		57	151
Haggai		57:1	151
2:20–23	99, 113	59	151
		59:1	151
Zechariah		59:16	129
3:8	113	60	151
4	113	60:1–2	151
6:12	113	63	151
		63:1	151
Malachi	78	69:6	173
1:6–2:9	216	70:6	59, 67
2:11–12	114	74:21	59
3:14	184	78:5	78
3:22	78	86:1	59, 68
3:22–24	76, 77, 78, 196	99:6	149
3:23	78	106:33–42	106
3:23–24	77	106:43–45	106
3:24	78	106:47	106
4:4–6	76, 77	107:27	129
		109:16	59
Psalms	14, 59, 74, 78, 89, 156, 157	109:22	59, 68
3	151	119:36	184
3:1	151	119:60	165
7:1	151	142	150, 151
18	151, 152	142:1	151
18:1	151	151–153	152
19	76		
19:9	166	Proverbs	124
30:1	151	1:19	184
30:10	184	7	113
34	151	12:15	124
34:1	151	15:27	184
35:10	59	17:6	78
35:11	60	21:2	124
37:11	59		
37:14	59	Job	101
40:18	59, 67	22:3	184
51	151		
51:1–2	151		

PRIMARY SOURCES INDEX

Ruth	88	9:13	173
1:1	89	9:15	173
4:17	113	10:10	173
4:22	113	10:19	173

Lamentations	211	Nehemiah	6, 18, 37, 88, 106, 122
		2:7–8	147
Qohelet	101, 156, 157, 158	7:5	147
1:16–2:10	155	7:7–8	32
4:11–13	155	8	37
5:1–2	155	8:1–5	185
6:4	156	8:5	147
7:26	156	8:6	147
		8:7	35
Esther	86	8:7–8	147
		8:13	148
Daniel	73	8:17	74
		9	148
Ezra	6, 18, 37, 87, 88, 94, 106, 122, 132, 147	9:1	114
		9:6–37	105
Ezra–Nehemiah	73, 84, 131, 142, 146–52, 211	9:13–15	131
		9:26–31	127
1:1–3	88	9:27–28	105
1:9–10	114	9:36–37	37
2:59–63	183	10:30	165, 166
2:62	147	11:20	117
4:1	106	13:1	114
4:1–3	216	13:23–30	114
4:2	106		
4:8	147	1 Chronicles	80, 149, 150
5:5	147	1–2 Chronicles	6, 19, 23, 25, 36, 37, 42, 74, 80, 87, 88, 101, 106, 111, 112, 113, 122, 149, 150, 153, 160, 189, 190, 197, 201, 210, 211, 212, 215
6:3	147		
6:14	147		
7–10	83		
7:6	132		
7:10	147	1–9	80
7:12–26	94	2	79
7:14	37, 94	2:16	177
7:25	37	3:19–24	99
7:25–26	37, 94	4	79
9–10	193	6:39–48	117
9:1	83	6:50–66	117
9:3–10:1	94	9:32	147
9:6	173	12:25–38	117
9:7	173	10	110

1 Chronicles (cont.)		30:16	43
11:39	177	30:23	217
17:1–15	110	32:32	212
17:3	111	33:10–19	211
17:4	111	34	200
17:5–6	111	34–35	39, 40
17:6	110	34:9	36
17:9–10	110	34:13	36, 42
17:14	111, 112	34:14	42
21	154	34:31	165
21:3	173	35:20–25	211
22:10	147	35:21–22	42
28:5	111, 112	35:22	174
28:8	166	35:27	212
29	151	36:8	212
29:19	165	36:20–21	23, 211
29:23	111, 112	36:22–23	88
2 Chronicles	42	Sirach	
6:3	174	24:23	44
8:13	42	31:31–32:13	146
9:8	111, 112	47:11	149
9:29	212		
11:6	177	1 Maccabees	
11:39	177	14:41–49	188
13:6–7	168		
13:8	111, 112, 168	Matthew	
13:9	168	5:5	59
13:15	168		
13:20	168	Qumran	
13:22	212	4QMMT	78
15:1–6	110	4QPs[a]	150
16:11	212	11QPs[a]	152
21:11	168	*Baba Bathra* 12 b	201
21:18	168		
23:18	42	Demosthenes	
24:6	43	53	180
24:9	43	54, 14–15	180
24:11	36		
24:20	166	Herodotus, *Histories*	
26:28	177	1.136	140
27:7	212		
27:24	177	Josephus, *Jewish Antiquities*	
28:26	212	11.6–12.1	86
29:6	174		

Lysias
- 1.29 — 180
- 1.30 — 180
- 1.37 — 180
- 1.49 — 180

Plato, *Laws*
- 810e–811a — 143
- 811a — 144

Plato, *Protagoras*
- 338e–339a — 143
- 339a — 145

Plutarch, *Moralia*
- 17d–38a — 145
- 23d — 145
- 34f–35c — 145
- 35d — 146, 152
- 36f — 156

Strabo, *Geography*
- 15.3.18 — 141

Xenophon, *Cyropadia*
- 1.2.6 — 141
- 1.2.6–8 — 140

Xenophon, *Symposium*
- 3.5 — 143

Modern Authors Index

Achenbach, Reinhard 2, 122, 130, 131, 225, 247
Adam, Klaus-Peter viii, 3, 20, 153, 159, 223, 225
Aejmelaeus, Anneli 159, 225
Albertz, Rainer 34, 122, 131, 225, 228, 243
Alkier, Stefan 137, 142, 241, 255
Alt, Albrecht 33, 183, 225
Alter, Robert 153, 225
Altmann, Peter 28, 225
Ames, Frank R. 210, 256
Amit, Yairah vii, 3, 17, 79, 103, 104, 105, 107, 108, 109, 112, 113, 124, 128, 209, 223, 226
Anderson, Robert T. 75, 226
Annis, Robert C. 10, 254
Arav, Rami 137, 226
Assmann, Jan 11, 226
Aucker, W. Brian 119, 191, 215, 233, 247
Auerbach, Elias 164, 227
Auld, A. Graeme 1, 42, 44, 149, 152, 189, 215, 225, 227
Baines, John 139, 227
Baltzer, Klaus 91, 227
Bar-Asher, Mosheh 112, 226
Barbour, Jennie 155
Barmash, Pamela 162, 227
Batten, Loring W. 105, 227
Becking, Bob 131, 228
Bellefontaine, Elizabeth 176, 182, 227
Ben Zvi, Ehud 3, 7, 8, 37, 46, 131, 132, 133, 134, 135, 136, 149, 198, 204, 205, 208, 209, 211, 212, 213, 214, 227, 234, 240, 241, 248, 251

Berding, Helmut 120, 236
Berge, Kåre 31, 32, 228
Berlin, Andrea M. 136, 237
Berquist, Jon L. 115, 116, 135, 228, 238
Berry, John W. 10, 254
Bertholet, Alfred 58, 61, 69, 228
Betlyon, John W. 142, 228
Betz, Hans Dieter 163, 240
Beyerlin, Walter 30, 228
Bickert, Rainer 171, 229
Bieberstein, Klaus 120, 229
Black, Jeremy 81, 229
Blenkinsopp, Joseph 105, 108, 109, 119, 183, 186, 212, 213, 229, 246
Blum, Erhard 186, 229
Böhler, Dieter 191, 248
Bolin, Thomas M. vii, 19, 133, 148, 157, 223, 229
Borgman, Paul 153, 230
Borré, Kristen 206, 230
Bösenecker, Jobst 188, 230
Botterweck, Johannes G. xi, 230
Boyer, Pascal 11, 230
Braulik, Georg 3, 230
Braun, Willi 205, 244
Briant, Pierre 140, 230
Brockington, Leonard H. 7, 105, 230
Brooke, George 108, 233
Buber, Martin 111, 230
Budde, Karl 164, 171, 230
Busto Saiz, José Ramón 159, 234
Butler, Trent 121, 230
Byrne, Ryan 139, 230
Campbell, Jonathan G. 78, 230
Cancik, Hubert 160, 230

-273-

Carr, David M.   7, 8, 139, 143, 144, 146, 148, 149, 152, 160, 185, 189, 230, 231
Carroll, Robert P.   210, 231
Carter, Charles   135, 137, 138, 142, 231
Charlesworth, James H.   x, 231
Choi, Soo Hang   10, 231
Clements, Ronald E.   191, 231
Cogan, Mordechai   217, 231
Combs-Schilling, M. Elaine   206, 231
Connerton, Paul   11, 231
Conrad, Edgar W.   88, 214, 231
Coogan, Michael D.   98, 139, 231, 241
Cook, Stanley A.   164, 232
Cook, Stephen L.   9, 249
Cortese, Enzo   90, 232
Crenshaw, James L.   139, 232
Crüsemann, Frank   111, 185, 232
Curtis, Edward D.   110, 232
Davies, Graham I.   138, 232
Davies, Philip R.   vii, 9, 12, 27, 28, 29, 33, 40, 42, 44, 82, 118, 123, 132, 134, 138, 151, 197, 204, 210, 223, 232, 233, 239, 241, 249
Day, John   139, 232
Dearman, Andrew   133, 233
Deist, Ferdinand   155, 233
Dietrich, Walter   164, 233, 254
Doniger O'Flaherty, Wendy   205, 206, 207, 214, 233
Dozeman, Thomas B.   2, 233
Driver, Samuel R.   61, 233
Edelman, Diana V.   vii, 1, 7, 30, 42, 46, 82, 108, 133, 137, 154, 204, 209, 212, 223, 228, 232, 233, 234, 240, 241, 248, 251
Edenburg, Cynthia   113, 234
Emerton, John A.   31, 138, 160, 171, 229, 236, 241, 250
Erll, Astrid   11, 234
Eskenazi, Tamara C.   131, 134, 234, 235
Exum, J. Cheryl   126, 234
Eynikel, Erik   153, 226
Fabry, Heinz-Josef   52, 55, 56, 58, 59, 234
Fensham, F. Charles   105, 234

Fenton, Steve   9, 234
Fentress, James   11, 234
Fernández Marcos, Natalio   159, 234
Finkelstein, Israel   79, 82, 135, 136, 234, 235, 239
Fischer, Irmtraud   172, 237
Fisher, Eli D.   184, 234
Flint, Peter W.   8, 249
Floyd, Michael H.   88, 235
Fohrer, Georg   33, 235
Fox, Michael V.   108, 246
Freedman, David Noel   ix, 153, 242, 243, 244, 251
Frevel, Christian   1, 4, 235
Frolov, Serge   vii, 15, 85, 87, 90, 91, 92, 93, 99, 101, 191, 223, 235
Frymer-Kensky, Tikva   184, 235
Galil, Gershom   103, 226
Galling, Kurt   163, 248
Garbini, Giovanni   134, 235
Gaster, Moses   75, 236
Geertz, Clifford   9, 236
Geller, Mark   103, 226
George, Andrew   81, 229
Gephart, Werner   119, 236
Gertz, Jan Christian   61, 62, 68, 173, 236
Giesen, Bernhard   119, 236
Giles, Terry   75, 226
Gillmayr-Bucher, Susanne   vii, 17, 115, 223
Gordon, Robert P.   139, 142, 232, 236
Gosse, Bernard   192, 236
Grabbe, Lester L.   33, 34, 37, 73, 123, 131, 132, 148, 210, 225, 231, 232, 236, 239
Graham, Patrick   133, 233
Groß, Walter   74, 115, 236
Guillaume, Philippe   2, 82, 87, 93, 115, 130, 236
Haag, Ernst   81, 243
Hagerdorn, Anslem C.   142, 236
Handy, Lowell K.   41, 237
Haran, Menahem   138, 237
Hardmeier, Christof   185, 245
Harris, William V.   138, 139, 140, 143, 146, 237

MODERN AUTHORS INDEX

Hayes, John H. 98, 255
Haynes, Stephen R. 85, 252
Heine, Heinrich 81, 237
Hempel, Johannes 58, 61, 62, 237
Henige, David 41, 237
Hentschel, Georg 172, 237
Herbert, Sharon C. 136, 237
Herion, Gary 29, 245
Hesseling, Dirk C. 144, 237
Hiebert, Theodore 139, 231
Himbaza, Innocent 191, 248
Hoftijzer, Jean 169, 237
Hoglund, Kenneth G. 135, 237
Holland, Martin 97, 237
Hölscher, Gustav 50, 51, 56, 58, 61, 65, 237
Holy, Ladislav 206, 249
Horton, Robin 10, 237
Hugo, Philippe 188, 191, 238
Iwawaki, Saburo 11, 231
Jacobson-Widding, Anita 10, 238
Jamieson-Drake, David 137, 238
Janzen, David 95, 238
Japhet, Sara 106, 109, 112, 114, 130, 238
Jeppesen, Knud 210, 238
Jobling, David 89, 238
Jonker, Louis 37, 241
Junge, Kay 119, 236
Kallai, Zecharia 117, 238
Kashima, Yoshihisa 11, 231
Kautzsch, Emil ix, 238
Keck, Leander 33, 105, 239, 255
Keel, Othmar 76, 78, 238
Kelle, Brad E. 210, 256
Kellermann, Diether 173, 174, 184
Kessler, John 135, 238
Kessler, Rainer 185, 245
Kim, Uichol 9, 253
Kissane, Edward J. 106, 238
Klein, Ralph W. 105, 110, 159, 168, 239
Klingbeil, Gerald A. 218, 238
Klostermann, August 63, 239
Knauf, E. Axel vii, 3, 4, 5, 14, 16, 30, 34, 36, 73, 74, 79, 81, 82, 86, 130, 209, 223, 239, 240

Knight, Douglas A. 1, 240
Knoppers, Gary N. 110, 122, 132, 149, 164, 189, 225, 227, 240, 243, 254
Koch, Ido 136, 234
Koester, Helmut 163, 240
Köhler, Ludwig 186, 240
Kokkinos, Nikos 79, 240
Kottsieper, Ingo 134, 192, 199, 227, 255
Kratz, Reinhard G. 1, 240
Kraus, Hans-Joachim 105, 240
Krüger, Thomas 155, 241
Kügler, Joachim 120, 229
Kuhnen, Hans-Peter 137, 241
Labuschagne, Casper J. 31, 241
Lasine, Stuart 163, 241
Leach, Edmund R. 212
Leith, Mary Joan Winn 98, 241
Lemaire, André 7, 79, 138, 241
Lemche, Niels-Peter 42, 135, 210, 241
Lenchak, Timothy A. 30, 241
Leuchter Mark 36, 37, 308, 241, 242
Leung, Kwok 11, 231
Levin, Christoph vii, 3, 13, 41, 44, 52, 56, 211, 223, 242
Levinson, Bernard M. 29, 31, 33, 51, 242
L'Hour, Jean 60, 61, 62, 65, 242
Lim, Timothy H. 119, 191, 215, 233, 247
Limburg, James 151, 242
Linville, James R. viii, 1, 23, 24, 203, 205, 209, 211, 216, 222, 223, 242
Lipiński, Eduard 173
Lipschits, Oded 79, 108, 109, 116, 119, 122, 130, 131, 135, 136, 137, 225, 226, 227, 229, 234, 238, 239, 240, 241, 243, 246
Lohfink, Norbert 30, 40, 52, 54, 58, 80, 81, 242, 243
Lyke, Larry L. 172, 243
Macchi, Jean-Daniel 1, 5, 86, 200, 240, 248, 249, 251
MacDonald, Nathan 28, 243
Macholz, Georg Christian 166, 176, 243
Mack, Burton L. 205, 208, 243
Madsen, Albert A. 110, 232

Magen, Yitzhak	109, 189, 243, 252	Oeming, Manfred	79, 116, 119, 130, 131, 137, 226, 227, 229, 234, 238, 239, 240, 241
Mandel, Sarah	153, 244		
Marrou, Henri I.	143, 144, 145, 244		
Marti, Karl	58, 61, 69, 244	Otto, Eckhard	2, 54, 58, 59, 65, 209, 246, 247
Martilla, Marko	149, 164, 244, 254		
Mathys, Hans-Peter	76, 244	Parpola, Simo	29, 247
Mayes, Andrew D. H.	56, 58, 61, 127, 128, 244	Perlitt, Lothar	51, 55, 56, 57, 63, 65, 67, 69, 247
Mays, James L.	1, 240	Person, Raymond F., Jr.	2, 149, 155, 189, 209, 215, 247, 250
McCarter, P. Kyle, Jr.	159, 244		
McCarthy, Dennis J.	29, 91, 244	Peters, Norbert	160, 247
McConville, J. Gordon	31, 164, 244, 254	Petersen, David L.	1, 240
McCutcheon, Russell T.	205, 206, 244	Platvoet, Jan	218
McKeating, Henry	162, 244	Polak, Frank H.	188, 247
McKenzie, Steven L.	85, 149, 209, 244, 252	Poortinga, Ype H.	10, 250
		Prosic, Tamara	211, 247
Mendenhall, George E.	29, 244, 245	Prothero, George W.	161, 248
Merendino, Rosario P.	58, 61, 62, 69, 245	Postgate, Nicholas	81, 229
		Pratchett, Terry	203
Meshorer, Yaakov	142, 245	Pury, Albert de	1, 5, 86, 200, 240, 248, 249, 251
Mildenburg, Leo	142, 245		
Millard, Alan	103, 226	Pyysiäinen, Ilkka	206, 248
Millard, Matthias	185, 186, 245	Rad, Gerhard von	33, 34, 162, 191, 248
Miller, J. Maxwell	98, 255	Radl, Walter	163, 248
Mitchell, Lynette	212, 234	Ranke, Leopold von	161, 248
Monroe, Lauren A. S.	208, 245	Rapp, Ursula	172, 237
Moor, Johannes C. de	142, 237	Reiterer, Friedrich V.	107, 226
Mor, Menahem	107, 226	Reuter, Eleonore	177
Mørkholm, Otto	142, 245	Reventlow, Henning G.	31, 228
Müller, Reinhard	185, 245	Reyes Lagunes, Isabel	9, 250
Murray, Donald F.	192, 245	Rezetko, Robert	119, 133, 191, 215, 233, 247, 248
Myers, Jacob M.	7, 110, 245		
Na'aman, Nadav	36, 40, 41, 82, 239, 245	Richards, Kent H.	1, 134, 235, 240
Naumann, Thomas	164, 233	Richter, Wolfgang	85, 248
Neef, Heniz-Dieter	118, 245	Ringgren, Helmer	x, 230
Nelson, Richard	4, 97, 208, 209, 245, 246	Ristau, Kenneth A.	132, 149, 227, 240
		Rofé, Alexander	176, 249
Nentel, Jochen	160, 246	Rollston, Christopher A.	139, 248
Niccacci, Alverio	89, 246	Römer, Thomas	viii, 1, 2, 3, 5, 22, 24, 29, 36, 40, 45, 86, 91, 108, 160, 187, 191, 192, 194, 197, 198, 200, 208, 209, 224, 232, 233, 240, 248, 249, 250, 251
Nicholson, Ernest W.	33, 246		
Niditch, Susan	134, 157, 246		
Nielsen, Flemming	153, 246		
Noonan, Benjamin J.	137, 246		
Noth, Martin	4, 45, 149, 183, 191, 246	Rost, Leonhard	163, 164, 167, 178, 179, 249
Oded, Bustanay	108, 246		

Roth, Martha T.	30, 249	Toorn, Karel van der	8, 9, 139, 148, 212, 253
Rütersworden, Udo	2, 235		
Ruwe, Andreas	185, 245	Triandis, Harry C.	9, 253
Ryle, Herbert E.	105, 249	Turner, Victor	219, 220, 253
Salzman, Philip C.	206, 249	Ulrich, Eugene	78, 253
Sanders, James A.	8, 249, 250	Van Keulen, Percy S. F.	188, 253
Scafuro, Adele C.	179, 180, 181, 250	Van Seters, John	30, 31, 144, 148, 149, 152, 252, 253
Schams, Christine	148, 250		
Schaper, Joachim	37, 250	Veijola, Timo	51, 52, 54, 56, 57, 58, 161, 164, 168, 171, 183, 243, 253, 254
Schenker, Adrian	187, 188, 190, 250		
Schiller, Johannes	172, 237	Waggoner, Nancy M.	142, 245
Schipper, Jeremy	192, 249	Waldbaum, Jane	142, 254
Schmid, Konrad	2, 73, 93, 192, 233, 250	Waldenfels, Hans	119, 236
		Watanabe, Kazuko	29, 247
Schmitt, Hans-Christoph	160, 250	Watts, James W.	186, 207, 229, 254
Schmitt, Rudiger	134, 192, 199, 227, 255	Weinfeld, Moshe	4, 29, 254
		Weinreich, Peter	10, 254
Schöpflin, Karin	129, 250	Weippert, Manfred	79, 254
Schroer, Silvia	76, 78, 238	Welch, Adam C.	33, 254
Schweitzer, Steven J.	212, 215, 251	Wellhausen, Julius	111, 183, 254
Seitz, Christopher	88, 251	Wells, Bruce	165, 254
Seitz, Gottfried	58, 61, 62, 65, 66, 67, 69, 251	Wenning, Robert	142, 254
		Wesselius, Jan-Wim	153, 255
Seow, Choon-Leong	155, 251	Westbrook, Raymond	165, 184, 235, 255
Simon, Uriel	164, 165, 176, 251	Westermann, Claus	1, 86, 255
Sinha, Jai B. P.	9, 251	Wette, Wilhelm M. L. de	49, 255
Smith, Anthony D.	9, 251	Whitelam, Keith	166, 175, 176, 255
Smith, Dennis	146, 251	Wickham, Chris	11, 234
Smith, Jonathan Z.	218, 251	Widengren, Geo	98, 255
Smyth, Françoise	199, 251	Williams, Prescott H.	139, 231
Soggin, J. Alberto	97, 251	Williamson, Hugh G. M.	7, 110, 139, 232, 255
Steck, Odil Hannes	196, 251		
Steiner, Richard C.	95, 252	Winter, Sarah C.	9, 249
Stern, Ephraim	142, 189, 252	Witte, Markus	2, 137, 142, 160, 189, 230, 241, 255, 255
Stern, Menahem	74, 252		
Steuernagel, Carl	56, 58, 61, 63, 65, 66, 252	Wörhle, Jakob	134, 191, 192, 199, 227, 255
Stott, Kathryn	41, 252	Wright, G. Ernest	33, 255
Stuchlik, Milan	206, 249	Wright, Jacob L.	210, 255, 256
Sweeney, Marvin A.	36, 41, 85, 91, 252	Würthwein, Ernst	41, 164, 171, 256
Tappy, Ron E.	139, 252	Young, Ian	139, 256
Tatu, Silviu	129, 252	Zenger, Erich	191, 256
Taylor, Bernard A.	188, 246	Zevit, Ziony	136, 256
Thomas, Rosalind	140, 146, 252		
Thompson, Thomas L.	152, 154, 252		

Subject Index

Aaron, 35, 42
Abel, 154
Abel Beth Ma'acah, 156
Abiathar, 188, 216
Abigail, 169, 172
Abijah, 112
Abimelech, 108, 151, 178
Abishag, 155
Abner, 162, 167
Abraham, 16, 75
Absalom, 20, 151, 162, 163, 167, 170, 171, 172, 173, 174, 175, 177, 178, 181, 182
Achaemenid era, 122, 140, 141, 152, 159, 160, 161, 186
Achan, 161
administration/administrators, 7, 21, 22, 31, 46, 47, 69, 94, 98, 140, 154, 182, 204, 216
admonition (genre), 15, 90
Adoni-bezek, 118
Adonijah, 177, 178, 179
adultery, 149, 180
agrarian society, 138
Ahaziah, 187
Ahijah, 195, 196
Ahimelech, 151
Ahitophel, 178
Ai, 83
Alexander, 86, 95, 100, 141
Alexandria, 74, 144
allusion, 8, 19, 28, 77, 155, 156, 157, 158, 171, 185
altar(s), 39, 80, 83, 104, 116, 217
Amasa, 167
Amaziah, 197, 214

Ammonites/Ammon, 83, 119, 125, 126, 164
Amnon, 163, 167, 172, 175, 177, 178, 182
Amorites, 83, 118
angel(s), 39, 107
annal(s) (genre), 145, 194, 212
Antiochus Epiphanes, 96
apostasy, apostate, 61, 62, 80
Arad, 7
Aram-naharaim, 151
Aram-zobah, 151
Aramaic, 140, 147
Arameans, 108
archaeology, 41
archive(s), 49, 136, 147
Aristotle, 163
ark 34, 35, 84, 150, 216, 219, 220
Artaxerxes, 186
Asa, 110, 111
Asahel, 162
Asher, 118, 120
Asia Minor, 19, 139
assassin, 125
asylum, 21, 163, 170, 174, 175
Athenian Empire, 95
Athens/Athenian/Attic, 142, 144, 146, 179, 181
audience, 2–3, 7, 8, 15, 20, 21, 22, 23, 24, 25, 27, 31, 32, 33, 46, 76, 78, 84, 85, 86, 87, 80, 92, 93, 94, 97, 101, 105, 109, 128, 129, 131, 133, 138, 145, 150, 152, 153, 154, 164, 165, 167, 170, 177, 186, 189, 194, 196, 200, 203, 204, 205, 206, 207, 208, 214, 220, 221, 222

authority, 2, 5–6, 7, 9, 10, 12, 13, 14, 16, 17, 18, 20, 21, 22, 23, 25, 27, 34, 38, 94, 95, 97–101, 104, 147, 150, 159–62, 166, 175–77, 182, 183, 184, 185, 188, 189, 190, 194, 195, 200, 201, 203, 204, 205, 207, 212, 213, 214, 215, 220, 222
authoritative, 20, 21, 22, 25, 36, 39, 46, 47, 50, 94, 105, 114, 115, 131, 133, 143, 148, 187, 204, 206, 214
author/authorship, 12, 25, 34, 93, 103, 104, 131, 138, 153, 155
Azariah, 110, 216
Baasha, 195
Babylon, 109, 123, 194, 199
Babylonia, 22, 33, 190
Bagawahyi, 83
Barak, 120
Bathsheba, 149, 151, 156, 163, 167, 182
battle report (genre), 90
Beersheba, 117
Behistun, 140
belief system, 6, 28, 37, 38, 153, 204
Benjamin, 19, 28, 79, 83, 106, 107, 108, 113, 118, 121, 122, 151
Bethel, 29, 107, 118
Beth-Marcaboth, 81
Beth-Zur, 137
Beyond the River, 37
biography, 4, 163
Bochim, 107
blessing(s), 15, 28, 30, 53, 54, 55, 58, 64, 67, 70, 80, 91, 94
Book of the Twelve, 45, 78
bribes, 184, 185
brotherhood, 13, 14, 49, 51, 52, 56, 57, 59, 62, 63, 64, 66, 67, 69, 70, 71
bullae, 136
bureaucracy, 15, 137, 146, 147, 157
Cain, 154
Caleb, 79, 80, 81, 93
calendar, 24, 31
Canaan/Canaanite, 4, 16, 31, 74, 80, 81, 83, 96, 97, 107, 116, 120, 215
canon, 7, 9, 11, 19, 20, 22, 45, 46, 73, 74, 75, 87, 89, 101, 105, 139, 152, 204

canonical/canonizing, 15, 29, 45, 46, 75, 76, 78, 87, 88, 90, 91, 92, 139, 145, 187, 201
case narrative, 20, 165, 166, 172, 173, 174, 175, 179, 181
census, 154
centralization of cult/religion, 12, 13, 31, 32, 34, 35, 38, 42, 50, 51, 70, 99, 194, 198, 201
chronicle, synchronistic (genre), 160
Chronicler, 20, 40, 42, 43, 44, 109, 110, 111, 112, 114, 169, 170, 189, 201, 211, 212, 215
citation, 8, 155, 156, 158
coinage/money, 15, 64, 82, 137, 142, 173
colonialism/colonial, 39, 131
colophon, 76, 77
commandment, individual, 15, 57, 58, 62, 63, 66
commandments (genre), 15, 37, 41, 53, 56, 90, 94, 95, 97, 165, 193, 196, 197, 198
comedy, Greek (genre), 181
concubine, 113, 121, 124
conquest, 13, 17, 24, 49, 55, 70, 80, 83, 90, 92, 97, 98, 99, 103, 107, 117, 118, 122, 123, 215
context, literary, 84, 85, 86
copyist, 110
court, 35, 36, 60, 62, 68, 69, 146, 159, 167, 171, 176, 179, 181, 182, 185, 186, 190
covenant, 4, 5, 13, 14, 21, 23, 24, 28, 34, 37, 44, 52, 56, 57, 70, 92, 106, 107, 127, 197, 207, 208, 214, 216, 219, 221, 222
Covenant, book of the, 31, 199, 222
Covenant Code, 13, 31, 50, 51, 54, 55, 60, 63, 64, 67, 70
covenant theology, 14, 56, 57, 61, 62, 65, 70
creation, 76
credit, agricultural, 15, 82
cult/cultic, 12, 13, 28, 29, 35, 36, 38, 39, 40, 83, 86, 97, 124, 127, 128, 131, 132, 140, 148, 150, 152, 157, 173, 186, 188, 189, 194, 198, 199, 201, 209, 216

SUBJECT INDEX

cultic reform, 38, 39, 40, 41, 42, 43, 198, 199, 201, 203, 207, 213
culture, 12, 28, 134, 139, 140, 142, 146, 148, 152, 153, 156, 208
cuneiform, 140
curriculum, 7, 8, 9
curse(s), 15, 24, 28, 30, 70, 75, 80, 91, 94, 186, 214, 219
Cush, 151
Cushan-Rishathaim, 108
custom(s), 9, 29, 32, 38, 132
Cyrus, 101, 130, 150
Dan, 117, 118, 119, 120, 121
Daniel, 192
Darius, I 95, 153, 154, 186
David/Davidic, 13, 16, 19, 20, 21, 22, 23, 36, 44, 51, 78, 92, 98, 99, 100, 101, 110, 112, 113, 130, 135, 149, 150, 151, 153, 154, 155, 156, 157, 160, 161, 162, 163, 164, 165, 166, 167, 168, 169, 171, 172, 174, 176, 177, 181, 182, 187, 191, 192, 193, 194, 197, 200, 210, 219
Deborah, 118, 120, 125, 127, 131
debt/debtor, 52, 55, 59, 67, 82
Decalogue, 50, 62, 70
deity(ies)/god(s), 19, 28, 29, 33, 36, 38, 39, 40, 50, 83, 86, 92, 93, 94, 104, 105, 116, 119, 123, 125, 139, 141, 145, 154, 193, 216, 218, 220
Demetrius, 188
Demosthenes, 180
deportees, 96, 108
Deuteronomistic collection, 3
Deuteronomistic History, 1–5, 17, 45, 74, 104, 105, 149, 153, 157, 160, 208, 209
Deuteronomist(s), 20, 36, 86, 160, 164, 171, 183, 185
devout poor, 59, 71
Diadochi, 100
Diaspora, 50, 71, 191, 218
divination/divinatory, 161, 183, 207
divine encounter(s), 15
divine judgment, 14, 59, 60, 61, 62, 67, 68, 71, 109, 195, 203, 220
Doeg, 151

drama, Greek (genre), 21, 161, 165, 178, 179, 181, 185, 186
dynasty/dynasties/dynastic, 16, 28, 92, 98, 99, 100, 112, 153, 161, 171, 191, 203, 210, 216
Ebal, Mt. 28, 80
economy/economic base, 64, 65, 86, 95, 122, 135, 137, 142, 146, 195, 216, 219, 220
Eden, 192
edition, 52, 66, 69, 103, 159, 160, 188, 209,
editorial activity/layers, 13, 25, 40, 46, 51, 52, 105, 108, 115, 130, 160, 171
editor(s), 17, 51, 52, 103, 104, 107, 109, 112, 113, 121, 194, 195, 197, 199, 201
Edom/Edomite, 79, 151
education, 6–7, 9, 11, 19, 21, 47, 78, 95, 96, 133, 134, 138, 139, 140, 141, 143, 144, 145, 146, 148, 150, 152, 153, 157, 158, 160, 185
Egypt/Egyptians, 6, 18, 19, 28, 38, 54, 75, 77, 83, 86, 95, 98, 119, 137, 139, 144, 148, 169, 215, 217
Ehud, 118, 125
'Ein Gedi, 17
Elides, 183
elders, 34, 46, 93, 125, 184, 219
election, 13, 52, 58
El 'Elyon, 44
Elephantine, 83
Elijah, 77, 187, 195, 196
elite(s), 19, 46, 83, 96, 98, 123, 133, 134, 137, 138, 139, 140, 141, 142, 144, 146, 147, 148, 150, 152, 153, 155, 157, 162
enculturation, 8, 10, 11, 19, 46, 139, 144, 152, 157
Enneateuch, 4–5, 15, 16, 22, 86, 87, 88, 89, 90, 91, 92, 93, 94, 95, 96, 97, 98, 99, 100, 101, 192
entrapment (literary device), 21, 170, 176, 179, 180, 181, 185
Ephraim/Ephraimite, 79, 92, 118, 119, 120, 121
epic (genre), 143

epithet, 145, 154, 176
Esarhaddon, 29, 30
eschatology/eschatological, 59, 71, 101, 200
ethic(s), 6, 13, 14, 49, 51, 52, 56, 57, 58, 59, 64, 65, 70, 71, 121, 128, 144
ethnicity/ethnic, 9, 17, 28, 29, 32, 35, 70, 71, 90, 115, 116, 119
ethnos/*ethne*, 22, 34, 38, 39, 65
exegesis/exegete(s), 49, 61, 68, 85, 155, 200
exile(s)/deportation, 5, 15, 18, 22, 23, 24, 84, 95, 98, 106, 109, 111, 117, 154, 167, 174, 175, 177, 181, 189, 192, 194, 207, 208, 209, 210, 211, 213, 215, 217, 221
exodus event/story, 13, 18, 24, 40, 73, 80, 81, 207, 215, 217, 218, 219, 221
Ezekiel (figure), 111
Ezra (figure), 199
fable, 141
farms, 137
feud, 162, 166, 167, 180, 182, 183, 185
feudalism, 38
fiefs, military, 15, 81
forefathers/ancestors, 4, 6, 9, 20, 28, 38, 43, 76, 93, 96, 106, 140, 148, 161, 196, 198, 216, 217
foreigner(s), 53, 56, 58, 64, 95, 104, 106, 116, 117, 186, 217
form criticism, 85, 163, 205
fortification texts, 140
fratricide, 167, 173, 177, 181, 182
Gad, 118
Galilee, 79, 81, 83
gate-keepers, 36
Gath, 151
genealogy(ies), 15, 28, 29, 38, 79, 90, 96, 117, 147, 149, 177, 183
Ger, 66
Gerizim, Mt., 12, 28, 46, 75, 80, 109, 189, 190
Geshur, 163, 170, 174
Gezer, 137
Gibeah, 113, 121
Gibeon, 83

Gideon, 108, 111, 113, 116, 119, 120, 125, 127
Gilead, 117, 118, 120, 125
Gilgal, 79
government, 39, 81, 95, 99, 100
governor(s), 38, 99, 113, 131, 154
Greece, 19, 21, 137, 138, 139, 140, 141-46, 148, 150, 151, 152, 153, 157, 161, 162, 165, 180
Greek pottery, imported, 19, 137, 141, 142
guards, 36
guilt, 20, 68, 168, 169, 170, 172, 173, 174
Hannah, 152
Hasmonean period, 80, 188
Hazar-Susa, 81
Hazor, 136
Hebron, 93
Hecateus of Abdera, 74
Hellenistic period, 3, 6, 13, 16, 17, 19, 21-24, 49, 51, 71, 86, 87, 93-95, 103-4, 114, 133, 135-37, 139, 144, 146, 149, 150, 154-55, 157, 158, 187-88, 195, 200, 201, 203-4, 207, 210, 217, 220
hero/heroic, 18, 20, 21, 42, 78, 108, 115, 124, 126, 127, 130, 144, 152, 161, 177, 192
Herodotus, 140, 141, 153
hero-lists, 20, 161
Hexateuch, 4, 16, 91
Hezekiah, 42, 43, 89, 98, 109, 128, 194, 195, 197
hierarchy/hierarchical, 82, 201, 219
historicity, 37, 41
historiography/historiographical, 1, 45, 46, 55, 153, 160, 168, 169, 170, 213
history-writing, ancient, 17, 103, 106
Hittite(s), 83, 94
holiness, 36
Holiness Code, 50, 71, 208
Homer, 6, 141, 143, 144, 145, 147, 152, 153, 154
homicide, 20, 21, 162, 163, 164, 165, 166, 167, 168, 170, 173, 174, 175, 176, 177, 181, 182, 184, 185

SUBJECT INDEX

Horeb, Mt., 24, 77, 195
Huldah, 40, 200
Hushai, 178
hybridity, 152
Hyrcanus, 79
Ibzan, 118
iconography, 142
Iddo, 212
ideal(s)/idealization, 6, 12, 18, 19, 21, 22, 23, 24, 37, 50, 55, 67, 69, 78, 120, 121, 124, 127, 130, 131, 132, 140, 145, 171, 182, 192, 207, 208, 216, 218, 220, 221
identity, 2,3, 6, 9, 11, 17, 18, 22, 23, 24, 28, 29, 32, 35, 38, 39, 47, 115, 116, 119, 121, 123, 124, 128, 132, 159, 169, 193, 199, 207, 211, 216, 219, 222
ideology/ideological, 23, 24, 36, 37, 40, 42, 45, 46, 47, 50, 86, 131, 154, 155, 156, 193, 205, 211, 214, 216, 218
Idumea, 79, 81
imperial authorization, 37
imperial bureaucracy, 15
imperialism, 7
incipit, 76, 77
individual memory, 10
inscription(s), 41, 99, 140, 199, 205
institutionalization, 10
interest on loan, 64, 65
interpolation/interpolator/insertion, 20, 44, 52, 55, 58, 63, 88, 89, 99, 101, 168, 171, 172, 190
interweaving literary technique, 5
Isaiah (figure), 88, 89, 212
Ishbaal, 162
Israel, 2, 3, 4, 11, 12, 13, 16, 17, 18, 19, 21, 22, 23, 24, 27, 28, 29, 31, 32, 33, 34, 36, 38, 41, 43, 46, 47, 52, 55, 58, 74, 75, 76, 77, 78, 79, 81, 83, 84, 91, 92, 93, 95, 96, 97, 98, 99, 100, 104, 105, 106, 107, 108, 110, 111, 112, 114, 115, 116, 117, 118, 119, 120, 121, 122, 123, 124, 125, 126, 127, 128, 130, 131, 132, 138, 148, 150, 152, 155, 157, 159, 160, 162, 166, 175, 176, 184, 187, 189, 190, 194, 196, 197, 198, 203, 204, 207, 209, 212, 213, 214, 216, 217, 218, 219, 220, 222
Israelite, 8, 14, 15, 16, 18, 30, 37, 38, 46, 65, 66, 74, 75, 79, 80, 92, 93, 97, 98, 101, 114, 115, 116, 121, 125, 133, 153, 159, 161, 166, 176, 187, 189, 193, 194, 197, 208, 211, 216, 217, 218, 220, 222
Issachar, 118
Jacob, 29, 32
Jebusite(s), 83, 107
Jehoahaz, 109
Jehoiachin, 99, 191, 192
Jehoiada, 42
Jehoiakim, 184
Jehoram, 168
Jephthah, 113, 116, 119, 121, 125, 126, 127
Jeremiah, 195, 200
Jericho, 75, 82, 83, 97, 137
Jeroboam I, 108, 112, 168, 194, 195, 220
Jerusalem, 7, 12, 13, 15, 16, 19, 23, 24, 39, 46, 51, 74, 79, 72, 82, 83, 86, 94, 107, 134, 135, 136, 137, 138, 146, 150, 151, 153, 154, 156, 157, 166, 187, 189, 193, 194, 198, 200, 204, 208, 210, 216, 217, 220, 221
Jew(ish), 11, 14, 16, 22, 46, 40, 70, 74, 80, 86, 88, 89, 93, 94, 95, 96, 97, 98, 99, 100, 101, 138, 159, 186, 207, 216, 220
Joab, 21, 149, 151, 156, 162, 167, 170, 171, 172, 175, 176, 177, 178, 181, 182
Jonah, 196, 212
Jonathan, 179 149
Jordan, West, 49, 55
Jordan River, 83, 92, 97
Jordan Valley, 82
Joseph, 92, 118, 190, 192, 220
Josephus, 86
Joshua, 14, 16, 17, 74, 75, 77, 80, 83, 88, 92, 93, 97, 104, 126, 215
Josiah, 13, 14, 30, 31, 33, 36, 39, 41, 42, 43, 44, 49, 98, 128, 160, 194, 198, 199, 200, 201, 203, 207, 208, 211, 213, 221, 222
Jotham, 128

Judah, 3, 7, 9, 17, 18, 19, 21, 22, 29, 32, 33, 50, 78, 79, 81, 82, 83, 94, 95, 95, 98, 99, 103, 104, 106, 107, 108, 112, 113, 118, 120, 121, 122, 123, 131, 151, 167, 168, 182, 183, 187, 195, 196, 201, 208, 211, 213, 216, 219, 220, 222

Judahite, 33, 40, 49, 51, 79, 103, 106, 107, 108, 113, 114, 159, 168, 182, 187, 188, 189, 193, 194, 210

Judaism, 4, 22, 50, 146, 159, 186, 193, 195, 199, 200

Judean(s), 14, 17, 19, 22, 23, 24, 33, 34, 40, 79, 80, 81, 105, 118, 131, 159, 183, 189, 190, 191, 192, 193, 204, 208, 211, 216, 220, 222

judge(s), 18, 19, 34, 35, 37, 43, 60, 61, 68, 89, 105, 107, 108, 110, 111, 113-15, 118, 120-27, 129, 130, 131, 141, 164, 165, 167, 172, 176, 177, 183, 184, 185, 194

judgeship, 98, 99

justice/judicial process, 21, 22, 33, 36, 38, 39, 46, 47, 62, 69, 104, 114, 127, 140, 141, 162, 163, 168, 169, 175, 184

Kadesh-Barnea, 7

Kedesh, 136

kidnapping, 65

king(s)/monarch(s), 7, 12, 17, 18, 19, 20, 22, 23, 24, 30, 33, 38, 39, 40, 41, 43, 50, 61, 74, 75, 82, 94, 98, 99, 100, 104, 105, 108, 109, 111, 112, 118, 125, 126, 127, 128, 129, 132, 139, 149, 152, 153, 154, 155, 157, 160, 161, 162, 165, 166, 167, 168, 169, 170, 172, 175, 176, 177, 181, 182, 183, 185, 188, 189, 191, 193, 194, 195, 197, 198, 199, 200, 201, 203, 212, 216, 217, 219, 200

kingship, 12, 18, 92, 98, 101, 110, 130, 151, 154, 156, 160, 184, 187, 194, 195, 197, 200

kingship, divine, 17, 111, 112, 114, 154, 199

kinship/kin, 9, 113, 163, 166, 169, 173, 175, 176, 181, 183

Kuntillet ʿAjrud, 7

lament, 151

land, 15-18, 28, 35-38, 43, 53-55, 58, 59, 64, 74-76, 79-83, 92, 93, 95-97, 99, 100, 105, 106, 117, 118, 120, 123, 124, 130, 160, 192, 198, 211, 217, 222

law(s), 5, 13, 21, 22, 30, 34, 35, 36, 37, 41, 43, 44, 45, 46, 50, 51, 54, 57, 60, 62, 63, 66, 67, 68, 70, 76, 94, 95, 104, 121, 128, 130, 132, 160, 162, 165, 166, 167, 174, 176, 179, 184, 186, 196, 199, 201, 220

law book/scroll, 12, 13, 14, 33, 39, 40, 41, 42, 43, 44, 49, 50, 51, 70, 76, 194, 198, 199, 201, 208, 214, 221

law code/collection, 12, 13, 14, 29, 30, 36, 38, 52, 146, 166, 173, 174, 175, 207, 220

law of Moses, 40, 42, 43, 44, 46, 197, 198, 201

law tablets, 35, 197, 219

leader/leadership, 14, 16-18, 92, 99, 100, 108, 110, 114, 115, 120–28, 130, 131, 132, 154

legality/legal, 20–21, 29, 32, 35, 55, 63, 64, 67, 68, 69, 137, 141, 146, 160, 162, 164, 165, 166, 167, 169, 170, 172, 174, 175, 176, 177, 179, 181, 182, 183, 185, 186, 219

leprosy, 65

Levant, Southern, 19, 28, 133

Levites/Levitical, 6, 8, 12, 22, 34, 35, 36, 37, 42, 46, 83, 97, 105, 121, 124, 147, 148, 150, 151, 157, 216

Levitical priests, 12, 34, 35, 39, 42, 43, 46, 47

library, 101, 144, 192, 195, 204

liminality/liminal, 219, 220, 221, 222

literacy, 133, 138, 139, 141, 146, 152

literary criticism, 42

literati/intellectuals/educated elite, 7, 17, 22, 32, 46, 96, 98, 101, 103, 105, 131, 132, 134, 138, 146, 147, 199, 204

liturgy/liturgical/worship, 47, 81, 87, 89, 151, 188

livestock, 62, 63, 64

loan, 52, 53, 57, 58, 64, 66, 67

lot-casting, 89
loyalty oath, 29, 30, 31
Lysias, 180

Machir, 120
Manasseh, 43, 79, 99, 118, 120, 189, 194, 195, 197, 198, 211, 213
marriage, 113, 162, 163, 165, 193
masora finalis, 87
Masoretic Text, 9, 22, 57, 88, 149, 150, 184, 187, 188, 189, 199, 204, 210, 217
mediation, 33, 208, 221
melodrama (genre), 163
Megiddo, 200
memorandum (genre), 147
memory/ies, social/collective, 2, 3, 9, 10, 11, 15, 17, 21, 22, 47, 84, 95, 119, 122, 125, 130, 132
mercy, 17, 18, 105, 106, 160, 217
Meribaal, 178
Merodach-Baladan, 109
Meroz, 120
Mesopotamia(n), 6, 96, 139, 140, 148, 160
messiah/messianism/messianic, 101, 130, 153, 160, 191
metaphor/metaphoric, 128, 129, 178
metaphorical tale, 128-29
Micah, 121, 124, 212
Micaiah, 212
Michal, 149
military leadership, 16, 33, 125, 126
minority/marginal group, 14, 59, 70
miracles, 15, 75, 78
Mishnah, 218
Mizpah, 121, 135
Moab/Moabites, 31, 41, 42, 82, 83, 114
Molech, 199
monarchic period, 2, 7, 9, 14, 29, 40, 43, 50, 83, 84, 110, 157, 186, 209, 214, 215, 216
monarchy, 12, 13, 16, 21, 22, 31, 32, 38, 39, 41, 51, 79, 92, 98, 99, 101, 112, 114, 128, 130, 150, 153, 159, 187, 188, 189, 190, 192, 193, 194, 210, 211, 213, 217, 219

monotheism, 28, 38, 160
Mordechai, 192
Moses/Mosai,c 4, 5, 12, 13, 14, 15, 16, 23, 24, 31, 34, 35, 36, 39, 40, 41, 42, 43, 44, 45, 49, 74, 75, 76, 77, 78, 88, 89, 90, 92, 126, 132, 147, 160, 185, 194, 195, 196, 197, 198, 200, 201, 214, 219, 220
motif(s), 5, 80, 161, 169,
myth, 23, 24, 108, 139, 141, 205, 206, 207, 208, 211, 214, 215, 217, 218, 220, 221, 222

Nabal, 162, 169
Naboth, 81
Naphtali, 118, 120
narrative (genre), 15, 20, 23, 36, 37, 45, 74, 75, 81, 82, 83, 89, 90, 93, 117, 124, 130, 139, 147, 149, 150, 151, 152, 153, 154, 155, 160, 161, 162, 164, 165, 166, 167, 169, 171, 172, 174, 175, 177, 178, 182, 183, 185, 189, 195, 199, 201, 204, 205, 214, 221, 222
narrative emplotment, 11
narrator, 92, 97, 125, 167, 168, 178, 190, 193, 201, 208, 214
Nathan, 129, 151, 169, 170, 172, 195
Near East, ancient, 19, 78, 82, 94, 134, 139, 141, 143, 146, 207
Necho, 42
Nehemiah (figure), 99
Neo-Assyria(n)(s), 17, 29, 30, 31, 94, 103, 106, 194
Neo-Babylonian Empire, 13, 32, 49, 81, 135, 191, 194
Neo-Babylonian period, 2, 123, 209, 210
Nob, 150, 162
norm(s)/normative, 6, 19, 23, 62, 94, 95, 97, 100, 101, 119, 121, 134, 139, 140, 144, 146, 147, 148, 156, 157, 158, 175, 206, 207,
obedience, 13, 18, 42, 43, 44, 53, 55, 128, 196, 220, 221, 222
officials/magistrates, 36, 37, 200, 216
Olives, Mt. of, 82
omen-texts, 139

Ophel, 136
oracle(s), 22, 29, 40, 62, 110, 129, 192, 194, 195, 200, 207
oral recitation/reading/performance, 8, 19, 21, 32, 46, 77, 141, 144, 146, 147, 148, 155, 158, 185, 186, 199, 200, 222
origin story/founding legend, 18, 29, 39, 119
Othniel ben Kenaz, 107, 108, 113, 118, 125, 127
palace, 139, 170, 172
Palestine, 133, 138
parable, 20, 21, 129, 163, 164, 165, 167, 170, 172, 175, 176, 177, 182
paraenesis, 90
paraphrase, 8
Passover, 13, 24, 38, 39, 41, 43, 44, 207, 215, 221, 222
patriarch(s), 29, 92, 99, 207
patron/patronage, 12, 33, 38, 127
pedagogy 134, 139, 140, 141, 143, 146, 147, 151, 153, 154, 157
Pentateuch, 4–5, 16, 21, 23, 27, 29, 32, 35, 43, 45, 54, 60, 61, 63, 66, 90, 92, 93, 100, 157, 189, 197, 199, 201, 215, 219
periodization, 19, 130, 209
Perizzites, 83
Persepolis, 140
Persian(s), 19, 46, 140, 154, 189, 209
Persian Empire, 12, 23, 46, 51, 79, 80, 81, 86, 94, 100, 130, 131, 137, 152, 153, 157, 183, 200
Persian period, 2, 3, 7, 9, 12, 13, 14, 15, 16, 17, 18, 19, 20, 21, 22, 23, 24, 37, 49, 52, 71, 79, 81, 82, 86, 87, 93, 94, 95, 98, 99, 101, 103, 104, 106, 109, 113, 114, 115, 121, 122, 123, 131, 133, 134, 135, 136, 137, 138, 139, 149, 150, 155, 157, 159, 160, 161, 162, 166, 169, 170, 173, 174, 183, 184, 185, 186, 187, 188, 189, 193, 195, 197, 198, 199, 200, 201, 203, 204, 207, 209, 210, 216, 217, 220
Peshitta, 60, 61, 63, 66, 184
Pharaoh, 42, 76, 200

Philistine(s), 113, 121, 126, 151, 161, 173
Phoenicia, 98
pilgrimage festivals, 13, 31, 32, 38, 46, 47, 207, 217
Plato, 143, 144, 145
pledge(s), 66, 67
plot-line/storyline, 5, 16, 24, 44, 146, 159, 160, 162, 163, 167, 171, 172, 175, 178, 180, 181
Plutarch, 144, 145, 152, 154, 156
poetry/poem(s), 143, 144, 145, 146, 148, 151, 152, 156, 157, 162
polemic, 107, 108, 113, 128, 189
political status/agenda, 11, 15, 17, 18, 22, 24, 28, 29, 80, 81, 82, 98, 99, 112, 138, 162, 192, 193, 195, 209, 210, 215, 216, 218, 219
poor, care of, 13, 49, 51, 52, 53, 54, 56, 57, 58, 59, 66, 67, 68, 69
postcolonial theory, 152
power 10, 11, 17, 86, 94, 98, 99, 100, 188, 192, 203, 205, 216, 217, 218
prayer (genre), 37, 105, 139, 151, 192, 217, 220
preamble/prologue, 15, 30, 45, 91, 170
priest, high, 16, 99, 188
priesthood, 216, 221
priest(s)/priestly, 6, 7, 12, 19, 22, 34, 36, 39, 42, 43, 60, 61, 83, 86, 101, 111, 148, 150, 157, 162, 168, 173, 183, 188, 200, 216
Priestly school, 36, 90, 186
Promised Land, 4, 5, 13, 16, 81, 92
prophecy 12, 41, 46, 78, 114, 200, 201, 213, 215
prophet(s), 4, 7, 12, 15, 16, 20, 22, 23, 24, 41, 44, 75, 76, 77, 78, 84, 100, 104, 111, 116, 150, 151, 161, 182, 187, 191, 194, 195, 196, 199, 200, 201, 203, 211, 213, 214
prophetic, 14, 23, 40, 45, 71, 80, 94, 120, 125, 129, 183, 192, 194, 195, 196, 207, 212, 213, 214, 216
prostitutes, 113
proverb (genre), 143

province, 13, 17, 18, 28, 29, 39, 46, 51, 79, 80, 95, 98, 105, 122, 131, 135, 138, 154, 189, 200, 220
psalm (genre), 19, 67, 71, 78, 149, 150, 151, 152
Pseudo-Philo, 150
Ptolemaic Empire/rule, 86, 100, 142, 155
punishment, 15, 60, 68, 69, 96, 109, 111, 121, 126, 168, 169, 170, 177, 182, 193, 196, 221
purification/purity, 168, 199, 216
Quatrateuch, 4, 5
Qumran, 87, 95, 150
Rabbah, 164
rabbi(s), rabbinic, 9, 101, 154, 204
Ramah, 184
Ramat Raḥel, 135, 137
rape, 163, 167, 174, 175
Ras, Khirbet er-, 137
reader(s), 18, 23, 24, 25, 32, 36, 78, 84, 85, 87, 125, 128, 131, 133, 134, 145, 150, 152, 154, 177, 178, 190, 197, 203, 204, 205, 206, 207, 208, 210, 214, 218, 220, 221, 222
reception, 161
redaction criticism, 183
redaction/redactional history, 4, 69, 80, 84, 85, 133, 134, 183, 209
redactional layer/level, 16, 30, 51, 55, 88, 151, 164, 213
redactor(s), 22, 214
regionalism, 9
Rehoboam, 168
release, legal, from debt, 52, 53, 54, 55, 56, 59
religion, 12, 13, 17, 28, 31, 38, 39, 86, 115, 156, 186, 199, 204, 207, 208, 214
religious/cultic community, 50, 51, 57, 65, 70
religious practice, 6, 9, 204, 219
retribution, 20, 43, 163, 168, 169, 170, 182
Reuben, 118, 120
revenge, 20, 21, 162, 163, 165, 166, 167, 168, 169, 170, 173, 174, 175, 176, 177, 181, 182, 185

revolt/rebellion, 96, 98, 100, 112, 151, 163, 175, 195
rhetorical device, 30
righteousness/righteous, 67, 68, 69
rite of passage, 219, 220, 221
ritual(s), 13, 23, 24, 28, 44, 47, 124, 205, 207, 208, 211, 214, 216, 218, 219, 220, 222
Roman period, 19, 101, 135, 136
Ruth (figure), 114
Sabbath, 23, 211
sacrifice(s)/sacrificial, 35, 38, 42, 43, 83, 125, 150, 154, 155, 156, 173, 189, 199, 216, 217, 220
sage(s), 78, 201
Samaria/Samerina/Samarian, 3, 12, 14, 18, 19, 28, 29, 32, 33, 34, 37, 39, 46, 79, 80, 81, 105, 122, 131, 187, 189, 193, 197, 201
Samaritan(s), 54, 60, 61, 63, 66, 75, 80, 86, 107, 189
Samson, 113, 116, 119, 121, 126, 127
Samuel 17, 104, 111, 149, 150, 156, 160, 184
sanctuary, 12, 32, 34, 35, 38, 50, 183, 189, 190, 193, 216, 221
Satan, 154
satrapy, 37
Saul, 20, 108, 110, 112, 113, 114, 124, 149, 150, 151, 153, 154, 157, 160, 161, 162
scribal training, 6–7, 9, 21, 140
scribe(s), 2, 7, 8, 9, 36, 40, 42, 46, 50, 91, 101, 132, 138, 140, 141, 146, 147, 199, 204, 210
Second Temple period, 50, 65, 83, 159, 204, 205, 208, 209, 211, 214, 215, 216, 218, 220
segregation, 22, 160, 193
Septuagint, 22, 25, 54, 57, 60, 61, 66, 88, 184, 187, 188, 189, 199, 210, 217
Seleucid Empire, 100
sermon (genre), 34, 185
servant, 43, 54, 66, 67, 76, 77, 173, 191, 195, 196, 197, 198, 199
Shealtiel, 114

Shechem, 80, 92, 108, 109, 113, 129
Shemaiah, 212
Shiloh, 79, 80, 83, 84
Simeon, 81, 107, 118, 120
Simon Maccabeus, 188
Simon the Just, 86
sin/sinner, 38, 43, 53, 59, 67, 68, 108, 109, 111, 160, 173, 193, 194, 197, 213, 221
Sinai, Mt., 13, 24, 40, 195, 215
singers/singing/song, 36, 43, 81, 120, 127, 129, 141, 147, 151, 152, 158, 173
slave, slavery, 38, 51, 52, 54, 55, 56, 57, 146, 180, 181, 221
social boundaries, 6, 24, 28, 204, 206, 219, 222
socio-historical context, 14, 21, 51, 78, 85, 133, 185, 186, 204, 207
Solomon, 19, 20, 22, 42, 99, 112, 155, 164, 165, 167, 168, 175, 178, 179, 192, 193, 194, 195, 197, 203, 212, 215, 216, 217, 218, 219, 220
source criticism, 159, 163, 164, 166, 167, 171, 173, 179
speech (genre), 13, 41, 45, 80, 97, 116, 128, 146, 160, 177, 178, 181, 185, 193, 194, 197, 215, 218
stipulations, 15, 30, 34, 91, 94
Stoics, 144
Strabo, 141
Succession Narrative, 153, 164, 178, 179
Sukkot/Booths, Festival of, 24, 38, 74, 217, 222
superscription, 88, 89, 149, 150, 151, 152, 156, 212
suzerain, 12, 15, 94
symposium, Greek, 146
synagogue, 199
Syria, 138
tabernacle, 216, 218
Talmud, 195, 201
Tamar, 163, 167, 174, 175
Targum, 184
Tekoa, wise woman of, 20, 165, 178, 181, 182
temple, 7, 8, 12, 13, 14, 15, 23, 24, 29, 36, 39, 40, 42, 52, 74, 75, 83, 101, 109 110, 139, 147–52, 154, 160, 189, 191, 193, 194, 198, 199, 200, 201, 204, 207, 209, 215, 216, 217, 218, 220, 222
temple community, 14, 70, 183
Temple Mount, 136
teraphim, 199
Tetrateuch, 45
textual criticism, 42, 159
theme(s), 5, 20, 21, 146, 153, 154, 160, 161, 162, 163, 164, 165, 195
theocracy, 18, 111
theodicy, 101
theology/theological, 15, 20, 57, 70, 78, 81, 82, 158, 188, 190, 193, 194, 209, 211
theophany, 195
threshing floor, 57
tithe, 35
Torah, 6, 7, 12, 15, 16, 17, 18, 23, 24, 35, 36, 37, 39, 41, 42, 45, 47, 50, 71, 74, 75, 76, 77, 78, 79, 80, 81, 83, 84, 87, 88, 91, 100, 126, 128, 131, 132, 147, 148, 160, 185, 194, 196, 198, 199, 200, 201, 207, 209, 214, 215, 222
town/locality list(s), 81, 82, 83, 90
trade, 65, 123, 137
tradition(s), 2, 7, 8, 16, 20, 21, 22, 30, 88, 101, 103, 115, 128, 131, 132, 139, 141, 153, 154, 157, 158, 159, 161, 162, 163, 188, 189 206, 212, 213, 214, 215, 220
tragedy (genre), 20, 126, 153, 160, 161, 162, 163
treasurers, 36
treasury texts, 140
treaty, vassal, 12, 13, 15, 29, 30, 70, 91, 94, 207
tribe(s), 17, 18, 19, 27, 28, 75, 81, 89, 92, 93, 97, 107, 108, 110-13, 116-27, 130, 131, 193, 216
urbanization, 137
Uriah, 20, 163, 164, 165, 167
usurper/usurpation, 163, 177
utopia, utopian, 12, 15, 32, 36, 37, 49, 59, 82, 215

value system/values, 11, 16, 17, 22, 46, 116, 128, 134, 140, 145, 146, 156, 157, 158
vassal, 12, 13, 50, 51, 94
violence/abuse, 20, 121, 123, 152, 162, 166, 169, 176, 177, 180, 181, 184, 203, 221
vow/oath, 155, 161
Vulgate, 53, 60, 63, 184, 199
wages of day-laborer, 66, 67
war/warfare, 39, 98, 100, 107, 110, 120, 121, 125, 126, 141, 149, 161, 200, 203
warrior, 21, 80, 127, 177, 178
Weeks, Festival of, 38
wilderness, 38, 43, 151, 215, 217, 218, 219, 221
wisdom/wise, 78, 147, 156, 170, 193, 203, 204
witness(es), 30, 60, 159
women, foreign, 17, 22, 94, 113, 114, 193
world upside-down, 128
worship/veneration, 23, 39, 40, 91, 93, 106, 116, 151, 189, 194, 198, 201
Xenophon, 140, 141, 143
Yael the Kenite, 113
Yehud, 3, 6, 9, 12, 13, 14, 17, 18, 19, 20, 22, 28, 29, 32, 37, 39, 46, 79, 81, 106, 134, 136, 137, 138, 140, 141, 142, 146, 148, 149, 154, 157, 158, 159, 162, 166, 183, 186, 190, 199, 200, 204
YHWH Elohim, 13, 35, 53, 54, 58, 64, 66
Zadok, 188, 216
Zebulun, 118, 120
Zechariah (figure), 113
Zenon papyri, 137
Zemaraim, Mt., 112
Zerubbabel, 99, 113, 154, 191
Ziphites, 151

www.ingramcontent.com/pod-product-compliance
Lightning Source LLC
Chambersburg PA
CBHW021834220426
43663CB00005B/245